Gladys Swartzell
Grade 7

24-14-4

Building health

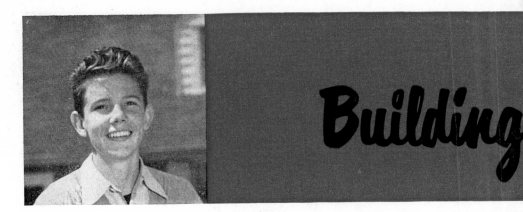

Building

The following members of the administrative and supervisory personnel of the Denver Public Schools have given counsel and advice in planning and preparing this material:

All royalties received from the sale of this book will be paid into the funds of the Denver Public Schools and devoted to the furtherance of instructional practices in the schools of the city.

KENNETH E. OBERHOLTZER
 Superintendent of Schools
ROY A. HINDERMAN
 Deputy Superintendent for Instructional Services
PETER C. HOLM
 Assistant Superintendent for Personnel Services
GRAHAM R. MILLER
 Assistant Superintendent for Business Services
LOUIS H. BRAUN
 Administrative Director, Department of Instruction
RUSSELL K. BRITTON
 Administrative Director, Department of Instruction
LELAND M. CORLISS, M.D.
 Director of Health Services
GERTRUDE E. CROMWELL, R.N.
 Supervisor of Nursing
NINA MAE DOLEZAL
 Director of Home Economics
MILDRED E. DOSTER, M.D.
 Assistant Director of Health Services
WILLARD N. GREIM
 formerly Director of Health Education
JAMES A. HALL
 formerly Director, Department of Instruction, presently Superintendent of Schools, Port Washington, New York
ARTHUR J. LEWIS, JR.
 formerly Director, Department of Instruction, presently Assistant Superintendent of Schools, Minneapolis, Minnesota
A. LOUISE McNIFF
 Supervising Teacher, Department of Instruction
MARY C. MOORE
 formerly Supervising Teacher, Department of Instruction, presently Dean of Girls, East High School

Second edition

Dorothea M. Williams

Cole Junior High School
Denver, Colorado

Drawings from the Studio of Waneeta Stevic,
University of Colorado School of Medicine

J. B. LIPPINCOTT COMPANY

Chicago, Philadelphia, New York

Preface

Improved health practices and knowledge is a major objective of education. Health instruction, however, has been a part of the school program for years, but too frequently has resulted in little change in the habits and attitudes of the boys and girls. In order to make health instruction effective it is necessary that it stirs emotions of boys and girls and makes them want to change their behavior.

It is our belief that this text, *Building Health,* will be effective in changing the behavior of boys and girls because of the fact that it is based upon the results of a study that was made in Denver of the health interests of children. In this book health needs are approached through the interests which this study shows are high during adolescence. In the junior high school "growing up" is a very high interest.

Reading and discussing are very important experiences for boys and girls, but *doing* is necessary to make any class vital. This text is designed to provide plenty of doing experiences which will enliven and make real the health principles enunciated in it. The text is adaptable for classes in which pupils and teacher plan together by discovering problems and seeking the answers. The text is so organized that it can be used as resource material and it is not necessary that it be used chronologically or that the subjects be covered in the sequence outlined in the book.

Each chapter has a "Picture Preview" which will be useful, we hope, for stimulating interest and providing the basis for co-operative planning. Through each "Picture Preview," classes are helped to set goals for their study and at the end of the study it can be used to help evaluate progress. Each chapter is also preceded by suggestions for individual and committee experiences, panels, research, and various activities at home and in the community.

Each chapter ends with a well-designed series of test materials that cover thoroughly the important health concepts developed within the chapter. Complete listings of other readings and filmstrips and moving pictures, also found at the end of each chapter, will be of great help to the teacher.

Dorothea Williams, the author, is an experienced junior high school classroom teacher. The suggestions made in the book are those practical suggestions which she has found to be effective in developing changed behavior on the part of boys and girls with regard to their health.

We are particularly indebted to the persons named on the title page for special assistance in the preparation of this volume. Their contributions consisted of assisting in the planning and in careful reading and revision of the material as it was written.

The pictures in the front pages of the book were obtained from the following sources: H. Armstrong Roberts, pages ii, iii, ix, x (left), xii, and 2; Philip Gendreau, page vi (top); Denver Public Schools, page vi (bottom), page viii (top); Ewing Galloway, page vii; United States Public Health Service, page viii (bottom); Harold M. Lambert, page x (right); American Red Cross, page xi.

Contents

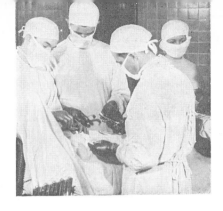

Contents, continued

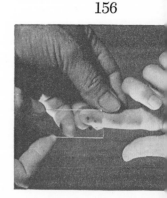

Contents, continued

Contents, continued

Building health

Health is a state of complete physical, mental, and social well-being and not merely the absence of disease or infirmity.

The enjoyment of the highest attainable standard of health is one of the fundamental rights of every human being without distinction of race, religion, political belief, economic or social condition.

The health of all peoples is fundamental to the attainment of peace and security and is dependent upon the fullest co-operation of individuals and states.

From the Constitution of the World Health Organization

What Does Growing Up Mean to You?

Step outside that body you are living in and take a good look at yourself. Do you like what you see? Would you like to have you for a friend? Are you the kind of person you admire? If you had the power would you make any changes before you stepped back into yourself?

Would you like to be better looking, stronger, and more graceful and accurate in your movements? Would you like to be able to work and play more successfully? Would you like to have more self-confidence and to be able to control your feelings better? Would you like to get along better with your family and friends?

A desire to improve is natural. Everyone has some things about himself he would like to change—even though some people are unwilling to admit it. But the really good news is that you *can* change. In fact you cannot keep from changing.

As you grow up you change, and the world around you changes. One thing you may be sure of is that you are different now from the person you were last year, or last month, or even yesterday. You will be different tomorrow and every other day.

Every day you build yourself—your body, mind, and spirit. As soon as you are old enough to think at all, you start solving problems, choosing ways to act. Every choice you make, everything you think and feel and do becomes a part of you. The problem of growing up is to make choices that will help you to be healthy and happy, both now and later.

Growing up gives you your big opportunity and responsibility. You can help yourself to be strong and attractive. As you grow up you can learn better methods of solving your daily problems. You can learn to use your mental ability and to control unhappy feelings. You can help yourself to be a healthy, happy person.

3

Picture Preview:
Chapter 1

Philip Gendreau

Do you ever dream of being a different kind of person in some ways? How would you like to change yourself?

How does planning make a trip more enjoyable? What other activities turn out better if they are planned?

United States Public Health Service

How can a study of health help you to grow up happily? What do you expect to study in health? Which questions in the table of contents interest you?

Books can be good companions and sources of information. How can they help you to grow up happily?

$\mathcal{C}hapter\ 1$

HOW CAN YOU HELP YOURSELF GROW UP?

$\mathcal{C}$an you imagine a man starting to build a house without any idea of the kind of house he wanted, without any knowledge or skill in carpentry, and without any information about the materials available? Would you like to sail on a voyage with a captain who did not know where he was going and who knew little about his ship or the sea on which he sailed? What chance does a pick-up football team without a system or a coach have against a well-coached, well-organized team?

Encyclopedia Britannica Films

A good builder works according to a plan. He knows his goal and what he has to work with. What plans do you have for growing up?

Almost everything we do requires a plan. A plan makes us more efficient, gives us a sense of security and satisfaction, and results in a superior product or achievement. Without a plan, we waste much time and energy, feel confused and bewildered, and may never accomplish anything worth while. One of the signs of growing up is an increased ability to plan for yourself. Do you make any plans for your daily activities? Can you manage your own spending money? Do you have any plans for the future?

What are important parts of any plan? A navigator must know not only where he is going but where he is and what kind of performance he can expect from his ship. He checks as he goes along to see if he is maintaining his course. A football quarterback must take stock of his position and make the most of the strong and weak points of his team and his opponents as he calls the plays.

Following a plan can help you to grow up. If your daily choices are based on straight thinking they are more likely to accumulate to build the kind of person you want to be. What

6

are important parts in a plan for growing up? You will need to take stock of your present position, choose worthy goals, and work out some plays that will move you successfully toward your goal.

What kind of person do you want to be?

An important part of any plan is its goal. Everyone has dreams or mental pictures of the kind of person he would like to be. Small children often think they would like to be something adventurous like cowboys or aviators or explorers. Older boys and girls often wish to be popular or glamorous. They imitate athletes and stars of radio, television, and movies. How do you think your dreams and goals affect your life?

Why are goals important? Goals are important because they help you to succeed. They give spark and direc-tion to your life. They help you choose what to do and give you a satisfying feeling that you are accomplishing something worth while.

If you study the lives of famous and successful people, you will find that each of them had a goal or purpose in life. To reach their goals they studied and worked. Often they gave up what seemed to other people the comforts and pleasures of life. Sometimes when we envy successful people we forget that back of their achievements are long hours, even years, of effort. Your favorite baseball star was not *born*

Denver Public Schools

A football team moves toward the goal by concentrating on one play at a time. Are you working on some definite plays to improve yourself?

7

with the ability to throw and bat a baseball! The boys and girls who seem so naturally friendly and self-confident acquired those skills by practice.

Most people do achieve any goal that is very important to them. A goal helps you to stick to difficult jobs. Athletes, students, and artists work long and hard to achieve their dreams. Have you ever enjoyed doing a difficult job because you were working for something you wanted?

Having a goal helps you decide what to do. A dancer's dream of being a star helps her decide what to eat and how to use her spare time. The football player's desire to play in the big game helps him decide whether to report for practice or go on a picnic with the gang. A desire to be liked by others can help anyone decide to pitch in and do his share of work.

Working for a purpose gives you enthusiasm and extra energy. It helps to make you successful. Success is getting what you want. Happiness is feeling that what you are doing is good and right. A happy person feels that he is living in harmony with other people, with his own best abilities, and with God. Do you think a goal could help you to be successful but make you unhappy?

What are reasonable goals? People have many different ideas of success and happiness. Some boys and girls dream of careers as artists or athletes. Some dream of serving as doctors, ministers, lawyers, teachers, mechanics, or salesmen. Some aim for wealth or fame or power. But all of us have some goals that are the same. Everyone wants to be a healthy, likable, responsible member of his group, whether that group is a family, a teen-age crowd, a community, or a nation. Everyone wants to feel worth while and to love and be loved by his family and friends. On these common goals we can all work together.

Some people choose goals that do not require their best efforts. They aim to fool others, to "get by," or to succeed at the expense of others. Even if they are successful they cannot be happy. Why not?

Some people try to achieve too much. If you expect yourself to be perfect, you are doomed to disappointment. We all can do many things well if we try, but no one can be perfect in everything. We all have many, many imperfections. We have physical defects and limitations. At times all of us are afraid, angry, jealous, or selfish. We behave foolishly. Sometimes we do a job poorly or fail completely. We attempt tasks not suited to our strength or ability.

All of us need to learn to face failure without discouragement. A football team expects that some of its plays will fail to gain. They try to diagnose the reason for failure and try again. Our efforts to be happy will not always be successful. We can learn how to try again.

To make us happy, goals should be high enough to challenge us, but not out of reach. A plan of life must take into account individual strengths and weaknesses.

Do goals change? As you grow up your dreams become more practical. You realize that success and happiness are the result of your own actions. You want to find out what you can do in order to be happy, now and in the future.

We move toward any goal a step at

a time. A football team uses a series of plays in order to score. Each play becomes a sort of temporary goal and sets the stage for the next play.

We move toward our goals of being happy, successful grown-up persons by a series of successful experiences. Being a successful, happy person now is the best way to plan for a happy future. The best thing a person can do for himself is to develop the skills and understandings appropriate for his own age.

Certain personal qualities help to make us successful and happy. No matter what our individual goals may be, good health will help us to reach them. Good health means more than being free from sickness. It includes your complete well-being in body, mind, and feelings. Healthy development means that each individual should develop a strong body, understand how to care for his own health and protect the health of others, assume responsibility for his own development and behavior, and establish habits that enable him to care for his health with little effort.

How can you work toward your goal? Daydreaming is a wonderful way to start directing your own growth. Everyone dreams, so that is easy. So easy, in fact, that many people stop right there. Idle dreaming that does not lead to action changes you, but not in a desirable way. Make sure your dreaming is only a step. When you know the kind of person you want to be, you can regulate your actions accordingly. When you have a decision to make, you can ask yourself, "How will this affect the person I want to be?"

The next steps are harder, but re-

Ewing Galloway

Have you ever worked long and carefully at a job? What attitudes and habits help you to stick with a job and do it as well as you can? How can you help yourself enjoy necessary work?

warding. Take a good honest look at yourself. Examine your appearance, your feelings, your actions, your wishes and dreams, and the things you wonder and worry about. Recognize your good features and your bad features. Pick out the characteristics that you would like to develop and those that you would like to change. Examining yourself is a difficult job. The test called "Take a Look at Yourself" (pages 31–33) at the end of Chapter 2 may help you to rate yourself and to see where you need to improve. Observing other people may help you to see yourself. Other people also live in families, go to school, try to make friends, and belong to groups. You are not the only person who is self-conscious, shy, and worried about grow-

9

Denver Public Schools

Your study of health will be more useful if you try some of the activities and experiments. What is an experiment? What are the boys above doing? What accurate measurements are they using?

Your study of health will certainly be of more practical use if you try out the directions and suggestions you find in this book. What are the boys and girls at the left doing? Why is it a good thing to know how to put on a bandage?

ing up and finding a satisfactory place in the world. If you are not too sensitive you may ask a trusted older friend to help you see yourself as others see you.

When you have some of your problems in mind, get all the information you can about yourself. Find out about your body—how it works, how it grows and develops, and how you

10

can help it work and develop at its best. Learn how your mind and nerves and feelings work; learn how they must change and develop if you are not to be a baby in a grown-up body. The more you know about yourself the better you will be able to help yourself be healthy and happy. You will better understand yourself and other people. You will be able to meet more successfully the problems of life in a changing world.

How can a study of health help you?

A study of health can help you to develop physically, mentally, and emotionally. It can give you information about how your body works and how you can help it work at its best. It can help you see that your problems and worries are similar to those of other people.

To develop and to learn you have to think and plan; you have to test what you read and hear in the light of your own experiences. To improve yourself you must make some changes in your ways of thinking and acting. A study of health can help you improve only if you are doing something with

Denver Public Schools

Are you planning to use films to help you understand yourself and how you can be healthy and happy?

the information you obtain. Books can help you only if you use them actively.

How can books help you change? Books can help you to dream. They can help you realize the remarkable powers of the human body and mind and spirit. Maybe you have been satisfied with too little or discouraged too easily. Many people become accustomed to poor health or unhappy living conditions. They do not realize life might be different—happier and more thrilling. For lack of imagination, courage, and self-discipline they lose their opportunity to develop and to live happy lives. Stories of boys and girls and of men and women who have made the most of themselves and who have overcome great handicaps can give you hope and courage.

Books can help you to recognize your problems. Anything you have to decide or any question you want answered is a problem. Big problems are made up of accumulations of little ones. Before you can solve them you must sharpen your ability to recognize the little parts. You may be too close to your own problems to see them. Anything very close to you looks large. You may just feel vaguely dissatisfied about your whole situation. To see someone else in a situation like yours may help you see your own problem more clearly. Stories and cartoons help you to gain perspective. Usually your problems do not seem quite so serious when you realize that everyone has them. Maybe you can even laugh at yourself a little. Problems and worries have a way of shrinking when you look at them squarely and tackle them with confidence.

After you recognize your problems and realize that you need more information, books can furnish you with facts and information. They can point out relationships that you may not have recognized. They can suggest ways in which you may use facts to solve your own problems. You probably realize that your comfort and appearance are related to your health; so are your personality and your behavior. But do you know just how and why and what you can do about it? How does food affect your complexion and your strength? How can you use information about muscles, skin, and various body systems to improve your complexion and to build a strong, attractive body? What does sleep have to do with your ability to play basketball? How can understanding your emotions help you to gain self-confidence or to have friends? How can you form habits that will make you a healthy, happy person?

How can you use this book?

First get acquainted with the book. Look it over and see what it contains. Find the table of contents, the page in front that lists all the chapter titles. Notice all the questions of the units and chapters. These are the problems of other boys and girls. Are some of them of particular interest to you? Find the index in the back of the book. Do you know when and how to use it? What other material is in the back of the book? What is it good for? Now look through the book. Notice the pictures and problems. Take a look at the previews at the beginning of each chapter.

This book can serve as a guide to your study of your own growth and development. It contains many facts and principles that you can use to solve your own problems. Unit 1 describes the importance of change and how you can adjust to it. It describes how growth and development take place and what is normal in growing up. Unit 2 contains descriptions of how your body is constructed, how it works, and how you can help it work and develop. Unit 3 contains information that will help you to use your body and mind efficiently and comfortably. Unit 4 describes some of the reasons why people behave as they do and has some suggestions that may help you to get along with people.

Do you want to make the best use of the time you spend studying health? The suggestions that follow may help you to learn more easily. You will find them helpful.

1. In a planning period, try to see how the problems discussed in the chapter fit into your life. Read and discuss the planning questions. See how much you have already learned in various ways about the problem and what additional understanding you want or need

2. Read the introduction to the unit and to the chapter.

3. Look over the "Picture Previews" and "Looking Ahead" sections. Pick out some that interest you. Write down your answers or reactions right away before you read any further or discuss the questions with anyone. Save your answers to read again when you finish studying the problem.

4. Discuss the pictures and problems in class. Find out other people's ideas. Do they give you new ideas, raise other questions in your mind, or remind you of other experiences related to the problem? If you can associate the problem with other experiences, in or out of school, it will have more meaning for you. Try to examine some of your old ideas in the light of new information.

5. Look at the suggestions for activities and start planning to do some of them. Everyone needs to know how to work alone and with others, how to read for different purposes, how to use the library, and how to talk with and exchange ideas with others. Some

Denver Public Schools

Reading is only one method of learning. What are some other methods?

13

of the activities will require reading, interviewing, observation, committee work, library work, experiments, and other worth-while methods of learning. Not all the activities will appeal to you. Do the ones that interest you at first. Later try some of the others. You may be surprised at how much you enjoy them, and the new experience may be just what you need. For example, if you have always been timid about talking with people, a carefully planned interview with the high school basketball coach or someone in the city health department may be just the experience you need.

6. Read the chapter rapidly to get the general idea.

7. Read the chapter again, more slowly for details. Test your understanding by trying to answer the questions under the pictures and in the headlines.

8. When you finish reading the chapter, get ready to contribute your share to the class discussion. Do some further reading and some of the activities.

Denver Public Schools

Can you think of other interesting ways of reporting to the class what you have learned?

9. Be ready to present some of your ideas to the class or to other classes, either alone or as part of a group. You might prepare an exhibit, a report, a panel discussion, an experiment, a story, a poem, a play, a radio script, or a cartoon. Make your presentation a helpful experience for yourself as well as for your audience—plan it and carry it through to the best of your ability. Give yourself a chance to practice some skills that you need. Give yourself the pleasure that comes from completing a job successfully.

10. Evaluate your work.

(a) What have you learned? Have you changed any of your ideas? Acquired some new ones? How are you changing? Is it in the direction you desire, or are you getting better at doing sloppy work, putting things off, and covering up your weaknesses? The learning that means the most to you is the learning that changes what you actually do. One good habit formed—drinking a glass of milk at lunch or stopping to consider other people's feelings before you speak or act—is more learning than if you memorized this whole book.

(b) If you are really learning, some of your ideas, attitudes, and behavior should change. Test yourself to see if you change in any way. Check yourself now on the self-inventory test, "Take a Look at Yourself," pages 31–33, in Chapter 2. Check again at intervals during the year. Keep a record of your physical growth. You may like to make a chart in your notebook to record at intervals your height, weight, and scores on various self-testing activities—jump, rope climb, etc. See your physical-education teacher for some self-testing activities.

Everyone needs to be able to work alone or with others. What kind of work is best done alone? When is a group better?

(c) *Some boys and girls like to keep a record by taking pictures. This record is even more interesting if you can include pictures from the time you were an infant. Pictures of your whole class taken at regular intervals make a very interesting study of growth. You will be amazed at changes in just a year or so. Perhaps you can plan such a series and note for yourselves the general pattern of growth as well as the wide variations among individuals. You may be able to plan your pictures to show growth in interests, activities, and duties.*

(d) *If you want to keep a record of your mental, emotional, and social growth, keep a diary. Include the things you do and how you feel about your experiences. By the end of the year you will have an interesting picture of yourself. Compare yourself "before" and "after."*

11. Evaluate the work of the whole class. Pick out good things you are doing and reinforce them. Strengthen weak activities.

Do you want to learn about health from other sources? You cannot learn all you want to know from one book. To obtain more information on some of the questions that interest you, read

15

Ewing Galloway

If you are making a trip you must constantly check your position. Tests at the end of the chapter help you check your progress.

Be on the alert for other sources of information, for opportunities to enlarge your point of view and to broaden your understanding. You can learn from cartoons, comic strips, movies, newspapers, television, plays, experiments, conversations, and your own observations. Many sources of information are not reliable, but they give you ideas you can check with more reliable sources. Keep your eyes and ears and mind alert and working. Most of all you learn what you live. The things you do every day are the things you are really learning. You are only fooling yourself if you say that you know better but continue to use poor daily habits of living. Check your own daily habits. Apply what you learn to yourself and to your own community.

Do you like to work with groups? You may like to use the plan of dividing into committees to help each other. Talk the plan over with your teacher and classmates. For example, you might like to have committees:

1. To locate books and arrange for the class to use them.

2. To locate and write for pamphlets and free material.

3. To locate films available from schools, health departments, government agencies, and commercial firms.

4. To arrange to show films, to prepare the class for them, and to conduct discussions.

5. To arrange for field trips or guest speakers; to investigate what your own community is doing, and what it might do better to help keep its citizens well and happy.

6. To collect materials and to prepare bulletin boards and scrapbooks

some of the other books that are mentioned. You will find references on sports, first aid, popularity, scientific discoveries, improving your looks, hobbies, how to get along with people, and many other subjects that have been interesting to boys and girls like you.

Some of the books are stories, real or imaginary. Stories often help you to see other people's problems and help you to understand people better. If you are observant you may be able to relate some of their experiences to your own life. Many old stories, if they are well written and describe how real people feel and act, have problems that still exist. In a world of change, some fundamental human problems always remain.

Committee reports can be made in a variety of ways. Demonstrations or exhibits can be lively and interesting.

These students are carrying out safe practices they learned in class. They are walking on the left side of the highway. Why? Keep a record of the health lessons you practice.

of drawings, clippings, statistics, pictures, cartoons, and the like.

7. *To keep the class safety conscious. Safety is no accident. It requires planning, alertness, and skill. The committee can keep busy all year helping you to apply what you learn to help you keep safe and active.*

Committees will need to watch the chapters ahead and be ready with materials when the class needs them. Chairmen can assign individual responsibilities. You can use part of a period each week for committee planning and reports.

When you finish your work on a problem, evaluate the work of the committees. Remember to make criticisms that will be helpful. Make criticisms kind and courteous. Improve your own ability to work with others.

Reviewing the chapter

Test yourself

Looking at questions that bother other boys and girls, comparing your attitudes with those of other people, and rating your own habits may help you to recognize your own problems more clearly.

Look at your attitudes and beliefs

What would you say to a person who made such statements as those listed below? Do you agree or disagree? Why? Do you have good reasons for your beliefs? Do you practice what you believe?

These are the statements for you to discuss:

A person should be entirely responsible for his own health.

Health articles in magazines and newspapers give reliable information.

Schools have no right to give medical examinations.

You can cure cancer by diet.

There should be a law to compel vaccination.

It is better to be popular with your crowd than to be approved by your parents and teachers.

Feeling tired and being tired are the same thing.

Some fatigue is good for you.

You can be farsighted without knowing it.

I would like to dance, but the others are so good they would make fun of me.

Do you know?

You are constantly having to make decisions—to do something. Good health information and habits can help you.

What would you do if:

You had an earache?

You thought you were overweight?

You woke up tired every morning?

Someone fainted?

Different people in a room wanted different temperatures?

Somebody asked to borrow your comb or towel?

You were so sore you could hardly move after the first football practice?

Your schoolwork seemed too difficult?

Your parents seemed to boss you too much?

You became excited and nervous when you had to recite?

You seemed to lack the pep to keep up with others?

You had frequent headaches?

You became angry often?

You felt that everyone treated you unfairly?

You had many colds?

You were troubled with pimples and blackheads?

What do you think are other common problems a study of health could help people solve?

Look at your habits

Are you trying to be the kind of person you like?

What are you actually doing about it?

Do you do as many things for yourself as you can?

When you fail, do you honestly try to find out why so you can do better next time?

Reading to help you grow up

Stories about other boys and girls may help you to see your own problems and to understand yourself.

This Happened to Me, by Helen Ferris, is a collection of short stories that touch such problems of teenagers as shyness, desire for popularity, being ashamed of one's home, and temper tantrums.

Out on a Limb, by Louise Baker, tells the humorous, courageous story of a girl who loses her leg in an accident at the age of eight. It offers new courage for those inclined to pity themselves.

Almost any biography, whether of an inventor, explorer, actress, pioneer, soldier, or saint, can help you realize that all people face problems and overcome handicaps.

Benjamin Franklin's *Autobiography* tells in detail of his own plan for self-improvement.

Triumph Clear, by Lorraine Beim, tells about adjusting to being physically handicapped.

Life and Health, by Wilson, and others, has an interesting first chapter discussing life goals and plans.

Films to help you understand

Wastage of Human Resources. Encyclopedia Britannica Films. Tells of the waste and unhappiness caused by society's failure to provide healthful, safe, and efficient living conditions. What can be done about disease, careless accidents, juvenile delinquency, unemployment, alcohol and drug addiction, mental diseases, crime, and war? Are these health problems?

Benjamin Franklin. Encyclopedia Britannica Films. Tells the highlights, the problems, the early struggles, and the success, of a famous man's life.

Encyclopedia Britannica Films

The surface of the earth changes all the time. What changes are going on now? What changes have you observed?

Encyclopedia Britannica Films

Can you describe some ways of life that are different from yours? Do people ever change their patterns of living?

How has the airplane changed the way people live? How have other inventions changed people's lives?

People change all their lives. How will these children change in the next five or six years?

Chapter 2

WHY IS CHANGE IMPORTANT?

$\mathcal{G}$rowing up is exciting. Life never stands still. You change and the world around you changes. Every day may bring new discoveries about yourself, the world, and your place in it. Every day you have the opportunity to see and to understand and to enjoy life.

Sometimes changes are sudden and dramatic. Sometimes they are gradual and seem so ordinary and natural that we do not realize how they affect our lives. A changing world makes life exciting, interesting, and hopeful. Can you imagine living in a world where nothing ever changed, where no change was possible?

Growing up changes you. Your body grows to adult size. You assume the proportions and characteristics of a grown man or woman. You develop in strength and skill and grace. Your developing mind, senses, and feelings increase your awareness, understanding, and enjoyment of the world you live in. As you grow up the world seems to expand. It offers adventure and happiness to those who can solve its problems.

Growing up is a challenging job. Change may be frightening to those who do not expect it and plan for it. An ever-changing, expanding world may be confusing and terrifying instead of thrilling. A changing world presents problems to be solved, offers opportunities to be grasped. Your changing self brings you problems as well as joys.

To be aware of and to understand changes in yourself and in the world will help you to grow up happily. You can learn how to adapt yourself to change and to adjust to new conditions. You can find out what changes take place and what causes them. You can take advantage of your ability to change. Especially in your teens, when growth and change are rapid, you have a wonderful chance to help yourself grow to be the kind of person you want to be. Why not start now on this important job?

Looking ahead

Questions and suggestions

Some questions and suggestions at the beginning of each chapter will help you to plan your study of the problem ahead. The questions will help you to understand the problem more clearly and to recall what you already know about it. The suggestions for activities will give you opportunities to learn in many ways. They will help you to apply your learning to your daily living.

1. Do you think that change is important? Why?

2. What things change?

3. What does change have to do with a study of health?

4. Read the topic questions in the chapter.

5. What is the main idea or purpose of the chapter?

6. Look over the two pages of pictures at the beginning of the chapter. What does "preview" mean?

7. Discuss the pictures in class. Your discussion may bring out some new problems you would like to investigate. Write the problems on the board as topics for reports.

8. What changes have you noticed in your community in your lifetime? Have the changes affected you? Have they affected your physical or emotional well-being?

9. How has your own private world changed in the past year or two? Has your home or school or circle of friends changed?

10. In what ways have *you* changed in the last year or two?

11. What brought about the changes?

12. Have the changes created any difficulties or problems for you? Do you think other people have similar problems?

13. How will you be changed at the end of this year?

14. Would you like to make some particular changes?

Committee planning

Some committees, like those for the library and bulletin board, will need to look ahead to have material ready when the class needs it. Sometimes experiments will be more interesting if presented when the class is just beginning to discuss a new problem. Committee members can look ahead; they can scan the chapters, read the suggestions at the beginning and the end of chapters, look over the books and films suggested, and plan their own work. Special suggestions are offered to some committees in each chapter. Use your own ideas, too.

Reading

Read rapidly through the entire chapter for the general idea. Then reread more carefully for details. Look at the pictures. Try to answer the questions at the end of the chapter. Write out in your own words the important ideas in the chapter.

Activities for everyone

When you have finished reading, make a plan that will help you to take part in class activities and discussion. You may do some of the reading the library committee has found, work on one of the activities suggested in the chapter and at the beginning of the chapter, and make plans for your committee. Be ready to present some of your ideas. Prepare an exhibit, a panel discussion, an experiment, a story, a cartoon, or some other kind of report.

23

To understand change you must first observe it and be aware of it. How observant are you? Do you notice the changes that are going on around you and within you? What changes do you think you will meet in your lifetime?

How does the world change? Imagine yourself living in the year 2000. What changes do you think will have taken place? Probably you will think first of new inventions, of ways of using atomic energy, of easier and faster ways of traveling and doing work, and of new designs and materials for clothing and buildings and other objects.

But other changes take place that make even bigger differences in the way people live. Do you think there will be any changes in the earth itself? Will there be changes in supplies of food and raw materials and in the way people are distributed over the earth's surface? Will customs, laws, manners, and habits of work and play be different? Will people change their ideas of what constitutes success, happiness, and good and bad ways of behaving? What traits of character will be most valuable and most highly regarded? In this uncertain, changing world there are some unchanging things. Laws of nature are the same now as they were when the earth was created. Knowledge of the eternal laws that govern all things in the universe help you to keep a sense of balance and security in a changing, bewildering world. What are some of the laws and ideals that remain unchanged?

Perhaps you can get a better idea of the way the world changes if you look backward instead of forward. Pictures, books, moving pictures, and memories can help you see changes that have already taken place. In what ways is the world today different from the world of a year ago? Try to think of changes in habits and customs and in beliefs and attitudes as well as changes in inventions and clothing. Try to imagine how an ordinary girl or boy would spend an ordinary day in the time of Columbus or Lincoln.

Encyclopedia Britannica Films

What changes in ways of living have taken place in two hundred years? Could we live like pioneers? Can we expect to go on living as we are now?

You do not have to read history or look at old pictures to see change. It is going on all the time, everywhere. You can see plenty of changes in a lifetime. Your grandparents can remember the first automobiles and radios and moving pictures. Ask your parents to tell you of changes that have taken place in their lifetime. If you are observant you can detect changes all around you. What changes have you seen in *your own lifetime?*

In what ways do you change? Even more exciting and challenging than a changing world are the changes in people. You are changing all the time. You cannot see the process, but the results are evident.

Look at yourself. Then look at a picture, real or imaginary, of yourself a year or several years ago. Picture yourself at various ages in the past and in the future. What changes take place in a lifetime?

You change in many ways, because human beings are extremely complicated. Your body changes, but, more important, your thoughts, feelings, and ways of behaving change. Like an actor you change the role you play in life. You change your ideas about yourself, about your relationships with other people, and about your place in the world.

The most noticeable changes are physical. You change in size, shape, and proportions. Organs function differently. A child is not a miniature adult; he is a completely different person. Do you know the ways he is different? If you observe carefully, or have a good memory, you may be able to describe some of the changes that take place as you grow up. You can read more about them in Chapter 4.

Byron G. Moon Company

What kinds of changes would you like to make in yourself? How can you make the changes you wish? How can you be sure they are changes for the better?

Since you were an infant your thoughts and feelings have changed as completely as your body. They will change even more as you continue growing mentally and emotionally all your life. Your childish experiences are still a part of you, like threads woven into a pattern that is repeated in new combinations. You change so completely you are really a whole series of different persons.

Can you remember any incident in your childhood? Try to recapture in your imagination your thoughts, feelings, and reasons for behaving as you did that day when you were younger. You probably will find it difficult to remember and understand the person you were just a few short years ago.

Change makes life exciting and challenging, hopeful and difficult. Life is a constant struggle to adjust to changes. Both you and your world change, so adjustment is continuous. Change brings problems to be solved and offers opportunities for improvement.

How is change exciting and hopeful? A changing world is important because it makes a difference in the way you live, and the way you live helps to make you the person you are. You cannot stand aside watching the world go by. You live in the world and you respond (answer) to it. A new invention or discovery may cause a city to grow. If your city grows, you respond by making changes in your way of life. You may have to move your home, travel long distances to work, make new friends, or learn a new job. To be important, changes need not affect the whole world. New members in your family, a different school, a new friend, or even a new fad or a new idea can make a big difference in your life. Your entire life is a series of adjustments to fit yourself smoothly into the changing world in which you live.

You are able to make adjustments because you have the ability to change and to learn. You can change your surroundings or yourself, or both. You can try different responses to situations and choose the one that works out best. As you grow in knowledge and understanding and skill you can react more expertly. You can figure out ways of responding that bring you more satisfaction and happiness.

Most people like change. Life without new experiences would be monotonous and dull. Living in a changing world is like taking a lifelong trip to new places. There are always new sights, new people, and new experiences. Even the old familiar places and faces and things to do stay fresh and exciting as you grow up and see them more clearly and understand them better. Change makes improvement possible. If you could not change you would remain forever the way you were born. To realize that

H. Armstrong Roberts

Changes are inevitable. If we are to live happily we must plan for change. What kind of planning makes old age a happy time?

26

Ewing Galloway

Do you think most people like change and new experiences? Why?

everything is changing and that you can help shape this future keeps you looking ahead, dreaming, and planning.

Why is change difficult? Change makes life interesting and hopeful, but it makes life difficult too. You never know what is going to happen next. New situations and new problems confront you continually. You must keep learning new skills and new ways of thinking. You cannot simply pick out one way of thinking, feeling, or acting and expect it to work all the time. The feelings and behavior that brought you satisfaction when you were three years old, or even when you were ten or eleven, may bring

nothing but unhappiness now. A baby can cry for what he wants. The boy or girl who uses that method is maladjusted (*mal* means bad). You must learn to adjust to changes in yourself, in your surroundings, and in what others expect of you.

Changes can be frightening and bewildering too. Things change whether you want them to or not. Change goes on all the time, giving you a new world to adjust to. Your body grows and develops. So does your mind and spirit. No matter how you respond to conditions and people around you, you are changed by your response. You may just become more the way you are, but you cannot stand still.

27

Encyclopedia Britannica Films

How do changes in a city affect the way people live? How can planning for change make life more pleasant? Does your community plan for the future? Can you offer any suggestions about how young people can help in such a plan? What changes has science recently brought about?

Denver Public Schools

Basketball is a fast changing game. How can a player be ready for the changes? A player has to be ready for split-second action. Do these boys look as if they are ready? How can you tell?

Even if you are satisfied with things as they are, you cannot keep them that way.

Many people have trouble adjusting themselves to change. Many may resist change, or close their eyes to it. They cling to habits and attitudes that were once useful but are no longer appropriate. They refuse to play the role of adults and try to remain children. They live in "the good old days." The failure to grow up is a common maladjustment. You probably know boys and girls your own age who cling to babyish ways and try to avoid the problems that are brought by change.

Not all changes are good changes. Change may move in any direction. Some cities and nations develop in size and riches as others decline. Some communities grow more beautiful; others run down. The world may grow better in some respects, but worse in others. You may develop satisfactory ways of solving some problems and unsatisfactory ways of solving others.

You cannot just sit back and say, "Tomorrow will be better." Tomorrow will be different, but it probably will not be better—*unless you do something about it.* Change offers you the opportunity to make the future better, but it also places great responsibility on you.

Living in a changing world is somewhat like playing in a fast-moving basketball game. You must constantly be aware of what is going on and what it means to you. You must be grounded in fundamentals, be in good condition, and be ready to make decisions promptly.

What can you do about change?

Change is sure to happen. You cannot stop it. But you *can* prepare yourself to keep your balance in a changing world and to solve its problems. You can try to find some of the unchanging laws that control everything that happens in the universe. You can learn to take advantage of your ability to change so that you will develop in the way you desire.

Can you change yourself the way you desire? Most boys and girls look forward happily to the changes that make them "grown up," ready to take a responsible, independent place in the world. But you will not wake up some morning to find yourself suddenly changed into the ideal of your dreams. You change slowly by growing and developing. Little changes that take place every minute gradually accumulate (pile up) to build the "grown-up" you. Everything you do, see, or hear and every thought and feeling you hold adds something to you, for better or worse. Your big opportunity and responsibility lie in finding out how you develop and how your own actions and failures to act affect your development. Then you can choose and practice habits and behavior that will make you develop into the person you want to be.

So far you probably have not given much thought to the changes that were taking place in you. You have just grown. Parents or other adults have tried to teach you practices and habits that would keep you well and happy. As a small child you were taught some rules and you learned some habits to govern your behavior.

Now you need to understand *how* and *why*. Then you can make your own decisions in new and changing situations, and you can accept the consequences of your own behavior without evasion or blaming others. You should know how your body works and develops normally. You should know how habits are formed. You should know some of the reasons why people (including yourself) act the ways they do. Then you can make up your own mind about what you should do to become the kind of person you admire and respect and like.

Previous poor training or surroundings need not discourage you, nor

H. Armstrong Roberts

How did you feel when you entered a new school? Do you like or dread changes in your life? Why?

29

These boys and girls are building a model City of Tomorrow. What do you think tomorrow's city will be like? Tomorrow's citizens?

should you blame or shift responsibility for your future development to others. Human beings often develop best when they have obstacles to overcome. Everyone has handicaps of some sort. You can read many true stories of people who have been happy and successful in spite of poverty, physical handicaps, continual discouragement, or poor early training and surroundings. The human spirit and will are able to accomplish wonders. Yours is the opportunity to become what you will, and yours is the responsibility.

What is your present position? To plan your life well you need an accurate picture of your present position. Such a picture will help you to strengthen or change weak traits and

to develop strong ones. It will help you to live up to your full possibilities and keep you from attempting the impossible. A picture of yourself should include a physical health inventory and a survey of personal qualities or characteristics, habits, attitudes, and interests. It should give you an idea of your physical, mental, and social development.

The self-inventories under "Test yourself" on pages 31–33 help you to know yourself. Be completely honest in answering the questions. Keep your answers and comments in a notebook. You may keep the results to yourself or you may want to discuss them with your parents, with your teacher, or with some older person who can help you solve them wisely. Mark the date on which you answered the questions. You may want to take the same tests later to see how much you have improved.

The important part of an examination is what you do about your discoveries. If the surveys show you do not have some weaknesses, you are a most unusual person. If you find many, do not try to make yourself over all at once. If you attempt too much you will probably become discouraged. Start with one thing and keep working on it every day. Consult the index for help in finding information that may help you.

Some defects may become worse if you delay treatment. Defects like decayed teeth and skin rashes should not be neglected.

Reviewing the chapter

Test yourself

TAKE A LOOK AT YOURSELF

For the following 85 questions allow two points if your answer is "always." Give yourself one point if your answer is "often." You get no points if your answer is "never." Be honest in your answers. You want to know how you really rate.

Is your body strong and healthy?

1. Are you full of pep during the day even when you are working hard?
2. Are you hungry at mealtimes? Do you enjoy your meals?
3. Are you free from frequent colds?
4. Do you have regular habits of elimination?
5. Do you take part in games and activities that require strength and endurance?
6. Are you free from headaches?
7. Do you wake in the mornings refreshed and rested?
8. Can you keep up with others your size?

Is you body attractive and comfortable?

9. Is your skin clean and clear?
10. Are your hands and nails clean and smooth?
11. Are your clothes simple, neat, and clean?
12. Are your shoes shined and in repair?
13. Is your hair clean and brushed?
14. Are your teeth clean and free from decay?
15. Do you change socks and underclothes frequently?
16. Do you use a deodorant when necessary?

Are you as alive mentally as you want to be?

17. Can you read as well as others your age?
18. Do you have good work habits in school and elsewhere?
19. Do you take pride in doing a good job?
20. Do you finish what you start?
21. Do you read the news regularly?
22. Do you have an active interest in art, music, and drama—either to take part or to enjoy another's performance?
23. Do you have at least one hobby?
24. Do you read some "good" books besides assignments?
25. Do you apply your learning to your daily living?
26. Do you find it easy to talk to people?
27. Can you accept criticism cheerfully?
28. Can you overcome discouragement?

31

29. Do you remember things you are supposed to do?

30. Do you make decisions promptly?

31. Do you plan your time to allow for necessary work and play?

32. Are you interested in school?

33. Do you have confidence in your ability?

34. Do people trust you to carry out assignments?

Are you growing up emotionally?

35. Do you accept responsibility for your share of work?

36. Do you make and keep close friends?

37. Do you enjoy the company of both boys and girls?

38. Do you have a favorite friend of your own sex?

39. Do you love and respect your parents and avoid unnecessary "revolts"?

40. Do you love your brothers and sisters and get along with them?

41. Do you co-operate with student leaders and adult authority?

42. Do you treat others with respect and kindness regardless of their race, their beliefs, or how much money they have?

43. Do you avoid spreading rumors and gossip?

44. Do you show emotional stability in times of stress?

45. Do you have a code of conduct to guide your daily actions?

46. Do you have a reasonably satisfactory belief about the meaning and purpose of life?

47. Do you make a sincere effort to practice your religious beliefs every day?

48. Do you like to be alone part of the time?

49. Do you expect to work hard for the things you want out of life?

Are you developing necessary skills?

50. Do you play at least two team games and two individual sports well?

51. Do you have good table manners?

52. Do you stand and walk easily erect?

53. Do you take part in group discussions?

54. Can you carry on a pleasant conversation?

55. Do you keep your clothes clean and neat?

56. Do you take care of your own room and of school and sports equipment?

57. Do you manage your own spending money?

58. Do you assume responsibility for some jobs at home and do them well?

59. Are you learning any new skills right now?

Do your habits help you to be healthy?

60. Do you eat at regular times?

61. Do you plan so you can come to meals rested and clean?

62. Do you go to bed at a regular time and get at least nine hours of sleep?

63. Do you have two hours of vigorous exercise daily?

64. Do you eat a hearty breakfast?

65. Do you drink four glasses of pasteurized milk daily?

66. Do you drink plenty of water daily?

67. Do you have regular habits of elimination?

68. Do you include foods from all the "Basic 7" groups in your daily diet?

69. Do you avoid large amounts of rich, sweet foods between meals?

70. Do you clean your teeth as soon as possible after eating?

71. Do you have regular medical check-ups—a general physical examination as well as examinations of eyes, ears, and teeth?

72. Do you wash thoroughly every day?

73. Do you wash your hands thoroughly before handling food and after going to the toilet?

74. Do you have two or three full baths a week?

75. Do you have your gym suit laundered regularly?

76. Do you keep your hands away from your face—avoid touching eyes and ears and pimples or infections?

77. Do you have several short periods of quiet rest during the day?

Do you do your share to prevent the spread of disease?

78. Do you stay away from people when you have a cold?

79. Do you cover your mouth and nose with a handkerchief when you cough or sneeze?

80. Have you had a recent smallpox vaccination?

81. Have you had a recent tuberculin test or chest X ray?

82. Do you use your own clean comb, towel, and make-up?

83. Do you help to keep your home and school clean and attractive?

84. Do you help to keep school and public washrooms clean?

85. Are you careful to patronize only clean stores, restaurants, and other public places?

Do you know?

1. What makes a good breakfast?

2. What foods help to build muscles and bones?

3. What the "Basic 7" food groups are?

4. Why you should avoid exercise after eating?

5. What "pasteurizing" means?

6. Why it is important that meats be cooked properly?

7. Why you should have a chest X ray?

8. If heart disease is the chief cause of death in the U. S.?

9. What is the chief cause of death among boys and girls your age?

10. What causes a poor complexion?

11. What rest does for your body?

12. How skills and habits are learned?

13. What personal qualities make a person popular?

14. The most efficient way to study and learn?

15. What skills and feelings are appropriate for teenagers? What are signs of failing to grow up?

Charting a course

Improving yourself can be an exciting game. Choose some definite goal to work on. Concentrate on one important improvement at a time. When you achieve one, select another. Did you find weak points to improve from the questions in the "Take a Look at Yourself" test?

Here are some other suggestions:

Would you like to: Improve your complexion? Take better care of your hair? Gain or lose weight? Avoid colds? Increase your "wind" and endurance? Improve your posture? Learn to play tennis or attain some other sports skill? Learn to study better? Develop habits of concentration? Develop habits of doing work promptly? Develop habits of doing work thoroughly? Learn to control your temper? Learn to get along with your brothers and sisters? Break some habit that is harming your personality? Develop the habit of being friendly and pleasant? Develop more self-confidence? Have more friends?

Committee planning

The safety committee can start right away trying to keep everyone aware of the smart, skillful, safe way to do things. A good way to begin would be to make sure that everyone knows and has a chance to practice school safety rules. What are the rules for traffic in the halls, in fire drills, on the playground, and in the lunchroom? A resourceful committee might make cartoon posters of safety rules for the classroom or school. Dramatize the safety rules, have quiz contests, or think of some other ways to make people safety conscious.

Other activities

1. A speaker could be invited to tell you about life in your community many years ago. How was life different? Were some problems of "growing up" the same?

2. If your community has plans for the future, you might enjoy learning about them. Invite a speaker from the planning committee to talk to you. Do you need to make plans for listening to a speaker? What questions would you like to ask? Do you know how to ask your questions?

3. Someone with a good imagination might like to try writing a play or a radio script picturing life in some other time or place, past or future.

4. Interview people from different places or different generations—perhaps your own parents or grandparents. How are your customs, schools, and problems different from the ones they knew?

5. Someone may like to investigate the unchanging things in our changing world. Interview people interested in science or philosophy to find out about unchanging natural laws that govern the universe.

6. A committee might like to make up a handbook of suggestions for helping new pupils adjust to your school.

7. A survey to see how your community is changing should be interesting. You may collect information from newspapers, from interviews, and from your own observation. You might like to make a map planning how your city could grow and improve. Do some housing areas need to be changed? Are there enough places for recreation?

8. Would you like to see how your classmates looked when they were younger? A display of baby pictures and grade-school pictures should be interesting. Can you recognize everyone?

9. The field-trip committee may be able to arrange a visit to a museum or to some historic place in your community. Does the committee know how to arrange trips? Are there school regulations? What about transportation? How can they prepare the class for a trip? Do you think a poorly planned trip could affect future expeditions?

Tests for pilots

Would you like to try some of the performance tests given to future pilots? Would you expect to do as well as a pilot? Why?

Eyesight. Read letters ⅜ inches high at a distance of 20 feet. Try each eye separately.

Breathing. Take a deep breath and hold it without becoming dizzy. A time of 20 seconds is passing; 25–35 seconds is fair; 35–40 seconds is good.

Relax. Let someone hold the entire weight of your relaxed, outstretched arm in the palm of his hand. When he unexpectedly removes his hand your arm should drop like a dead weight.

Balance on either foot with eyes closed 15 seconds.

Trembling. Stand with arms outstretched—fingers spread with no trembling.

Co-ordination. Practice each of the following exercises once: 1. Touch nose with right index finger. 2. Touch nose with left index finger. 3. Touch hands together until fingertips meet. 4. Touch left knee with right heel. 5. Touch right knee with left heel.

After you know the order, do the five movements above with your eyes shut.

Reading to help you grow up

Reading can help you to see and understand our changing world. Books are magic carpets that can carry you to faraway times and places.

Would you like to know how the surface of the earth has changed? Are you interested in lost cities and continents and civilizations and in imaginative stories of the future? Then you will like these books:

Lost World—Adventures in Archaeology by Anne Terry White. The discoveries of explorers who look for the ruins of lost civilizations of legend and tradition—of Troy, of ancient Crete, of the Pharoahs, of Yucatan, of the Tower of Babel, and of many others.

Living in Ancient Times by Robert Speer and others. Stories of how people lived in prehistoric times and in ancient Egypt, Babylonia, Greece, and Rome.

How the Earth is Changing, by Rudolf Bretz, tells of the making and unmaking of lands.

Stories Read from the Rocks by Bertha Morris Parker.

Are you interested in stories of how people lived in other countries or other centuries; how people change their ways of living to adjust to new conditions? These books will interest you:

Farmer Boy by Laura Ingalls Wilder. A story of pioneer life in the middle 1800's.

Caddie Woodlawn by Carol Brink. A story about a girl of a pioneer family.

The Little House, by Virginia Lee Burton, shows changes in a neighborhood as a city grows.

Petar's Treasure by Clara Ingram Judson. The story of a courageous immigrant family.

Films to help you understand

How We Think the World Came To Be. Jam Handy.

Growth of Cities. Encyclopedia Britannica Films.

Early Settlers of New England. Encyclopedia Britannica Films.

Pioneers of the Plains. Encyclopedia Britannica Films.

People of Hawaii. Encyclopedia Britannica Films.

Airplane Changes Our World Map. Encyclopedia Britannica Films.

Earth's Rocky Crust. Encyclopedia Britannica Films. Basic facts of building up and tearing down land.

Our Changing World. John Ott Film Library, Inc. 72 minutes. In color, with sound. The best theories of science concerning the origin, development and present state of our earth and the life upon it. Time-lapse photography shows cell division and growth. Animated drawings show the work of glaciers and volcanoes. Informs the mind and expands the imagination.

Denver Public Schools

All people are alike in many ways. Yet no two people are exactly alike. What are some of the ways these boys and girls are alike?

These identical twins start out in life with the same physical equipment. Will they be exactly alike as adults? Why?

Ewing Galloway

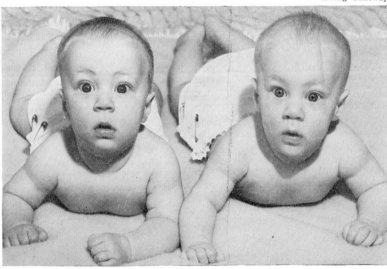

What traffic hazards do you meet around school and on the way to school?

H. Armstrong Roberts

Could the pilots of these planes use the same map to make a flight across the United States? How would their flight plans be different?

Ewing Galloway

37

HOW DO PEOPLE CHANGE?

The secret of your ability to change and to adjust to change lies in the mysterious process of growth. You are able to change because you grow. So if you want to improve yourself in order to be a happy and well-adjusted person, you need to understand growth.

Growth is many-sided because a human being is a complex creature. He lives, grows, thinks, feels, and believes. Most important of all he has a spirit that lives forever. He is exactly like no other thing in the universe. However, in some respects he is similar to many other things. He can be included in groups that are like him in some ways. He is a living thing: an animal, a mammal. He is all these things and much more. Knowing something about the living material of your body will help you to understand yourself.

Growth is an amazing process that changes an almost invisible speck into a complicated independent person; growth goes on changing a person every moment of his life. Growth cannot be completely understood by man. However, scientists have carefully observed and studied the process. They know that it is orderly and purposeful, proceeding toward a goal. They can describe the series of orderly changes that take place when growth is proceeding normally, and they can recognize signs that indicate retarded or abnormal growth. They have discovered the things that are necessary for growth and the things that are harmful.

We are so accustomed to growth that most of us pay little attention to it. How much do you know about growth after experiencing and observing it all your life? Is there a pattern that everyone follows? Do you grow all the time? How is it possible for your body to grow? Can your mind and feelings develop? Can you do anything about your own growth or are you just carried helplessly along?

38

Looking ahead

Questions and suggestions

1. Make an outline on the board or in your notebook of the important problems in the chapter. You can use for your outline the questions that introduce new topics. What are the three large problem-questions?

2. Discuss the outline-questions. Try to recall what you already know about living things and how they grow.

3. Do you know what heredity is?

4. How are you like your parents or grandparents? Do you think the likenesses are due to heredity? What else could account for them?

5. What kind of environment do you believe provides the best opportunity for growing up healthy and happy? This topic might provide an interesting panel discussion.

6. Do you know of people who have overcome handicaps of heredity or environment?

7. Why do people grow and develop the way they do?

Committee planning

1. Are your committees figuring out efficient ways of working? Can they plan their work so that it does not interfere with individual responsibilities? Be careful not to attempt too much. One job well done is more enjoyable and worth while than several done sloppily.

2. Does the library committee have a simple satisfactory method of taking care of books and making them available to other members of the class?

3. Is the movie committee planning far enough ahead to have material when the class needs it?

4. Are you a smart, safe traveler? The safety committee can help the class develop the alertness and skills that will protect them on their way to and from school. What are the traffic hazards and the safety rules in your neighborhood and community? Do traffic problems change as a community grows?

5. Are the field-trip and speakers' committees on the alert to find out how your own community fits into the problems you are investigating? What kind of an environment does your community provide for growing up? What is its health record? What kind of houses do the people live in? Does your community have a juvenile delinquency problem? Does it have good water supplies, good garbage and sewage disposal, and good recreation facilities? Any one of these problems will provide interesting trips and reports and will provide chances to apply what you are learning.

Reading

1. Are you developing the habit of reading rapidly through the chapter to get the main ideas, then reading again more slowly for details?

2. Do you use all the helps to learning: the glossary (dictionary) on page 417 for words you do not know; the pictures; the questions and tests to check your learning; and the additional readings to broaden your understanding?

Activities for everyone

When you have finished reading make a plan that will help you enter into class discussions. Do some of the extra reading and some of the activities suggested; or work with your committee.

How is growth possible?

All living things grow. They have the power to take in food materials and to change them into living substance which becomes part of themselves.

What are the characteristics of living things? Everything in the world can be divided into two groups—living things and nonliving things. Living things may be of any size or description. They have certain powers not possessed by nonliving things: (1) They react to their environment. (2) They can sense and respond to changes. (3) They breathe and need food. (4) They can change food into the material of their own bodies. (5) They grow. (6) They have the power to reproduce (to produce other living things like themselves).

Scientists have discovered that all living things are composed of cells. A *cell* is like a tiny living building-block. Cells vary in size from those barely visible to those that can just be seen with the most powerful microscope. Some plants and animals consist of only a single cell. Larger, more complex living things have hundreds and even billions of cells. All the activities of life are carried on by a single cell, but "life" itself is a mystery. As far as can be told, dead and living cells are chemically alike. You may be interested in studying more about cells.

Living things reproduce in a variety of ways. Some simple ones divide in half. More complex ones may produce buds, branches, or seeds. Some animals lay eggs. Others nourish the reproductive cells in special organs in their own bodies and produce living young. You may be interested in reading more about the way living things reproduce. Do you know how all these living things reproduce: germs, tulips, roses, dandelions, flies, fish, snakes, chickens, and rabbits?

Living things can be divided into groups—plants and animals. These groups can then be divided. Animals are divided into groups like insects, reptiles, fish, amphibians, birds, and mammals. Can you give examples of animals in all those groups? Man has the physical characteristics of the mammals. Mammals are born alive, are warm-blooded, have hair on their bodies, and nourish their young with

National Safety Council

Are you an expert bicycle rider? Do you know the rules and obey them? What suggestions would you give to a beginning rider?

milk. Do you know how plants are divided into groups? If you are interested in plants, this would make an interesting report.

How is your body built? If you examine your body you find it composed (made up) of many different kinds of materials—skin, fat, muscle, bone, blood, and other substances. If you examine these materials under a microscope, you find that all of them are composed of cells. It has been estimated that the average human body is made up of about 30 trillion cells.

Cells vary in size and shape according to the work they do. Skin cells are flat and close together. Nerve cells (for sending messages) are like wires, sometimes three or four feet long, but so fine it would take from one thousand to five thousand of the cells side by side to cover an inch. Cells in bones are far apart and surrounded by hard deposits which they produce. Muscle cells are long and fastened together side by side in bundles so they can pull together.

A group of the same kind of cells doing the same work is called a *tissue*. For example, skin is a tissue. So is muscle or bone. Several tissues working together to perform a special function (work) are called an *organ*. The stomach, with its muscles, glands, nerves, and blood vessels working together to help digest food, is an organ. Organs that work together to do a special job form a *system*. The mouth, esophagus, stomach, digestive glands, and intestines make up the digestive system. Other important body systems are the circulatory, the respiratory, the excretory, and the nervous systems. Do you know the organs in these systems and the work they do? They are explained in Unit 2. The systems specialize in various kinds of work, but they are not independent. They depend on each other and work together to keep the body alive.

How do cells make growth possible? Each cell is living and can do many of the things your body can do as a whole. Each cell can breathe, use food, eliminate waste, and grow. The billions of cells in your body working together carry on all life activities. To keep your body healthy you need to see that the cells are furnished the materials and conditions they need to work well. By experiments scientists have discovered that all cells need (1) oxygen, (2) food, (3) water, (4) means of eliminating waste, (5) favorable temperature, and (6) freedom from poisons and injury. Other chapters in this book describe how your body furnishes these necessities to all the cells, and suggest some ways you can help.

Almost all the cells in the body can make others like themselves (reproduce) by dividing in half. The new cells in turn grow and divide to make other cells. Some cells go on dividing as long as you live. Not all new cells are used to make the body larger. Many are used to replace cells that wear out. Cells are constantly wearing out. Red blood cells, for example, lead such active lives that they live only about 30 days. Billions of them must be replaced every day.

Do cells ever stop dividing, or divide too fast or too slow? At birth a person has all the organs and parts he will ever have. The organs are small and some nervous connections are not

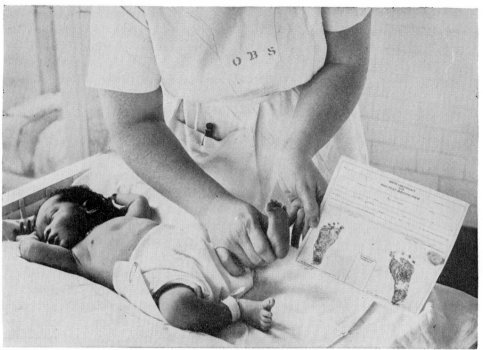

At birth a baby has all the organs and parts he will ever have. How is it possible for him to grow and change?

complete. Growth continues as cells grow and divide. Boys continue growing until they are about twenty-five years old, girls until they are about twenty. After physical maturity is reached, cells continue dividing, but only for repair and replacement.

Every cell grows in an orderly way, governed by laws of nature unknown to us. As long as cells follow an orderly development, growth is normal and the body is healthy.

Located in various parts of your body are certain organs called *endocrine glands*. Glands secrete (produce and pour out) chemicals called *hormones* (exciters) into your blood. Hormones act as regulators to speed up and to slow down many body processes. Some hormones regulate

the way organs function. Others play an important part in controlling rate of growth.

Individuals differ as to the amount of hormones produced and the time they are produced. Everyone seems to inherit a certain glandular time schedule. People grow different amounts and at different times. Usually girls develop adult characteristics earlier than boys.

During a person's teens the glands are particularly active. Some time between the ages of ten and fourteen most girls increase rapidly in height and weight. They develop a more rounded body and softer skin. Some time between the ages of thirteen and fifteen, most boys increase rapidly in height and weight, begin the growth

42

of a beard, and acquire deeper voices. These and many other changes are stimulated by gland secretions. They are signs of normal development into young manhood and young woman-hood. In other chapters of this book you will find more about glands, what they are, how they work, and how you can help keep them working normally.

Why does each individual develop the way he does?

Some of the reasons an individual grows as he does are beyond his control. He inherits some natural physical traits. Most of his characteristics, though, are acquired or developed by the way he lives. The way he lives is due partly to where he finds himself and partly to his own character and spirit.

How does growth depend on inheritance? The boundaries of your growth are set by your ancestors—your parents, and your grandparents for generations back. The single cell from which an individual develops contains from both parents substances called *genes*. Genes determine all the characteristics with which an individual is born. Because they have the same ancestors, members of a family usually have many characteristics which are similar. They may be alike in body build, shape of head, length of arms and legs, shape of nose, or other characteristics. Characteristics which are handed down from one generation to the next are called *hereditary*. They make up a person's inheritance.

The process which hands on the traits from countless generations of ancestors to every new individual is a complex one. You may like to read more about it from some of the books mentioned at the end of this chapter.

A child may inherit a short skeletal framework from one grandparent, blue eyes from another, curly hair from another, and fine skin texture from another. He will inherit certain combinations of nerve and brain and gland cells that will influence to some extent even his capacity for thinking and feeling and acting.

Characteristics which have not been inherited will not be handed on to the next generation. The loss of an arm or leg is not passed on from parent to child. Abilities and habits acquired by experience and education will not be inherited. A man may be a skillful surgeon, but his child will not be born knowing all about medicine. The child who displays a temper "just

Encyclopedia Britannica Films

Is artistic ability inherited? What things do we inherit? What do we learn?

like his father's" probably developed the temper by imitation or because he learned it was useful to get his own way.

Scientists generally agree that most diseases are not inherited. You may inherit certain cell weaknesses that make it easier for you to contract a disease if you are exposed to it.

How does environment affect growth? Your home, your family, your neighborhood, your friends, your school, the books you read, the movies you see, and all the other things and people that surround you are your *environment*. How much do you think your environment affects your growth?

Although you inherit certain physical structures, the way you live does much to determine the way you grow and develop. A poor environment can stunt and cripple a strong body. A good environment may overcome many of the effects of a poor inheritance.

Many of the ways in which your environment affects your growth and

Encyclopedia Britannica Films

Your home is an important part of your environment. Why? Do comfortable homes like these always provide the best environment? Why?

development are easily observed. You can see how size and strength are affected by the food you eat; by the exercise, rest, and sleep you obtain; and by the diseases and accidents you are exposed to. Look at the muscular development of people who get hard physical exercise. They did not inherit those muscles. Look at pictures of people who have been deprived of food, rest, or exercise. What do they look like?

Other ways in which your environment affects your health are not so easily seen. Some people fail to develop mentally and emotionally, partly because of poor environment. They have few opportunities to gain self-respect, to assume responsibility, to become independent, to develop concern for others, and to develop worthy life goals.

From your environment you learn ways of living. You may think that your way of life—the way you eat, sleep, exercise, and get along with people, and all your other activities—

Encyclopedia Britannica Films

There are many different ways of life in the world. How do we learn the customs and habits that seem so natural to us?

is "natural." Actually you learned all those things. You learn from your parents; from your brothers and sisters; from neighbors; and from schoolmates. You learn from books, movies, radio, television, and all your other experiences. You might be surprised if you looked up some "natural" ways of doing things in other times and places.

The living habits you learn from your surroundings have a great influence on the way you grow and develop. Many boys and girls and adults are weak and sickly because of their living habits. A diet may be expensive and delicious but lack the materials your body needs. Poor eating habits can make you as poorly nourished as a famine does. Lack of proper habits of rest and exercise can leave you as weak as a hospital invalid.

Good environment is not a matter of wealth. It is a matter of providing the necessities for normal growth and development. These necessities are inexpensive. Many homes may be poor in money and yet provide more nourishing meals, better opportunities for exercise and rest, better opportunities for developing responsibility and unselfishness, and more love and security than many wealthy homes do.

What can you do about growth? Each person develops in an area bounded by the laws of nature, by the cells he inherits, and by his environment. Inside that frame he is free to choose his course of development, to set a goal or ideal, and to work toward it. Some people have more freedom of choice than others because they have a bigger frame in which to develop. They inherit stronger bodies and minds. Their environment is more favorable. It offers them more opportu-

Encyclopedia Britannica Films

Your friends and recreation help to make you what you are. Dull games in unpleasant surroundings will soon make these boys restless and dissatisfied. What kinds of recreation do you really enjoy?

nities. But every normal person, endowed with intelligence and will, has much freedom and many opportunities to direct his own growth. With the freedom comes responsibility. It is up to each of us to choose worthy goals, to gain necessary knowledge, to form desirable habits, and to exercise the self-control necessary to make the most of himself.

We are often tempted to shrink from personal responsibility for our own development. It is easier to blame others for our shortcomings. We say that circumstances made us what we are. We say that we could not help ourselves. True, we may be limited in our development. We cannot, for example, change the color of our eyes— but we can use them to better advantage. We are affected by our environment, but we also affect our environment! We are a part of it, but it

45

Ewing Galloway

In what ways do children resemble parents? What parts of the resemblance are due to heredity? To learning?

encounter with a poor environment, one person may emerge stunted, bitter, and resentful. From the same experiences another person may develop strength, tolerance, and sympathy.

You read every day of people who have become outstandingly successful in spite of poverty; physical handicaps; bad training, companions, and surroundings; and continual discouragement. Thousands of others who never become famous lead happy and successful lives after overcoming obstacles that seemed to doom them to failure and unhappiness. Do you know any such people?

affects us only as we react to it. We may react in different ways. From an

How do people grow?

No two snowflakes are exactly alike. No two people grow up in exactly the same way. But behind the countless unique individuals is an underlying pattern. We can learn about ourselves from studying other people. We can learn about other people if we understand ourselves.

Are all people alike? In many ways all people are alike. A general description of a human being fits all of us. Our bodies are built of the same materials, according to the same design. A skilled surgeon can transfer parts— like skin, blood, and bone—from one person to another. Our bodies obey the same natural laws. They are alike in needing food, air, rest, and exercise. They are alike, too, in their weak-

nesses: the diseases and the accidents which may affect them.

All human beings are alike in their human nature. That is, they have need for security, for affection, for a feeling of individual worth and dignity. The men who wrote our Declaration of Independence expressed some of the ways in which human beings are alike when they wrote: "We hold these truths to be self-evident, that all men are created equal, that they are endowed by their Creator with certain inalienable rights, among which are life, liberty, and the pursuit of happiness." Our government exists to protect these natural rights, inherent in every individual.

We are alike too in our human feel-

46

ings. Any of us may have trouble in controlling feelings of fear and pride and anger and jealousy. We all try to find ways of satisfying our physical and our human needs. We struggle to maintain our lives and our feeling of self-respect and personal worth.

Scientists who study human beings agree with the religious principle that all men, regardless of race or color, are brothers. They have the same physical structures and needs. They are created in the same likeness and endowed by their Creator with the same needs and rights of their common human nature.

People are fundamentally alike, but they are different too. Each person is a unique individual exactly like no other person in the world. People differ in appearance and personality, in their ways of satisfying their needs and solving their problems. They are as individual as their fingerprints.

It would be too bad if we did all fit a pattern. We would be like a batch of gingerbread men. The little variations from the standard model make people interesting and able to make unique contributions. Variation gives us poets and engineers, leaders and followers. A democracy is based on a belief in the dignity and worth of every individual. As democratic citizens, we must guard our individual human rights. We must be on the alert against attempts of persons or groups who would suppress individual differences or ignore individual dignity and human rights.

Does growth follow a pattern? Everyone follows a general pattern of growth in which there are small individual differences. It is as if many airplanes were flying around the world,

checking their course by flying over certain cities. All would follow a general pattern of flight, but no two would follow exactly the same plan. All the pilots could use the same general map, but each would make individual plans about altitude, speed, stopovers, refueling, and the like. Each would take into consideration factors like weather and the type and condition of his plane. Each would have his own individual flight plan.

In the same way, to be happy and comfortable while you are growing up, and to check your progress, you can use a general map of growth and development; but you must adapt it to fit yourself. Charts of normal height, weight, skills, abilities, and behavior at different ages fit no one exactly. They can guide you but are not meant to be followed in detail.

Human beings grow in a continuous, orderly way throughout their lives. Normal growth is controlled by natural forces and laws. Because people are extremely complex, they grow in many ways. Their bodies change not only in size and strength but in shape and functioning (working). People increase in ability to control their bodies, to do mental work, to control their emotions, to get along with others, and to solve their problems. From birth to death they develop certain characteristics. Can you tell the approximate age of a person from his size? From his mental ability? From his emotional control? From his beliefs about his place and purpose in life?

No one can predict or map your growth exactly, because variations from the general plan are to be expected. You can compare your devel-

47

H. Armstrong Roberts

How are his dreams of the future affected by his heredity? By his environment? To what extent is he responsible for his own happiness and success?

opment and progress toward maturity with the achievements of other boys and girls. You need not worry if you develop more slowly or more rapidly than your friends. Everyone has his own special design for growth.

Do you grow smoothly? You change and grow all your life, but not at a uniform speed. You grow continuously and gradually, but you do not grow a certain amount each day or month or year. Sometimes you grow rapidly, other times slowly.

One period of very rapid growth occurs sometime between the ages of ten and fifteen. When a boy's growth schedule arrives at the time for this spurt, he grows rapidly. In a single year he may increase as much as four to six inches in height and 15 to 25 pounds in weight. If your design for growth causes you to have your period of rapid growth when you are ten or eleven years old, for several years you may be quite a bit larger than your friends. If you have a late schedule you may be smaller than most of your friends for a while.

Not only do you grow in spurts, but parts of you grow at different times and at different speeds. Consequently your appearance changes considerably. You have only to look at a baby or small child to see that some parts of him will have to grow faster than others if he is to develop the proportions of an adult. An adult with proportions of a baby would look clumsy and ridiculous with a large head, small chin and mouth and teeth, and spindly arms and legs.

Perhaps you have heard or used expressions like these: "He is a big baby." "Act your age." "Why don't you grow up?" "He is old for his years." What facts about growth do people recognize when they use these expressions?

We recognize that different ways of thinking, feeling, and behaving are appropriate at different ages. We grow up mentally and emotionally as well as physically. Mental and emotional growth goes on all during life. It offers the greatest opportunity for happiness.

Other kinds of growth require more conscious effort and direction than does physical growth. Consequently they may lag behind physical development. Often people are childish in some respects and more mature in others. You probably know physically mature men and women who behave childishly. People who fail to develop mentally and emotionally can cause great unhappiness both for themselves and others. What are some signs of lack of emotional and mental development? Other chapters in this book discuss this more fully.

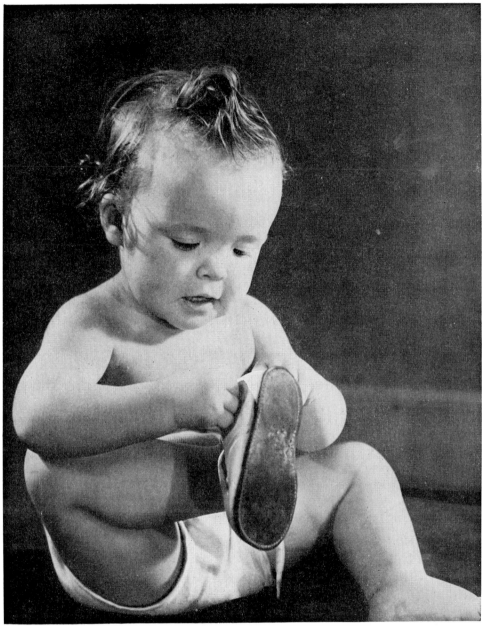

Ruth Nichols

We learn all our lives. What things does a baby have to learn? What must you learn? It is necessary to be patient with a child while he is learning to do new acts. Why? Children differ in appearance and personality almost as much as grownups do. This difference in abilities and feelings must be understood when you are a baby sitter.

Reviewing the chapter

Test yourself

I

Complete the following sentences by supplying the missing words. Do NOT WRITE IN THIS BOOK.

1. Everything in the world can be divided into two groups, ... and ....
2. All living things are composed of ....
3. .... cells may be three or four feet long.
4. Every living cell can .... , ... , ... , and ....
5. Hormones are produced by ....
6. Most girls develop adult characteristics between the ages of .... and ....
7. Most boys develop adult characteristics between the ages of .... and ....
8. An individual grows and develops the way he does because of his .... , ... , and ....
9. Governments exist to .... our natural rights; they do not give them to us.

II

What would you think, say, or do in the following situations?

1. If you heard someone say "Tuberculosis runs in families"?
2. If you heard someone say "That boy has bad blood. His father is in jail"?
3. If someone said that only wealthy, well-educated parents should have large families?
4. If someone asked your opinions about the importance of heredity and environment?

Other activities

1. A special committee might arrange some experiments with a microscope. The committee may have to learn and instruct the class in the skillful use of a microscope. Does your school have a projector for microscope slides? The committee can arrange slides to examine such things as a drop of pond water, cells in onion skin, mold, or perhaps prepared slides from a biology laboratory. The class can sketch what they see in the microscope for inclusion in their notebooks or for display on the bulletin board.
2. Some members of the class who are interested in biology may like to report on the various classes of animals. A chart that shows each class, with pictures and brief descriptions, would be interesting for class discussion.
3. Do you like to play Twenty Questions? It offers a good example of classifying objects into smaller and smaller groups until finally only one object is included. A panel might like to offer a demonstration in classification and straight thinking by trying to guess some object chosen by the rest of the class.
4. How do you suppose cells were discovered? Do you think it would make an interesting report?
5. Have you heard of diseases that are inherited? Look them up and see what doctors believe about their causes.
6. Many interesting reports can be made about people who have overcome handicaps. Posters, radio scripts, or two-minute talks about people like Thomas Edison, Helen Keller, Theodore Roosevelt, Franklin Roosevelt, Charles Steinmetz, Glenn Cunningham, Elizabeth Barrett Browning, Abraham Lincoln, or Eddie Cantor can help you understand how courage and perseverance can overcome handicaps.

7. Members of the class interested in government, law, and peace might like to report on the natural rights of every person as set forth in the Charter of the United Nations, the Bill of Rights in the Constitution, and other writings.

Reading to help you grow up

Interesting health books with more detailed descriptions of cells and body systems are the following:

Your Health and Safety by Jessie W. Clemenson and William R. LaPorte.
The Human Body by Clifford Lee Brownell and Jessie F. Williams.
Growing Up Healthily by W. W. Charters and others.

These books have interesting discussions of traffic safety:

A Sound Body by W. W. Charters and others.
Building Good Health by J. M. Andress and others.

For good readers:
Biology for Better Living, by Ernest R. Bayles and R. Will Burnett, has an interesting discussion of how living things change.

Films to help you understand

Living Things. Filmstrip. Society for Visual Education. Characteristics of common plants and animals.
Backward Civilization. Encyclopedia Britannica Films. Daily life in a primitive environment.
Heredity. Encyclopedia Britannica Films. Describes inheritance of characteristics in animals.

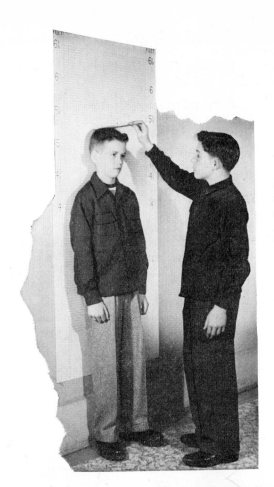

Picture Preview:

Chapter 4

How much did you increase in height last year? Do you grow about the same amount every year? How much do you expect to gain in height and weight in the next year or two?

Philip Gendreau

This is a group of boys and girls about twelve years old. What do you notice about their sizes? How do you think they will change in the next few years?

Denver Public Schools

Denver Public Schools

Compare this group of high school boys and girls with the twelve year olds. What happens as you grow up?

How rapidly do infants gain in height and weight? How do the proportions of an infant's body differ from those of an adult?

Colorado State Department of Public Health

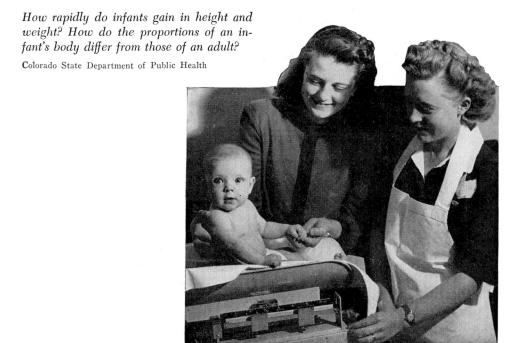

Chapter 4

WHAT HAPPENS WHEN YOU GROW UP?

In what ways have you changed during the past year? How much have you gained in height and weight? How much have you grown in ability to control your emotions and to get along with others? Have you developed new skills? Are you more responsible and dependable?

Growth is a process of change. Naturally you are most concerned with the way you are changing now. You will understand these changes better if you see them as a part of a lifelong series of changes. Look back at the growth you have already accomplished. Look ahead to the kind of person you hope to be. Are you moving in the right direction?

The steps you take toward maturity are just as right and normal and enjoyable as maturity itself. Every age has its own appropriate growth and skills. Failure to develop skills appropriate for your age may make life difficult. Expecting to achieve skills before appropriate growth has taken place can lead to unhappiness.

Doctors and psychologists have studied thousands of children as they grew up. They have kept records of physical measurements, skills, and behavior at all ages. Their information has been assembled in books, tables, and charts. Although no two children developed in exactly the same way, most of them had a certain stage of development at various ages.

This chapter describes some of the characteristics of boys and girls at various ages. You can find out how growth usually progresses and check your own development. As you read, remember that the descriptions represent *average* development. This means that most of the children who were studied had achieved that growth, or performed in that way, at that particular age. Other perfectly normal boys and girls might be as much as two years ahead of or behind the average. Every individual has his own special schedule of growth. There is no definite rule for all, although the average can be used as a guide for study.

Looking ahead

Questions and suggestions

1. Suppose that someone asked you the question, "What happens when you grow up?" What would you answer?

2. What clues do you use to help you guess a person's age? How do actors on the stage, on radio, on television, and in the movies give you an idea of a character's age?

3. What do you mean by chronological age, mental age, emotional age, and physical age?

4. Can you from your own experience describe the normal development of a child? What would you expect him to be like at various ages?

5. People of all ages have accidents. What kinds of accidents do you think are most likely to occur at various ages? Why?

Committee planning

1. Accidents are by far the greatest cause of death during school years. The safety committee can bring to the attention of the class ways of preventing the accidents most common for boys and girls your age.

2. The library committee can collect some of the references suggested at the end of the chapter. Do they know how to locate other references about any subject? Can they use the card catalog, or the *Reader's Guide to Periodical Literature*? Several magazines regularly have interesting pictures and articles about problems of growing up. The committee may be able to make a collection of current and old issues of magazines like *Today's Health* (formerly *Hygiea*), *Parents' Magazine*, *Ladies' Home Journal*, and others.

3. The movie committee can arrange to show some of the films suggested at the end of the chapter. Can the committee suggest the names of some good movies showing how people act at various ages? Maybe they can locate some home movies showing members of your class when they were younger.

4. Would you like to take a look at real boys and girls, younger and older, growing up? The field-trip committee can arrange some interesting trips. Perhaps you can visit a preschool or some of the lower grades in school. You might like to visit a high school. You could observe how the schools as well as the boys and girls change.

5. Can you learn from other peoples' experiences? The speaker's committee can invite a panel of high school students to give you tips on what high school is like. They may be able to tell some of the mistakes they made and the problems they solved when they were in your shoes a year or so ago. They may be able to help you make plans for learning and developing some skills that will make your high school days more enjoyable.

6. Perhaps a committee from your class could visit an elementary school to give them some tips on junior high.

Reading

1. Do you keep the purpose of the chapter in mind as you read through it rapidly?

2. Do you read it the second time, more slowly for details? Do you try to see how each topic fits into the entire problem?

3. Check yourself by trying to answer in your own words each of the topic questions. (The topic questions are the headings in dark type like those on pages 56, 62, and 67.)

How does your body change as you grow?

As you grow up, your body changes in many ways. It changes in size and shape. Various parts change in the way they work. Do you know what changes take place? Could you make a series of drawings showing the differences in size and appearance of a child at the age of two years, eight years, and fourteen years?

What is normal growth? As you continue your study of growing up,

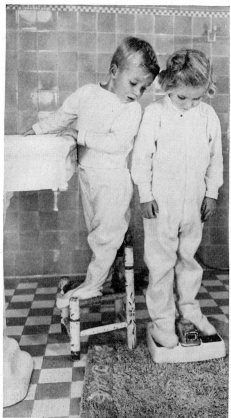

Nitey Nite Sleepers

Have you ever noticed the proportions of a small child? His head forms about what fraction of his total height?

try to keep in mind the general characteristics of growth. To simplify explanations books often describe parts of the body or aspects of growth as if they existed independently. The following are important facts to remember:

1. A person lives, grows, and behaves as a whole. Each organ affects others. Mind, feelings, and body act on each other.

2. Growth occurs physically, mentally, and emotionally.

3. Growth goes on all the time, at changing rates, like the flow of a river.

4. Growth accumulates. Each step is affected by all that have gone before. Each step influences future steps.

5. Growth moves in the direction of adult characteristics: mature body, self-control, independence, self-confidence, responsibility, concern and consideration for others, and recognition of worthy life purposes.

6. Growth follows a general pattern with a special, unique timetable for each individual.

Most of this book and your study of health will deal with the changes that are taking place and with the problems that you are trying to solve right now. But first let us see where your present problems fit into the entire picture of your life and growth.

Problems that you are trying to solve now seem large because they are so close to you and mean so much. They will seem less difficult if you can look at them from a little distance. Re-

56

member they are part of a long series of changes and problems.

Problems are nothing new. You have been solving them and will continue solving them all your life. The way a person succeeds in solving his early problems determines the kind of person he will be at a later stage.

Although growth is a continuous process we often describe it in sections or steps: we commonly speak of *infancy, childhood, youth,* and *adulthood.* We recognize that everyone takes these steps in order but at different speeds. Each stage has its own characteristics and problems. Growth is orderly but extremely complex and varied.

Look back on the growth you have already accomplished; look forward to the ways you will continue to grow. As you look back, try to recall how you learned the different tasks of your childhood. If you have small brothers or sisters, you have a wonderful opportunity to watch growth. Do you think you can help them grow?

How fast does your body grow? People do not grow at the same rate. During two periods of life—infancy and early youth—they grow most rapidly. Why would you need extra amounts of food and rest at these times? Could you do other things to help your body? Adults are responsible for furnishing an infant what he requires for healthy growth. Boys and girls must assume some of the responsibility for helping themselves develop during their second growth spurt.

Boys and girls do not follow the same kinds of growth patterns. Can you tell from your own observations how their general growth patterns are

Harold M. Lambert

The most noticeable changes in growing up are in size. What are other important changes that take place?

different? You might like to make a line graph on the blackboard showing the heights of boys and girls in your class.

You will never again grow as fast as you did during your first few months of life. At birth an average baby weighs about 7 pounds and is about 20 inches long. By the time he is five months old, he will usually double his birth weight. How much would you weigh by now if you had continued to double your weight every five months?

The rate of growth gradually decreases. By the time a baby is a year old his birth weight is usually tripled. By the end of the second year, he gains about 6 more pounds. He gains about 5 pounds his third year and 4 pounds the fourth year. For the next few years, up to the time of puberty, when the body begins to grow more rapidly and to develop characteristics of adulthood, a child gains steadily but more slowly. The rate will vary, depending upon inherited characteristics, general health, and care that is given the body.

Increases in height gradually slow down too. A baby usually gains about an inch a month for the first six months. The next six months he gains about ½ inch monthly. After that the rate slows down to about 3 inches a year. When a child is about five years old his height in inches is about equal to his weight in pounds. For instance, a 41-inch child will weigh about 41 pounds. From that time on, weight in pounds increases faster than does height in inches. If this were not true, when you weighed 90 pounds you would expect to be 90 inches tall, and that is improbable—except for giraffes!

You may like to weigh and measure some children. You may be able to collect records of heights and weights of

Most eight year olds like to imitate older activities. Boys like group games that do not require much skill. What are the typical activities and social groups of third graders?

How have the proportions of these children changed since they were smaller?

some children and see how closely they follow the general pattern.

How fast do teenagers grow? After the comparatively slow and steady growth of childhood another period of rapid change occurs in the early teens. Then, sometime between the ages of about ten and seventeen, everyone has another period of more rapid growth. Most girls begin to grow rapidly between the ages of ten and twelve. They may gain 15 or 20 pounds and increase several inches in height in a single year. They continue growing but not quite so rapidly for two or three years. Most girls grow only a little after they are sixteen or seventeen years old.

Most boys begin their growth spurt when they are between twelve and fourteen years old. Some may speed up earlier and some may start a year or so later. But for a while in the early teens, most girls are taller and more mature than boys the same age.

Teenage boys may gain 4 or 5 inches and as much as 25 pounds in a single year. By the time they are fifteen or sixteen most boys are taller than girls their age. Boys usually continue to gain an inch or two in height and 7 to 15 pounds a year until they are eighteen or nineteen years old. Many continue growing into their early twenties.

Rapid changes in size are accompanied by many other changes. The body changes in shape. Some organs work differently.

Boys become wider through the shoulders. Their bones and muscles are larger and stronger in order to do heavy work. Voices deepen and hair begins to grow on the face and body.

Girls become more rounded. Hips become broader. Their skin becomes softer and clearer.

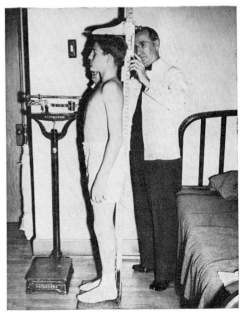

How rapidly does a teenager grow? Are all parts of his body growing at the same rate?

59

Many boys and girls worry when they find themselves much larger or smaller than friends of the same age. Remember, this is a general pattern of development with variations for everyone. Some boys and girls start their growth spurt as early as their tenth year. Others grow more slowly and grow up most rapidly after they are fifteen or sixteen. Many different sizes are perfectly normal during the teen-ages.

If you are concerned about your own development, consult a physician. Do not worry needlessly. If something is interfering with your normal development, the doctor can help you correct it. If you are developing normally, the reassurance will relieve your mind. Yearly physical check-ups are helpful for most people. They help them to choose suitable food and activities as well as to find defects early while they can be remedied.

What are some other physical changes? The proportions of your body change during these growing years. A child's head does most of its growing before birth. An infant's head is about one-fourth the length of his whole body. It grows slowly during childhood and achieves adult size at about the age of nine or ten.

On the other hand, the legs and arms of an infant are comparatively short. They remain comparatively short during childhood and lengthen rapidly before or during the teens. Teenagers who are growing rapidly sometimes feel they are "all legs and arms." Some who grow faster than their friends may feel conspicuous. Sometimes they try to disguise their new height by slumping. Others realize that the growth spurt will soon be over. They help their bodies develop normally by giving them a balanced diet and extra amounts of rest. They participate in activities that will help them to develop skill and strength.

Changes in teeth follow a well-known pattern. The first teeth usually appear when a baby is about six months old. They have been growing in the jaws since about 30 weeks before birth. All 20 of the first set of teeth usually appear before a child is three years old. When he is about six, four additional molars appear. About the same time a second set of teeth begins to replace the first set of 20. Four additional molars appear around the age of twelve, and four more—

Denver Public Schools

Many kinds of useful skill bring you a sense of satisfaction and self-confidence. Now is a good time to be learning some. What skills are you learning or improving?

60

By the time they are four or five years old children enjoy simple group activities that require no skill. They are learning to take turns and obey simple rules. Why is it important for children to have playmates?

called "wisdom" teeth—usually appear sometime after the age of sixteen.

Changes in body shape and size are accompanied by many other changes not so easily observed. Bones harden and some grow together. Muscles increase in size and strength. The nervous system improves its control of muscles and sense organs. The heart beats more slowly and with greater force. During adolescence the increased demands for food needed for growth and activity, as well as the increased size of the stomach, may cause greatly increased appetite. Boys and girls who learn to eat balanced meals may save themselves from the dangers of overeating or undereating. They can learn to enjoy a wide variety of foods and can establish regular efficient eating habits.

All parts of the body do not grow at the same rate. Some boys and girls may feel awkward or tired, or they may have digestive upsets, as they adjust to rapid changes. Much of the awkwardness teenagers experience is probably due more to feelings of em-

61

barrassment or fear concerning their maturing bodies than to poor physical control. The body does a marvelous job of keeping itself balanced and attractive through all its changes. Knowledge of how your body works and grows can help overcome much self-conscious awkwardness.

How do you grow in skill?

As a child's body grows he develops rapidly in strength and skill. Growth in size depends mostly upon the structures and the growth timetable you inherit. Growth also depends upon how well your body is provided with everything it needs—food, rest, exercise, and freedom from disease. Growth in skills depends partly upon bodily growth. It also depends upon practice and experience.

How do you develop muscular skill? All new babies are helpless and lack muscular control. They can make only uncontrolled movements and a few necessary movements like feed-

Clapp's Baby Food Division

A six-month's-old baby seems very helpless. He has really learned a great many muscular skills in a short time. What are some of the things he has learned?

62

ing, sneezing, coughing, and crying. Everything else must be learned. For the first seven or eight months babies develop chiefly in strength. They slowly learn to co-ordinate and control their movements.

The important task in gaining skill is learning to make muscles work together and to work as they are directed. Muscular skill develops in an orderly way, starting with muscles at the top of the body. First the eyes become co-ordinated and learn to follow objects. Muscles in the neck permit increasing control of the head. Then the shoulders, arms, and hands gain co-ordination and control. Babies notice their hands and attempt to grasp objects. Later they gain control of their lower trunk and legs. They sit, swaying, with legs wide apart. They notice their toes and move their legs. They scoot, creep, and stand alone. Finally, when they are about thirteen or fourteen months old, they walk.

Skills cannot develop until the necessary muscles mature. Children need plenty of freedom to exercise and should not be forced to attempt skills before they are ready.

Children learn to use large muscles first. By the time they are five they can walk, run, slide, climb, skip, jump rope, and throw and catch a ball. They continue to improve these skills as they grow up. They fit them into new patterns like games and dances. They react more rapidly and precisely. When children enter school, they have fair control of larger muscles. Their fingers are still awkward.

During childhood boys and girls improve greatly in strength and precision. During the teens they begin to show greater differences in muscular

Denver Public Schools

Between the ages of twelve and fifteen boys and girls like games requiring skill. They can stick to rules and understand scoring. What are some favorite games and activities of boys and girls in your class?

ability. Boys have wider shoulders, longer arms, bigger hands, and larger muscles. They are more concerned with muscular development and generally surpass girls in physical achievements. Girls mature more rapidly. Frequently they have greater muscular control and co-ordination for fine, precise movements.

Most boys and girls do not make the most of their physical capacity to continue improving in strength and skill. Watch little children as they learn some new skill. Do you remember when you learned to ride a bicycle, to

63

Kindergarten children have fair control of their large muscles. They run and skip, throw and catch a large ball, use crayons and simple large tools. Why are reading and writing difficult for them?

Natural growth forms a basis for developing mental skill. As a child grows he can do increasingly difficult mental tasks. His memory improves. He can pay attention for a longer time. He learns to look ahead. He observes and imitates. In order to develop his natural mental ability a child needs opportunities to learn and to think.

From experience a child learns to interpret what he sees, hears, feels, tastes, and smells. He learns to judge distance and to touch and grasp objects. He learns to put experiences to-

skate, or to play baseball? Do you still approach new skills to be learned with the same eagerness, willingness to practice, and ability to laugh at your mistakes and try again? Many teen-agers seem to forget that life is constantly changing. We cannot stop with skills appropriate for children. To live happily in a changing world, we learn new skills or improve old ones all the time. The things you want to learn now, such as dancing and behaving with poise and self-confidence, can be learned the same way you learned to walk or to play basketball.

How do you grow in mental ability? Everyone is born with a certain capacity for learning. These capacities must be developed in much the same way as physical abilities. Both physical and mental abilities depend partly upon inheritance and partly on experience and practice.

How much sense of color and shape do small children have? How well can they use their fingers? How do they improve these abilities?

gether and accepts water as wet, ice as cold, and thousands of other facts.

Children naturally accumulate many experiences. They are curious and adventurous. They look and listen; they touch and taste everything

Do you think increasing mental ability is an important part of growing up? How can you help yourself improve in mental skills—ability to concentrate, to learn, to think, and to express yourself clearly?

H. Armstrong Roberts

Are you increasing your ability to enjoy sound, shape, and color as are the boys and girl in the picture below? Do you give yourself a chance to enjoy new activities by learning more about them? What are your interests and hobbies?

Denver Public Schools

they can. All their impressions accumulate to help them interpret new experiences.

Ability to speak is an indication of increasing mental ability. Most children can say a few simple words when they are about fourteen months old. Many are able to learn to read when they are about six years old. Their ability to read, to receive ideas from others, and to express themselves can improve steadily if they have opportunities to learn and if they practice.

Mental development can increase throughout life. Practice in observing, remembering, and reasoning help to develop skill. Many people fail to develop their mental ability. They do not make the effort to add to their experiences by looking, listening, reading, studying, and trying to understand. Expanding your mental frontiers can be an exciting, satisfying lifelong occupation. In later years you will discover the truth of this. Even now you can find that it is fun to learn.

How do you grow up emotionally?

Your feelings and interests change as you grow up. Can you remember your big interests and problems of last year? How have they changed? Your feelings and interests are expressed in the things you do. Descriptions of how people behave and of the kind of people they like may help you to understand changes in your own feelings.

Clapp's Baby Food Division

Small children occupy themselves at their own play. They are self-centered and do not care about group games.

How do you develop socially? An infant starts life completely self-centered. He is interested in his own comfort and pleasure. As he grows up he accumulates ever-widening circles of interest in other people. He remains interested in himself but slowly sees himself as part of a world of people.

His world first expands to include his mother. Then he becomes interested in his father and other people who help to keep him happy. Small children show little interest in playmates. Often they will play in the same room with other children but pay no attention to them. Slowly they learn to play with others their own age, to share, and to take turns. Children in elementary grades are usually interested in playmates about their own age, both boys and girls.

Later boys and girls become more interested in activities of their own sex. They like group and informal team games. Often they form small social groups or "gangs." Gangs may be informal neighborhood groups or more highly organized clubs like the Boy Scouts and Girl Scouts. In gangs boys and girls develop social skills, such as loyalty to the group, judging people, sharing with others, and being able to give and take. Usually they learn to share more completely the feelings of one or two close friends. They learn what other people like and think.

As the physical development which changes boys and girls to young men and women speeds up, changes in interests and feelings occur too. So for a year or two as they enter their teens, boys and girls have some quite different interests and feelings. Girls grow up a little sooner and may think boys their own age are lazy and childish. Boys often think girls are silly and act too grown-up.

In the early teens circles of interest and friendship widen to include many friends of both sexes. The gang expands to become a "crowd," composed of both boys and girls. Boys and girls who have many friends and who learn to know and understand all kinds of people are ready to develop more mature social interests. They can share the feelings of others and love others unselfishly. Later they will marry and establish their own families.

The most mature social development is concern and sympathy for the welfare of all people. Social development moves from complete selfishness through accumulating stages of interest and concern for others. Selfishness or selflessness is one of the best indications of how grown-up a person is. Some people never grow up emotionally. They always put their own convenience and comfort first. Selfish, im-

Denver Public Schools

Do you think dancing is a skill that you need to learn as you grow up? Why? How do you go about learning a new skill?

mature people are most likely to fail in their relationships with other people, in friendships, in school, in business, and in marriage.

What are problems in growing up? Every stage of growing up is normal and important. Each stage prepares for the next. It has its own decisions and adjustments to be made. When you are very young, adults help you to improve in physical and emotional skills. Wise parents give children plenty of opportunities to practice using their muscles. They give them opportunities to learn to do things for themselves. They teach them to get along with other boys and girls. Childhood is the natural time for learning many physical skills that form a foundation for future activities.

Teenagers can help themselves to grow. They can check up on their present position along the road to growing up. All of us develop faster in some ways than in others. Most boys and girls your age have developed

Ability to avoid simple hazards, to follow rules, to use machines safely and skillfully are signs of growing up. Do you know good safe places to play in your community?

considerable skill in games and activities. They have developed mental skills. They can pay attention, stick to a job, study efficiently, and learn satisfactorily in school. They have widened their interests and their friendships. Usually they have some close friends among members of their own sex and can get along well with many people. They are ready to tackle new problems with confidence.

Now boys and girls are ready to become more independent. From taking small responsibilities they have learned to assume larger ones.

Through friendships with members of their own sex, they have learned some of the skills that will help them to get along in mixed crowds. They have given up childish habits of crying and fighting and having temper tantrums. From experience they have learned more effective ways of controlling their emotions and solving their problems.

If you lack some skills and self-confidence, now is the time to catch up. You can overcome poor training and lack of development. You can help yourself gain physical, mental, and emotional skills. You can improve your health, your ability to play and work, your ability to study and learn, and your ability to get along with people.

How do activities like belonging to the Boy Scouts, being on a team, and going camping help you to grow up? What groups do you belong to? Are activities like these available in your community?

Denver Community Chest

Reviewing the chapter

How do you grow in understanding?

Growing up is more than waiting for the years to roll by. You must add to your interests and skills and habits. How many of these abilities have you mastered? Probably you will find yourself advanced in some ways and retarded in others.

Most *ten-year-olds* have mastered these abilities: Handle simple tools. Help with routine jobs like raking, washing dishes, and making beds. Read for pleasure. Go about the community freely.

Most *twelve-year-olds* have these abilities: Like to play difficult games with rules and scoring. Have interest in books and newspapers. Write short letters. Buy some of their own clothes. Can do things well with their hands. Can be depended on for ordinary chores and errands.

Most *fourteen-year-olds* have these abilities: Can write interesting letters. Behave well without close supervision. Manage their own spending money. Assume responsibility for keeping themselves clean and neatly dressed.

Most *fifteen-year-olds*: Have considerable skill at games such as basketball and tennis. Are active members of teams and groups. Attend parties and are learning to dance. Perform responsible, routine jobs without urging.

Most *sixteen-year-olds*: Look after their own health without fussing. Like personal responsibility. Make practical plans for school and work. Have good standards and conform to them in everyday living. Enjoy the company of opposite sex.

Are you outgrowing these childish attitudes?

For the following questions allow 2 points if your answer is "often" and 1 point if your answer is "sometimes." You don't get any points if your answer is "never." A score of 9–16 is about average for a fourteen-year-old.

1. Do you become angry enough to scream or hit?
2. Do you become bored with daily routine?
3. Do you feel jealous?
4. Do you find it difficult to get along with other people?
5. Do you like to daydream?
6. Do you give up quickly, ask for much help?
7. Do you feel depressed by setbacks?

69

8. Do you dislike people who do not agree with you?

9. Do you attribute it to a person's lack of brains if he gets in trouble?

10. Do you spend much time thinking about past mistakes?

11. Do you fear many things, become frightened easily?

12. Do you have to have grand things to make you happy?

13. Do you try to avoid the opposite sex?

14. Do you get jittery when you have to spend time alone?

15. Do you refuse to help in group and community work?

Other activities

1. A special records committee might take some class pictures or movies. They will be interesting now but even more fun to look at later, perhaps when you are ready to leave junior high.

2. Could you, from your own observation and reading, make a list of problems and things to be learned at various ages? A panel discussion of the steps to be taken in growing up should be lively and helpful.

3. One of the baby sitters in class could report on taking care of children.

4. You might like to start a growth record of members of your class. Weigh and measure everyone at regular intervals throughout the year.

5. Some of the mathematicians in class might like to figure out the fractions that compare length of head, or leg, to total height. Can you show how proportions change as you grow up?

6. Budding artists or sculptors can draw or model figures to show typical body shapes and proportions at various ages.

7. The bulletin-board committee can arouse lots of interest with baby pictures, or with an artist's impressions of your classmates several years from now. Or

they might illustrate every year of someone's life. How he looked and acted; what he liked to eat and play; his interests in people, in reading, and in clothes; his big problems and accomplishments at each age.

Reading to help you grow up

Many interesting stories describe how it feels to grow up. You will like these:
The Yearling by Marjorie Kinnan Rawlings.
Going on Sixteen by Betty Cavanna.
Linda Marsh by Adele DeLeeuw.
Meet the Malones by Lenora M. Weber.

Descriptions of what happens when you grow up are found in these books:
Growing Up Healthily by W. W. Charters and others.
Your Health and Happiness by Burkhard and others.

Girls will find answers to some of their problems in the following:
Very Personally Yours and As One Girl To Another. International Cellucotton Products Company.
Growing Up and Liking It. Personal Products Corporation.

Facts about accidents can be learned from publications of the National Safety Council.

Many companies issue free or inexpensive booklets and other helpful material. A committee may write to several for lists of their publications and begin to assemble a classroom library. Often you will be able to obtain material for every member of the class.

A film to help you understand

Life With Baby. March of Time Forum. Interesting explanation of how children grow physically and mentally.

How Can You Help Your Body in Its Work?

Have you ever felt your palms sweat and your heart pound when you were frightened or nervous? Do you know of occasions when emotions or beliefs have made it possible for individuals to ignore pain, or to be capable of more than normal feats of physical strength or endurance?

You probably have recognized and made use of the fact that a person who is tired or hungry or sick is likely to be more irritable and harder to please.

It is important that you do realize that a human being is much more than a body, more than a collection of chemicals and cells endowed with a force called life. He is a combination of body and spirit. He has characteristics that make him different from all other creatures. A human being can reason and judge. He is conscious of himself as an individual. He dreams and plans and works for the future.

Although a human being is much more than a body, his body is an important part of him. A healthy body helps you to have strength, skill, good looks, and personality. Knowing how your body works helps you to understand yourself. It helps you to make decisions based on facts and to form habits that will help your body to work well.

Boys and girls need to form a firm foundation of health information, attitudes, and habits. When they can trust their bodies to function as they should, they can see health in its proper perspective. Health is a desirable and helpful foundation for a good life, not an end in itself. Adults who practice good health attitudes and habits need to spend only a little time and thought on health. They can use most of their time and energy for other activities.

People of long ago learned about their bodies by observation. What modern devices help us to examine the body more accurately?

United States Public Health Service

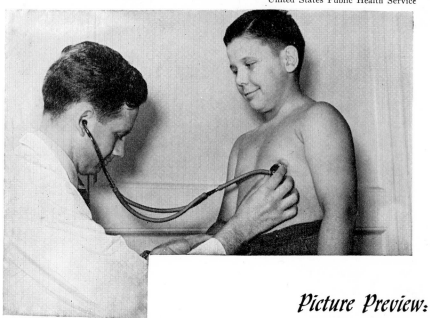

Picture Preview:

Chapter 5

Denver Public Schools

This is an experiment to measure the intensity of light. How is an experiment different from ordinary observation?

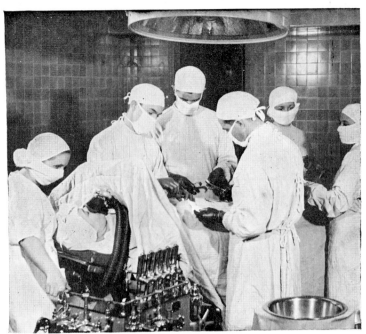

Ewing Galloway

In a modern operating room all the accumulated skill and knowledge of centuries helps to protect the patient's well-being. Why are the masks, caps, and rubber gloves used?

Dr. Jonas E. Salk, who developed the polio vaccine. Can you name some other health heroes?

National Foundation for Infantile Paralysis

Chapter 5

WHAT IS KNOWN ABOUT THE HUMAN BODY?

Today we take for granted much knowledge about our bodies. Modern boys and girls know about such things as digestion, vitamins and minerals, circulation, germs, and antiseptics—things that were not known even by the wisest men a few generations ago.

It is hard to realize that there was a time when even the most learned did not know how the human body is constructed and how it works. It is hard for us to believe that people once believed that the arteries contained air or that blood was burned in the heart to heat the body.

Only a little over 300 years ago William Harvey demonstrated that blood circulates (travels in a circle) and is used over and over in the body. Less than 100 years have gone by since Louis Pasteur proved that germs cause infection and many diseases. He laid the scientific foundations for immunization, antiseptic surgery, sanitation, and preventive medicine.

You may like to look up the health beliefs and practices of people of other days. You probably will be surprised to learn how new is some of our information. You may also be surprised to find that some of our modern ideas are thousands of years old. People often had theories before they were able to prove facts experimentally.

You may be surprised to find out that there is still a great deal we do not know about how the human body works. You may be interested in looking up some of the research that is being carried on. Find out some of the latest facts and ideas about such common problems as colds, tooth decay, tuberculosis, heart disease, polio, and cancer.

Many people today still try to protect their health more by superstition than by using the best information available. Your study of health can give you information that will help you judge methods of protecting and improving yourself.

74

Looking ahead

Questions and suggestions

1. Recall your discussions about how you can help yourself grow up. What are some important steps you can take?

2. Unit 1 helped you to take an airplane view of growing up, to see you own position and problems more clearly. Unit 2 will help you to gain information about how your body works. How can you plan to use the information in your own daily living?

3. Look at the table of contents. The next eight chapters help to answer the question "How Can You Help Your Body in Its Work?" Do you think it is worth while to find out how your body works? Why or why not?

4. What are some superstitions people still believe in?

5. Do you know any stories of the heroes in man's fight against disease?

6. You often hear that we live in the age of science. What do you think science is?

7. Why is it difficult to find out how the human body is constructed and works? How were men able to discover some of the ways a living body works? Are there still some things they do not know?

8. The field-trip or speaker's committees can arrange to investigate your own community health organizations. How does your community protect the health of its citizens? Do you have a public health department?

9. How does a changing world bring new health problems? What are some problems we are working on today?

10. How can you help in the search for knowledge and health?

Committee planning

1. The library and correspondence committees can build an interesting class library about health discoveries. Several companies publish interesting booklets about health progress and discoveries. Magazines and newspapers have many stories of recent research and discoveries.

2. How can you use scientific discoveries to help you prevent accidents and illness? The safety committee can report on scientific ways of protecting yourself on a camping trip, for example. How can you have safe drinking water and food, take care of small cuts and blisters? Should you take other precautions?

Reading

1. After you have read the chapter once rapidly, tell the purpose or main idea in your own words.

2. After you have read the chapter more carefully for details, try to answer the topic questions.

3. Take the test at the end of the chapter. In a day or so take the test again. Do you remember what you read?

4. When you finish reading, do some of the extra reading or activities. There are many articles about new health discoveries and research. Are you keeping a file of the interesting health and safety material you find in magazines and newspapers?

Activities for everyone

Many people still believe in fortunetellers, astrologers, lucky charms, blood tonics, luck, and other kinds of magic. Make a collection of advertisements and articles that show how much superstition still exists.

The simplest way we learn how our bodies are constructed and how they work is by observation. What can we find out by observation? What other methods of obtaining knowledge and understanding do we use?

What can we learn by observation? You can learn a great deal about your body by examining it. You can see that it is divided into distinct parts—head, neck, arms, trunk, and legs. Each of these large parts is made up of smaller parts. The head, for example, contains hair, eyes, ears, neck, and mouth. You can see that the body is made of different materials. Some of these materials are hard, some soft, and some

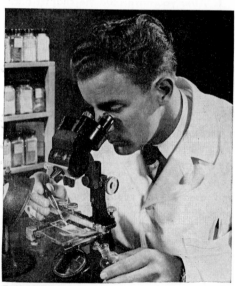

Ewing Galloway

Modern scientists use the microscope to examine parts of the body invisible to the naked eye. Why did some explanations of disease have to wait until the microscope was discovered?

liquid. Skin, hair, fingernails, teeth, lips, and eyeballs—all are different.

Further observation shows that the body changes continually. It may become larger, stronger, and more efficient; or it may become weak, deformed, and less efficient. Lack of air, food, water, or sleep cause poor functioning and finally death. Disease and loss of blood also cause weakness and, in extreme cases, death.

Observation was the most important way people of long ago found out about their bodies. We still obtain much of our information by observation and experience. Scientists have improved methods for examining people. They have microscopes, fluoroscopes, X-ray machines, stethescopes, electrocardiographs, and many other instruments and techniques.

Observation is a valuable means of obtaining information, but it has many limitations. It tells what the body looks like and a little about how it acts. But observation tells almost nothing about why or how things are, what they are, or why they act as they do.

How can you explain what you observe? People have never been satisfied with observation alone. They make up tests and invent instruments to see what makes the observed facts occur. They want to know how they can be stronger and more comfortable; they want to know why their bodies become unhealthy and what can be done about it. From early times people have tried to explain *how* and *why* their bodies use food and air and rest, *how* and *why* they become weak and diseased or stay strong and healthy. They have worked out many answers that seem to be reasonable explanations.

Reasoning (right thinking) gives reliable information if it is based on accurate observations and reliable ideas. Reasoning may lead to incorrect conclusions unless carefully tested. Some early explanations of how the body works and some early methods of keeping healthy were based upon accurate observation and good reasoning and are still useful. Many early facts and ideas are included in new scientific explanations.

Many other explanations were based on incomplete or faulty observation or upon incorrect ideas—and have been proved false. For example, we no longer believe that certain foods cause mumps or that malaria is caused by bad air. Do you know of some more recent changes in our ideas about health?

Reasoning is an important part of any method of gaining knowledge. Man's ability to use his mind to think, to imagine, and to reason makes progress possible. Accurate, systematic thinking is called logic. Great thinkers have discovered principles or rules of logic that help to make thinking accurate and systematic.

The ability to think logically has always been one of the most valued of human accomplishments. Every piece of knowledge is first an idea. Experience and experimenting merely add evidence to prove or disprove ideas. Ideas point the way, tell us what to look for. The important step in any scientific discovery is the reasoning that discovers why a thing happens.

You can develop your ability to think logically and to live reasonably in much the same way you develop other skills. You can study the principles of good thinking and practice them at every opportunity.

How do superstitions originate?

Often when people cannot find a natural cause for some happening, they try a short cut. Instead of reasoning logically, they imagine some magical cause. Ancient peoples often believed that spirits, good and bad, caused almost everything to happen. They believed evil spirits entered the body to cause sickness and evil. Sometimes in their attempts to drive out evil spirits, they stumbled on something that had good results. The good results strengthened their belief in their magic.

Gradually many explanations of how the body works—some reasonable and reliable, others unreliable—were built up. Some of the explanations were believed and taught by the wisest men of the times. Often the explanations came to be regarded so highly that they were difficult to contradict. New evidence that made old explanations seem unreasonable was suppressed or ignored.

Even today many people hesitate to change from old ideas. They are not willing to accept new ideas that have

How did early people decide what to eat? The modern sciences that help to keep people well fed are based on much research. Do you know what to eat to be healthy?

been made possible by new discoveries. Many people still believe in old superstitions and magic cures. They buy "cure-alls" and support astrologers. They prefer to explain happenings and behavior by short-cut methods that require no reasoning. Instead of looking for natural causes behind events and actions, they accept explanations of luck or fate. What do you think about luck?

Old ideas or new ones? On the other hand, many people are too quick to believe any new idea. Every new idea is not necessarily better than every old idea. Change is not always for the better. Some modern ideas are not even new. They are revivals of old ideas long ago proved false.

It is true that new ideas have certain advantages. People today have instruments that help them observe more accurately. They have microscopes, telescopes, and X rays. They can use the accumulated knowledge and techniques of people who have gone before. However, people still can make errors in observation and mistakes in reasoning. They may become so enthusiastic about a new discovery that they weave elaborate explanations and theories around it.

Old ideas have some advantages too. They have been tested by time and experience. Many have been thoughtfully considered by brilliant minds. They have been expanded to include new evidence. Many old ideas are real discoveries of laws of nature, true for all times and all places. New discoveries of science will only strengthen them with additional proof.

In a world flooded by facts and ideas—true, half-true, and completely false—everyone needs to have some means of judging facts. Our problem is how shall we choose what is true. You can make better decisions if you know the difference between facts and theories. You need some knowledge of ideas of the past. You need to examine some of the facts and theories about how the human body works. You must let your ideas grow and expand to include new information as you grow in knowledge and understanding.

All these things have for years been known by educators, who do all they can to introduce young people to the best ways of thinking, learning, and doing. That is why you are now in school. But teachers and schools, to help you, also need help from the one person most interested—yourself.

How has our knowledge grown?

Although our scientifically proved information is new, much practical knowledge has been known and used for a long time. When you read about some of the ancient peoples—Egyptians, Babylonians, and Hebrews—you may be surprised at some of their modern health practices. They were familiar with surgery, narcotics, sanitation, purification by fire, and isolation of those with infectious diseases. And yet they had very little knowledge of how the body works and how diseases are caused.

What did ancient peoples believe? What causes disease and death? What can be done to relieve and prevent pain and suffering? How can you have a strong, healthy body and mind? People have always tried to answer these questions.

As you know, when people were unable to find natural causes, many of them turned to explanations that evil spirits caused disease. They used charms to drive evil spirits away. Not all their treatments were pure superstition. Many were based on observa-

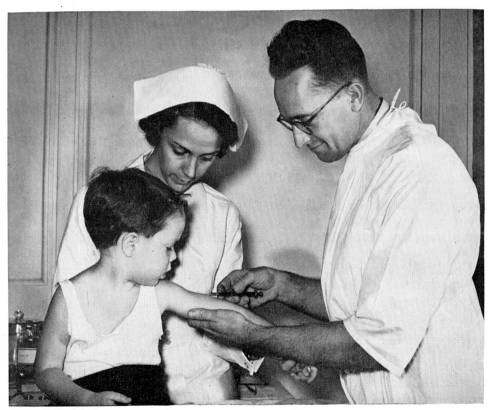

Denver Public Schools

Today scientists know many ways of protecting us from disease. What are some of them?

tion and reasoning. Experience taught them the value of some medicines and treatments. Much of their treatment was based on sound understanding of man as a whole, composed of body and spirit. Prayers and dances often gave patients the confidence and hope needed to help them recover. Modern medical practice again recognizes the value of TLC (tender, loving care) in addition to medicine and surgery in helping people get well.

Three thousand years ago the Egyptians had rules of *hygiene* (personal care) and *sanitation* (public cleanliness). They bathed regularly. They had food inspection. Their surgeons performed amputations, used instruments purified by fire, and used narcotics to dull pain. They relieved pressure on the brain by cutting a piece of bone from the skull.

In the time of earliest recorded history, the ancient Babylonians reported simple surgery like opening boils and tumors. Some of their beliefs seem strange to us, but they were reasonable in terms of the few facts they had. For example, they believed that the heart was the center of feeling and understanding and that blood came from the liver. They thought that there were two kinds of blood. Why was that a reasonable belief?

Hindu doctors in 800 B.C. suggested that mosquitoes might spread malaria. Many centuries later this belief was proved true.

Many of our modern ideas of hygiene and public health date back to the ancient Hebrews. Their guiding principle of health was that the body was a home for an immortal soul, and should be kept pure in the sight of God. On this religious basis they developed rules for cleanliness; for disinfection, including even the burning of buildings and clothing that were contaminated; for isolation of diseased persons; and for food inspection and preparation.

The early Greeks, too, were influenced in their daily living by the nearness of their gods. They, too, believed in a close relationship of body and spirit. They were interested in developing healthy, beautiful bodies as well as in preventing and curing disease. Their rules of physical training taught the value of exercise and of self-discipline in building strong bodies. Their treatments by bathing and resting in beautiful temples were the forerunners of modern treatments in sanitariums and health resorts.

Why is Hippocrates the "father of medicine"? Ancient Greece was noted for her philosophers—men who tried to find answers to the age-old puzzles of what man and the universe are like. Many were accurate observers and logical thinkers. They believed that everything in the universe obeyed natural laws. They said if man could discover these laws of nature, he would know how and why things happen.

Hippocrates (Hĭp·ŏk′ra·tēz), often called the father of medicine, was born in Greece in 460 B.C. (What was the world like at that time? Do you know how the people lived in Greece? In other parts of the world?) Hippocrates looked critically at all the accumulated medical knowledge and beliefs of his day. Most of it was based on reasoning, without much accurate observation. Early peoples did not dissect (cut apart) and knew almost nothing about the anatomy of the human body.

Hippocrates began to organize medical knowledge. He and his pupils made careful observations and recorded them in detail. He believed in a world of orderly happenings and tried to figure out how the normal body works and how to help the body work naturally.

Many of Hippocrates' discoveries and explanations were brilliant. Some of his writings are full, accurate descriptions of disease. Many have never been improved upon—and they are over 2000 years old! His students carried on his work of careful observation and search for natural explanations. Hippocrates made medicine an art and a science. His oath, setting forth the ideals and responsibilities of a physician, is still recited by young men beginning a career in medicine. You might like to read this oath with its strange mixture of references to ancient gods and the practical duties of a physician.

Naturally Hippocrates made many mistakes. His opportunities and instruments for studying the human body were limited. In attempting to explain things that could not be observed, he reasoned out some incorrect theories.

Like earlier people, Hippocrates believed that the heart was useful for distributing air. He thought that air entered the heart from the lungs. In some mysterious way the heart gave "life" to the air and sent it through the arteries to the parts of the body. In the tissues the "living air" united with blood from the liver to become living tissue. He also thought that some blood went to the heart where it was burned with "living air" to keep the body warm.

Denver Public Schools

Psychology is a study of human behavior. Why is it difficult to experiment with human beings?

Greek physicians, who followed the traditions of Hippocrates, were highly regarded in all the ancient world. Even in mighty Rome, the most famous physicians were Greeks.

The big contributions of the Romans themselves were in the field of public health. The Romans drained swamps, devised sewage systems, and established hospitals and public baths. They built and maintained a great water-supply system. They had rules about cleaning houses and streets, inspecting markets, and disposing of the dead. They knew nothing about germs, but observation and reasoning often precede scientific explanations and proof.

What did Galen contribute to medicine? From the third century to the sixteenth century, medical knowledge was based upon a book written by a man who had never completely examined the inside of a human body. Galen, a Greek physician, lived from A.D. 131 to A.D. 201. He took care of the gladiators wounded in the Roman arenas. He was a brilliant physician, eager to learn about the structure of the body.

Galen lacked the necessary instruments and knowledge to look inside a living human body. It was against the law to examine human bodies after death. So Galen studied the bodies of animals. He worked out explanations for almost everything that goes on in a human body. He made no attempt to prove his explanations.

Some of his explanations were correct. He discovered that blood moved in the body; he found out that arteries contain blood, not air. He traced accurately many nerves, including some in the brain.

Galen made many mistakes. His reasoning was based on the false idea that human bodies were exactly like those of the monkeys and pigs he dissected. He tried to explain more than his evidence supported. Some modern scientists make the same mistakes. They may build elaborate explanations, or theories, on too few facts. They may experiment on animals and assume, without proof, that the same facts apply to humans.

Galen collected all his facts and explanations into a book. This book, containing truth, half-truth, and error, became such an authority that upon it was based all medical teaching from A.D. 200 to A.D. 1543.

For hundreds of years after Galen's time, little was added to the knowledge of how a human body is constructed and how it works. Physicians were trained and hospitals established. Experience and skill were gained in treating wounds, fractures, and abcesses.

The great improvement of printing about 1450 helped to spread the knowledge that had accumulated. About the time Columbus discovered America, a great artist, Leonardo da Vinci, studied human muscles and bones to help him make his paintings more lifelike.

How has experimenting added to our knowledge? Experiments are observations so carefully controlled and so accurately described that they can be verified by other scientific workers. An experimental scientist attempts to break a problem into simple parts that can be carefully studied one at a time. He relies only on explanations that can be tested, on accurate measurements, and on careful observation.

The year 1543 is important because of the publication of two books. Both were based on experimentation and investigation. Both pointed out mistakes in beliefs that had been long accepted. They started people thinking along new lines. One of the books, by Nicolaus Copernicus, proved that the earth revolves around the sun. The other, by Andreas Vesalius, was a detailed description of the human body.

Andreas Vesalius was a young professor of anatomy at a great medical university in Italy. He was the fifth physician in direct line in his family. Vesalius worked with his students dissecting the dead bodies of criminals. He traced out every muscle and nerve, examined every organ. He set down all his findings in a book full of beautiful, exact drawings. Vesalius is still considered the greatest anatomist of all time. His accurate drawings may still be used.

Vesalius' book was a bombshell. It proved Galen wrong on many details. It opened the way for new inquiries.

Vesalius made people acquainted with the way the human body is built. He knew little about how it worked and accepted most of the explanations of Galen. Much remained to be learned, but man's knowledge had taken a big step in a new direction. Curious men were experimenting in other fields and discoveries came rapidly.

How has science advanced our knowledge of ourselves? As the method of experimental science became established, discoveries of new facts accumulated rapidly. Each new discovery and invention opened the way for others. As knowledge accumulated, it had to be divided into sections or areas, in order for individuals to become acquainted with what was known.

Today the field of scientific knowledge is divided and subdivided almost endlessly. The two big areas are the *physical* (or nonliving) *sciences* and the *biological* (or living) *sciences.* Each of these in turn has many fields. You might like to find out what kinds of knowledge are included in such special fields as physics, chemistry, botany, zoology, physiology, anthropology, psychology, bacteriology, medicine, or any of the many other sciences.

As the experimental method gained acceptance, men from all nations and all walks of life added to the ever-accumulating store of knowledge. Some discoveries were made almost at the same time by men working independently—often in different countries. Some discoveries may be credited to several people. Sometimes discoveries were made, and then forgotten and not used for many years. Sometimes new ideas that look good, but were later proved false, put men off on a wrong track. Knowledge advanced on some fronts and slipped back on others, but always curious minds keep research to its true meaning of **re**-search (that is—search *again and again*).

In about the middle of the 1800's Louis Pasteur, a French chemist, and Robert Koch, a German bacteriologist, working separately, proved that tiny living organisms cause fermenting, souring, decay, and certain diseases. (Here is something to think about: *Why did such proof have to wait until the discovery of the microscope? Why did not the man who first used the microscope to see germs develop the germ theory? What is necessary for a theory to be developed?*) Their experimental work was so accurately done and so logically reasoned that it became a model for future experimenters. Discoveries of other disease germs followed rapidly.

Who are some other scientists who made important discoveries in health? Discoveries of experimental science in

Denver Public Schools

Chemistry is a branch of science that is concerned with what things are made of. What are some other sciences?

the field of health are tremendous. Many are well known. Others, just as important, are almost unrecognized or unknown. The pieces of knowledge fit together, like pieces in a puzzle. Many of the parts are still missing. In the following paragraphs are named a few of the great workers for a healthier mankind.

Ambroise Paré, born in 1510, is known as the father of surgery. His knowledge and his humane treatment of his patients lifted surgery to the dignity of a profession.

In 1616 *William Harvey* demonstrated that the heart is a pump causing blood to circulate. Before Harvey it was commonly believed that blood came from the liver, was warmed in the heart, and disappeared in the tissues. Can you figure out how Harvey was able to prove that blood circulated? You may enjoy reading descriptions of his demonstration before the court; you can read his own account of his experiments.

Harvey proved that blood circulates, but he was unable to understand how it got from arteries to veins. A few years later the microscope had been so improved that *Marcello Malpighi* was able to see and describe the capillaries that join arteries and veins in the lung of a frog.

Harvey proved that blood circulates, but no one knew why. It took many years and the careful work of many men, experimenting in many fields, to furnish the answer to the *why. Antoine Lavoisier, Robert Boyle, Robert Hooke,* and many others added evidence bit by bit.

Edward Jenner, born in 1749, demonstrated a method of vaccination against smallpox. He had no knowledge of germs.

Louis Pasteur, who has been called "the most perfect scientist," in 1864 demonstrated the part bacteria play in disease. After Pasteur, discoveries followed rapidly in bacteriology, chemistry, antiseptic surgery, and vaccines.

Crawford Long and *William Morton* demonstrated the use of anesthetics in operations. Can you find out if this was the first use of anesthetics?

Florence Nightingale, during the Crimean War, restored nursing as a humane and honorable profession in England. What can you find out about the history of nursing and hospitals?

In the last century much has been done for public health by applying scientific medical facts to our living habits. Life in a modern city is made safe and comfortable only by constant effort. A modern city needs an alert, well-trained health department to provide pure food and water supplies; to furnish healthful conditions for living, playing, and working; and to prevent disease and accidents.

The health discoveries mentioned above are only a selected few. There are many others. You may like to see if you can find some interesting ones that are not so well known. In the library you will find stories about famous scientists.

In the last few years many new "wonder" drugs have been discovered, such as the sulfas and the antibiotics. Vaccines have been developed for some of our most dangerous communicable diseases. New techniques in surgery, "refrigeration" anesthesia, space medicine—all offer interesting stories you may like to read and tell. Men and women from all nations and times have contributed to our store of knowledge. Scientific discoveries are greatly hindered in a world where free interchange of ideas and information is not possible. One scientist must be able to build on the discoveries of another.

What has science contributed?

Science has made possible our amazing modern world of electricity, radio, airplanes, and atomic power. It has lengthened the span of life and made life more comfortable. Sometimes science is used to mean merely experimental science—the testing of theories by observation and exact measurement. At its best, science is an attitude of curiosity, of belief in a universe of law and order. It seeks to discover the laws of nature and to extend man's mastery over them. It is a method of finding facts and of testing theories. It is a search for truth best done without interference from ideas of personal gain or glory and without outside pressures to control it.

What is the scientific method? A scientist works in much the same way a detective does. He has a problem to solve. He collects clues and ideas related to the problem. Then he works out a possible solution, called a *theory.* He tests his theory by further observation, by logic, and by experimenting. The results of his testing determine his next step. Experiments may show that his theory is wrong. He changes the theory to include his new clues, and then he tests the revised theory. His experiments may prove conclusively that his theory is correct. If so, he has established a *scientific fact.* More likely, his experiments will add evidence that support his belief without proving it conclusively.

You may like to read about some of the mysteries and puzzles solved by great scientists. More thrilling than made-up stories are these adventures of men who fight pain and disease and death, who search for mysterious killers of mankind, and who discover the laws of nature.

The unique contribution of the modern scientific method is its faith in *testing* theories by experimenting. In the physical (nonliving) sciences, where it has been most successful, the scientific method follows strict

Denver Public Schools

Why is measurement so important in experimental science? How can we measure length, weight, time, temperature, the loudness of sound, the brightness of a light, or the amount of electricity? What are some of the numbers and measurements used to describe tests of how your body is working?

rules. A fact is not considered proved until it has been demonstrated beyond all possible doubt. Identical circumstances must always produce an identical event. Such demonstrations require precise and accurate measurement of all the things involved. To establish a simple fact, like the temperature at which water boils, requires exact measurement of the purity of the water, of the air pressure, and of the temperature of the water.

Sometimes such proof is impossible. The circumstances are too complex or too delicate to be duplicated in an experiment. In such cases, physical scientists will grudgingly admit evidence based on the accurate observation of a tremendous number of identical events. Individual pieces of evidence are like pieces of a jigsaw puzzle. They must be fitted together by reasoning to have any meaning.

Human beings are hard to analyze and to measure. In the field of human health, science is at a stage where it has an abundance of evidence but few experimentally proved facts. Scientists are only at the beginning of many research jobs.

What are scientific facts? People today believe many different kinds of facts. In the field of health only a few facts are supported by enough experimental evidence to be generally accepted by all scientists. Do you think descriptions of parts of the body would be acceptable scientific facts? Why? What about descriptions of how they work?

A great many opinions believed today are scientific theories. They are not supported by final experimental evidence. Some have enough evidence in their favor to be widely accepted.

Many such theories are of great practical use, scientific or not.

The scientist keeps an open mind on theories. He believes that we can never be sure that we have the last scrap of information. New evidence may show that a theory is wrong, entirely or in part. Even in the physical sciences, where experimental evidence is most abundant, scientists have had to change a great many theories in the last few years to fit them in with theories of relativity and atomic energy. In an orderly universe all truths fit together.

Some theories are supported by very little evidence. Some questions about human beings are so complicated that the evidence is difficult to collect. The evidence is so confusing that totally different theories may be based upon the same pieces of evidence. For example, there are several theories about how people learn, how habits are formed, how the nervous and glandular systems work, and how the brain works. Some theories seem to be based on more evidence or on better evidence, but all have many missing pieces.

Theories that cannot be proved experimentally may be tested by practical experience and by time.

What is the role of science today? During the last century experiments were being carried on in many fields. Man seemed on the way to conquering germ diseases and to discovering all of nature's laws. Particularly in chemistry and physics, discoveries came thick and fast. No wonder people became enthusiastic.

Scientists themselves, for the most part, proceeded slowly and accurately, piling up facts and testing

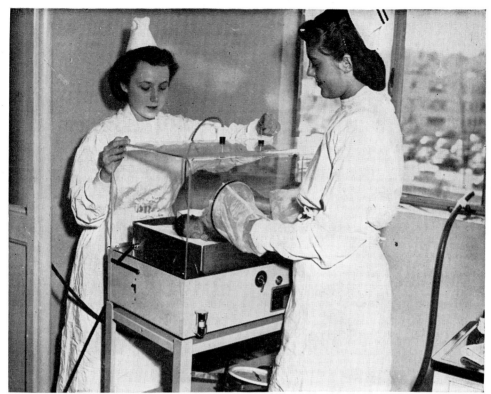

University of Colorado Medical Center

This new-born baby is being kept alive in an incubator. What knowledge about the human body makes such a device practical?

theories. Many other people were not so careful. Science had added so much to our comfort and knowledge that they believed it could answer all our questions. People abandoned many old ideas because they had not been proved experimentally. They accepted any piece of evidence, any explanation that was labeled scientific. Experimental science became as highly regarded as Galen's beliefs had been in his day. People believed that science would automatically build for us a perfect world.

Today mankind is not so sure that we are on the road to perfection. We have knowledge and comfort and power never dreamed of a few years ago. But we still have problems and questions. We are beginning to listen to the thoughtful men who have been trying to tell us that scientific discoveries must be used with intelligence. Man still needs moral standards and a philosophy of life to guide his decisions. We need some of the old ideas that had been discarded because they could not be measured and proved in a laboratory.

Science can never answer all the questions about a human being. Science works by studying the parts of things. It accepts only data that can be accurately measured. Some truths are never found in parts. A person is more than a collection of separate parts. Science cannot measure or explain the most important abilities of a human being—his ability to think, to will, to believe, and to plan. Life itself is still a mystery though we accurately know some aspects of it.

Reviewing the chapter

Test yourself

I

You should answer "yes" to the following questions:

1. Do you keep your eyes and ears open to learn for yourself what is going on in the world?
2. Do you keep an open mind toward new ideas?
3. Do you stop to think about attractive-sounding new ideas and methods?
4. Do you like to experiment to find out how things work?

II

Can you arrange the following list of names of men and events in the correct order of time?

(a) discovery of circulation of blood
(b) Louis Pasteur
(c) Hippocrates
(d) magic
(e) Vesalius
(f) Galen

III

Complete the following sentences by supplying the missing words. DO NOT WRITE IN THIS BOOK.

1. Instruments that aid observation are ...., ..., and ....
2. A wrong guess that people continue to believe is a ....
3. Carefully tested observations are called ....
4. The science that studies living things is ....

5. Scientific theories are reasonable guesses that have not been ....
6. Both science and religion believe in an .... world and natural laws that are ....

IV

What would you think, say, or do in the following situations?

1. If someone said that only doctors and nurses ought to study how the body works?
2. If you read an advertisement about a sure cure for headaches?
3. If someone boasted about his good health even though he broke many laws of healthful living?
4. If someone said that what was good enough for his parents was good enough for him?
5. If you heard someone say that scientific inventions had done more harm than good?

Other activities

Lives of scientists and other health workers, scientific discoveries, and ancient health practices provide material for interesting reports, charts, dramatizations, and discussions. Besides the men mentioned in the chapter you might be interested in the contributions of Benjamin Franklin, Anton Leeuwenhoek, William Osler, Joseph Lister, Alexander Fleming, Walter Reed, Clara Barton, Dorothea Dix, Florence Sabin, and scores of others. Use encyclopedias and card files in the library.

Reading to help you grow up

You can read of thrilling scientific discoveries in these free booklets:

Men of Science. The Westinghouse Corporation.

Ventures, Voyages, Vitamins. The National Dairy Council.

Health through the Ages and *Health Heroes.* The Metropolitan Life Insurance Company.

If you are interested in medicine you will enjoy these books:

The Story of Medicine by Joseph Garland.

How Man Discovered His Body, by Sarah R. Riedman, describes the experiments and discoveries that have added to our knowledge of ourselves.

Health and Human Welfare, by Burkhard and others, has interesting stories of scientific conquests in health, old and new.

For good readers:

Biology for Better Living, by Bayles and Burnett, has an interesting account of the scientific method, and the history of science.

Other interesting stories of heroes of science and medicine are found in *Men against Death* and *Microbe Hunters* by Paul DeKruif.

Films to help you understand

Health Hero Series, Filmstrips. Metropolitan Life Insurance Co.

Anesthesia. Association. How anesthesia was discovered.

Men of Medicine. March of Time Forum. Training a doctor.

White Angel. Teaching Film Custodians. Story of Florence Nightingale.

Man against Microbe. Metropolitan Life Insurance Co.

Modest Miracle. Bakery Engineers. History of science of nutrition dramatically portrayed.

Have you ever looked out over a familiar place from an airplane or a hill? How does it give you a different idea of the country?

Ewing Galloway

Picture Preview:

Chapter 6

Ewing Galloway

Teamwork enables a player to make a spectacular run. How do parts of your body work as a team?

Parts of several body systems are shown in the drawing. What are they? What are some systems not shown? In what order would you encounter the systems if you could see into a body?

FAO Information Division, United Nations

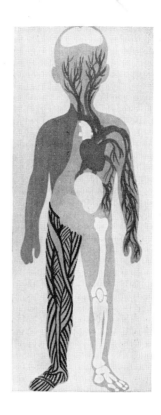

These boys are learning how an automobile engine works. Your body is much more interesting and more complicated. How can you learn how it works?

Chapter 6

WHAT ARE THE BIG JOBS OF THE BODY?

Have you ever looked down from a high place—a hill or an airplane—at the earth spread out beneath you? What happens to a scene if you go high enough to see a large area all at one time?

Your body is extremely complex. You will understand it better if you see it from many different angles and heights.

Since a person can think of only a limited number of things at a time, it is easier to study your complex body part by part. Chapters 7, 8, 9, 10, 11, and 12 describe various body systems one at a time in detail.

At the same time you need to keep in mind that a person lives and acts as a whole. This chapter will give you an airplane view of how your whole body works. You can see the important jobs performed by each system without losing sight of the whole pattern.

The jobs that must be done to keep a person alive are called the vital processes. The systems that perform these jobs are the vital systems. They provide food and oxygen, eliminate waste, and enable cells to work together. No system works alone. Each helps other parts of the body. Each depends upon other parts.

Your tissues and organs are not what they appear to be. If you look at the parts of your body under a microscope, you will find that each is made of cells. Each cell is a living unit. It requires food and oxygen, eliminates waste, and can grow and make others like itself. How is your body organized so that each of these billions of cells can get what it needs to live and work? How can the cells work together for the common good? How can they maintain the beautiful order and balance we call good health?

Looking ahead

Questions and suggestions

1. What is the purpose of the chapter you are about to read?

2. What does *vital* mean? From what Latin word does it come? What are some other words derived from the same Latin meaning?

3. Do you remember what cells, tissues, organs, and systems are?

4. What are the body's vital systems?

5. Do you know the organs in each system?

6. Can you compare the work and organization of your body with that of an army?

7. You probably have heard parts of your body compared to various machines. Name as many body parts as you can that resemble machines in some way.

Committee planning

1. The field-trip committee may be able to arrange a trip to a museum or hospital or school that has a model of the human body. You can see how the various body parts and systems are related to each other. If you cannot locate a model, perhaps you can find some charts.

2. A special committee may be able to obtain from home or from the butcher shop some animal internal organs or a piece of chicken. Can you identify different kinds of tissues? Can you see how blood vessels and nerves send branches to all parts? The finest branches of these systems can be seen only with a microscope.

3. Science committees can do some simple experiments to show: (1) that air has pressure, (2) that burning uses oxygen, and (3) that pure oxygen speeds up the rate of burning.

4. In many sports your body needs special protection. The safety committee can demonstrate some of the equipment and rules that protect athletes in such sports as football, basketball, swimming, boxing, and baseball. They can discuss the dangers of taking part in sports without adequate equipment and knowledge of rules and skills.

Reading

Try to keep in mind the purpose of the chapter as you follow your usual plan of reading once rapidly, then again more slowly for details.

How is your body organized?

Your body is more complicated than any machine ever built. Each organ is like a delicate precision instrument, finer than any machine made by man. In your body all the organs, made up of billions of cells, work together performing all the different functions of your body.

How can the parts of your body work together? In order to work to-gether the cells must be able to communicate with each other. Like the separate soldiers and units in an army, cells must respond to orders from some organizing authority. The body's communication and organization center is the *nervous system*. The nervous system sends its threadlike branches to all living parts of the body. It is so organized that it controls all parts of the body, co-ordinates them, and keeps you in touch with the outside world. All body activity, even though it may be carried out by other systems, depends upon the nervous system to set it in motion and to regulate it. No cell works without a message or stimulus.

Something of the structure of the nervous system has been known for a long time. Early anatomists traced the threadlike paths of many nerves. The nervous system is often compared to a telephone system. The nerves are like wires, the spinal cord is like a great connecting cable, and the brain is like a switchboard or control center. This comparison may help you get a general idea of the structure. You

Denver Public Schools

Which parts of your body work together to help you make a strike? How are they able to work together?

need to remember that the comparison is greatly oversimplified.

The brain and spinal cord and the nerves leading from the brain and spinal cord are called the *central nervous system*. Sometimes they are called the *voluntary nervous system* because they control the voluntary muscles (those which respond to your conscious direction). The central nervous system also functions in all activities of the mind and sense organs.

A special, partly independent system of nerves, called the *autonomic system,* controls activities of the internal organs like the heart, lungs, and stomach. These internal activities go on automatically; that is, they cannot be controlled by your conscious direction or will. Do you think it is important to have vital processes automatic?

You are able to receive messages from outside your body through sense organs. These are specialized organs for receiving impressions of sight, sound, taste, smell, and touch. Sense organs are said to be sensitive to anything that causes them to send a message to the brain. For example, the eye is sensitive to light, the ear to sound. Certain other cells are sensitive to heat, cold, pressure, or pain. Where are some of them located?

Anything that causes a message to travel along a nerve is called a stimulus. The action that takes place because of a stimulus is called a response.

No one knows exactly how the nervous system works. No scientist has any proof based on fact as to how consciousness, thought, feeling, and will arise from nervous activity. The efficient functioning of all body parts

94

is dependent upon healthy nerves. Some theories seem to explain at least part of the work of the nerves and furnish a basis for improving our use and control of our minds, thoughts, feelings, and will.

Helping the nervous system to control and regulate the body are certain glands knows as endocrine glands. Endocrine glands send chemicals called hormones into the blood. Hormones have many wonderful powers: they can make midgets or giants; they prepare the body to meet emergencies by increasing the rate of heartbeat and of breathing; they control growth and weight and the changes that occur when sex organs mature and boys and girls change into young men and women.

The nervous and endocrine systems are important factors in personality. They influence mental ability and emotions which together help determine the way you act. Like other parts of the body they need proper food, rest, exercise, and freedom from irritation or disease. They grow, develop, and can be trained. You can learn how to help your nervous system develop and work at its best.

What is the body's transportation system? One of the first things people realized about the body was that the heartbeat is a sign of life. They did not know what caused the beat or why it was so important, but they knew that when it stopped life was gone. Many words and expressions indicate the ancient belief that the heart is the special place where dwells man's life, spirit, affections, and emotions. Can you think of some words or expressions that use "heart" to convey such a meaning?

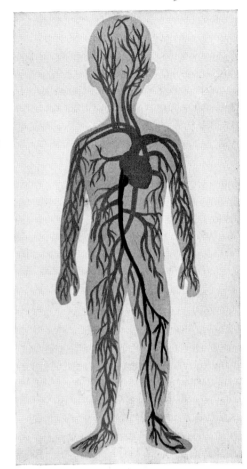

FAO Information Division, United Nations

How can you tell this is the body of a child? What does the circulatory system do for the body? What are parts of the circulatory system? Why is it called "circulatory"?

About the time John Smith was founding his colony in Virginia, another Englishman, named William Harvey, was proving that the heart is a pump which keeps blood circulating through tubes, or blood vessels, and back to the heart. The vessels that carry blood away from the heart are called *arteries*. Those that carry blood back to the heart are called *veins*. The

95

microscopic, thin-walled tubes that connect arteries and veins are called capillaries.

Apparently the heartbeat is essential because it keeps blood circulating. Immediately other problems arose. Why does a cell need a constant supply of fresh blood? How does material pass back and forth between cells and blood vessels? How is the blood kept fresh—supplied with essential materials and kept free from wastes? What kind of theory could you work out to answer these questions? How could you test the parts of your theory?

We have now found out that the cells that make up your body are like tiny islands almost touching each other. Winding in and out among the cells are the smallest blood vessels, the *capillaries*. The walls of the cells and the walls of the capillaries are thin enough so that certain substances can pass right through them.

Surrounding the cells and the capillaries is a salty liquid called *lymph*. The blood flowing through the capillaries releases into the lymph materials needed by the cells. Cells soak up the materials they need and send wastes into the lymph. Some of the lymph re-enters the capillaries. Some of the lymph flows along through the body in its own circulation system.

Your circulatory system does many other jobs. It helps to regulate body temperature. It helps to maintain the necessary water balance in your body. It distributes disease-fighting agents and chemicals that regulate the activities of the cells.

No part of the body can be healthy without a constant supply of clean healthy blood; nor can the circulatory system operate without help from the other body systems. Chapter 8 explains in more detail how the heart beats, how blood circulates, and how you can help your circulatory system function well.

What are other vital systems?

Branches of the communication and transportation systems extend to every cell in the body. Other vital systems must also contribute their special jobs to keep you alive. Three of these are the digestive, respiratory, and excretory systems. We will discuss these systems now.

How does your body use air? The use of air in the body was one of the hardest problems scientists had to solve. It was easy to see that air was drawn in and forced out of the body by movements of the chest and that people died when air was cut off. But why was air necessary? Many scientists added facts about air that helped to solve the problem.

In 1660 Robert Boyle discovered that when air was removed from a jar that contained a candle and a mouse the candle flame and the mouse both died. Apparently air is necessary for both processes—living and burning. Another scientist discovered that both burning and breathing used only part of the air. The part of the air used by breathing and by burning was called *oxygen*. He discovered that in pure oxygen a smoldering candle burst into brilliant flame and a living animal had more pep for a time. Other scientists

H. Armstrong Roberts

All kinds of body activity require oxygen. What are signs your body needs more oxygen? Which vital systems furnish oxygen to the cells?

have analyzed air that is breathed into the body and air leaving the body on the out-breath. In-going air contains about 21 per cent oxygen and .04 per cent carbon dioxide. Air leaving the body contains about 16 per cent oxygen and 4.5 per cent carbon dioxide. What has happened?

Then the French scientist Antoine Lavoisier proved that activities of living cells are made possible by a slow burning in the cells, similar to the burning of fuel in an engine. Burning requires fuel and oxygen, produces heat and energy for activity, and produces carbon dioxide and other wastes. Burning in the body cells, called *metabolism*, requires food for fuel to be combined with oxygen taken from the air. It too produces heat and energy and wastes.

How do you breathe? The large body cavity inside the trunk is divided into upper and lower sections by a muscular partition called the *diaphragm*. The lower cavity, called the abdomen, contains organs of digestion and excretion. The upper section, called the chest, is enclosed by ribs and diaphragm. It holds much of the respiratory and circulatory systems.

The muscles that enclose the chest can move to change the size of the chest cavity. When the diaphragm

Burning requires oxygen from the air. How can you build a fire so that it gets a good supply of oxygen?

moves down and the ribs up, the chest cavity is enlarged. Air outside the body rushes in. It travels through the organs of the respiratory system, the nose, throat, windpipe (or trachea), and bronchial tubes into the lungs. The lungs are like clusters of millions of tiny air sacs. They occupy most of the space in the chest. In the lungs the exchange of oxygen for carbon dioxide is made.

The whole complicated process of breathing is timed and regulated by the nervous system. The part of the brain that controls breathing is called the respiratory or vital center. Damage to it may cause instant death.

How does your body use food? Another puzzle for people not so long ago was how food could be changed so that it could be used by the body. By dissection of dead bodies scientists had discovered the organs through which food traveled. The name *alimentary canal* was given to the continuous series of tubes composed of the mouth, the throat, the esophagus, the stomach, and the small and large intestines. Other organs—the liver, pancreas, and gall bladder—had tubes and ducts leading into the food canal.

Somehow in passing along the alimentary canal food was changed into a liquid. It was picked up by the blood to be carried to the cells. There it was used for growth and energy. The process which breaks food down into substances that can go into the blood stream is called digestion. The organs chiefly involved are those of the digestive system.

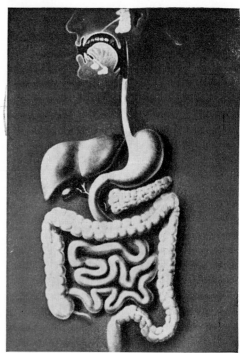

The digestive system prepares food for all the cells in the body. What are the organs in the system? How does food get from the digestive system to the cells?

Even after men knew the organs of the digestive system, they could not tell how they worked. Countless experiments have gradually added to our picture of how the body uses food.

About 125 years ago Dr. William Beaumont, a U. S. Army surgeon, treated a Canadian woodsman, Alexis St. Martin, for a bullet wound in the stomach. The wound healed in such a way that the stomach had an opening directly to the outside. Through this opening Dr. Beaumont watched the stomach work. He collected the digestive juice secreted by the stomach and experimented with it. He dangled food in the stomach and watched what happened. He learned how long various kinds of foods must remain in the stomach to be digested. He watched the effects on digestion of exercise, fear, anger, rest, alcohol, and the chewing of food.

Since Dr. Beaumont's time, scientists have invented other means of studying digestion and have learned many things.

Other experiments have added to our knowledge of how food is used in the body, what kinds of food are necessary, and how other factors affect digestion.

You may like to examine X-ray machines, fluoroscopes, and other scientific instruments. You may like to read about other discoveries of how your body uses food. Chapter 10 tells in more detail how digestion takes place and how you can help your digestive system do its important work.

What are some other jobs your body does?

Your body does many things besides just staying alive. It can move. It receives impressions from the outside world. It fights enemies and adapts itself to change. It has the power to hand on its heritage of life to new human beings. Somehow from its workings arise thoughts, feelings, dreams, and hopes.

How can you move? The most conspicuous body systems are the bones and muscles. They give your body form and shape. They enable it to move.

Your skeleton is composed of 206 bones of different sizes and shapes. The bones are fastened together by strong cords called ligaments. They are fastened in such a way as to make a framework for your body. They protect vital organs and permit a wide variety of body positions and movements.

Muscles are elastic-like fibers that bring about body movements. There are three kinds of muscle fibers. Voluntary muscles, which obey conscious direction, are attached to the bones and can move them. Involuntary muscles, which do not obey the will, are found in the internal organs like walls of the stomach, the small intestine, and blood vessels. The heart is made of a third special kind of muscle cell.

The entire body framework is covered by sheets of muscle fibre. Can you move the muscles in your arms and legs? Those across your abdomen? Those in your head? Muscles are fastened to the bones by tough cords called tendons. Each muscle is made up of thousands of tiny cells.

Each cell is stimulated by a nerve and nourished by a blood vessel.

Through careful study experts have discovered many things about muscles: how they grow and develop, how they become tired, and how they co-ordinate (work together). You can use many of their discoveries to increase your own muscular strength and skill.

How does your body protect itself? In order to work well, your body must maintain favorable conditions for all its cells. It must protect them from extremes of temperature. It must maintain proper balance of water and various necessary chemicals. It must get rid of harmful materials. Coverings of bone and muscle protect the vital organs from outside dangers.

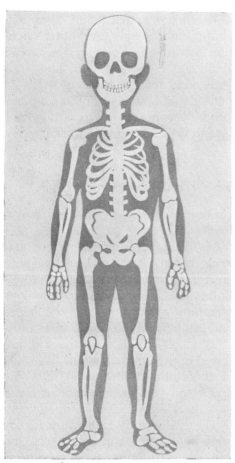

FAO Information Division, United Nations

Is this a child or an adult? What are the big jobs performed by the bones? With what other systems do they work?

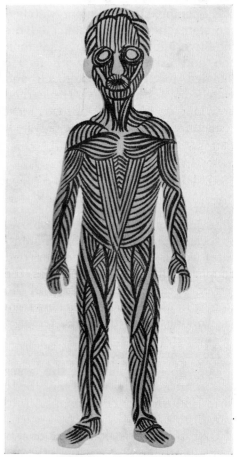

Courtesy FAO Information Division, United Nations

What kinds of muscles are shown in the drawing? What other kinds of muscles are in the body?

H. Armstrong Roberts

Your body has many natural protections. What are some of them? When does it need extra protection? How do equipment and coaching help to protect your body?

Your *skin* is one of the most important protective devices. It is a sensitive, tough, elastic covering that contains sweat glands, oil glands, hair roots, and nerve endings. It serves to keep out all kinds of irritating substances. Sweat glands help eliminate waste and help to keep the body cool. Special structures arising from the skin, like hair and nails, also help to protect the body.

Blood has many special protective uses. It helps to regulate body temperature. It keeps a water balance in the cells. It carries white corpuscles and chemicals that fight disease, poison, and infection. It carries hormones that can speed up or slow down body activity.

The *lymphatic system* protects your body from germs and aids in the production of blood cells.

Your *sense organs* protect you. Even pain, that may seem unnecessary to you, protects your body. How? Your whole nervous system protects you by detecting changes inside and outside the body and by stimulating appropriate responses. Can you give some examples?

101

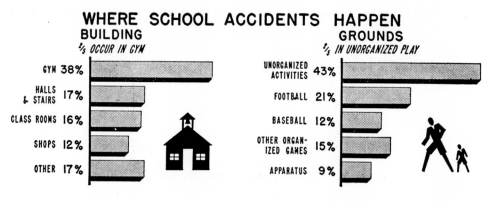

WHERE SCHOOL ACCIDENTS HAPPEN

BUILDING
⅖ OCCUR IN GYM

GYM	38%
HALLS & STAIRS	17%
CLASS ROOMS	16%
SHOPS	12%
OTHER	17%

GROUNDS
⅖ IN UNORGANIZED PLAY

UNORGANIZED ACTIVITIES	43%
FOOTBALL	21%
BASEBALL	12%
OTHER ORGANIZED GAMES	15%
APPARATUS	9%

National Safety Council

Discuss some ways of preventing accidents in each of these activities.

Encyclopedia Britannica Films

The man is demonstrating an artificial larynx. Do you know how talking and hearing are accomplished?

Reviewing the chapter

Test yourself

Complete the following sentences by supplying the missing words. Do NOT WRITE IN THIS BOOK.

1. The body's communication and organization center is the ....

2. The parts of the central nervous system are the ...., ..., and ....

3. The .... helps the nervous system to control and regulate the body.

4. Blood vessels that carry blood away from the heart are called ....

5. The smallest blood vessels are ....

6. Organs of the respiratory system are ...., ..., ..., ..., and ....

7. Organs of the alimentary canal are ...., ..., ..., ..., ..., and ....

8. Your skeleton is composed of .... bones.

9. Muscles which follow your conscious directions are called .... muscles.

Reading to help you grow up

Working Together for Health, by Burkhard and others, has an interesting description of the body as a factory.

How Your Body Works by Herman and Nina Schneider. An easy interesting book with many drawings and simple experiments that show how your body works.

The safety committee will find many good suggestions for activities in these books:

Road to Safety Series by Mann and others.

Outwitting the Hazards by Bacon.

Your Health and Safety by Clemenson and LaPorte.

Films to help you understand

Human Biology Series. Five filmstrips. Society for Visual Education. The digestive, circulatory, respiratory, glandular, and nervous systems.

Good form in any sport calls for muscular control. It requires co-ordination and practice.

Ewing Galloway

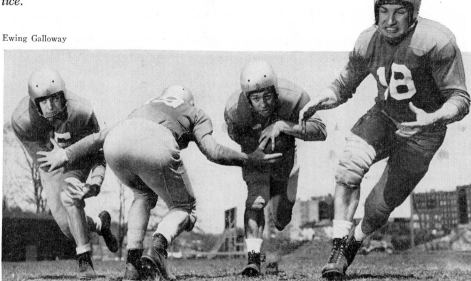

Picture Preview:

Chapter 7

Healthy, well-developed bones and muscles give you a graceful attractive body. What foods help you to have strong bones and muscles?

Emma Willard School

No one is born strong and grace-ful. How do small children learn to control their muscles? How can you continue to improve your co-ordination?

Milk is the most nearly perfect food. Why is it especially important for young people?

Muscles develop with use. What are some activities that use many muscles?

Chapter 7

WHAT DO BONES AND MUSCLES DO FOR YOU?

*D*o you admire people with well-developed, graceful bodies? Do you enjoy watching acrobats, skaters, and dancers perform with grace and skill? Have you experienced the thrill of feeling your own body respond with power and accuracy as you hit a home run, or served an ace, or walked across a stage or into a room? Back of all these feats of grace, strength, endurance, and skill are healthy muscles and bones.

Together bones and muscles give your body its shape. Well-developed muscles covering strong, well-formed bones give your body an attractive, streamlined look, free from unsightly bulges and flabbiness. Muscles help to hold your bones in position. Bones held in their proper alignment give you an attractive, comfortable posture. Your body is balanced and all its parts are in positions where they work well.

Lift your heel from the floor. Can you feel muscles pull? Bones act like levers. They are moved by muscles pulling on them. Strong, graceful movements depend upon well-developed muscles working together smoothly under the control of healthy, well-trained nerves.

Not all people inherit equally strong bodies. Few make the most of what they do inherit. Look up the stories of some sports champions. You will probably be surprised to see how many of them overcame serious physical handicaps.

Most of you probably will not use the time, effort, and attention necessary to become a champion in any athletic sport. You do want to have a body strong, attractive, and skillful enough to enable you to enjoy life. You want to be able to play and work without getting too tired.

Experts have learned a great deal about how your body is lined up for efficient movement, what makes bones strong, how your muscles work, and what kind of care and training will develop your body. You can profit from their findings. You can form habits that enable your body to develop at its best.

Looking ahead

Questions and suggestions

1. Can you locate some of the bones and joints in your own body? How many can you locate in your arm and hand? Why are there so many in your hand?

2. What movements can you make with your wrist, elbow, shoulder, and trunk?

3. How are your joints constructed so these movements are possible?

4. Do you remember the meaning of these words: voluntary, involuntary, stimulus, and response?

5. Where are the voluntary and the involuntary muscles?

6. What gives your upper arm its shape? Watch and feel your upper arm as you extend your forearm, then bend your elbow. How do muscles work?

7. Have several people extend their arms straight out from their shoulders and hold them motionless. Have others move their arms leisurely up and down. Which group tires more quickly? Why?

8. Good posture is attractive, comfortable, and efficient. Do you know how to recognize good posture? Chapter 16 has some suggestions. You might like to check your posture now and try to improve if necessary. Later in the year you can check to see if you have improved.

a trip to a museum to look at one. Large charts are helpful if you cannot find a skeleton.

3. A committee can collect a variety of bones from the butcher. There are several suggestions in this chapter that will help you to plan a bone show. You can show bone construction; the living and the mineral part of bone; special shapes; joints; cartilage; fractures; marrow; attached muscles; and channels for nerves and blood vessels.

4. Artists in the class may like to trace profiles of individuals of different ages and you can notice the change.

5. The speaker's committee may be able to have an expert help you with problems of developing strength and skill and endurance. Do you have some flabby muscles? Do you tire easily or feel awkward? An expert can help you choose activities that develop all muscles. He can give you expert advice on conditioning muscles, avoiding muscle soreness and strain, and using your body efficiently.

6. The field-trip committee may be able to arrange with physical-education teachers to give your class tests in some fundamental muscular skills. Do you perform as well as most boys and girls your age? Each person can keep a record of his speed, skill, strength, and endurance and recheck sometime during the year.

Committee Planning

1. Have the library, movie, and bulletin-board committees planned ahead so they have materials ready for the class?

2. Can someone locate a skeleton for the class to examine? Perhaps you can arrange

Reading

Read rapidly through the chapter for the main ideas. Read again for details. Test yourself by answering topic questions and the test at the end of the chapter.

Bones serve as a framework and a support for the muscles. They protect important organs. They act as levers which can be moved by muscles to cause body movements.

What do your bones do for you? Your body is built around a skeleton framework of bone just as a building is built around a framework of wood or steel. Without this skeleton you would be as shapeless as a rag doll and as unable to move. If the bones that make your skeleton are weak or crooked or underdeveloped, you will be weak and unable to move gracefully.

The main support of the skeleton is the backbone, or spinal column. Can you feel your backbone running down the middle of your back? At the top of the spinal column is the skull (the bony case which holds the brain and forms the face). Just below the skull is the part of the backbone forming the neck. Below the neck is a bony ring, made by two collar bones and two shoulder blades. The arms are suspended from this ring or shoulder girdle. Below the shoulders is a cage for the heart and lungs, formed by the spinal column, a breastbone, and 12 pairs of ribs. At the lower end of the spinal column is a ring of heavy bones, called the pelvis. The pelvis holds up the organs in the abdomen. The legs are suspended from the hip bones, which form part of the pelvis. Can you locate all these parts of your skeleton?

What kinds of bones are in the skeleton? The 206 bones making up the adult skeleton vary in size and shape according to the work they have to do. Long heavy bones help support the body and make large movements. In the arm are three long bones. The upper arm has one, and the lower arm has two. The bones in the leg correspond to those in the arm, except that the knee is protected by a kneecap. Can you find the long bones in your arms and legs?

Small, short bones are for short, fast movements. In the wrist are eight small bones. Each hand has five bones, each finger has three, and each thumb has two. The ankle has one bone less than the wrist. The bones of the foot correspond to those of the hand. Can you find the short bones in your hands and fingers?

Specially shaped flat bones help to protect important organs. Can you find specially shaped bones that protect the brain? The heart and lungs? The organs in the abdomen?

The chest is formed by 12 pairs of ribs, the spinal column, and the breastbone. All the ribs are attached to the spine. The top seven ribs are fastened in front to the breastbone or sternum. The next three ribs are attached in front to the ribs directly above. The lowest two are not attached at all in front and are called "floating" ribs.

The hip girdle, or pelvis, is formed by the next to last bone of the spinal column and two heavy hip, or pelvic, bones.

The eight bones which enclose the brain are the cranium. Together with fourteen facial bones they make up the skull. In an infant the cranial

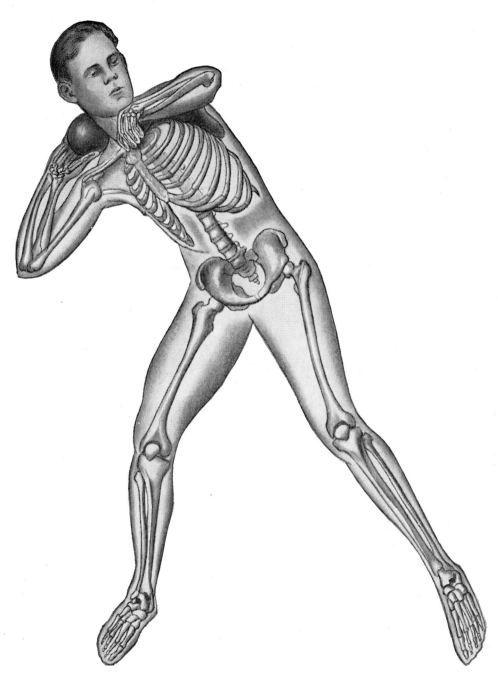

Your body is built around a skeleton framework of bone. Where are internal organs especially well protected by bones? Can you tell how many there are in the body? What is the big difference—besides size—between your bones and the bones of a baby?

The bottom two, the sacrum and coccyx, are more rigid. Seven vertebrae at the top form the neck, the next 12 are attachments for the ribs, and the next five are the small of the back.

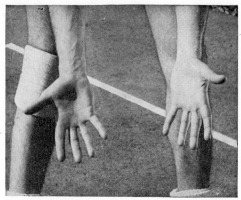

Human hands can do a wide variety of activities. How does their construction make them so useful? How many bones are in your hand?

bones have small spaces between them filled with membrane (soft tissue). These small spaces, called fontanels or "soft spots," gradually fill with bone until the entire skull is firm at about eighteen months of age. If you examine a skull, you can see the jagged lines where the cranial bones meet and have fused. Some of the bones in the face are hollow. The hollow air spaces, called *sinuses*, make the head lighter and allow air from the nose and throat to circulate through them.

How is it possible for the backbone to be so flexible? Have you ever wondered how it was possible for your back to be flexible enough to bend in any direction, yet be rigid enough to hold you upright? The backbone is made of 26 bones, piled one on top of the other to make a column. Pads of cartilage, called discs, separate the bones. Tough cords called *ligaments* hold them in position.

The 24 upper bones are separate and movable and are called *vertebrae*.

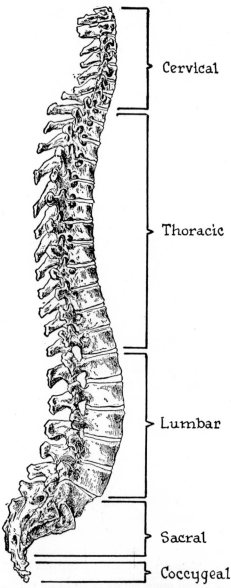

Cervical

Thoracic

Lumbar

Sacral

Coccygeal

A side view of an adult vertebral column shows the natural curves. How are the vertebrae held in position?

110

Each vertebra is an irregularly shaped flat bone with a hole in the center. The holes fit over each other to form the spinal canal. Through the canal runs a cable of nerves called the spinal cord. The spinal cord sends out cables of nerves from between each two vertebrae. Each cable supplies nerves for a special section of the body. Individual nerves branch out from the cables to cells in all parts of the body. The nerves are well covered by a protective sheath; and the openings between the vertebrae allow plenty of room so that in a normal spine nerves cannot be pinched or injured.

Viewed from the side, the spinal column takes the shape of a long, slender S, the upper end pointing forward. This curvature of the backbone eases the jolts that come from walking and other body movements. If the muscles that support the backbone become weak, the curves may become exaggerated. When the curves are exaggerated the body is not so well balanced. It is not as attractive and tires more easily.

How do you bend? Your body can bend only at the joints, where one bone meets another. At the joints, the ends of the bones are enlarged and covered with smooth, tough cartilage. Strong bands called ligaments, attached above and below the joint, hold the bones together. One large ligament encloses the whole joint in a sac which secretes synovial fluid. This fluid lubricates the joint and helps the bones slide over each other smoothly without pain or friction.

Move your shoulder, your elbow, and your wrist. Can you make the same kinds of movements with all joints? The kind of movement you can make depends upon the way the bones are fitted together. Hinge joints, which open only one way like the hinge on a door, are found in fingers, elbows, and knees. Ball-and-socket joints, which allow movements in many directions, are found in the shoulders and hips. Bones with nearly flat surfaces, like those in your wrist, allow gliding movements. Your body has many kinds of joints to permit a wide variety of motions. In some joints, like those in your skull, bones are movable at first to accommodate changes at birth. Later these joints become rigid and allow no movement.

How can you develop a strong body framework?

A strong, erect body and graceful movements are admired by everyone. To have a strong, graceful body you need a straight, strong, well-balanced framework. You can find out how your bones grow and develop so you can help them.

What are bones made of? Bones are made of about one-third living material and two-thirds nonliving material. In the living material are cells, blood vessels, fat, and a tough celluloid-like substance called cartilage. The mineral matter, or the nonliving material in bones, is chiefly calcium and phosphorus. The living material enables bones to grow and to repair themselves. The mineral material makes the bones strong and rigid.

If you can get some bones from the

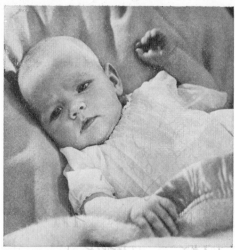

Clapp's Baby Food Division

A baby's bones are mostly soft cartilage. What are the "soft spots" on a baby's head?

butcher you can study the characteristics of these two kinds of material—organic and mineral. Soak a bone in strong vinegar or dilute acid for several days to dissolve the mineral matter. The part of the bone that is left is organic matter. You will find it looks like the original bone but is tough and flexible instead of hard and stiff. You can bend it easily. To study the mineral part, bake another bone in an oven for several hours. The part of the bone that remains after heating is mineral. You will find it light in color and weight, brittle, and easily crushed.

A baby's bones consist mostly of the living, rubber-like cartilage. As a child grows older, if his diet is right, the tiny bone cells grow and harden by taking minerals from the blood. As minerals are deposited in the bones, the skeleton gradually becomes more rigid until finally not much cartilage is left, except as a covering on the ends of the bones. You can feel some of the cartilage left in your own body in your ears or nose. In old age, bones become very brittle, and an old person needs to be very careful to avoid falls that may break bones.

How does a bone grow? Look at a long bone cut crosswise. The outer part looks hard and solid and the inner part looks spongy and full of holes. These holes are the cut ends of canals that carry blood vessels and nerves. Surrounding each canal are living bone cells. The bone cells take *phosphorus* and *calcium* from the blood. These minerals make a hard substance which is deposited in layers around the cells to harden the bones. As a bone grows larger, longer, and harder, living bone cells remain scattered through it for upkeep and repair.

The long bones contain a spongy substance called *marrow*. You can see the marrow if you break open a chicken drumstick or examine the round bone in a slice of ham. You can pick out the soft marrow with your finger. The marrow running up the center of the bone is yellow and composed mostly of fat. The marrow in the ends of the bones is red and contains thousands of tiny blood vessels that manufacture red blood cells.

A break in a bone, or fracture, heals in much the same way as a bone grows. Blood accumulates in the tissues around the broken bone, causing the flesh to become swollen and inflamed. The accumulation of blood provides larger amounts of bone-building materials. Bone cells around the break produce new cells of cartilage, which gradually change to bone. By the end of the healing period the

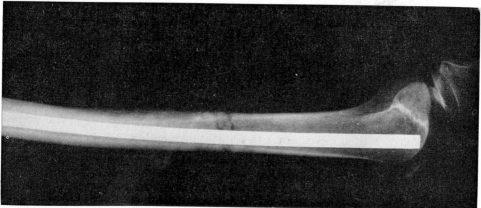

University of Colorado Medical Center

These X-ray pictures show a fractured thigh bone, before and after it has been set. Notice the overlapping ends of the broken bone in the first picture. In the second picture you can see the metal rod that has been driven through the bone to hold it in place until the bone grows together.

bone is as strong as ever with a new deposit of minerals over the fracture.

How can you help your bones grow straight and strong? To grow larger and become stronger, bones must have large supplies of the minerals calcium and phosphorus. The very best source of both calcium and phosphorus is whole milk. About the only other foods that contain much calcium are milk products and a few vegetables. Many foods contain phosphorus. Boys and girls who are still growing need at least a quart of milk a day.

In order to build bones and teeth from calcium and phosphorus the bone cells must be provided with vitamins C and D. Vitamin C is found in citrus fruits (oranges and lemons),

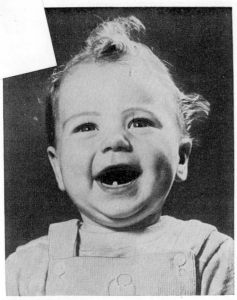

Hansen's Laboratory

Why are baby teeth important? Small children should have regular dental examinations to prevent decay and loss of teeth.

tomatoes, cabbage, and some other raw fruits and vegetables. Vitamin D is made by the body when certain short rays of the sun, called ultraviolet rays, shine on the bare skin. It is not found in foods except in certain fish-liver oils, like cod-liver oil, and in milk which has been treated by exposure to ultraviolet rays or has had vitamin D added to it.

While bones are growing, children need three or four times as much mineral and vitamin supply as adults. The best way to help yourself develop strong, well-shaped bones is by drinking at least a quart of milk a day, eating lots of vegetables and fruits, and exercising outdoors in the sunshine. Vigorous exercise helps the blood circulation carry the minerals to the bone cells.

In the winter all children who cannot be exposed outdoors to the sun should receive some type of vitamin D, such as cod-liver oil, or milk with vitamin D. Great care must be exercised in exposing delicate skin, particularly the skin of a baby, to the direct sunlight. Learn more about the effects of sunlight on the skin before you try an unusual amount of strong sunlight.

How can you care for injured bones? Most injuries to bones need to be treated by a competent physician. He can find out if the injury is a fracture (broken bone), a dislocation, or a sprain. Often an X-ray photograph of the injury may be necessary.

A *fracture* is set (put in place) by pulling the ends of the bone into place and binding them. If the ends of the bones slip out of place, the bone may not heal, or it may heal in the wrong position. An X-ray picture during healing enables a physician to see if the bone is setting correctly.

Some fractures require special care. A bone broken near the end—near a joint—may swell and cause permanent stiffening of the joint. A broken bone that breaks through the skin is called a *compound fracture*. Infection is the great danger from a compound fracture. Why?

Moving a person with a broken or dislocated bone may make the injury worse. What is the best thing to do if you are with someone who injures a bone?

A *dislocation* is a bone pulled out of place at a joint, but not broken. The bones must be replaced in the joint and held in place until the torn ligaments are healed.

When a joint is pulled so that liga-

114

ments are stretched or torn, the injury is called a *sprain*. Since no bones are broken or out of place, a sprain does not have to be set. A firm binding tends to keep down excess swelling and prevents movement of the joint. At first the joint should be moved very little to prevent further injury. Later it should be gradually exercised in order to counteract stiffness and to increase circulation.

What changes take place in your skeleton as you grow? As you grow your skeleton gets larger, stronger, and more rigid. Your body becomes less flexible because minerals replace cartilage in your bones, and also because some bones grow solidly together. For example, bones in the head unite; so do those at the bottom of the spinal column. Children have 33 vertebrae. Adults have only 26, because the lowest four unite into one vertebra to form the coccyx and the next five unite into one vertebra to form the sacrum.

Because different parts of your skeleton grow at different speeds and at different times, your body proportions change. A little baby looks very different from an adult. He is top-heavy, with a head one quarter his entire body length, a short neck, a large abdomen, and short arms and

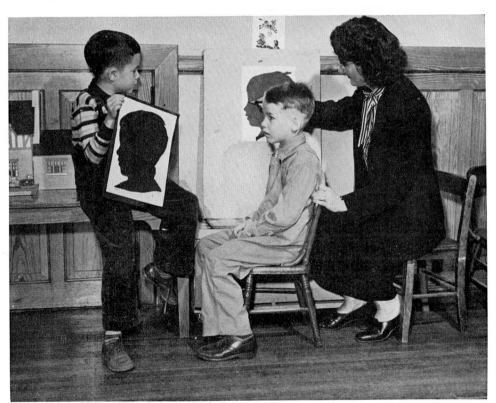

Bones in your body grow at different times and different rates. How do the bones in a child's head differ from an adult's?

legs. A baby's head grows slowly during infancy and achieves its final size when a child is nine or ten. The trunk is relatively large at birth. It grows rapidly for a few months and then grows slowly until adolescence. It does not attain its final size until late adolescence.

The bones in the arms and legs are comparatively short at birth. They grow steadily during childhood and lengthen rapidly in early adolescence. Boys grow broader through the shoulders; girls grow wider through the hips. A boy's whole skeleton grows heavier; that is why boys can engage in more strenuous sports and do harder work than girls. For a while individuals may be high waisted because their legs grow faster than their trunks.

The face changes gradually in size and shape. It grows most rapidly in early adolescence. The upper part of the face usually develops faster, and the jaw is often the last feature to attain adult size and shape.

As long as bones are soft, pressure can change their shape. Bones which are not used and exercised may not grow normally. However, most poorly formed bones are a result of malnutri-

Denver Public Schools

How does exercise in the sunshine help you to have strong bones? If you cannot have sunshine on your skin every day, how can you obtain the vitamin D you need?

tion. A person may have poorly formed bones because, in early childhood, he did not get enough calcium or vitamin D. If you furnish your body with a good diet and plenty of outdoor exercise in the sunshine, it will develop at its best.

Many boys and girls are self-conscious and worried about their growth. Some think they are growing too rapidly; others think they are growing too slowly. Their arms and legs and hands and feet seem out of proportion and hard to handle. Girls are sometimes ill at ease because they are taller than the boys in their class; boys worry because they are small. But rapid changes and great variations in size among boys and girls of the same age are perfectly natural. Give your body the food, rest, and exercise it needs to grow properly. Have a physical examination and follow the suggestions of the doctor. Then relax! In a short time the rapid changes will be over.

Take advantage of these growing years. Participate in many activities. Have fun and prepare for the future at the same time. By practice you learn co-ordination and skill and self-confidence.

Learn to know people, to get along with them, and to like them. Don't let yourself drop out of things because you are growing. Growing offers you your big opportunity to learn to be skillful and happy.

How do muscles do their work?

What you call flesh on your body is really muscle, along with some fat. Healthy, well-developed muscles give you a smoothly rounded appearance which keeps you from having that bony look. Muscles help hold your bones in place, hold the body in position, and make it possible for you to move. You can help your muscles develop strength, skill, and endurance.

How do muscles cause body movements? The muscles covering your body are attached to the bones of the skeleton by tough bands called tendons. In order to move a bone a muscle must also be attached to another bone. Can you understand why? See how the muscles of your upper arm are attached to the shoulder blade and to the bones in your lower arm. The muscles attached to your skeleton are controlled by nerves from the voluntary nervous system. Muscles and nerves work in such close teamwork that they are often called the *neuromuscular* (nerves and muscles) *system*. Muscles work only when they receive a stimulus from a nerve.

If you feel the muscle in your upper arm, you can learn the shape of most muscles. Can you tell that it has a thick middle part which narrows toward the tendon at each end?

A muscle works by contracting (becoming shorter). When it is stimulated by a nerve impulse it gets shorter, and the middle part gets thicker and harder. When a muscle shortens, it pulls on the bone to which it is fastened, causing it to move. When a muscle is not working it is

117

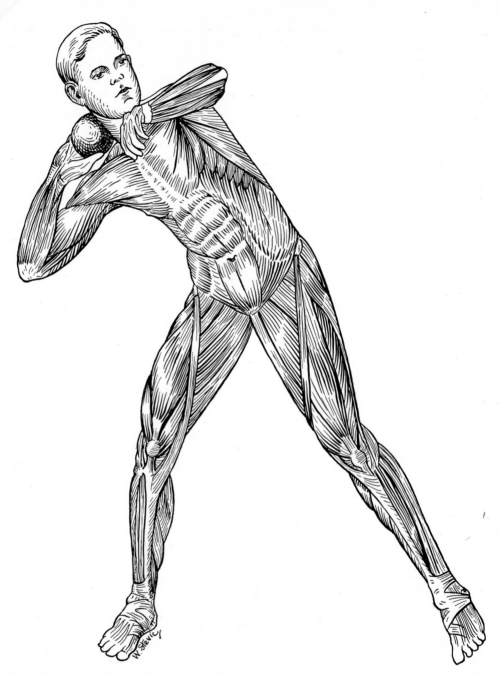

Your entire body framework is covered by muscles. How are muscles attached to bones? Like all living material, muscles are made of cells, called muscle fibers. These fibers are bound together in bundles to make the muscle. Can you identify the biceps in this drawing? See also the drawing on page 119.

relaxed. It is longer, thinner, and softer. Muscles can only pull, so they usually work in pairs. While one muscle contracts and pulls, its opponent muscle relaxes. In your upper arm these opposing muscles are called the *biceps* in front of your arm, and *triceps* at the back of your arm. Touch the muscles in your upper arm lightly as you lift the edge of your desk; then touch them as you push down on it. Can you feel the opposing muscles contract and relax? Try other muscles; for example, clench your fist, then straighten your fingers.

How is it possible for muscles to work? Like all other living material, muscles are made of cells. The cells, called muscle fibers, are long and threadlike. Hundreds of them are bound together in small bundles, about the size of a pencil lead, and wrapped in connecting tissue. The bundles extend from tendon to tendon; so each miscroscopic cell can exert its own pull. The bundles are grouped into larger bundles and all are fastened together to make the muscle.

Blood vessels and nerves send microscopic branches to each muscle fiber; so each cell is supplied with food and oxygen, is kept free of wastes, and is able to receive nerve impulses. When a single muscle fiber is stimulated by a nerve, it contracts

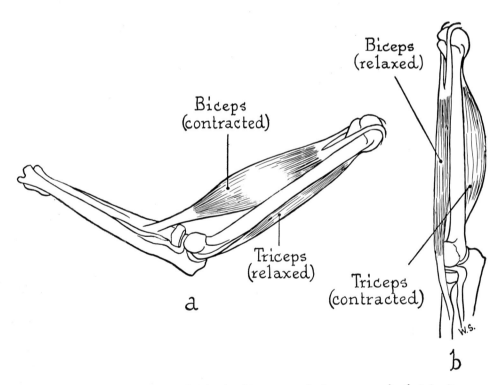

In bending the forearm upward (a), the biceps muscle is contracted—that is, it grows broader and thicker—and the triceps muscle is relaxed. What happens when the forearm is extended (b)?

completely, then immediately relaxes. Usually one nerve branches to supply a group of cells; so each small group acts as a unit. Skillful muscle action depends upon stimulating sets of muscle fibers one after the other in smooth rhythm. The athlete or graceful person uses less energy because he stimulates only as many fibers as he needs to perform action. Notice how a baby or a person learning a new skill uses too many muscles and makes many unnecessary motions due to lack of muscle co-ordination.

Contracting muscles burn food, producing energy, somewhat in the same way an engine burns gasoline. Tiny blood vessels bring food and oxygen to each muscle cell and carry away the wastes produced by the burning. A spark from the nervous system sets off the action. Between contractions a muscle cell prepares for its next action. It takes new supplies from the blood and gets rid of wastes. One of the remarkable features of the body machine is the ability of a muscle to convert part of the waste back into fuel if it has a good supply of oxygen. Why is rest so important in building muscle?

What is muscle tone? In a healthy individual muscles do not relax completely but maintain a slight degree of contraction, somewhat like an automobile with its motor idling. This slight contraction is called tone. Muscles not exercised regularly lose tone, become flabby, and respond sluggishly and weakly, like a cold motor. When muscles in the arms and legs are flabby, it is likely that muscles in the heart and other organs are flabby also. In a large degree, the food, rest, and exercise that improve the tone of one set of muscles improve the tone of all.

Why do muscles tire? When your muscles work hard or for a long time, the activity in the cells produces more than the usual amount of waste products.

Wastes interfere with the burning in the cells in somewhat the same way ashes clog a stove. When wastes accumulate you feel tired. When muscles are tired they do not respond quickly and accurately to messages from the nervous system. They lose their strength and co-ordination.

What causes muscle strain and cramps? Under extreme stimulation a muscle may go on working even when very tired. Enough waste may accumulate to cause a mild soreness. Rest and warmth to increase circulation help relieve sore muscles. Muscles may be strained (stretched or torn) by excessive stretching, violent efforts, or overuse. Strained muscles may be relieved and helped to recover by rest, warmth, and sometimes the use of a support, such as a bandage, tape, or splint.

A muscle spasm, or cramp, may result when stimuli come so fast that a muscle does not get a chance to relax. Prolonged or violent exertion, cold, or an unnatural position may cause a cramp. To relieve a cramp, remove the cause (get out of cold water, straighten the limb, etc.) and stimulate circulation by massaging in a direction toward the heart.

You can usually avoid sore, strained muscles. Work up gradually to hard exercise. Keep warm and relaxed. Can you think of other training rules?

How can you help muscles develop?

Modern life tends to make human beings "soft." Passive forms of recreation, like radio, television, movies, and reading, take much of the time of young people. Exercise, proper food, and rest are too frequently neglected. Muscles develop by use and are strengthened by continued use.

Why do muscles need food? Like most body tissues, muscles are made of a kind of material called *protein.* So for growth and repair they need a constant supply of foods containing protein. Some foods contain all the materials needed to build cells and are called complete proteins. Complete proteins are animal products— milk, cheese, eggs, fish, and especially meat. Poorer quality proteins, such as those in peas, beans, cereals, and gelatin, if used in enough variety, can provide all the materials to build cells. Certain vitamins and minerals found in fresh fruits and vegetables are necessary to keep muscles healthy and in tone.

Working muscles need a constant supply of food that furnishes fuel for energy. Starchy and sweet foods, called *carbohydrates,* are the chief foods used for quick energy. These are some common carbohydrate foods: cereal grains, such as wheat, rye, corn, and oats; foods made from cereal grains, such as flour, bread, cake, pastry, and macaroni; some vegetables and fruits, such as potatoes and bananas; and sweets, such as candy, jam, sirup, and honey. *Fats,* such as butter, oleomargarine, cream, chocolate, and fat meat, are also used as fuel. The amount of fuel furnished by food is measured in *calories.* By careful experiments scientists have figured out the amounts of fuel needed by the body for various activities. An average girl between thirteen and fifteen needs about 2600 calories a day. An average boy between thirteen and fifteen requires about 3200 calories a day. The amounts vary with size and amount of activity. Why?

The amount of a food does not tell you how many calories it has. Some foods contain much water and other substances that are not used by the body for fuel. Fats furnish almost twice as much fuel as other kinds of foods do. If you are interested in calories you can look up charts in other books. The following list will give you an idea of the fuel value of some

Fruit Dispatch Company

Sweet or starchy foods, called carbohydrates, and fats furnish fuel for the body. Can you name ten carbohydrate foods?

121

foods. *Each of these items of food furnishes 100 calories:*

1 medium hamburger
1 large potato
2 large heads of lettuce
¾ cup of peas
1¼ cups of cornflakes
3 tablespoons of Grapenuts
Small glass (⅝ cup) milk
1 tablespoon of butter or margarine
1 tablespoon of mayonnaise
½ cup of cocoa
Thick slice of bread
2½ heaping tablespoons of ice cream
2 tablespoons of sugar
1 large piece of fudge

Harold M. Lambert

It takes practice to become graceful and well co-ordinated. What skills are you practicing daily?

The more active you are, the more food for fuel your muscles need. Active boys and girls need plenty of carbohydrates. However, sugars and starches are very incomplete foods, totally lacking other things your body needs for building, repair, and regulation. Excess carbohydrates are stored as fat. They cannot help you grow. Especially during your teens, when you are growing rapidly, you need to be careful to eat the proper food. Do not allow your appetite for sweets, or the food habits of your gang, to crowd out other foods you need. Your diet should contain plenty of meat, milk, fruits, and vegetables, as well as sweets and starches, if you want your body to grow and develop normally.

Why do muscles need exercise? Muscles need exercise to develop. Exercise increases circulation. It helps carry blood to the muscles to furnish them with food for growth and energy and to carry away wastes so they can recover from fatigue. It causes muscles to become larger and stronger. Muscles that are used develop strength and endurance.

To develop strength, muscles must be given tasks of increasing difficulty. Muscles become very little stronger if they are not used in activities difficult enough to require some effort.

To develop endurance, muscles must be exercised for longer and longer periods. You must exercise long enough to become somewhat tired.

Exercise improves the ability of muscles and nerves to work as a team. Skaters, football players, and musicians must all practice to keep muscles and nerves working right. Practice helps even in simple matters like moving the tongue and jaws in speaking,

Denver Public Schools

Muscles used for fine movements need practice too. What are you doing to improve your finger skill and co-ordination?

lifting a spoon to the mouth, driving a nail, and writing.

To develop skill you must use the same muscles over and over in the same activity. The muscles must be trained to respond smoothly and quickly to stimuli from the nerves.

Muscular exercise stimulates all body functions. During exercise, heart action and circulation throughout the body are increased. This results in a general speeding up in the supply of blood to all the organs. Reserve heart strength is built up. Digested food and oxygen are brought to the cells. Fewer waste products are found in the blood because it is traveling rapidly and throwing off wastes.

Reasonable exercise improves digestion and helps to overcome constipation, headaches, and poor complexion. It clears the mind, steadies the nerves, and leads to better co-ordination of all bodily activities. You will feel and look better if you have at least two hours of vigorous outdoor exercise every day. Planning can help you get your exercise. Walking or riding a bicycle instead of riding in a car or bus; working in the yard; or playing with younger brothers and sisters —these are only a few ways in which you can combine exercise and routine duties to increase your own health and fun.

How does a warm-up help muscles? Muscles work best at normal body temperature, which is about 98.6° Fahrenheit. When they are cooler they do not respond as quickly or smoothly. They are like an engine that does not respond as well when it is cold. Muscles can be warmed by light exercise. Muscle contractions, like other burning, produce heat as well as energy for movement. Massage, direct sunlight, or a warm covering are helpful. Warm-up exercises serve the addi-

123

Denver Public Schools

How do athletes avoid injuries from falls? How do they avoid muscle strains and injuries?

tional purpose of speeding up breathing and circulatory mechanisms to correspond with muscle speed. It is dangerous and fatiguing to attempt strenuous exercise too suddenly.

Muscles warmed by exercise need to cool slowly. Experienced athletes have learned to keep their bodies covered after exercising so they do not cool off too rapidly.

Why do muscles need rest? Muscles need rest to give the cells a chance for growing, to store up energy, and to get rid of wastes that cause fatigue. All body movements are brought about by muscles, and some muscles in your body are working all the time. Involuntary muscles, which do not re-

spond to your conscious direction, perform all the movements essential to life. They work all the time, moving blood through your veins, moving food through the digestive system, bringing air into the body, and so on. Some voluntary muscles (those which respond to your will) work continuously for hours, or even all day. Which muscles work when you are sitting and standing? Individual muscle fibers have short intervals of rest, but all the muscles need longer periods of relaxation that are provided only when you sleep and all body processes slow down. Young people especially use great quantities of energy and need 9½ or 10 hours of sleep daily.

If you are getting enough sleep you should feel refreshed and full of energy in the morning. If you are getting too little sleep you are not giving your body a fair chance to grow and to restore the energy used during the day. Very active boys and girls need even more sleep than others. There is nothing childish about getting to bed early enough to get sufficient sleep. It is a sign of growing up mentally and emotionally to be realistic and independent enough to find what you need to be at your best and to take the responsibility of doing something about it. It is really childish to close your eyes to facts and "do as you please" just to show your independence. Sometimes in trying to show how independent you are, you only prove that you are not yet ready for independence and the responsibility that goes with it.

How do muscles develop? A newborn baby is the most helpless of all creatures. His muscles are small and weak, and he is unable to control them. But with proper food and exercise he develops in size and strength. His first movements are almost uncontrolled wavings of arms and legs. Gradually he learns to hold up his head, to support his body in a sitting position, to creep on hands and knees, to grasp objects with his hands, and to walk. Notice how much energy and extra body motion a baby puts into taking a step or reaching for a ball.

Growth in muscle size makes him ready to learn a skill. Practice strengthens and co-ordinates muscles to make him skillful. Notice how active children are. They are always climbing, throwing, jumping, hopping, skipping, and balancing. By these activities they exercise their muscles. Some children do not acquire as much skill as others. If parents keep children from getting enough practice by waiting on them too much, because they are afraid to let them take the falls and bumps that come with learning, children may fail to develop emotionally and socially as well as physically. They do not develop the ability to learn, from failure, the independence and self-confidence that spring from successfully mastering tasks suitable for one. They lack the feeling of being a worthy, skillful, and competent member of a group.

Teenagers sometimes forget that practice is necessary to develop muscular, mental, or emotional skills. Some of them act as if certain lucky individuals are born with, or are suddenly endowed with, the ability to play basketball, to dance, to make a speech, to recite in class, to attract and keep friends, to control their tempers, and to assume independence and responsibility. They withdraw from activities because they are afraid others may laugh at their awkwardness. So they fall farther and farther behind in developing skills appropriate for their age. If one has fallen behind, it takes a great deal of courage and determination to look honestly at one's failures, to stop making excuses, and to start developing the necessary skills. But it can be done. Other chapters in this book have some suggestions that may help.

During childhood, boys and girls show constant improvement in strength and skill. Early in adolescence muscles grow more rapidly in size than in strength. They need plenty of rest and exercise to develop strength and skill. Muscles depend upon many other body systems to keep them strong and healthy. Conse-

American Red Cross

Most home accidents are the result of falls. How can you prevent falls in your home?

quently, anything that helps to keep you healthy in general helps to make your muscles strong and efficient. The heart and lungs and the organs in the digestive system develop in strength more slowly. They need plenty of rest and care to be able to meet the demands of a body increasing so rapidly in size. Teenage boys and girls are often misled by their larger size to overdo—to work and play too long and too hard. Adults also often expect too much of adolescent boys and girls because they are large. If you are demanding too much of your body and not supplying it with the proper kind or amount of food, exercise, and rest, it may not be able to do its work well. You may suffer from some of these ills: chronic fatigue, indigestion, poor appetite, constipation, or skin troubles. You may become irritable, un-able to concentrate, subject to emotional or nervous outbursts, or easily discouraged. Worst of all, the body's resistance to disease is lowered.

Muscles continue in adult years to develop in strength, skill, and endurance. But many people do not continue developing. About the time their bodies stop growing, they stop participating in outdoor exercise. They become spectators. Girls especially often neglect exercise for new interests as they grow up. Consequently, they fail to develop strong, attractive, and graceful bodies. They miss much of the companionship, fun, and sense of joy and well-being that accompanies outdoor exercise. Boys and girls who look ahead will learn some recreations and outdoor exercises that they can enjoy when they are fully grown.

Reviewing the chapter

Test yourself

Copy these statements on a piece of paper. Write a plus sign (+) before each good habit. Write a minus sign (−) before each bad habit. Do NOT WRITE IN THIS BOOK.

1. Drink a quart of milk a day.
2. Come into the school when you arrive early on pleasant days.
3. Carry heavy loads of books habitually with the same arm.
4. Take sun baths in summer and cod-liver oil in winter.
5. Drink coffee for breakfast.
6. Stand and walk with hands in pockets.
7. Stand with weight on one leg.
8. Sit only in seats which support the lower part of the back.
9. Relax several times a day.
10. Exercise outdoors in the sunshine.
11. Practice new activities slowly at first.
12. Put on a sweater when you are warm from strenuous exercise.
13. Depend upon others to get you up in the morning.
14. Compete with larger and stronger boys and girls.
15. Rest just before strenuous activity.
16. Eat milk, fruits, or vegetables between meals.
17. Sleep 9 or 10 hours a day.

Other activities

1. The safety committee can report on causes and methods of preventing injuries to bones and muscles. How do falls and accidents occur at school, at home,

and on playgrounds? Can you help to make your school and home safer?

2. Scouts or a group interested in first aid may demonstrate emergency methods of taking care of injured bones and muscles.

3. Someone interested in medicine, nursing, coaching, or other professions that require a knowledge of anatomy may like to report on the Latin names of bones. Are there any advantages to retaining the Latin names for bones?

4. A committee may like to test dexterity on hand and finger skills.

5. You may be interested in finding out if your regular diet furnishes you with the material needed to build healthy bones and muscles. A diet committee can find out how much protein and minerals are required by growing boys and girls and what foods supply the necessary materials.

6. Class surveys to check on daily habits can provide interesting activities for several committees. They can work out check lists of good habits of eating, resting, and exercising and see what habits need to be improved. Perhaps some group activity will help individuals improve their habits. A milk-for-lunch club or some activities that get everyone out in the sunshine before or after school or at noon might help.

Reading to help you grow up

If you are interested in more technical names for bones and muscles, you will enjoy these books:

Health and Human Welfare by Burkhard and others.

Working Together for Health, by Burkhard and others, has an interesting section on sports, athletics, and games.

Your Health and Safety, by Clemenson and LaPorte, has interesting discussions of how to make various sports safe.

A Sound Body, by Charters and others, has chapters on bones and muscles, and treating injuries to bones and muscles.

Discussions and charts for measuring calories are found in the following titles:

Building Good Health by Andress and others.

Working Together for Health by Burkhard and others.

Builders for Good Health by Burkhard and others.

Films to help you understand

Body Framework. Encyclopedia Britannica Films.

Muscles. Encyclopedia Britannica Films. Animated drawings help to illustrate structure. Discusses exercise and posture.

How to Avoid Muscle Strains. Bray.

Improving Your Posture. Coronet. Helps to overcome individual posture faults.

Posture and Exercise. Encyclopedia Britannica Films. How the muscles act.

Healthy blood is necessary for the well-being of every cell in the body. How does it help you to be vigorous and attractive?

Good athletes wear clothing and equipment that protect them from injury. Why do they wear warm-up suits after vigorous exercise?

Picture Preview:

Chapter 8

Doctors often tell the rate of heart beat by timing the pulse in the wrist. Can you feel your own pulse? Can you feel it other places besides your wrist? Why is this?

What can you see if you examine a drop of blood under the microscope? What useful information can a doctor obtain from a microscopic examination of blood?

How is the heart affected by exercises? Is the same kind of exercise good for everyone? How do you choose your own activities?

Chapter 8

HOW CAN YOU UNDERSTAND YOUR HEART AND BLOOD?

We no longer believe that love and courage originate in the heart. We know that spirit and feelings belong to a person as a whole. However, the blood and heart still are of great importance. A great deal of research is being carried on to find out how they function in keeping the body healthy, and why they become unable to function.

The heart pumps blood through a continuous network of tubes or blood vessels to every cell in the body. Cells receive from the blood everything they need to grow and maintain life. They return to the blood all their waste products. By studying the blood, physicians can receive information about the condition of all body cells. They can tell if some cells or organs are not doing their work well. They can detect the presence of many diseases.

A healthy blood supply is the body's best defense against disease. The blood contains cells that fight disease. It manufactures chemicals to fight certain diseases. In recent years blood has been increasingly used in treatment of the sick and injured. Transfusions of whole blood, or of certain parts of the blood, may be given.

Even while scientists are learning more about the blood and heart, the death toll mounts from diseases of the circulatory system. Heart disease is now the leading cause of death. Other diseases of the circulatory system including the blood vessels and kidneys are among the chief causes of death today.

Although they do not know everything about the heart and blood, doctors can offer many suggestions that will help you to care for your circulatory system. If you understand how your circulatory system works, you can establish habits that help it to work efficiently.

Looking ahead

1. Have some class members or a panel tell what they already know about the heart and blood. Why are the heart and blood important? How do they work? How may they be injured? How can you care for injuries? What are blood types? What are transfusions?

2. Listen carefully. Jot down for discussion anything that you disagree with and questions you would like to have answered by the speakers.

3. Locate the pulse in your wrist. You can locate it most easily by holding the tips of your fingers along the inside edge of your wrist. Using a watch with a second hand, count the pulse for a half minute before and then after exercise. Notice how soon after exercise the heartbeat becomes normal. Put the various pulse rates on the board to see how much variation there is. What is the average normal pulse rate?

4. Can you locate veins in various parts of your body—at the temple and inside the elbow, for example? Why do they appear blue? Hold your arm down and open and close your hand vigorously several times. What happens to the veins in your hand and arm?

5. How many words and expressions can you think of that use the heart as a symbol of love or courage or feeling?

Committee Planning

1. Library, movie, and correspondence committees can have ready some of the materials suggested at the end of the chapter.

2. A biology committee may be able to dissect an animal heart for the class. They can get a beef or pig heart from the butcher shop. If they use a sharp knife and work carefully they can cut the heart open lengthwise to expose the chambers. Where are the chest walls thickest? Can you find arteries, veins, valves, muscle, and fat tissue?

3. The field-trip committee may be able to arrange a trip to a blood bank in your community.

4. The speaker's committee may invite a doctor to talk to the class about the heart and blood. Perhaps he will demonstrate some of the instruments and techniques for listening to heart sounds, estimating or counting red blood cells, and measuring heartbeat and blood pressure.

5. The safety committee can demonstrate methods of caring for bleeding wounds, fainting, and shock.

Reading

This chapter is rather long. Can you concentrate and keep yourself working until you finish a difficult job? Set definite reasonable goals for yourself.

How can you help your heart?

Your heart is a remarkable organ that works and adjusts to changing conditions during every minute of your life. You can help it work long and well. You can strengthen it, protect it from disease and injury, and make its work easier.

What is the heart like? The heart is a powerful hollow muscle shaped somewhat like a pear and about the size of your fist. It is located near the middle of the chest cavity behind the breastbone. The small end points downward and toward the left. We usually think the heart is on the left side of the chest because we can feel its beat most strongly there.

A partition completely separates the heart into two chambers, right and left. The right side pumps blood only to the lungs; the left side pumps blood to the rest of the body.

Each of the two separate chambers is divided into two smaller chambers connected by a door, called a *valve*. Each upper chamber, called an *auricle*, receives blood from the veins. Each lower chamber, called a *ventri-*

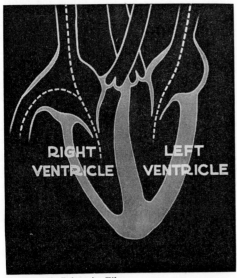

Encyclopedia Britannica Films

The heart is a double pump. Blood returning from the body enters the right side of the heart and is pumped to the lungs. Blood returning from the lungs enters the left side and is pumped to the rest of the body. Which side of the heart is larger and has thicker walls? Why? Can you locate the valves? Why are they necessary?

cle, pumps the blood out into the arteries.

How does the heart work? It may help you to understand how the heart works if you think of it as two pumps set side by side. The left pump receives blood from the lungs and sends it to the body. Because it has more work to do, the left side of the heart is larger.

When the heart beats, it contracts, driving blood out into the arteries. It then relaxes, permitting blood from the veins to flow into the heart. Blood flows from the heart to the farthest parts of the body and back in one-third to one-half minute. To illustrate how the heart works, let a little water run into a small bag or balloon held in your relaxed, loose fist. Now squeeze your hand quickly into a tight fist. Just as the contraction of your hand forced the water out of the bag or balloon, the contraction of the ventricles in the heart forces blood out of the heart into the arteries. The pulse is the rhythmic swelling of an artery resulting from the heart's action.

In the interval between contractions, the valves between the auricles and ventricles stay open as the heart relaxes and fills with blood. This is a rest period. When the ventricles contract, the valves close, and each ventricle forces out about one-third cup (2½ ounces) of blood into its artery. This blood pushes ahead in waves to keep the whole stream moving forward. The valves keep the blood from flowing backward.

Valves that do not close tightly allow some of the blood to seep backward and cause a heart leakage at the valves. The heart has to work harder to repump the blood, and the added exercise may gradually cause the heart to become enlarged. The enlargement may compensate for the leaky valve and enable an individual to live normally if he does not subject his heart to sudden or severe strain. A trained physician can tell from heart sounds how the valves of the heart are working. An X ray or fluoroscope will reveal the size and shape of the heart. Anyone who plans to participate in strenuous work or play should make sure that his heart is normal.

How fast does your heart beat? The rate of heartbeat varies so greatly with individuals there is no single normal rate. Among adults, the rate may be normally as low as 50 or as high as 90. The rate varies with age. On the average, it is about 140 at birth, gradually slowing down in youth to about 85, and becoming rather stable in adult life around 72. It is slightly slower for men than for women.

The rate of heartbeat varies greatly with the position of the body and the amount of activity going on. When you are lying down, your heart does not have to pump against gravity; so it can slow down. When you are sitting it beats about four times a minute faster than when you are lying down. When you are standing it beats about ten times a minute faster than when you are lying down. When you are asleep all your body activities are slowed down, so your heart does not have to work so hard. Vigorous exercise makes your heart beat so hard and rapidly you can feel it all over your body. Feelings of fear, anger, or excitement also speed up the heart rate.

Each heartbeat is started by nerves in the heart itself. Two other sets of nerves can change the rate at which the heart beats. One set connected to the base of the brain slows the heart. Another set of nerves (accelerators) can speed up the heart rate as needed in emergencies. Nerve impulses caused by excitement, anger, and fear can indirectly cause the accelerator nerves to increase the rate of heartbeat. Have you ever felt your heart speed up when you were excited or afraid?

What does the heart need to function and develop at its best? Everytime the heart beats it pumps about 5 ounces of blood into the arteries. If the heart averages 72 beats a minute, how much blood does it pump in a day? Actual measurements show that the heart of an average man lying at rest for 24 hours does about the same amount of work that his leg muscles would do in climbing a mountain 1300 feet high. More than any other muscle in your body, your hard-working heart must have rest, exercise, and a rich supply of food and oxygen.

Many people believe that the heart never rests, but it does. It rests after each contraction, while it is relaxed and filling with blood from the veins. When the heartbeat slows, the rest periods between contractions are longer and the heart muscle has an opportunity to recover and develop. During sleep, the heart rests about 28 seconds of each minute.

Are you likely to injure your heart? The human heart is amazingly strong. Doctors believe that even strenuous activity will not injure a completely normal and healthy heart, but you cannot be sure your heart is without defect unless you have a careful medical examination. You should insist on such an examination before taking part in any strenuous or competitive sports. If your heart is normal do not worry about it. If it has a weakness you are lucky to find out about it. Proper care may overcome the weakness or at least enable you to live a happy normal life. People with heart defects may not be able to play as long or as hard as people with normal hearts, but by forming a few good habits, they often can live just as long and as happily. They usually must have extra hours of rest and sleep, must protect themselves from colds and other infectious diseases, and must avoid undue excitement or sudden and violent exertion.

The valves and muscle of the heart may be weakened, usually only temporarily, by such diseases as tonsillitis, severe colds, diphtheria, and scarlet fever. During the time you are ill with any high temperature, your heart will beat faster; therefore you should remain quiet even up to 24 hours after the fever has been lowered. Following any illness, strenuous exercise should be avoided for a time and periods of rest and sleep should be extended.

Rheumatic fever is a disease that often results in permanent damage to the valves of the heart. Recovery depends on complete rest in bed, often for several months. Rheumatic fever is a leading cause of death among school-age children. It follows "strep" infections. So early and adequate treatment of all "strep" infections by means of antibiotic or sulfa drugs prevents rheumatic fever. Children who have had rheumatic fever should continue medical treatment until they are 18 years old. In addition to adequate diet and rest, they should have daily dosages of a sulfa drug or penicillin.

How can you protect and strengthen your heart? Anything that is good for your health in general—balanced diet, rest, and exercise—helps your heart work and develop at its best.

You can keep your heart toned up and able to meet emergencies by regular exercise which is vigorous enough to increase the rate of heartbeat, but which is not too strenuous. Athletes have found that the best way to develop strength and endurance is by building up gradually to a peak of activity. They also give their heart a chance to speed up gradually by warm-up activities. You cannot train your heart by giving it sudden hard tasks to do. A sensible balance between exercise and rest is essential for developing a strong heart.

In the early teens the skeleton and muscles increase in size faster than the heart increases in power. Many adolescent boys and girls become unusually tired even from light activity. Demands on the heart are great, and it needs plenty of rest to grow and develop. Nine to ten hours of sleep are usually needed and the best athletes often get more.

Physical strength and endurance require the co-operation of a heart that has all the reserve power possible. Boys and girls who want strong, skillful bodies avoid unnecessary strains on their hearts. Tobacco temporarily increases the heartbeat as much as 10 beats a minute. Alcohol indirectly speeds up the heart by deadening the nerves that slow it down. Some patent medicines such as sleeping powders, "pep" pills, and "pain killers" contain drugs which affect the heart. Excite-

134

ment, fear, and anger also make the heart beat faster for no useful purpose. If you are trying to grow and develop normally and to keep your body in the best possible condition, you will avoid unnecessary strains on your heart. You will avoid tobacco, alcohol, patent medicines, and prolonged periods of emotional upset. Follow the examples of skillful athletes, dancers, and models: get plenty of vigorous outdoor exercise daily; stop exercising when you begin to get tired or feel breathless; alternate periods of activity and rest; get in condition by gradually increasing the amount and difficulty of your exercise; and get plenty of sleep.

Denver Public Schools

Why should you avoid chilling or strenuous exercise after a heavy meal? Why are the swimmers warmer than the boys standing around? Is swimming a sport that may cause unnecessary strain on the heart?

How does your blood work?

Your heart pumps blood to every cell in your body. Why is it so important that every cell is supplied with blood? What does your blood do for you?

What is your blood like? If you look at a drop of blood under a microscope, you will see a colorless liquid in which are floating hundreds of circular discs and many odd-shaped specks. The circular discs are the red corpuscles, which give the blood its color; the odd-shaped specks are white corpuscles and blood platelets; the colorless liquid is called plasma.

Red corpuscles are round and thin and slightly dented in the center, like a candy mint. They are so small you could put about 50,000 on the head of a pin, but the ordinary person has so many of them that if they could be spread out flat they would cover almost an acre.

The most important part of the red corpuscle is the *hemoglobin*, a spongy red material composed mostly of iron. When exposed to air, hemoglobin absorbs oxygen. The red corpuscles can take a load of oxygen to the body cells and exchange it there for carbon dioxide. They carry the carbon dioxide back to the lungs to be released from the body in the exhaled breath. Hemoglobin carrying oxygen is bright red. When carrying carbon dioxide, hemoglobin is dark, bluish red. The veins visible through the skin look blue because the "red" corpuscles are carrying carbon dioxide. The blood vessels which carry oxygen are deeper below the surface. Why is this construction of advantage to your body?

The *white corpuscles* are living cells, of irregular shape, about one-third larger than the red corpuscles. They are defenders against infection,

135

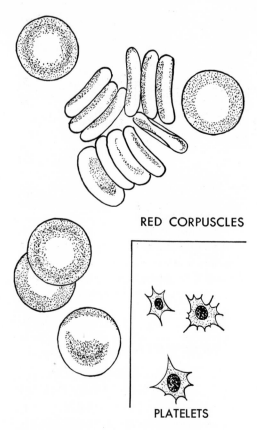

RED CORPUSCLES

PLATELETS

Red corpuscles are the most numerous of the blood cells. What gives them their bright red color? Platelets are smaller. What work is done by the red blood cells and by the platelets?

hormones, waste materials, disease-resisting substances called antibodies, and minerals necessary for growth and functioning of all the kinds of cells.

Are any foods good for the blood? Red blood corpuscles lead such active lives that they wear out in from 20 to 60 days. Millions of them wear out daily and must be removed from circulation and replaced by new ones. New red corpuscles are constantly being manufactured in the red marrow, which is found in the ends of the long bones. The iron which is the principal part of the red corpuscles is obtained partly from the worn-out corpuscles and partly from food. A person whose daily diet is deficient or lacking in iron will not be able to manufacture enough healthy red corpuscles. His blood will not be able to carry enough oxygen, and his body cells will become tired and weak. Teenagers need extra amounts of iron in their diet, not only to replace corpuscles worn out by strenuous activity, but also to manufacture larger supplies for their rapidly growing bodies.

Many people suffer from lack of pep, pale complexion and lips, and a reputation for laziness just because they need more iron. Most foods like fruits, vegetables, and meats contain some iron. If you eat a wide variety of such foods, you will probably have enough iron. Active, growing boys and girls can make certain they have a good supply of rich red blood by eating foods unusually rich in iron, such as liver; sea food; meat; eggs; poultry; molasses; green, leafy vegetables, like broccoli and salad greens; whole-grain bread and cereals; dried beans and peas; and dried fruits like

fighting germs by surrounding and destroying them. The usual number of white corpuscles is about one to every six or seven hundred corpuscles. They increase in number when the body is fighting a severe infection.

The *flat platelets* in the blood help the blood congeal or clot when a blood vessel is broken.

The *plasma* in which corpuscles and platelets float is about 90 per cent water and contains more than a hundred dissolved substances, such as foods,

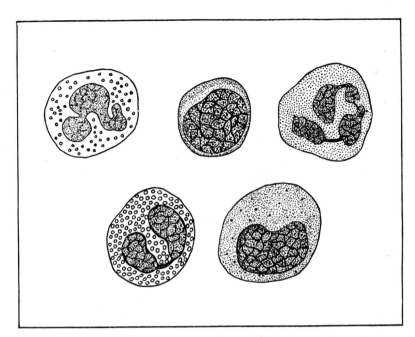

White corpuscles are larger than red ones, but are fewer in number. They can change their shape, move through the spaces between cells of the thin-walled blood vessels, and penetrate to all parts of the body. Some of them can devour germs that enter the body. Others have functions not well understood. Why may a high white count indicate the presence of infection?

raisins, prunes, apricots, figs, and dates.

What is anemia? A person who has too few red corpuscles or corpuscles with too little hemoglobin in them is suffering from a disease called anemia. He will probably be pale and thin and will tire easily because not enough oxygen is being carried to his tissues. Oxygen is needed to combine with food to form new cells, to enable cells to grow, or to produce energy. A physician or trained laboratory worker can tell if your corpuscles are too few or are poorly formed. You may be interested in having a doctor explain how he counts red corpuscles or finds the amount of hemoglobin in your blood.

The most common cause of anemia is a poor diet. However, in some people the red marrow produces imperfect corpuscles, causing a serious, prolonged kind of anemia called *pernicious anemia*. Pernicious anemia was a very serious, often-fatal disease until 1925 when scientists discovered a substance in the liver that helps the red marrow produce healthy red corpuscles. Now pernicious anemia can be treated by the use of animal liver as a food or by injections of liver extract.

What are blood vessels like? Blood flows through the body in a continuous system of tubes, or blood vessels. The blood vessels vary in size and construction from the largest artery, which is ½ to 1 inch in diameter, to

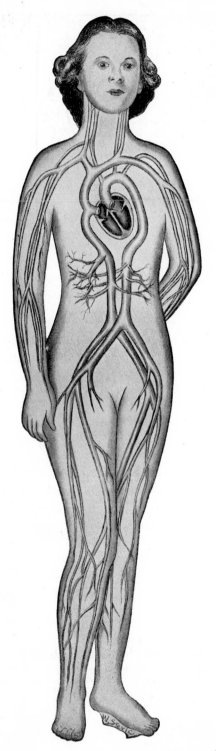

capillaries, which can be seen only with the aid of a microscope. Arteries, which carry the blood away from the heart under great pressure, have thick elastic walls. Veins, carrying blood back to the heart under less pressure, have thinner walls. The large veins contain valves to keep the blood from flowing backward. Capillaries, which join arteries and veins, have walls only the thickness of a single cell. They are so thin that materials can pass back and forth through them between body cells and the blood stream. Some veins may be seen near the surface of the body. Most arteries are deep in the body; the tiny capillaries penetrate every cell, deep and surface.

The network of arteries is often compared to a tree. The trunk is the large artery, called the *aorta*, which opens out of the left ventricle. Main branch arteries go to the head, arms, legs, and abdomen. Each of these branches divides into smaller and smaller arteries that reach every part of the body. The walls of the tubes become thinner and thinner as the arteries become smaller in diameter. Finally the tiniest arteries open into still finer blood vessels, the capillaries.

Capillaries average about $\frac{1}{25}$ of an inch in length and are so small in diameter that in many of them, blood corpuscles must pass thru in single file. They form a network much finer than a spider web, reaching every liv-

The heart and blood vessels form a continuous transportation system carrying supplies to every cell in the body and carrying wastes away. Blood is pumped by the heart into arteries, through the networks of capillaries, and returns to the heart through veins.

ing cell in the body. You cannot prick any part of your skin with a fine needle without drawing blood. It is estimated that there are so many capillaries in your body that, if they were joined end to end, they would form a tube that would reach around the earth two and one-half times.

Capillaries open into the tiniest branch veins which in turn open into even larger branch veins which finally open into two large veins that lead into the right auricle. This is the drainage system like another tree carrying blood back to the heart.

How do materials get in and out of the blood stream? If the blood simply circulated around through the body in a closed system of tubes, it would accomplish no useful purpose. In order to do its work, blood must be able to take on cargoes of food and oxygen and any other materials needed by the tissues; to release these supplies to the individual cells; and to take on in exchange wastes produced by the activities and wearing out of the cells. Then the blood must have some way to get rid of the wastes to purify itself.

The exchange of materials between cells and the blood stream takes place in the capillaries. Through the thin capillary walls oxygen and small quantities of plasma seep into the spaces between the cells; so all the cells are constantly surrounded by a liquid called lymph. A good example of lymph is the watery liquid which collects between layers of skin to form a blister. Lymph is very much like blood except it has no red corpuscles. Red corpuscles do not pass through the capillary walls, although white ones do.

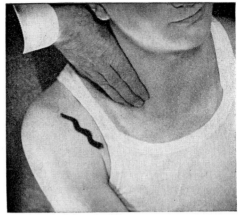

Encyclopedia Britannica Films

Severe bleeding from an artery is extremely dangerous. Often it may be checked by pressing with the fingers where the artery lies close to a bone. These places are in front of the ear, along the jawbone, on the side of the windpipe, behind the collarbone, inside the arm, and in the groin. Why must you press between the wound and the heart?

Food and oxygen from the lymph seep through the thin cell walls into the cells. Wastes enter the lymph from the cells. Part of the lymph seeps back into the capillaries. The rest flows into lymphatic capillaries and flows slowly back toward the heart through lymphatic vessels, which empty into veins below the neck. Scattered along the course of the lymph vessels are small oval-shaped structures called lymph nodes. They act as filters removing harmful bacteria or other impurities from the lymph. Sometimes they become inflamed if the white corpuscles cannot keep up with their work of digesting bacteria. There are many nodes in the neck and under the jaw. Larger groups appear in the armpits and groins. In some infections nodes may become swollen and painful.

139

From the fine network of capillaries, blood (now bluish-red because it has lost oxygen and added carbon dioxide) flows into the tiniest veins, into larger and larger branch veins, and finally into the right auricle of the heart. From the right auricle the blood flows to the right ventricle and at the next beat is forced into the pulmonary (lung) artery. In the capillaries in the lungs it gets rid of carbon dioxide and takes on a fresh supply of oxygen.

The fresh, bright-red blood returns to the left side of the heart to start a new journey through the body. This is the most efficient pumping system and food-supply line in the world.

How does the body maintain good circulation?

Every cell in your body must be continuously supplied with fresh red blood. If anything interferes with the circulation to any organ, the cells there will become less efficient, and in extreme cases will die. Pains and general ill health can result from poor circulation in the lungs, stomach, liver, intestines, and other parts of the body.

How is circulation regulated? Good circulation means that blood flows rapidly enough to nourish the cells in all parts, speeds up when the body is more active, and is suitably distributed according to the needs of the various parts. The needs of the various organs vary from time to time, and the blood supply must be changed to meet changing demands. When might the muscles need more blood? When might the digestive organs need more blood? The body has many devices for insuring good circulation automatically; it has signals that warn an individual that his circulation needs some help. Do you know some of the signals that tell you circulation is poor in some part of your body?

Your body regulates the blood supply to any organ by changing the size of the arteries and capillaries through which blood flows to the organ. Nerve impulses from the brain and spinal cord stimulate the involuntary muscles in the walls of the small arteries to contract. The contraction makes the arteries smaller and cuts down the amount of blood flowing through them. How can these nerves make you turn pale? Another set of nerves relaxes the muscles, enlarging (dilating) the blood vessels and permitting more blood to enter them. How can these nerves make you blush?

In general, the nerves dilate blood vessels in organs that are being used and contract vessels in inactive organs. For example, after a heavy meal, arteries to the digestive system dilate so that more blood flows to those organs; other arteries constrict, so you feel sleepy and lazy. But during exercise, more blood flows to the muscles and less blood flows to the digestive system. Why should you avoid strenuous exercise for an hour or two after a heavy meal? During periods of inactivity, blood often collects in the large vessels in the abdomen. If you rise suddenly after lying down, momentary lack of blood supply to the brain may make you feel faint or dizzy.

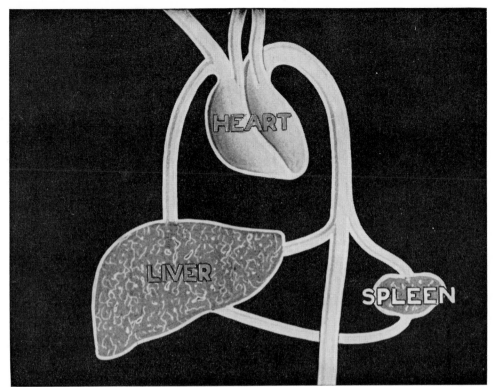

The spleen and liver serve as storage place for blood. Usually they contain about one-fourth of the blood in the body. It is believed they also destroy worn-out red corpuscles. What are some other jobs of the liver?

How can blood flow "uphill"? With each beat your heart forces some blood into the aorta in a powerful spurt. This blood, moving at a rate of about 1 foot per second, pushes on all the blood ahead, to keep the whole stream moving. But as the arteries branch and become smaller and more numerous, the force of the flow gradually becomes less.

The force with which blood pushes against the walls of the blood vessel is called *blood pressure*. It may be measured by an instrument which increases air pressure in a sack around the arm, until it counterbalances the blood pressure, and stops the flow in a large artery. You may like to have a physician demonstrate a blood pressure instrument and explain what blood pressure indicates about the condition of the circulatory system. Blood pressure in the arteries should be great enough to drive blood to all parts of the body.

By the time the blood reaches the billions of capillaries, it is traveling at only a fraction of its original speed and pressure. On the return trip blood in the veins has little pressure. It flows smoothly and more slowly than in the arteries. It needs some extra help to return to the heart, especially where it must flow "uphill," as in parts of the

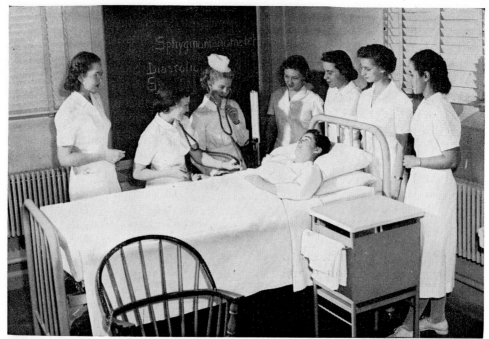

Student nurses practice measuring blood pressure.

body below the level of the heart. So veins are constructed with valves, and placed among muscles. Valves prevent backflow and keep blood flowing toward the heart. When muscles contract, they change shape and squeeze the veins which are located among them, pushing the blood along. Deep breathing helps circulation by alternately pressing and releasing large veins in the chest and abdomen.

These veins fill from below by the vacuum principle used in filling a fountain pen.

Lymph returning through its own system of lymphatic vessels also moves slowly. It is not propelled by the heart. Muscle action squeezes it past valves that keep it moving toward the places it re-enters the blood stream. Without muscle action lymph may collect in ankles and feet and cause them to swell. Exercise helps to keep it moving along.

What causes fainting? Anytime the blood supply to your brain is inadequate, a feeling of faintness, dizziness,

These portions of veins show how the valves operate. How does the action of muscles and valves keep blood flowing back to the heart?

or even unconsciousness may result. Standing still for long periods, or sudden change of direction such as occurs when an airplane spins or dives, may cause blood to leave the brain and collect in large veins in the abdomen. At such times circulation can usually be promptly restored by lowering the head. An airplane pilot wards off "blackout" by holding his abdominal muscles firm or by wearing a wide, firm belt around his waist and abdomen. What is the explanation for this?

If you have to care for someone who feels faint, keep him lying down. Why? See that he has plenty of air. Loosen any tight clothing. Smelling salts or aromatic spirits of ammonia or a sprinkle of cold water on the face may stimulate deep breathing. Steady pressure on the abdomen will help prevent blood from collecting there. If unconsciousness lasts more than a few minutes, call a physician at once. Fainting and dizziness may be due to other causes than poor circulation. Any marked or repeated attacks should be investigated by a physician.

Can you improve your circulation? Poor circulation may cause feelings of pain, cold, numbness, loss of efficiency, and, in extreme cases, degeneration or gangrene (death of tissue in certain areas). It can be the cause of pale complexion and colorless lips, fainting, dizziness, varicose veins, and general ill health. Fortunately, many conditions that interfere with good circulation can be easily avoided.

It is hard for blood to force its way through pinched blood vessels. Tight collars, garters, armbands, and belts are particularly harmful, and tight shoes may impair circulation in the feet. Any nonelastic clothing should be adjustable and no tighter than necessary. Veins in the legs may be enlarged or injured by constant pressure on the back part of the leg and knee from chairs or from crossing the legs at the knees. Any cramped or slumped position may pinch blood vessels.

You can help your digestive organs obtain blood to aid in digestion by avoiding strenuous exercise after a heavy meal.

Some people have enlarged and painful varicose veins in their legs as a result of overworking the veins in their legs by long periods of standing. You can help circulation in your veins in several ways. Regular exercise keeps muscles and blood vessels in tone. When you stand for long periods, move about a little so the muscle action can help force blood out of the veins. Periods of rest with your feet elevated are often helpful.

Circulation may be impaired in older people when arteries lose their elasticity (power to stretch) and become partially blocked by deposits of calcium. The actual causes for "hardening of the arteries" are not known. However, excesses of various kinds— overeating, overworking (physically or mentally), uncontrolled emotional outbursts, excessive use of alcohol or tobacco, as well as some infections and poisons—seem to contribute to the hardening. The best way to protect your circulatory system, as you grow older, is to be moderate in eating, working, and playing. Try to do your best from day to day without undue exhaustion, excitement, or worry. Keep a sensible balance between exercise and rest.

Sometimes it is necessary to increase circulation in certain parts of

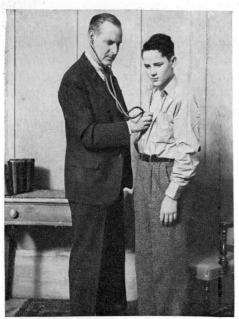

H. Armstrong Roberts

Have you had a physical examination recently? Why are examinations particularly important for athletes and young persons?

the body. In general, you can increase circulation by exercise, massage, and heat.

Any exercise or movement helps circulation. Heat allows more blood to flow to the heated part. Cold contracts the vessels and reduces the blood supply. Cold packs help prevent swelling. Alternate hot and cold packs stimulate circulation and often relieve pain. Exposure to extreme cold may freeze parts of the body. The frozen part should be warmed quickly by gently wrapping in warm blankets or placing in lukewarm water. Too much heat or rubbing may increase the damage to tissues.

You can help your body maintain good circulation by exercising daily vigorously enough to stimulate the flow of blood; by wearing loose, comfortable clothing; by working and playing moderately; by avoiding long periods of standing or sitting; by getting adequate rest and sleep; and by maintaining tall, relaxed body positions that do not cramp blood vessels.

Good circulation will make you feel more comfortable and alert. How many of these habits do you practice?

How does your blood get rid of the wastes it collects?

To get rid of the useless and harmful wastes it collects from the cells, the blood stream must make several special detours. As you know, it makes a special trip to the lungs to eliminate carbon dioxide and renew its supply of oxygen. To obtain its cargo of food, one branch of the aorta goes to the small intestine and then on to the liver to store part of the food and to get rid of wastes. Blood from another branch of the aorta goes to the kidneys to be purified. Chapters 9 and 10 will explain how the blood functions in the intestines and lungs. This section will tell you how the liver and kidneys help keep your blood stream free of accumulated wastes.

What is the work of the liver? If your liver and kidneys stopped working for even a few minutes, the wastes of cell activity accumulating in your blood would cause changes throughout your entire body. At first you would probably feel pepless; then gradually headache and nausea would

144

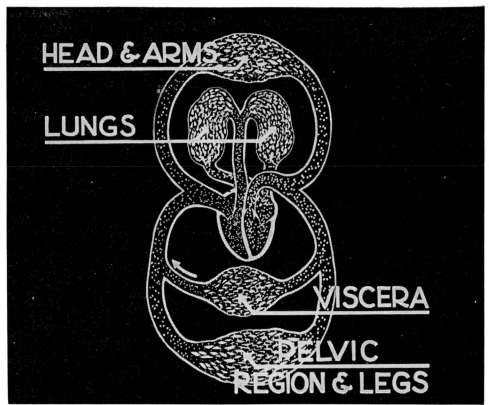

Can you trace the various paths a corpuscle might travel from the time it leaves the right ventricle until it returns to the right auricle?

develop. After a few hours you would have convulsions and die. Since the liver and kidneys are so important, you should learn something about them and how to keep them in good condition.

As blood leaves the small intestine on its return trip to the heart, it follows a special route through the liver. The liver extends from front to back on the right side of the abdomen just inside the lowest ribs. It is the largest solid organ in the body and performs a greater variety of functions than any other organ. Among its other duties, the liver takes sugar from the blood and stores it in its own cells. When the body needs extra amounts of fuel, the liver releases its stored sugar into the blood stream. It secretes into the blood stream materials necessary for digesting fats, for helping in the manufacture of red corpuscles, and for clotting blood. One of its most important functions is to help remove poisons and wastes from the body. In the liver these wastes are changed into new substances. The changed wastes are carried on by the blood stream until they reach the kidneys, where they can be eliminated from the body.

What do the kidneys do? The kidneys are two bean-shaped organs

145

about the size of your fist. They are located in the upper part of the abdomen on either side of the backbone. Blood from a branch of the aorta flows into the kidneys. In the kidneys the blood flows through vast numbers of tiny coiled capillaries. Excess water and the wastes that have been treated in the liver pass through the capillary walls. Each capillary is surrounded by a tiny tube. The liquid waste, called urine, flows through the millions of tiny collecting tubes to the center of the kidney. From there it flows through two tubes, 10 or 12 inches long, into a muscular bag called the bladder. Urine is stored in the bladder until it is released from the body. The

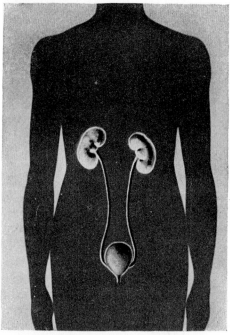

Kidneys are two bean-shaped organs lying on either side of the backbone in the upper part of the abdomen. Liquid wastes taken from the blood flow from the kidneys through two tubes into the bladder.

outlet from the bladder is controlled by a circular muscle which can relax to permit the urine to leave the body. Usually this muscle can be voluntarily controlled after the age of two years.

The average healthy adult secretes about three pints of urine daily. However, the amount is variable. Anything that increases blood circulation through the kidneys will increase the rate at which they secrete urine. The amount of water a person drinks and the amount of water he loses by perspiring also affect the urine output.

Can you help keep your blood pure? Since your blood is purified by your liver and kidneys, anything you do to help them work better will help keep your blood clean and pure.

You can avoid overworking your liver by eating moderately. Too much fat or rich food overstimulates the liver to produce bile for digesting fats. Too much protein makes the liver work harder to eliminate the excess. Protein is not stored by the body. Too much carbohydrate overtaxes the liver's storage capacity. All this extra work interferes with the ability of the liver (1) to produce materials necessary for the manufacture of red corpuscles and (2) to change wastes into substances that can be eliminated by the kidneys. Help your liver to function well by eating a well-balanced diet in the quantities your body needs.

You can help the blood circulate freely through your liver by maintaining good posture and by getting plenty of exercise. Sitting and standing tall keeps the blood vessels from being pinched and helps the blood flow freely. Exercise and deep breathing keep the blood moving through the capillaries in the liver by the

146

squeezing action of the diaphragm, alternately pushing down, then releasing the pressure on the liver.

Kidneys seem to be harmed by too little rather than too much water. The wastes removed by the kidneys must be dissolved in large quantities of water. Drinking six to eight glasses of water a day keeps the wastes well diluted so they are not irritating to the delicate tubes in the kidneys. Much more water is needed if a person has a fever, cold, or other disease in which the kidneys have to eliminate unusual amounts of wastes and poisons. More water is needed, too, by persons exercising strenuously or losing much water through perspiration. In a healthy person, thirst is usually a good guide to need for water. If you seem to have an abnormal thirst, you should see a doctor.

Wastes from all the cells in the body eventually go into the urine. Doctors can find out much about your body by making chemical tests of urine to find out what substances are being removed from the blood. It is a good idea to have a urinalysis every year with your physical check-up. By such an analysis a physician can often detect diseases and inefficient functioning of organs before the illness had advanced so far as to cause pain or other symptoms. Diabetes and kidney troubles are diagnosed by tests on the urine. Early treatment of disease can save much suffering.

The best way to help keep your blood pure is to help your liver and kidneys be healthy and active by (1) eating a moderate, balanced diet, (2) drinking sufficient water, (3) maintaining good posture, (4) exercising vigorously every day, and (5) having a yearly physical check-up including a urinalysis.

How does the blood help control body temperature? Any body activity produces heat. You can demonstrate that muscle activity produces heat by running or by swinging your arms vigorously. You may have done this to keep warm on a cold day. An athlete's temperature may rise three to four degrees during a strenuous event.

Your body operates best at a temperature of about 98.6° Fahrenheit. It maintains that temperature by making adjustments that balance the heat produced in the body with the heat lost. Not every living creature maintains an even temperature. The so-called "cold-blooded" animals, such as turtles, fish, and snakes, have the same body temperature as the air around them. In cold weather their body activities slow down and they fall into a deep sleep.

For human beings much variation from normal temperature is dangerous. Slight variations, as usual, are perfectly normal. Infants, young people, and old people usually have about one degree higher temperature than adults. Women often have a slightly higher temperature than men. However, life can be maintained for only a short time at a body temperature below 95° or above 104°. Any lowering of body temperature slows down cell activity and weakens the protective forces of the body. Chilling makes you more susceptible to disease. A temperature above normal, called a *fever*, is usually a warning that the body is fighting disease. You can help it fight by getting plenty of rest in bed and calling a doctor if it continues.

Your blood carries heat through your body like a hot-water heating system. It is warmed by contact with working cells. It is cooled by circulating near the skin. The skin is cooled by contact with cooler air and by evaporation of perspiration. The temperature of the body surface is always a few degrees cooler than internal parts of the body. If your hands or feet perspire freely they may feel very cool. Have you ever been nervous and excited and felt your hands become damp and cold?

When it is necessary for the body to lose more heat, blood vessels near the surface dilate so that more blood can flow through them. That is why the skin becomes warm and flushed when you exercise vigorously. In cold weather, the blood vessels near the skin dilate to warm the skin. If the heat loss is too great, they contract to prevent excessive chilling of internal parts of the body. Have you noticed your face get red in cold weather? What is happening? What happens if you are exposed for a longer time or to intense cold?

How can you avoid chilling? You can help your body maintain normal temperature by applying a few principles you have learned. You know that anything that increases the rate of burning in the cells—that is, any activity—will increase body temperature.

You can warm yourself by muscle action. Shivering is a method your body uses to produce heat by tiny muscle contractions. You can help by using larger muscle actions and moving your arms and legs briskly. Brisk exercise warms you up, but during exercise blood vessels near the surface of the body are dilated, and the skin becomes flushed and bathed in sweat. When you stop exercising you lose body heat very quickly and can become chilled unless you take steps to prevent it.

Good athletes know that is is important to wrap up warmly after exercising, until the sweat has evaporated and the flush caused by dilated blood vessels has subsided. If possible, athletes take a shower, a brisk rubdown and put on dry clothing. Your body loses heat through the skin being in contact with cooler air. It also loses heat by evaporation of moisture from the skin. You may become chilled by wearing wet clothing or by sitting in a draft when you are perspiring.

Very cold air absorbs body heat too rapidly, chilling the body. Very warm air increases perspiration and dilates the blood vessels in the skin. A temperature between 68° and 70° F. in a room is the happy medium. Below 68° not enough heat is produced by ordinary muscular activity to balance the amount of heat lost through the skin. You can protect your body from loss of heat by covering your skin. Do you know the kind of clothing that best protects the body from heat loss?

Some people have the dangerous,

Rabbits are warm blooded. Turtles are cold blooded. What would you expect the rabbit's temperature to be as air inside the box is cooled? What will happen to the turtle's temperature? Can you tell the difference between them by touching them?

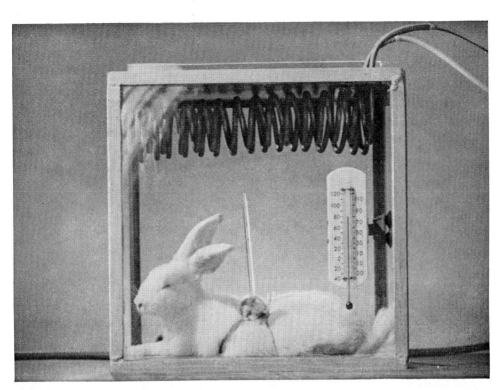

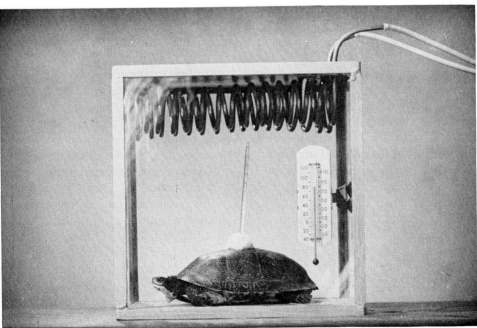

University of Colorado Medical Center

Blood banks take blood from the vein of a healthy person. It can be stored and kept for transfusions for about three weeks. What is blood plasma? When is it useful?

mistaken notion that a drink of whiskey or other drink containing alcohol will keep them warm on a cold day or after a chill. Alcohol causes blood vessels in the skin to dilate, and more blood flows to the skin. The drinker looks flushed, and his skin feels warm, but a flow of blood to the skin is the body's method of losing heat. The very thing that makes the drinker feel warm is actually lowering his body temperature. Heavy drinkers show a high death rate from pneumonia. If you do become chilled, the best thing you can do is to take a drink of hot milk or cocoa and wrap up warmly.

What are blood transfusions? Sometimes in great loss of blood from bleeding, or in certain diseases, lives are saved by transferring blood from one person to another in a transfusion.

In older methods of transfusion, a direct connection was made between the vein of the patient and the artery of the donor (person giving his blood). In modern methods blood is drawn from the vein of a donor into a sterile container. Properly treated blood may be refrigerated and kept for several weeks.

For transfusions, the red blood cells of the donor must be of a type that are not injured by substances in the patient's blood. There are four main types of blood. The proper type must be used for every transfusion.

Nearly every wounded person, even without actual loss of blood through an open wound, suffers from shock. In such a condition plasma flows out of blood vessels into tissues. Once this process starts, it is hard to stop and the volume of blood flowing in the blood vessels may fall so low that death results. Introducing plasma into the blood vessel restores the volume and also helps to bring back fluid which has escaped into the tissues.

150

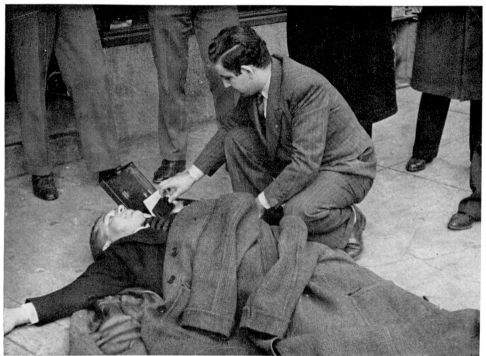

Encyclopedia Britannica Films

In accidental emergencies the person injured should be placed in a comfortable position lying down and covered to keep him warm and prevent further injury and shock.

Plasma contains no red corpuscles, so it need not be typed. Any plasma can be safely put into a person's body under the necessary surgical precautions. Plasma may be frozen or dehydrated. Blood and plasma banks keep whole blood and both liquid and dried plasma ready for immediate use.

Any severe pain, extreme nervous upset, or excessive loss of blood may result in shock. The patient is usually pale and his breathing is shallow. He should be kept as quiet as possible, lying down with head low, and kept warm, but not overheated, until a physician arrives.

Reviewing the chapter

Test yourself

I

You should answer "yes" to the following questions:

1. Do you eat foods which contain iron each day?

2. Do you have a physical check-up each year?

3. Do you give your heart a good balance of rest and exercise?

151

II

Which of the following statements are true and which are false? Reword each false statement to make it true:

1. The heart pumps blood through miles of blood vessels.
2. Blood is carried away from the heart in the veins.
3. Blood flows back to the heart in the arteries.
4. Food and air leave the circulatory system from the network of capillaries.
5. The cells are surrounded by blood.
6. The lymph comes from the blood.
7. The liquid part of the blood is clear.
8. Red corpuscles are chiefly made of carbon dioxide.
9. Blood changes from blue to red in the lungs.

III

Complete the following sentences by supplying the missing words. Do NOT WRITE IN THIS BOOK.

1. Foods rich in iron are ...., ... and ....
2. Diabetes can be detected by a ....
3. Shock may be treated by transfusions of ....

Other activities

1. Some of the microscope experts may like to examine blood under a microscope. Sterilize a needle by wiping it with sterile cotton dipped in alcohol or by passing it through a flame. Wipe your finger with alcohol. Prick your finger with the needle and place a small drop of blood on a slide. Place a coverglass on the blood and examine it with the low power, then the high power of the microscope. The tiny discs floating in the liquid are red corpuscles. Here and there you may see a corpuscle with a silvery appearance. This is a white corpuscle. Make a drawing of what you see. If the slide is not prepared quickly, the red cells may lose water and appear rough and knobby.

2. Other class scientists may report on or demonstrate the following experiments: How temperature is measured and what Fahrenheit is. How to use a thermometer to measure body temperature. How evaporation causes cooling. How a pump works and why valves are important.

3. Obtain from the butcher a beef heart. Note the shape and color of the heart, the fat embedded in the walls, and the blood tubes leading to and from the heart. How do the arteries differ from the veins? Locate the valves between auricles and ventricles. Force water into the ventricle until the valves leading from the auricles are closed. Cut the heart open lengthwise and locate the four chambers. Which chamber has the thickest walls?

Reading to help you grow up

Interesting chapters on the heart and blood are found in these books:

Working Together for Health by Burkhard and others.
A Sound Body by Charters and others.
The Human Body by Brownell and Williams.
How Your Body Works by Schneider.

Films to help you understand

Circulation of the Blood. United World.
A Life in Your Hands. American National Red Cross. Shows how blood banks work.

Heart and Circulation. Encyclopedia Britannica Films. Also filmstrip.

Control of Body Temperature. Encyclopedia Britannica Films.

Work of Kidneys. Encyclopedia Britannica Films.

Human Heart. American Heart Association. A March of Time production.

Before the Doctor Comes. Central Washington College. A chart of arteries showing pressure points and how to control bleeding and treat shock.

Control of Bleeding. Encyclopedia Britannica Films.

Friends Magazine

Why is control of breathing so important in swimming? Why does a swimmer breathe in through his mouth?

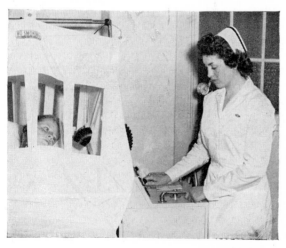

Your body uses only a part of air called oxygen. Why is it sometimes helpful to give the body extra supplies of oxygen?

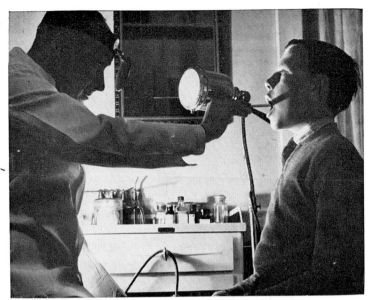

The doctor is examining the patient's throat. Why are throat infections so dangerous? Are tonsils of any use?

Your voice is produced when moving air causes the stretched vocal cords in your larynx to vibrate. Why do they not vibrate all the time?

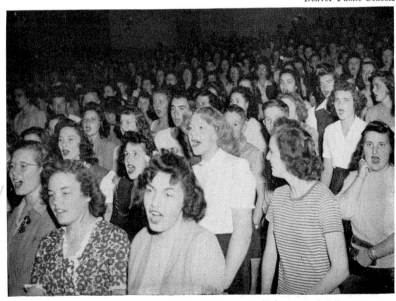

155

Chapter 9

HOW DOES YOUR BODY OBTAIN AIR?

Have you ever felt drowsy and depressed and unable to work or to think, then been refreshed and cheered when you went out into the fresh air? Do you feel cheerful and full of pep after brisk outdoor exercises? There is a reason for that feeling of well-being when you have a good supply of fresh air.

To remain alive and working, every cell in the body must have a constant supply of oxygen. Complete lack of oxygen causes death in a few minutes. Partial lack of oxygen results in decreased ability of the cells to work.

Brain cells are particularly delicate. Even a mild shortage of oxygen may cause changes in mental ability, disposition, and ability to concentrate and to co-ordinate fine movements. Progressive symptoms of a shortage of oxygen in the tissues are a tired feeling, mental dullness, changes in breathing, a bluish tinge to the skin, loss of muscular control, and finally unconsciousness and death.

Normally your body obtains a sufficient supply of oxygen from the air.

Can you think of circumstances where there might not be sufficient oxygen in the atmosphere? Sometimes the oxygen is present, but your body cells are not able to receive good supplies. Can you think of accidents or diseases that make it difficult for the body to secure oxygen or carry it to the cells? If oxygen from the air is not available, artificial supplies of pure oxygen may be used.

The special system in your body that takes oxygen from the air and makes it available to all the cells in the body is called the respiratory system. It is a series of tubes and passages through which air travels to microscopic air sacs in the lungs. From the air sacs oxygen goes into the blood stream.

Like other vital systems the organs that make up your lifeline have many natural safeguards and protections. However, they are exposed to many dangers and abuses. You can help them to work efficiently and safely. You can form habits that protect them from injury and disease.

156

Looking ahead

Questions and suggestions

1. Before you read the chapter about how your body obtains and uses air, try to recall what you already know about the subject.

2. How long a list can you make of activities and subjects that come to your mind as you think about breathing? These may help you to get started: artificial respiration, mountain climbing, colds, and talking.

3. Can you locate your Adam's apple (also known as the larynx or voice box) with your fingers? What happens when you swallow? When you hold air in your lungs? When you make a sound? Hum up and down the scale. Do you notice any changes? How does your larynx produce sounds?

4. Speak while holding your nose. What happens?

5. Spread your fingers across the front of your waist as you breathe in and out. What happens? Can you breathe without noticeably moving your ribs?

6. Put the ball of your thumb across one nostril at a time. Do you breathe as freely through one nostril as the other?

Committee Planning

1. The safety committee can illustrate and report on water safety—swimming, diving, and boating.

2. The speaker's committee can invite a voice teacher or expert to give you some tips on developing a more pleasing voice.

3. The field-trip committee may be able to arrange a trip to inspect an iron lung, an oxygen tent, a plane with a pressurized cabin, or other devices that aid respiration. If you can make a trip to a swimming pool, you can experiment with your ability to float, to tread water, to breathe properly in swimming, and to swim underwater.

4. A committee of Boy Scouts or first-aid experts can demonstrate and explain artificial respiration.

5. A committee may report on dangers of suffocation and methods of emergency treatment.

6. A committee can conduct breathing experiments. Below are several activities that you can try.

Measure your chest just under the arms while you breathe out. Measure your chest again after taking a deep breath. Compare the measurements.

Time the breathing of a person at rest, then after vigorous exercise, then 10 minutes after exercise. If you can, time the respirations of a young baby.

Examine your throat with a mirror. Can you find your soft palate? Yawn and see what happens. Can you see your tonsils?

Hold the mirror near your nose and exhale. Are the steamy areas on the mirror about the same size and shape? Why?

You can experiment with your voice. Arrange to meet in a room with a piano. Find the highest note you can produce with your voice. The lowest. How far apart are they?

Blow up a toy balloon. Stretch the neck so that as air escapes it makes a sound. What causes the sound? How does your larynx produce sound?

Reading

After your first rapid reading, try to answer the test questions at the end of the chapter. Now read again more carefully. Can you answer the test questions more satisfactorily?

What are the parts of the respiratory system?

The organs that supply the body with air make up the respiratory system. They require special protection because they are subject to some of the most frequent and most dangerous diseases and disorders.

What does your nose do? The duty of the nose is to clean, warm, and moisten the air taken in from outside the body. The nose protects the other parts of the system from materials in the air that might cause irritation or infection. If you clean carefully around the opening of the nostril with a piece of cotton or tissue you can see some of the materials stopped by the nose.

The entire nasal passage is lined with a delicate membrane. This membrane is richly supplied with blood vessels which warm the air. It secretes a sticky fluid called mucus which moistens the air and catches germs and dust particles from the air.

The nasal passages are separated from the mouth by the palate. The hard palate, or roof of the mouth, is bone. Further back is the muscular soft palate. Can you locate these?

A thin wall of bone and cartilage, called the septum, divides the nose into two short passages. These bones, which branch out into the upper part of each passage, increase the air-conditioning surface. The facial bones near the nose contain cavities or air spaces called sinuses. Sinuses are lined with mucous membrane which is a continuation of that in the nose.

What does your throat do? From the back part of the nose, air passes into the throat, or pharynx. Air may enter the throat through the mouth, but nose breathing is more healthful. Why?

The throat is an open space back of the mouth. It is a meeting place for six tubes or passages. One of the tubes is the *esophagus,* down which food travels to the stomach. The other five are air passages. The upper part of the throat has the openings from the two nasal passages, and two more from the Eustachian tubes leading to the middle ears. At the lower end of the throat is the opening to the *larynx* or voice box. The larnyx is the top part of the windpipe which leads to the lungs.

Care of the throat is particularly important, because from it infections can spread in so many directions. The throat has natural protections from infection including the mucous membrane lining with its secretions, and a generous supply of lymph nodes. One lymph node high on the back of the throat is called the adenoid. Two others lower down on each side by the tongue are called tonsils. Can you see them? The mucous membranes which cover the tonsils and adenoids are wrinkled and pitted to increase their surface and enable them to catch germs entering the throat.

What happens in the windpipe? From the back of the throat, air enters the *trachea,* or windpipe. The windpipe is located in front of the food canal. It is a rigid tube about an inch in diameter and four or five inches long. Layers of U-shaped rings of cartilage make the trachea non-collapsible. You can feel the rings in the front of your neck. How does the structure of the windpipe protect your life?

158

Safe and expert ways to enjoy a canoe. Top left: What are safe ways to get into a canoe? Top right: What are safe ways to ride? Lower left: Why is standing or moving dangerous? Lower right: The safest boats will support several people even when they are overturned or submerged. If you ride in a boat that will not float after capsizing, what precautions should you take?

The *epiglottis,* a small cover or lid of cartilage, attached to the base of the tongue, keeps food from entering the windpipe. When you swallow, the upper end of the windpipe moves upward until it is covered by the epiglottis. After swallowing is completed, the windpipe moves down again, leaving the air passage open. If you try to eat and talk at the same time, food may go down the wrong way into the windpipe; then strong muscles contract to make you cough and expel the food. Can you feel the top of your windpipe move up and down as you swallow?

At the top of the windpipe is the voice box or larynx. Its walls are made of cartilage and form a V in front called the Adam's apple. The vocal

159

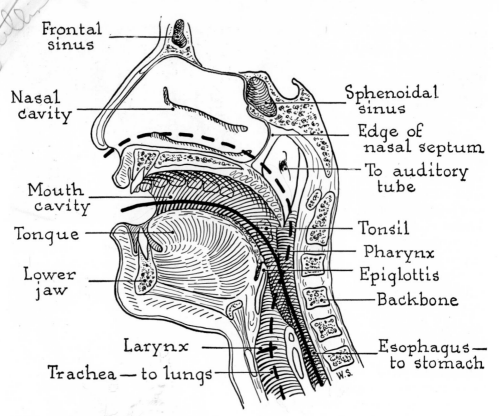

Frontal sinus

Nasal cavity

Mouth cavity

Tongue

Lower jaw

Larynx

Trachea — to lungs

Sphenoidal sinus

Edge of nasal septum

To auditory tube

Tonsil

Pharynx

Epiglottis

Backbone

Esophagus — to stomach

In this view through the middle plane of the head, the air path is shown by a broken line. The food path is shown by a solid line. The two paths cross in the lower throat. How is food kept out of the windpipe?

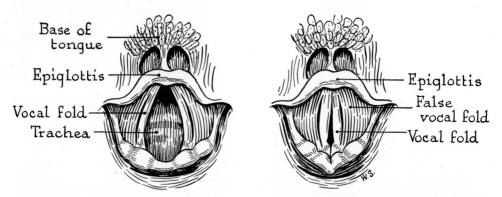

Base of tongue

Epiglottis

Vocal fold

Trachea

Epiglottis

False vocal fold

Vocal fold

The interior of the larynx, viewed from above, looks something like these drawings. Left, the vocal folds are separated. Right, during singing the vocal folds are brought together. Air forced through the slitlike openings causes the cords to vibrate and produces sound.

cords (two elastic bands covered with mucous membrane) stretch across the larynx from front to back. When the voice is not in use, the bands are relaxed against the sides of the larynx. When you speak or sing, tiny muscles spread the vocal cords toward each other, into the current of air expelled from the lungs. The air current makes the cords vibrate. The vocal cords produce sounds in the same way as a vibrating violin string, clarinet reed, or drumhead. Muscles that change the tension on the cords help to change the pitch of your voice. In adolescence a boy's vocal cords lengthen and the pitch of his voice changes. The vocal cords of the average man are about three-quarters of an inch long. Those of women are shorter.

What are your lungs like? At its lower end, the windpipe divides into two branches called the *bronchial tubes.* One branch enters the right lung, the other the left. In the lungs, the bronchial tubes divide and subdivide into smaller and smaller tubes, like the branches and twigs of a tree. Finally each tiny tube ends in a little group of thin, elastic air sacs resembling little clusters of microscopic balloons.

The millions of little air sacs which make up the lungs are enclosed in two big bags of membrane (a layer of thin soft tissue) and suspended in an airtight chest cavity. Blood vessels enter the lungs at the top of the chest cavity where the lungs are fastened to the body. The blood vessels branch until a network of capillaries surrounds each microscopic air sac. Oxygen from the air in the lungs passes (diffuses) through the thin walls of the air sac

Denver Public Schools

How does a violin produce a sound? How do other musical instruments—a clarinet, a trumpet, a drum—produce sound? How does your voice box produce sound?

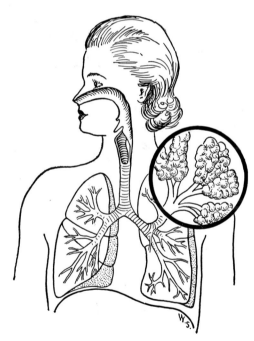

The lungs are two big elastic bags divided into millions of air sacs. In the lungs the air and blood are separated only by the very thin walls of the capillaries and the air sacs. The walls are so thin oxygen and carbon dioxide easily pass through them.

161

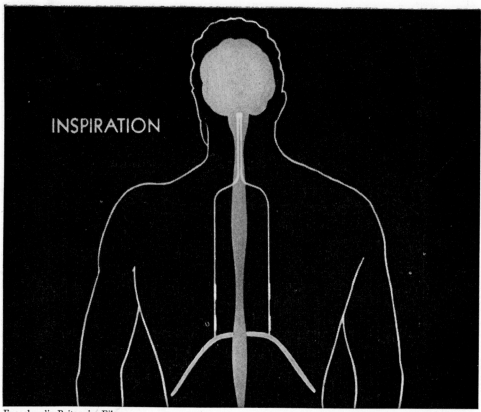

INSPIRATION

The drawing above shows how the chest cavity enlarges in order that you can breathe in. Breathing in is called inspiration. Breathing out is called expiration. See the other picture on the opposite page.

and through the capillary walls into the blood. Carbon dioxide travels in the reverse direction. Blood containing a fresh load of oxygen returns to the heart to begin its journey through the body. What color is blood in the veins returning to the heart from the lungs? Why?

What happens when you breathe? You breathe in (inhale) and out (exhale) by changing the size of your chest. The chest is an airtight chamber with movable walls and floor. It is en-closed by the spinal column, the ribs and the breast bone, and the muscles around and between them. Its movable floor is a thin muscular sheet called the diaphragm. A continuation of the *pleural* (chest) *membrane* surrounds the lungs and lines the chest cavity. A painful condition of the pleural membranes, called pleurisy, sometimes follows lung infections. The lungs fill most of the space in the chest and almost completely surround the heart. Consequently, any change

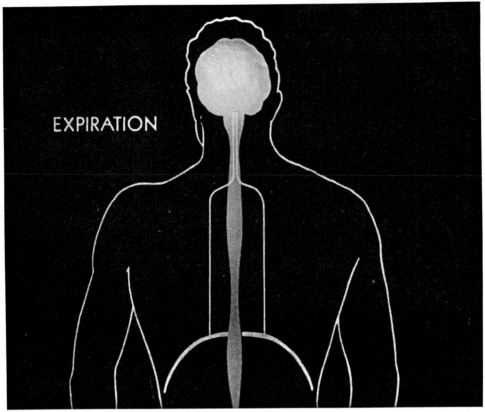

EXPIRATION

This drawing shows how the diaphragm moved upward, making the chest cavity smaller, and causing air to be forced out. This forcing out is called expiration. What muscles beside the diaphragm affect the size of the chest cavity?

in the size of the chest cavity increases or decreases the amount of air space in the lungs.

The *diaphragm* is attached to the side of the chest cavity at about the level of the lower ribs. It curves upward when relaxed because of the upward pressure of organs in the abdomen (lower part of the body cavity). When the diaphragm contracts, it becomes flatter, making more space in the chest cavity. At the same time other muscles between the ribs move

the ribs and breastbone forward and up, increasing still further the size of the chest cavity. Air, which has a pressure of about 15 pounds to the square inch, moves in and expands the lungs to fill the enlarged space. When you breathe out (exhale), the diaphragm rises, and the ribs are lowered to make the chest cavity smaller and force air out of the lungs. Put your hands on your ribs and feel these movements as you breathe.

Although you can modify the mus-

163

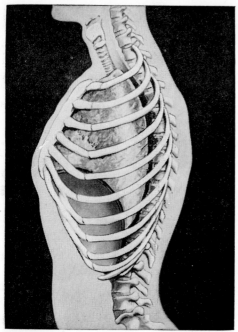

This is a view of the lower part of the respiratory system. Notice the dome-shaped diaphragm muscle. Notice the bony cage that protects organs in the chest.

An average adult breathes about 16 to 18 times a minute. An increase of carbon dioxide in the blood acts on the respiratory center to cause it to speed up the breathing impulse. Carbon dioxide accumulated during vigorous exercise may continue to stimulate rapid breathing for some time after the exercise stops.

Excitement and fear can also speed up breathing. The gland secretions caused by feelings affect the nerves in the respiratory center. Shock, or a dash of cold water, may stimulate a deep breath or gasp. How might this be helpful if a person had fainted? Slowing down of bodily activity decreases the rate of breathing. During sleep the rate may be only 12 to 13 times a minute.

cular movements which regulate breathing, they are largely automatic. It is impossible for anyone to hold his own breath long enough to suffocate. Nerves located in the respiratory center in the lower part of the brain automatically stimulate the breathing muscles to contract. Destruction of nerves in the respiratory center causes death because breathing stops. How does an iron lung work to aid breathing when these nerves have been damaged?

The rate of breathing varies considerably in individuals according to their age, size, and activity. A newborn infant breathes 40 to 70 times a minute. The rate gradually decreases.

In cases of near drowning or electric shock where breathing has stopped, it often may be started again by immediate artificial respiration. Details of the back pressure-arm lift method should be learned and practiced under qualified instructors.

How can you help your breathing apparatus to work well?

Good breathing is the natural result of clear air passages, good posture, and strong chest and diaphragm muscles. Air passages may become blocked because of enlarged or misshapen bones, swelling of mucous membranes, or enlarged tonsils or adenoids. Most obstructions can be prevented or corrected.

How can you guard against colds? Infections of the membranes lining the air passages cause pain, swelling, and obstruction. The nose is frequently affected by an infection of the mucous membrane called the common cold. Most colds are thought to be caused by small organisms. Every time an infected person coughs, or sneezes, or even talks, he expels many of these organisms from his respiratory tract.

The best protection from colds is to avoid all contact with infected persons or with articles they have used. At times when colds are widespread avoid crowds. Keep yourself in good condition by getting plenty of good food, rest, and outdoor exercise. Avoid overtaxing your body by getting chilled.

If you have a cold, give yourself and everyone a break by staying home in bed. Stay away from other people as much as possible. Use clean handkerchiefs or disposable tissues to cover your mouth and nose when sneezing

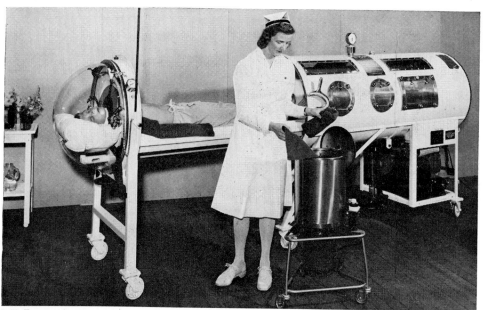

J. H. Emerson Company

If the nerves that control chest and diaphragm muscles are damaged by disease or injury, natural breathing stops. A respirator may be used to enable the patient to breathe. How does it work?

or coughing. To protect yourself from serious infection, you should rest in bed and drink increased quantities of water and fruit juices. When your body is resting it can use all its strength fighting infection. If fever or signs of spreading of the infection develop, a physician should be called. The greatest dangers from colds are that they may spread or that more serious diseases in their early stages may be mistaken for a common cold.

Influenza, or flu, may start like a cold, but develops fever, headache, backache, and extreme weakness. There is some influenza during every winter. At intervals, great epidemics have spread over the world. In 1918 over a quarter of a million Americans and about 10 million people in the world died of influenza. At the first sign of flu it is wise to go to bed and to drink plenty of water and fruit juices. Remain in bed a couple of days after the temperature has returned to normal.

How can you avoid other respiratory infections? Infection of nasal membranes may extend into the sinuses. Here they are difficult to treat because the small openings become closed. Sinus infections are very painful and need to be treated individually by a physician.

You may be able to prevent some infections from spreading by cleaning the mucus from your nose correctly. Cover your nose with a clean handkerchief and blow *gently* through *both* nostrils. Blowing hard with the lower nostrils closed may force infected mucus up through the Eusta-

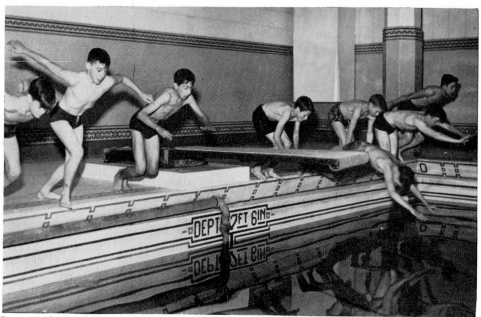

Denver Public Schools

Inexperienced divers may force water into their ears and nasal passages. Why is this dangerous? How can it be prevented?

chian tube, which leads to the ear, or through any of the other respiratory passages.

Vitamin A helps to resist infection in mucous membranes. Important sources of vitamin A are whole milk, butter, eggs, green leafy and yellow vegetables, liver, apricots, and bananas. Vitamin C also increases resistance to infection. Especially good sources of vitamin C are oranges and other citrus fruits. Tomatoes, potatoes, green pepper, raw cabbage, and onions, and some other fruits and vegetables, contain vitamin C.

Infections of the membranes lining the air passages may spread into the middle ear. How? Earache is a sign that such spreading has occurred. Infections in the ear may have serious complications, including deafness. A physician should be seen at once.

Often a sore throat develops with a cold. Gargles give temporary relief because of the cleansing effect.

Infection may spread to the larynx, bronchial tubes, and lungs. Such infections as laryngitis, bronchitis, and pneumonia may begin like a common cold. New methods of treating pneumonia have greatly reduced the death rate, but it is still a dangerous and deadly disease.

Lung cancer is now a leading cause of cancer deaths among American men. Scientists are trying to find the cause for the sharp rise in this disease. Some believe it is mostly due to pollution of the air from exhaust fumes and industrial smoke. Statistics show that heavy cigarette smoking is closely associated with lung cancer. Heavy cigarette smokers have a much higher death rate than nonsmokers, not only from lung cancer but from other

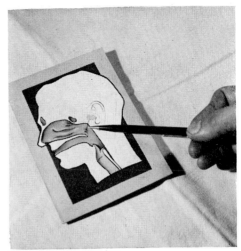

Encyclopedia Britannica Films

The pencil points to the Eustachian tube. What is the use of this tube?

forms of cancer and from diseases of the arteries. At best, smoking is a dirty, expensive, and irritating habit, and is of no help to health. It may be very dangerous.

What are other dangers to breathing? The membranes lining the breathing passages may become irritated or swollen from causes other than infections. Some of these are excessive dryness, dust, prolonged or strained use of the voice, allergies, smoking, sudden chilling, and unbalanced diet.

Those who want to keep their breathing apparatus in top condition avoid anything that irritates the delicate membranes. Particularly careful are athletes and people who work in high altitudes.

Air passage may be blocked by enlarged or infected tonsils or adenoids. Tonsils and adenoids are useful as long as they are healthy. Why? But they may become swollen or diseased

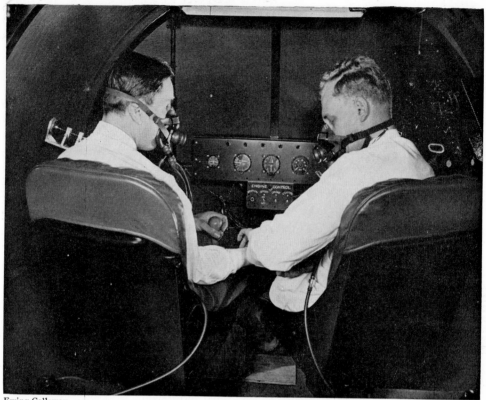

In a high altitude pressure chamber, a doctor checks the pilot's pulse and heart action. Why does high-altitude flying require well-developed lungs and heart?

when they have too much work to do, as when an individual has frequent colds or sore throats. Occasionally they may become infected and spread poison through the lymph and blood vessels to cause trouble in other parts of the body. The adenoids may become so enlarged that they block the passage between the nose and throat and cause mouth breathing. You should try to keep these protectors of your throat healthy and efficient. Badly infected or enlarged tonsils and adenoids are more a danger than a protection and should be removed by a surgeon.

How can you develop good breathing habits? Good posture, sitting and standing tall with the shoulders straight and chest lifted, gives the lungs room to expand fully. Exercise can help your breathing by developing the muscles which hold you erect and which expand the chest cavity. Exercises like hiking, swimming, and active games are better than deep-breathing exercises because they stimulate the whole body. They increase circulation and speed up the rate at which oxygen is being used and carbon dioxide produced. Bodily activity increases the rate of breathing naturally. Some athletes, such as marathon runners and distance swimmers, develop such a large lung capacity that even during strenuous exercise their breathing is only slightly speeded up.

Breathlessness, or rapid breathing, is a signal that the body needs rest. Good athletes, and all individuals who want to keep their bodies in good condition, pay attention to such warnings and signals by their bodies. They exercise regularly. Their exercise is vigorous enough to increase their rate of breathing, but they stop it when their breathing becomes rapid or labored. By daily exercise they strengthen their chest muscles and gradually increase their breathing capacity. A good coach or trainer does not permit athletes to enter strenuous activities without a physical examination and a program of gradual conditioning.

Mouth breathing is bad for several reasons. It gives a person an unattractive appearance, making him appear stupid or dull. It fails to take advantage of the air-conditioning system in the nose, hence it increases the possibility of colds and sore throat. It dries the mouth, often causing irritation and coughing.

Breathing through the mouth may be a bad habit or may be caused by an obstruction in the nose. If you breathe through your mouth and cannot form the habit of nose breathing, the best plan is to get the advice of a physican. Sometimes the nose passages are blocked by enlarged or crooked bones. Try breathing in and out while closing first one nostril and then the other, by pressing gently with the finger against the outside of the nostril. Are both passages free and unobstructed?

Denver Public Schools

The greatest amount of oxygen is used during strenuous exercise. Breathing becomes more vigorous, circulation speeds up, and the whole body is benefited. What are signs that the body needs more oxygen?

Encyclopedia Britannica Films

By breathing on a mirror, observe the temperature and moisture of the air you exhale. How does breathing help to regulate body temperature?

Reviewing the chapter

I

You should answer "yes" to the following questions.

1. Do you always breathe through your nose?
2. Do you exercise each day vigorously enough to increase your breathing?
3. Do you blow your nose carefully?
4. Do you follow the rules to avoid catching and spreading colds?

II

Complete the following sentences by supplying the missing words. Do NOT WRITE IN THIS BOOK.

1. The .... system and the .... system working together supply the cells with oxygen and remove carbon dioxide.
2. The nose is lined with ....
3. Air-conditioning surfaces are increased by .... and ....
4. Tubes opening into the throat are the ...., the two ...., the two ...., and the ....
5. The windpipe branches at its lower end into two ....
6. A powerful muscle, the ...., enables you to breathe naturally.

III

Which of the following statements are true and which are false? Reword each false statement to make it true.

1. The mouth prepares the air for the throat and lungs.
2. Sinuses are cavities in the lungs.
3. The epiglottis closes the windpipe when we swallow.
4. Red corpuscles are the food carriers of the blood.
5. Rest is the best "medicine" for a cold.

6. Tonsils are of no use to the body.
7. Active games are better than breathing exercises to increase breathing capacity.
8. Mouth breathing may be simply a bad habit.

Other activities

1. From a doctor or a health magazine approved by doctors find the latest information on preventing and curing colds. What can you find out about the antihistamines?
2. The class may be interested in a project to try to avoid colds the rest of the year. Can a committee draw up some rules and suggestions? Another committee can keep track of all the colds. How many people have them? How long do they last? Perhaps you can get some all-school figures to compare with the record of your class.
3. Many interesting reports can be made on subjects related to breathing. Are you interested in how other animals breathe, and how people and animals breathe in such situations as in submarines, in high mountain climbing, in swimming, in diving, in poison gas, in high-altitude flying, in flight beyond the atmosphere, or in diseases like pneumonia, hay fever, and tuberculosis? Look up some of these subjects in books and pamphlets gathered by the library committee, in encyclopedias, or in other books you find yourself.
4. Committees interested in science might like to demonstrate air pressure or the production of sound by different methods of causing objects to vibrate.

Reading to help you grow up

Three pamphlets published by the Metropolitan Life Insurance Company offer interesting and practical sugges-

tions for protecting yourself from respiratory diseases. The pamphlets are listed below:

"Colds, Influenza, Pneumonia."

"Just a Cold? Or—"

"Respiratory Diseases."

Man in the Air, by Herbert Zim, tells how flying affects man's body and mind and has interesting chapters on oxygen masks, pressure cabins, effects of speed, tests of physical fitness, and safety suggestions.

Our Ocean of Air, by Bertha Morris Parker, has interesting simple experiments to perform with air.

Films to help you understand

Breathing. Encyclopedia Britannica Films.

How We Breathe. Bray.

The Common Cold. Encyclopedia Britannica Films.

Artificial Respiration. Castle. Filmed by the United States Navy. In color.

Back to Life. Aetna. Artificial respiration. In color.

Fire. Encyclopedia Britannica Films. Explains principles of burning, use of air, and fire hazards.

Picture Preview:
Chapter 10

H. Armstrong Roberts

How may a good breakfast affect a close decision? Why is breakfast so important? What makes a good breakfast?

Have you ever tried to swallow when you were standing on your head? Can you do it? Why? Does food fall down through your esophagus to your stomach?

Denver Public Schools

How do you think your personality and vigor are affected by your digestive system? Does your disposition affect your digestion?

Ewing Galloway

Rinsing your mouth immediately after eating, especially after eating sweets, helps to prevent tooth decay. Why?

Byron G. Moon Company

Chapter 10

HOW CAN YOUR BODY MAKE USE OF FOOD?

$\mathcal{M}$ ost of your plans to improve yourself, to be the kind of person you want to be, depend partly on the food you eat. Food is used by every part of you. It helps to give you strong muscles, straight bones, shining hair, an attractive smile, a clear complexion, and pep and energy to work and to play.

Your body needs foods containing protein to grow and to repair itself. What are some good sources of protein? It needs carbohydrates and fats to burn for heat and energy. What are some foods containing carbohydrates and fats? It needs special kinds of foods—minerals and vitamins—to help it do special building and operating jobs. For example, red blood cells must have iron. Bones require calcium and phosphorus and vitamin D.

Since ancient times man has been accumulating evidence about the kinds of food necessary to keep his body working well. He has tried to answer questions about what happens to food in the body. How does it get to the cells that need it? Can extra food be stored?

In order to be used by the body food must be broken down into simpler parts. These parts must be able to dissolve so they can be carried by the blood stream to every cell. The process of changing complex foods into simpler, soluble foods is called digestion.

The organs that help in the process make up the digestive system. Most of them are constructed so that they form a continuous tube, called the alimentary canal. Foods moving through the chambers of the canal are chopped and churned, acted upon by chemicals, dissolved in water, and finally passed through the canal walls into the blood stream. Food not digested is eliminated from the body.

Scientists have discovered much about how the digestive system works. You can use some of this information to help you establish habits that will keep your digestive system healthy and efficient.

174

Looking ahead

Questions and suggestions

1. Can you remember some advertisements from radio or magazines for products that are supposed to help your digestive system? Do you think digestive troubles are very common?

2. What are some of the symptoms that indicate the digestive system is not working well?

3. How many organs of the digestive system can you name? Do you know what jobs each does? Do you know where each is located in the body?

4. What is the difference between the stomach and the abdomen?

5. Can you make your mouth water? Can you tell where the saliva enters your mouth? How does saliva help your body use food?

Committee Planning

1. Newspapers and magazines advertise many products that are supposed to aid digestion and elimination. A special committee can collect some of these advertisements for class discussion and for putting on the bulletin board.

2. The Food and Drug Administration enforces the Federal Food, Drug, and Cosmetic Act which controls the purity, safety, and labeling of foods, drugs, and cosmetics which cross state lines. A special committee can give a report on the ways in which its work protects health.

3. The field-trip committee may be able to arrange a trip to some place that prepares or serves food—to a bakery, dairy, restaurant, or cannery. How do they make sure food is pure and safe?

4. The speaker's committee may be able to have someone from your local health department tell you how your community makes your food safe.

5. The safety committee can show the class how to avoid poisoning, how to protect others from poisoning, and how to give emergency treatment in case of poisoning.

How does the digestive system work?

Part of digestion is a *chemical process* of changing complex substances into simple ones that can be dissolved in water. Chemical digestion is accomplished by juices secreted by digestive organs. Part of digestion is a *mechanical process* of breaking and churning food so it can be reached by digestive juices.

What happens in the mouth? Digestion begins in the mouth. There the food is ground by the teeth and mixed with a digestive juice called saliva. Saliva is secreted by three pairs of salivary glands. One pair of glands, called the *parotid salivary glands,* is located in the jaw, just under each ear. These are the glands that commonly swell when a person has the mumps. Ducts, or tubes, from the two other pairs of glands open into your mouth just under your tongue, in back of your front teeth.

Saliva moistens and softens all food and acts chemically on starches. Starch cannot dissolve in water, but sugar can. Saliva changes starchy foods to simple sugars. If you chew a cracker or piece of toast for a few minutes, you can tell by the taste

175

that the starch is being changed to a sweet sugar. All starch is not changed to sugar in the mouth. The saliva mixes with the food and keeps on working after food reaches the stomach.

What happens in the esophagus? From the back of the mouth, the tongue pushes food into the throat. There the muscles in the esophagus can move it along. The esophagus is a tube which extends down the back of the chest, through the diaphragm, to the stomach. Rings of muscles in the walls of the esophagus contract and relax, one after the other, producing a wavelike motion known as *peristalsis*. Peristalsis occurs throughout the length of the alimentary canal, in the esophagus, in the stomach, and in the intestines. It seems to be produced automatically whenever the sides of the canal are pressed upon by their contents. Sometimes the peristaltic wave starts at the stomach and works backward causing vomiting. Vomiting is a protection for the body. How?

What happens in the stomach? Food flows from the esophagus into the stomach, a saclike enlargement of the alimentary canal. The stomach is a pear-shaped elastic bag. It is very small when empty but is able to stretch enough to hold a quart or more of food. The stomach is in the abdomen, mostly on the left side of the body with the large end on top well up under the ribs.

Food enters in the center of the stomach; food already present is pushed out toward the stomach walls. Glands in the stomach walls produce a fluid called gastric juice. Gastric juice starts the digestion of protein foods. In the center of the stomach saliva mixed with food continues the digestion of starch.

Peristaltic waves from both ends of the stomach churn the food, mixing it with *gastric juice*. After one to six hours the food is reduced to a soupy mass containing small lumps. The soupy mass collects in a pouch near the outlet that leads to the small intestine. A valve opens to permit small quantities of the partly digested food to enter the small intestine.

Many scientists have studied the action of the stomach and of the gastric juice. You may be interested in looking up the stories of Dr. William Beaumont or René de Réaumur to see how they devised ways of studying the stomach in action and experimented with gastric juice. Dr. Beaumont's work is mentioned briefly on page 99.

How does food get into the blood? Most of the digestion of food takes place in the small intestine. The small intestine is a long, hollow tube coiled in the abdomen. It is about 1 inch in diameter and from 20 to 30 feet long. Like the esophagus and stomach, it has muscular walls which continue peristaltic action.

As the partly digested and partly liquefied food from the stomach is pushed through the small intestine, it is mixed with three digestive juices. *Intestinal juice,* produced by the walls of the small intestine, and *pancreatic juice,* which enters by means of a duct from the pancreas, complete the digestion of starches and proteins and begin the digestion of fats. *Bile,* a bitter, greenish liquid produced by the liver, helps digest fat. Bile, or gall,

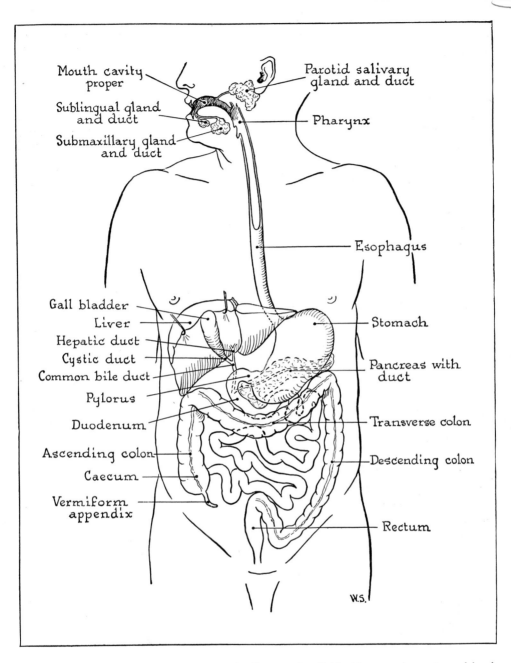

In this diagram of the digestive system, the liver and gall bladder are shown turned back and to the right. Look again at the picture on page 98 and see if you can name the organs shown there.

enters the stomach from a small storage pouch called the gall bladder. The yellow color of urine comes from bile pigments which have been absorbed into the blood from the intestine.

Food usually takes about eight hours to move through the small intestine. As a result of all the mechanical and chemical action in the mouth, stomach, and small intestine, all the usable parts of food are changed into a thin, milky liquid. The digested food dissolved in water can pass right through the walls of the small intestine into the blood stream. Some foods are ready to pass into the blood stream more quickly than others. Carbohydrates digest most rapidly as they begin the process in the mouth. Some simple sugars, such as those in ripe fruits, need almost no digestion. They are ready to be absorbed quickly and form a source of quick energy. Fats are the slowest foods to be digested.

The small intestine is especially constructed so that digested food, dissolved in water, can pass right through its walls. The mucous membrane lining the small intestine lies in countless folds. It is indented with thousands of tiny, finger-like projections called *villi*. Villi makes the inner surface of the small intestine look like velvet. The wall of each villus is very thin. Just outside the intestine, extending up into each villus, is a network of capillaries and lymph vessels. Foods in solution pass through the walls of the villi. Fat is taken into the lymph vessel. All other foods are absorbed into the blood in the capillaries. From the capillaries the blood flows into larger vessels and finally to the liver. In the liver, part of the sugar is changed to glycogen and stored. The rest of the food goes into general circulation, eventually to the cells. Excess fat and glycogen are stored in various places under the skin and around some organs.

What happens to food which is not digested? Food which is not digested for absorption finally enters the large intestine. The large intestine, usually called the colon or bowel, is shaped something like a hurdle. It joins the small intestine just in front of the right hipbone. Near the junction of the small intestine with the large intestine is a small, finger-like projection called the appendix. The appendix apparently has no function in the human body. Bacterial action in this organ may produce inflammation and pain called appendicitis.

The large intestine is shorter but larger than the small intestine. Peristalsis through it is slower. The large intestine is about two inches in diameter and about four feet long. From its junction with the small intestine, it goes up the right side of the abdomen to the lower ribs, crosses the upper abdomen to the left side, then curves down and to the center of the lower abdominal cavity. The lower end is called the rectum, and the outside opening, the anus.

Material entering the bowel is a watery solution of parts of food which could not be digested, digestive juices, bacteria, and mucus. The chief work of the colon is to absorb water from the watery materials, reduce their bulk and eliminate them in comparatively solid form. Mucous glands in the walls of the intestine help to lubricate the mass to prevent friction as it moves along. It usually takes materials

12 to 24 hours to travel through the colon and collect in the rectum.

When enough wastes (feces) accumulate, they press on the sides of the rectum to bring about a natural desire for elimination. If the signal is not heeded and waste remains in the bowel, more water may be absorbed, and elimination may become more difficult. Elimination is accomplished by peristaltic action of the rectum. Most healthy persons have a regular elimination, or bowel movement, daily. Regular movements at other intervals, even every two or three days, may be perfectly normal.

How can you help your digestive system?

The organs of the digestive system are well supplied with natural protections and controls to keep them healthy and to help them work efficiently. The best way to prevent digestive upsets is to give the organs a chance to work naturally.

How do your feelings affect digestion? The flow of digestive juices may be influenced by your feelings. You have probably noticed your mouth "water" in the presence of appetizing foods and odors, or noticed a sudden dryness when you were frightened or angry. Have you ever had an upset stomach or a heavy feeling after eating when you were tired, or worried, or angry?

Mealtime should be as pleasant as possible. Every member of the family can help make it happy by coming to meals promptly and cheerfully, dressed neatly, with clean hands and face and well-brushed hair. Older boys and girls may enjoy helping to prepare attractive meals and keeping up a pleasant conversation at mealtime. Leave worries and quarrels to be settled somewhere else. Allow plenty of time to enjoy the food and companionship. A clean, attractive table, appetizing food, good manners, and pleasant talk help the body to digest food.

How can a good breakfast help? A regular schedule for eating is the first step in good digestion. The digestive tract, like the rest of the body, works better if it has regular alternating work and rest periods. Omitting or slighting any meal is likely to cause overloading at another meal. The food for the day should be fairly evenly divided between the three.

The longest time the body goes without food is between the evening meal and breakfast. Food eaten for breakfast must supply the energy for the day's activities. If you have a good breakfast you should be at your best during the morning hours. You will be rested and refreshed and supplied with plenty of fuel for all your cells. Fruits or fruit juice supply energy almost immediately. Why? Other foods digest more slowly and continue furnishing food to the cells over a longer period of time.

Unfortunately, breakfast is the meal many people think they can do without. Many people omit breakfast. Many have a quick breakfast of poor foods. Some girls and boys claim they have no appetite for breakfast. They

Are you an expert camper? How can you keep healthy and happy on a camping trip? What kind of a routine helps to prevent illness?

try to do their morning's work without supplying their muscles and nerves with food for energy.

Appetite is partly habit. You can improve a sluggish appetite for breakfast. You can help by following a morning schedule that allows you plenty of time for eating. Good stimulants to appetite are light exercise, a bath, or a drink of water on rising. A little thoughtfulness and a few minutes of your time can also help other members of your family get off to a good start in the morning.

Many boys and girls take pride in contributing to family efficiency and happiness by preparing and serving good attractive breakfasts. Fruit, cereal, toast, and a milk drink are easy to prepare and offer many ways of providing variety. Occasional additions of hot breads, eggs, or bacon can make breakfast the most enjoyable meal of the day. Good breakfasts make you cheerful, efficient, and alert all day. They even improve your personality. How?

What other habits help? During the first half-hour or so after a meal, the stomach needs extra blood to work on large quantities of food. Strenuous exercise which draws blood to the muscles and away from the stomach may delay digestion and cause discomfort and incomplete digestion.

Your body will be more comfortable and efficient, and you will get more good from your food, if your schedule allows plenty of time for meals. Give yourself time to clean up and calm down before meals. Eat slowly and enjoy your meal. Give your food a chance to digest by avoiding strenuous exercise after meals. What kinds of activities would be sensible?

You can form the habit of choosing and enjoying foods that help you to keep healthy. You do not have to eat the things advertisers tempt you with. Eating between meals satisfies hunger. It may cause a person to fail to eat foods he needs. If you eat between meals, be smart. Eat some foods that supply you with proteins, vitamins, and minerals, as well as energy. Eat something that digests easily. Drink a glass of milk or eat some fruit. Fruits are really "glamour" foods. Many of them were the highest-priced delicacies a few years ago. Get acquainted with all kinds.

Fresh fruits and vegetables and

Encyclopedia Britannica Films

Good foods to take along on a hike or picnic provide quick energy and a good share of the day's proteins, carbohydrates, minerals, and vitamins. What is wrong with the lunch in the picture?

181

whole-grain cereals help digestion and elimination because they contain bulky indigestible parts which stimulate peristalsis. How? They also contain vitamin B, which is important in maintaining muscle tone in the intestines.

Habits of sitting and standing tall allow blood to circulate freely to digestive organs and give the organs room to work. Exercise which involves muscles in the waist and abdomen helps to maintain muscle tone.

How can you help your body eliminate wastes? Some regularity of elimination is necessary for good health. If all the digestive organs are working well, evacuation of bowels is regular and natural.

Irregular or delayed elimination is called constipation. Many people have an unnecessary fear of constipation, probably the result of exaggerations in advertisements for laxatives. Constipation is not a disease, but a symptom or signal of something wrong. If the other symptoms mentioned in the ads —headache, nervousness, bad breath, coated tongue, loss of appetite, and "tired feeling"—really do occur, a physician should be consulted to locate and treat the cause.

Constipation usually is caused by loss of muscle tone in the intestines. Such weakness may be caused by eating too much, by drinking too little water, by a poorly selected diet, by lack of exercise, by irregular habits of elimination, or by too frequent use of laxatives.

Habitual use of laxatives will increase the tendency to constipation. Harsh laxatives may irritate the bowel. Some laxatives may cause intestinal muscles to depend upon them

for extra stimulation. Muscles lose their tone and their power to respond to natural stimulation.

The best way to prevent or cure constipation is to establish good habits of diet, exercise, and elimination.

Because of peristaltic action, elimination is usually easier 15 or 20 minutes after eating. Most people find it easy to establish the habit of having a bowel movement after breakfast each day. Peristaltic action started by eating breakfast continues into the rectum and helps remove material which has accumulated during the night and preceding day.

Daily meals which include plenty of roughage and water are an aid to regularity. Fibers from fruit, vegetables, and whole grains provide necessary bulk or roughage. Very harsh rough fibers may irritate the intestinal tract.

What causes indigestion? We are not conscious of digestion if it proceeds as it should. An uncomfortable feeling, a pain, or any other digestive disturbance is abnormal. Digestive disturbances are usually warnings of incorrect eating. A coated tongue, canker sores, headache, belching, heartburn, or feeling of discomfort or pain may mean too much or too little food, wrong type of food, contaminated food, improper eating habits, or a clogged intestinal tract.

One of the commonest causes of indigestion is gas on the stomach. Some air is always swallowed with food. When more than usual is present it causes an uncomfortable feeling of fullness. Sometimes reverse peristaltic waves from the stomach expel excess gas back into the esophagus and mouth to cause belching. Ex-

182

cess gas may be formed in the stomach by the action of bacteria, causing some foods to ferment.

Some bacteria are always present in the intestines. They act on food to produce various substances, mostly harmless. Sometimes harmful bacteria enter the alimentary canal with contaminated food or drink. Food and drink may become contaminated in various ways. Milk may contain germs of tuberculosis, typhoid fever, diphtheria, septic sore throat, dysentery, undulant fever, or diarrhea. The possible dangers from the presence of any of these bacteria may be greatly reduced by pasteurization.

Meat may carry germs of paratyphoid fever, botulism, tuberculosis, or the parasitic worms—tapeworm and Trichinella. Inspection by federal, state, and local health agencies helps to eliminate diseased meat and other bad meat from the food supply. The purchaser of meat should always look for the government stamp that reads "U. S. Inspected and Passed." Thorough cooking is an additional safeguard against disease germs or parasitic worms in meat.

Any food may become contaminate during preparation, storage, or handling. Shops and restaurants that handle food should be inspected and supervised to insure sanitary conditions. Medical examinations should be required of people who handle food. Many foods, especially milk products such as custards and cream pies, should be kept cold. Both in the home and in public eating places, communicable diseases may be carried from person to person on unscalded dishes.

You can help protect yourself from

Denver Bureau of Health and Hospitals

Pasteurization destroys the disease-carrying germs which may be present in milk. One method holds milk at a temperature of 143° Fahrenheit for 30 minutes. Newer methods heat milk rapidly to 161° Fahrenheit for 15 seconds. Milk is then cooled quickly to below 50°. Pasteurization does not change taste, odor, digestibility, or food value of milk.

digestive infections and upsets. Buy from stores that handle food in a sanitary manner. Thoroughly wash any food that is to be eaten raw. Cook meat, especially pork, thoroughly. Use only pasteurized milk. Use only water that has been tested and approved, or boiled. Wash your hands thoroughly with soap and water before handling food. Use food soon after purchasing or keep it stored in a cold place. Never eat any food that looks or smells suspicious.

Any foreign material may irritate the intestines and cause pain. Pain may cause the body to hasten elimination and material will be eliminated in a watery state. This condition is called diarrhea. Like vomiting, it is one of the body's ways of protecting itself by expelling harmful material quickly.

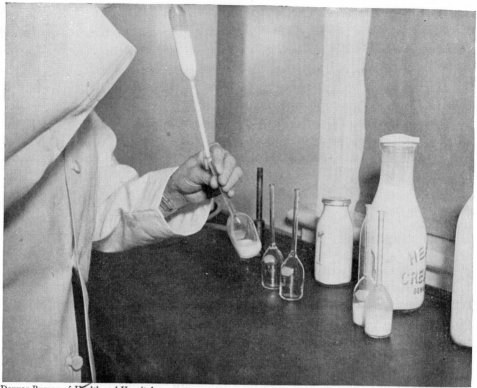

Denver Bureau of Health and Hospitals

Milk sold by dairies should be inspected and graded. What are the laws in your community regarding the sale and labelling of milk?

Heartburn is an irritation of the lower end of the esophagus near the heart. It is caused by an upward movement of digestive juices in the stomach, often combined with the expulsion of gas.

Most digestive disturbances are temporary. If they persist for several hours, or occur repeatedly, a physician should be consulted. Most of them can be avoided by habits of cleanliness, regularity of elimination, and moderation in eating.

What about medicines? The digestive system is much too complicated for you to "doctor." Indigestion, constipation, and other upsets may be due to many causes. Pain or other symptoms of indigestion may be caused by lack of any of the digestive juices from the stomach, liver, pancreas, or intestine; by loss of muscular tone; by diet deficiencies; by poor circulation; by abnormal growths; by introducing harmful and unnecessary medicines that interfere with natural controls; by nervous stimulation; and by a variety of other defects. Only a trained physician can diagnose (find) the real *cause* of digestive trouble and help you restore the natural functioning of the body.

Patent medicines and home remedies usually treat the symptom, not

184

the cause. They may be useless but harmless. In such cases the natural protections of the body work. The patient recovers as he naturally would have recovered without the medicine. The medicine was just an unnecessary expense.

Sometimes medicines are harmful. Medicines that you buy without consulting a doctor may irritate delicate or injured parts of the body. They may deaden pain so that necessary skilled treatment of the cause of the pain is delayed. If you have a pain that persists for several hours or returns at frequent intervals, find out what causes it. See a physician.

What about appendicitis? If you study the drawing on page 177, you will see near the beginning of the large intestine a small curved projection or pouch called the appendix. The appendix may develop infection and inflammation known as appendicitis. When the appendix is inflamed, pain may be felt in any part of the abdomen before it finally centers in the region near the appendix. The intestine will probably constrict to prevent food from passing and further irritating the appendix. The patient may be constipated. The use of heat, massage, or a laxative may further irritate or even rupture (break) the appendix. A ruptured appendix releases bacteria which may spread through the whole body cavity and cause death. Physicians estimate that 7000 lives might be saved each year if individuals would not use laxatives for abdominal pains. So this is a serious example of the use of home remedies that may cause death.

Remember that the symptoms of appendicitis are usually persistent abdominal pain, nausea, and fever. In any abdominal pain, do not use a laxative, massage, or hot-water bottle. If pain persists, call a doctor.

How can you care for your teeth? Chewing is an important part of digestion and is almost completely under your control. You can get more good out of your food and make the work of your digestive system easier, if you chew each mouthful of food slowly and thoroughly. Gulping down large mouthfuls of food without proper chewing may cause indigestion. Why? It makes you an unattractive and unpleasant companion at meals.

You can do a much more attractive and efficient job of chewing if you have a full set of sound, even teeth. A clean, healthy mouth with straight, sound teeth is well worth the time and effort it requires. It improves your appearance and personality as well as your health. When your mouth and teeth are well cared for, you feel more comfortable and self-confident, smile more often, and present a more pleasing appearance.

The part of each tooth visible above the gums is protected by a layer of *enamel,* the hardest substance in the body. Below the gums each tooth has one or more *roots* which holds it securely in place. The main body of the tooth is *dentine.* In the center is the *pulp cavity* containing nerves and blood vessels.

Probably the most important factor in maintaining a healthy mouth and good teeth is diet. Teeth are built from the minerals calcium and phosphorus, with the help of vitamins A, C, and D. Vitamins A and C also play a part in keeping the mucous membranes

185

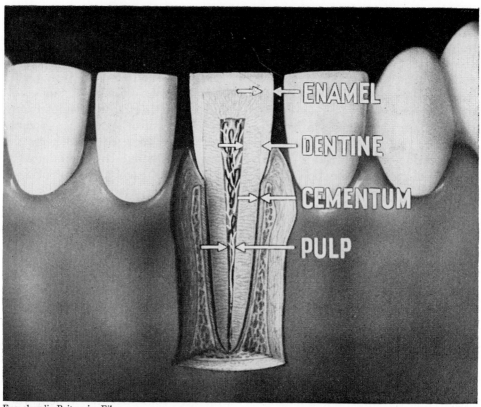

The hardest substance in the body, enamel, protects the visible part of your teeth. Enamel may be broken accidentally or be dissolved by acids produced when bacteria in the mouth act on sugar. How can you protect tooth enamel?

of the mouth and throat healthy, and in keeping the gums firm. If you eat all the different kinds of foods you need for the growth, repair, and general good health of your whole body, you will supply your teeth with plenty of building materials. Especially important are daily supplies of milk, fresh fruit, green vegetables, oranges, and tomatoes.

Special attention may be necessary to get adequate supplies of vitamin D. If you are not exposed to sunlight every day, you may need some food especially enriched with vitamin D, such as vitamin D milk or cod-liver oil. Canned or evaporated milk often has vitamin D added to it. Look for such information on the label.

Are baby teeth important? Teeth develop in the gums long before they come into their permanent positions. The structure of temporary, or baby, teeth is determined in part before birth. The 20 teeth in the first set generally have appeared by the time a child is three years old. Between the ages of six and twelve, temporary teeth are replaced by permanent teeth. New molars erupt to bring the

Good teeth depend upon both diet and care. Why?

number of teeth in the permanent set to 32. The last molars, the 4 wisdom teeth, may not appear until you are between seventeen and twenty-five years old.

It is important to keep temporary teeth in good condition. They not only maintain a child's appearance and comfort, but maintain a proper shape to the jaw and help permanent teeth to come in straight. If the teeth in the upper and lower jaw meet accurately in biting and chewing, the *occlusion* (meeting) is said to be good.

Proper occlusion is important. Irregularly spaced teeth are difficult to keep clean. They chew less efficiently. They are more likely to decay. Poor digestion, defective speech, and unnatural facial expression often result from defects in jaws and teeth.

Teeth that are irregular may be straightened by the dentist. Naturally this is a slow process. Straightening is more easily accomplished while an individual is young. Why?

How can you prevent tooth decay? Tooth decay is still the physical de-

fect found most often among boys and girls. The causes of tooth decay are not well understood. The tendency to decay has been blamed on improper diet, lack of exercise in chewing, and excessive sugar.

One favorite theory is that bacteria, which are always present in the mouth, work on sugar to produce an acid which dissolves small areas of enamel. Once the hard enamel dissolves, bacteria enter the tooth, and decay progresses rapidly.

Theoretically we could prevent decay by (1) making the teeth harder, (2) preventing acids from forming, (3) neutralizing the acids, and (4) keeping the mouth scrupulously

Regular brushing helps to keep your teeth sound and attractive. It removes food particles and prevents unattractive accumulations of tartar. What is tartar? How may it be removed?

187

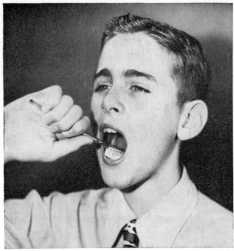

Brushing the inside and chewing surfaces of your teeth removes food from crevices and helps to prevent decay and bad breath. Why is it best to brush your teeth immediately after eating?

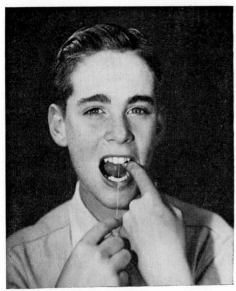

Dental floss helps to remove food particles from surfaces not reached by a toothbrush.

clean. Scientists are experimenting with all these methods.

A good diet makes teeth harder. Individuals with a diet deficient in calcium or vitamins A, C, or D often develop dental troubles. A good diet is necessary for the health of gums, roots, and living parts of the teeth.

Interesting experiments are being carried on to see if a mineral called *fluorine* will prevent tooth decay. There seems to be less decay in communities where a certain small amount of fluorine is in the drinking water. In some places dentists are painting the teeth of boys and girls with solutions containing fluorine. It is believed that the fluorine acts on the structure of the tooth to harden enamel during the years when the teeth develop. You may want to get the latest scientific reports of fluorine from your dentist or some other reliable authority. Are newspapers and popular magazines reliable scientific authorities?

For people whose teeth are already formed, the main hope for preventing decay seems to be in controlling what comes in contact with the teeth. Much evidence seems to indicate that sugar may be one of the main causes of decay.

Acid is produced in the mouth almost immediately when sugar is eaten. To prevent the destruction of enamel, teeth should be cleaned immediately after eating sugar or carbohydrates. In other words, teeth should be cleaned after every meal. Some toothpastes and powders have been developed to neutralize the acids. A thorough cleaning and rinsing with clear water or a solution of

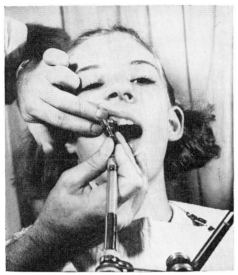

A dentist can remove accumulated tartar from your teeth. He can detect small cavities and stop decay before it has a chance to cause much damage. When were your teeth examined? How often should they be examined?

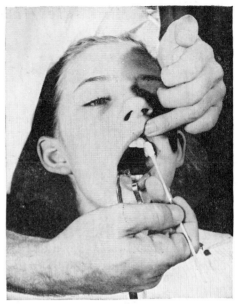

The dentist is painting teeth with a fluoride solution. Research evidence indicates that teeth treated with fluoride during the growing period are more resistant to decay.

salt and soda is just as effective in eliminating enamel-dissolving acids. *When* you clean your teeth is more important than *what* you use. If you cannot brush your teeth after eating, you can at least rinse your mouth thoroughly with clear water.

The best method of cleaning teeth and stimulating circulation in the gums are pictured on pages 187 and 188. The important points to remember are to be thorough and to be careful. Take enough time to clean all the surfaces. Be especially watchful for those tiny crevices in molars and the spaces between teeth where food is likely to lodge. Brush away from the gums, and use dental floss carefully in order not to injure delicate gum tis-

sue. Clean teeth look and feel better. They contribute to a fresh taste in your mouth and to a pleasant breath.

Even when you give your teeth all the materials they need and keep them clean, you need to see a dentist regularly. Only a dentist can find and repair decayed places and straighten crooked teeth. If you visit him twice a year he can repair defects when they are just beginning and save you much grief and expense.

Pyorrhea is a disease of the gums and bones around the buried parts of the teeth. It often causes teeth to be lost. Normal gums are pink, dense, resist pressure, and have a flat edge. Bleeding gums should be a warning for you to consult your dentist.

Reviewing the chapter

I

You should answer "yes" to the following questions.

1. Do you eat slowly and chew food well?
2. Do you avoid hard exercise immediately after a meal?
3. Do you eat at regular times?
4. Do you avoid eating when excited or tired?
5. Do you wash your hands before eating?
6. Do you brush your teeth after eating?
7. Do you rinse your mouth well after eating if you cannot brush your teeth?
8. Do you have regular bowel movements?

II

Complete the following sentences by supplying the missing words. Do NOT WRITE IN THIS BOOK.

1. Digestion begins in the ....
2. Food is pushed along the digestive tract by a wavelike motion called ....
3. Digested food in the small intestine is absorbed by the ....
4. Organs of the alimentary canal are ...., ..., ..., ..., ...
5. Some foods like .... digest very quickly.
6. Digestive juices from the .... and .... enter the alimentary canal to aid digestion.

III

What would you think, say, or do in the following situations?

1. If you were very excited or tired just before mealtime?
2. If someone started a heated argument during dinner?
3. If your friends wanted to swim or play ball right after lunch?
4. If someone in your family had a severe abdominal pain, and you were asked to go buy a laxative?
5. If you were troubled with constipation?
6. If your family left the care of your teeth up to you?

Other activities

1. Look through a microscope at bacteria from the hands.
2. Demonstrate attractive table settings.
3. Demonstrate and practice the proper way to hold and use table silver.
4. Demonstrate and practice acceptable table manners.
5. Take a trip to a grocery or market to see a variety of meats, vegetables, and fruits.
6. Make a collection of labels from packaged food. Discuss the information to be found on the labels.
7. Visit a dairy.
8. Make a map showing the sources of food you had for breakfast, or lunch, or dinner.
9. Practice choosing meals from restaurant menu cards.
10. Plan "budget meals" to serve at home.
11. Experiment with foods kept refrigerated and at room temperature to see which keeps longer.

12. Collect pictures showing attractive ways of serving foods.

Reading to help you grow up

Interesting experiments to show how food is digested are found in the titles listed below:

How Your Body Works by Herman and Nina Schneider.
A Sound Body by Charters and others.

For good readers:
Biology for Better Living by Bayles and Burnett. The chapter "How the Body Uses Foods and Removes Wastes" is helpful.

Films to help you understand

Alimentary Tract. Encyclopedia Britannica Films.
Digestion of Foods. Encyclopedia Britannica Films.
Save Those Teeth. Encyclopedia Britannica Films.
Teeth (Development and Care). Encyclopedia Britannica Films.

H. Armstrong Roberts

The ball carrier is able to gain because other members of his team carry out their assignments. Every part of your body depends upon other parts. How can they all work together?

Picture Preview:

Chapter 11

Muscles learn to obey orders and to work together by practice. Anyone learning new movements is awkward at first. How can you overcome awkwardness?

Philip Gendreau

Exercise develops harmonious action between muscles and nerves. It makes it possible for you to use your muscles easily and effectively. What games do you play?

A complicated network of nerves in the brain helps us to receive impressions from our senses, to think, and to send orders to our muscles.

Nerves and muscles working together make you a skillful, alert, safe bicycle rider. Can you control your bicycle well? Do you notice and obey traffic signals and laws?

193

Chapter 11

HOW IS YOUR BODY CONTROLLED?

Have you ever thought about all the activity that goes on in your body? To remain alive, all the billions of cells in your body must constantly be supplied with food and oxygen, have wastes carried away, maintain a favorable temperature, and grow and repair themselves. But your body is more than a machine, mechanically making the same set of motions over and over. It is an extremely sensitive, responsive organism, continually making new adjustments to changing conditions. Even the motions that seem most automatic, like your heartbeat, breathing, digestion, and balancing to walk and stand, are constantly changing.

Some of the changes are easily observed. You know how your heart and breathing speed up when you are exercising. Have you ever noticed the tiny balancing movements a person makes even when standing perfectly still?

Scientists have observed thousands of other small but important adjustments your body makes in response to changing conditions. The nervous system is responsible for all these.

To stay alive all the billions of cells in your body must be able to work together. They must be able to communicate with each other, to act as a team. Every cell must do the right thing at the right time. Special kinds of cells, called nerves, stimulate cells to act and enable parts of the body to communicate with each other.

Nerve cells are organized into a system, somewhat as soldiers are organized into an army. In special centers nerves come together to communicate with each other. From the centers orders go out to proper groups of cells to cause them to act. The nerve centers communicate with each other in increasingly complex centers. The final high command for voluntary actions is the brain.

Your nervous system makes the other parts of your body usable. Knowledge of how the nervous system works and what can be done to help it work efficiently is important to everyone.

194

Looking ahead

Questions and suggestions

1. What does "voluntary" mean?

2. What voluntary movements are you making at present? What muscles are you using that would be relaxed if you were asleep?

3. What involuntary activities is your body carrying on?

4. What is co-ordination? Can you give some examples? How can members of a football team work together? How can units of the armed forces work together? How can the billions of cells in your body work together?

5. Have someone tap you sharply with the side of his hand just below the kneecap. What happens to your leg? Do you know any other responses your body makes automatically?

6. Write your name. Now try to write it using your other hand. Do you find it hard to do? Why is there a difference in control and co-ordination?

7. Have you learned some new skill recently? How did you go about it?

8. Test your own neuromuscular control by trying to do the following:

(a) Lace a shoe while standing on one foot.

(b) Walk 30 feet on a chalkline or narrow rail.

(c) With eyes blindfolded stand on your left foot, right heel against left knee, arms horizontal, and balance yourself. Repeat, not using your arms.

Committee planning

1. Everyone in class can experiment by learning a new skill. You can learn to knit, to do a simple dance step, to throw a ball through a basket, to ride a bicycle, or to do something else that interests you. Notice your false moves and tensions, the steps by which you acquire skill. Everyone can teach someone else a new skill.

2. Do muscular co-ordination, skill, alertness, and reaction time have anything to do with safety? The safety committee can arrange a demonstration or exhibit to show skills and safety rules for bicycling, walking in traffic, and using public transportation.

3. The speaker's committee can invite an athlete, dancer, or coach to explain how particular skills and co-ordinations are learned.

Reading

This chapter is long and parts of it require slow, careful reading. However, you should be learning to concentrate and to read difficult material. Follow these four steps in reading this chapter:

1. Read rapidly through the entire chapter to get the main ideas.

2. Then read again slowly for details. Try to understand each topic before you go on to the next.

3. When you finish reading, test yourself. Restudy some parts if necessary.

4. Then try some of the extra readings or activities suggested.

How do nerves control your body?

So much about the human nervous system is still unknown that many theories have been advanced to explain how and why the nervous system acts in originating and controlling thoughts, feelings, and actions. If you are interested in the experiments, evidence, and reasoning back of these theories, you can read some of the books described on page 215.

Scientists have experimented and collected much data. They know enough facts to be able to offer helpful advice about taking care of your nervous system. They can also offer some suggestions about learning and about forming habits.

What is the nervous system? Your nervous system is really a double-control system. One set of nerves and command centers, called the central nervous system, enables you to direct your body as you will in all its activities. The other set of nerves and centers, called the autonomic system, automatically handles all the vital functions (those necessary to maintaining life and well-being).

The *central nervous system* coordinates and controls the voluntary muscles, the sense organs, and the mind. The central system brings you into contact with the world and enables you to respond to it. The parts of the central system are the brain, the spinal cord, and the nerves extending from them. Sometimes it is called the *cerebrospinal* or *voluntary system*.

The *autonomic* division of the nervous system operates without conscious direction to control activities essential to life itself. It controls activities of the internal organs. Among other activities it regulates digestion, circulation, the sweat glands, and the pupils of the eyes. The autonomic system consists of the small, self-controlled centers and the nerves extending from them.

Some of the autonomic nerves are centered in two chains of ganglia on either side of the spinal cord. Other autonomic nerves center in a network called a "plexus." The solar plexus just below the stomach is one of these nerve centers. A blow to the pit of the stomach may temporarily paralyze these nerves and cause a person to be unable to get his breath.

Autonomic centers, although not directly controlled by the central nervous system, are connected to it. They also have some sort of complicated relationship with the endocrine glands in the body. Thoughts, feelings, and sensations influence the activities of the internal organs. Have you ever had thoughts or feelings make your heart race or your hands perspire? Of course, the internal or-

Ewing Galloway

The nervous system may be compared to a system of telephone wires leading into a central exchange—the brain. Communication is broken down whenever any part of the system is damaged.

196

gans in turn influence our feelings and moods. How?

What is the spinal cord? The brain and spinal cord are a complicated network of nerves. They enable you to move, to feel, and to think. They occupy the best protected locations in the body, inside the bony protection of the spinal column and the skull.

The spinal cord runs through a channel in the backbone from the lower part of the back to the brain. It is a collection of nerves enclosed in a tough outer covering. The spaces between the large nerve cable and the outer covering are filled with a salty fluid (spinal fluid) which protects and cushions the cord from shocks and jars.

Pairs of nerves branch out to parts of the body from openings between each two successive vertebrae. The openings are plenty large. The nerves are well protected by layers of fat and membranes and a tough covering. In accidents where there is a chance that the backbone may be broken, the victim should be kept perfectly quiet to avoid possible injury to the spinal cord.

What are the jobs of the brain? Where the spinal cord enters the skull it widens and is known as the brain stem. The lower part of the brain stem, next to the spinal cord, is called the *medulla oblongata*. The medulla is the nerve center in charge of breathing and rate of heartbeat.

Above the medulla the brain stem bulges more to form the little brain, or *cerebellum*. The cerebellum is the center that controls and co-ordinates muscles in much practiced and well-known movements like balancing, walking, sitting, writing, and driving.

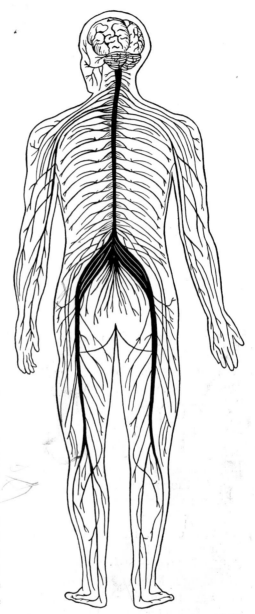

The central nervous system consists of the brain, the spinal cord, and the nerves branching from them.

Feelings, emotions, and urges to act originate here.

The largest part of the brain, the *cerebrum*, fills all the skull above the

197

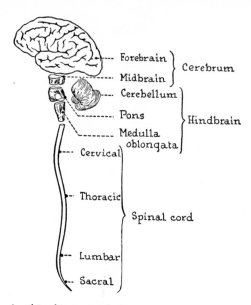

Forebrain ⎫
Midbrain ⎬ Cerebrum
Cerebellum ⎫
Pons ⎬ Hindbrain
Medulla oblongata ⎭
Cervical
Thoracic
Spinal cord
Lumbar
Sacral

In this diagram of the nervous system the nervous parts of the brain and spinal cord have been separated from one another.

level of the eyes. The cerebrum is the center for the highest type of mental activity—memory, learning, consciousness, judgment, conscience, will power, and reason. The most outstanding difference between human beings and other living things is this part of the brain. The cerebrum in man is so much more complex than any other brain that it is practically a different organ. No one knows how brain cells act to produce mental activities like reasoning, judgment, and will power. Man's ability to reason, to judge, and to do as he wills affects all his behavior. It makes him more free than other living things, but it gives him greater responsibilities.

An intricate network of nerves connects the various control centers of the nervous system to each other and to sense organs, muscles, and glands all over the body.

What is a nerve? Like all other parts of the body, the nervous system is composed of cells. The little white cord we see in chicken legs, for instance, and call a nerve is really thousands of nerve cells, wrapped together like the wires in a telephone cable. Like other cells, nerves are alive, require food and oxygen to burn for energy, and must get rid of wastes.

A nerve cell has a special shape in order to perform its special work of carrying messages. It is long and thin. A single cell may be long enough to run from your toe to the middle of your spine. Some nerve cells in the nerve centers are microscopic in length and make connections with other small adjoining cells.

Each nerve cell is called a *neuron*. It consists of a cell body with two or more branchlike fibers extending from it. The cell body is the life center of a nerve cell. Branches die when cut off from the cell body. The cell body remains alive, and may even, in a very long time, grow new branches. The cell bodies are located mostly in the central nervous system. Here they are well protected by the bones of the skull and the spinal column. Cell bodies are gray in color and make up the "gray matter" of the brain and spinal cord.

From its protected location in the central nervous system, each cell body extends a nerve fiber to a sense organ or muscle. The fibers are like tiny wires, so fine that it would take about 5000 of them side by side to measure an inch. Other branching fibers extend from the cell body toward other cells in the nerve center.

Thousands of nerve fibers are

wrapped together to make what we call a nerve. Some nerve bundles are as thick as a pencil lead and contain millions of fibers. Each fiber is protected by a fatty cover or sheath of thin membrane. The sheaths give the whole bundle a smooth white appearance.

Nerve fibers connecting the central nervous system and the sense organs and muscles can carry messages in only one direction. Nerves carrying messages from sense organs to the nerve center are called *sensory* nerves. Nerves carrying orders from the nerve centers to the muscles are called *motor* nerves.

If a sensory nerve is damaged, the part of the body it serves is without sensation or feeling. Sensory nerves may be made inactive temporarily by certain drugs which produce *anesthesia* or loss of feeling. If a motor nerve is destroyed or injured, the muscles it serves will be paralyzed (unable to move).

How do nerves carry messages? What are nerve messages, or impulses? How do they act? No one knows. They are thought to be like tiny electric currents traveling along a wire. Scientists believe they travel more slowly than electricity, probably a little over 200 miles per hour.

When you put your finger on a hot stove, sensory nerves ending in the skin are stimulated. The message travels along the nerves to the spinal cord. In the cord the message is transferred to other nerves. Motor nerves which receive the impulse carry the message to a muscle in your arm, causing it to contract to jerk your hand away. This simple reaction, called a *reflex*, does not need direc-

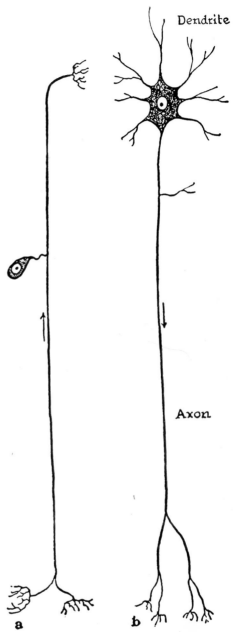

Dendrite

Axon

a   b

Nerve cells consist of a cell body with branching fibers, like a tree. Sensory nerves (a) carry impulses from a sense organ. Motor neurons (b) carry impulses to muscles. How can messages from sense organs cause muscles to respond?

199

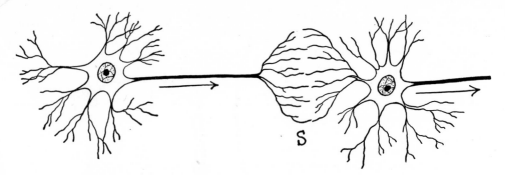

A synapse (S) is the place where the branches of one neuron meet branches from many other neurons. The impulse may jump to one or more of the nearby neurons.

tions from the brain. Nerves going to the brain carry the message to higher centers to be recorded and interpreted.

Very few responses are as simple as the one described. Most of the time a person does not respond so quickly or so predictably. You cannot be sure how a person will act in most situations. The same stimulus may cause different actions. Apparently nerve impulses do not have to follow a set path through the central nervous system. There are many possible connections.

Several paths are available to nerve impulses because the nerve fibers split into branches at the ends. These endings, or terminals, resemble the frayed ends of a rope. In the control centers, the terminals of one neuron make connections with terminals from many other cells.

According to the most popular theory of nerve functioning, the nerve branches come very close to, but do

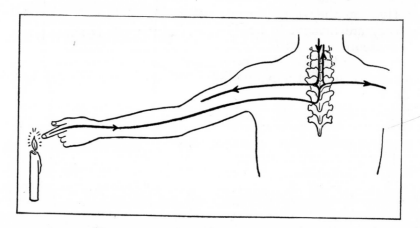

When you touch a hot object, the impulse travels from the sense organ in the finger along a sensory nerve to the spinal cord. There it connects with other nerves. Muscles of the arm jerk the hand away even before the sensation of pain is felt.

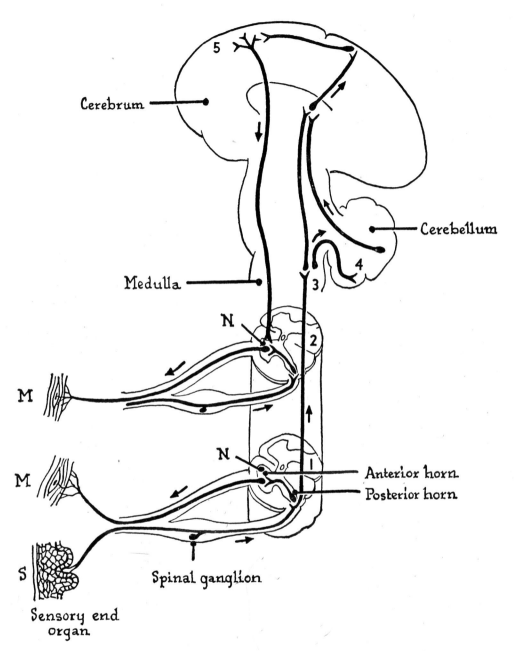

Cerebrum

Cerebellum

Medulla

N

Anterior horn
Posterior horn

Spinal ganglion

Sensory end
organ

An impulse from a sense organ (S) has many pathways open to it. (1) It may transfer to a motor nerve in the spinal cord. (2) It may travel along nerves in the spinal cord to the medulla where it is transferred to other motor nerves. (3) It may reach the medulla, or (4) the cerebellum, or (5) the areas of sensation and thought in the cerebrum before it passes to a motor nerve. What kind of reaction takes place at (1)? At (5)?

not touch, branches of other cells. The microscopic gaps between nerve endings are called *synapses.* Impulses traveling along a nerve can jump a synapse, just as an electric current can spark across a small gap. Nobody knows what causes them to jump one gap instead of another. Once a gap has been crossed, it apparently is easier to cross thereafter. Repeatedly crossing the same gap seems to make a path, so some responses are easier than others thereafter. This is the way a habit is formed.

Some nerve cells in the central nervous system seem to serve as switches or relays. They make connections between incoming sensory impulses and outgoing motor impulses. These relay nerves are also connected with many other nerves in the brain and spinal cord. An impulse from a sense organ has many paths open to it. It may transfer directly to a motor nerve cell in the spinal cord. It may travel along other nerves to any part of the brain before it is transferred to a motor nerve.

How are movements controlled?

How the nervous system produces precise yet ever-changing responses to ever-changing conditions is still beyond our understanding. Scientists believe that no simple explanation is possible. The system as a whole somehow governs the activities of all parts of the system. A person's feelings, purpose, insight, and will are powerful determiners of his actions, even of many actions that seem automatic.

Are some actions automatic? Activities of internal organs are governed by the autonomic system. By chemicals in the blood or by other means, autonomic centers are alerted to send out orders to vital organs. These paths seem to be fixed and responses are automatic and predictable.

Some other responses seem automatic. Certain situations call forth the same quick reaction from all normal human beings. You blink your eye when an object comes near it. You pull a hand or foot away from

heat or a sharp knife. These are examples of such automatic or reflex actions. The knee jerk is another familiar example of a reflex. Has a doctor tapped sharply just below your kneecap during an examination? What happened? Doctors sometimes do this to test the functioning of the nerves of the legs and the lower part of the spinal cord.

A reflex action does not have to be learned. Apparently the pathways are already formed when you are born. In some instances a reflex cannot be controlled because the connections between sensory and motor nerves are made so quickly in the spinal cord that the brain does not have time to send out a controlling impulse. If you unexpectedly touch a hot stove, reflex action enables you to jerk your hand away before your brain even records the sensation of pain. Most reflex actions can be controlled if the brain has advance knowledge of what is going to happen. Can a person hold on to something hot deliberately?

Fortunately, we have only a few responses as automatic as the knee jerk. Human beings can guide their actions, vary them, learn new ones, and choose appropriate ones to accomplish what they want.

What movements are learned? In a reflex act the simplest possible nerve connections are made. The path followed by the nerve impulse is probably (1) sense organ, (2) sensory nerve, (3) central nerve cell in spinal cord, (4) motor nerve, and (5) muscle. Cells in the brain seem not to be involved, except to record the event and sometimes to start other actions.

Very few acts are this simple. Most nerve pathways are formed by conscious direction and by practice. Nerve cells in the brain control the transfer of impulses. For example, imagine you are about to catch a ball. Your eyes send impressions of the ball to your brain. Somehow your brain recalls other experiences you have had catching a ball. It judges speed and location and decides on appropriate action. It switches the impulse to the proper motor nerves. If the brain's judgment is correct, and the muscles in your arms and hands are well co-ordinated, you catch the ball.

Watch small children of different ages catch a ball. Notice how their judgment and co-ordination improve with experience. All your skills and habits have to be learned. Even a simple skill, like balancing in order to sit or to stand, must be learned. Balancing requires the co-ordination of many impulses originating from

Denver Public Schools

Rhythm is an important part of co-ordination and skill. Rhythmic movements are smoother and less tiring. Why? How is rhythm used by a football team, a boxer, or a swimmer?

the eyes, ears, joints, muscles, and pressure on the skin.

Human beings are born the most helpless of all creatures. They have to learn practically every response. Probably only the responses necessary to keep them alive have established pathways at birth. New-born infants make random, unco-ordinated movements. Even their eyes do not work together. If you have a chance watch an infant from day to day as he gradually learns to control his movements. Watch children of all ages as they develop skills and habits.

How are skills and habits learned? A skill is a learned ability to act easily, efficiently, and gracefully. Like a habit, it is a tendency to respond in a certain learned pattern of movements with little or no conscious control.

Denver Public Schools

Are you learning to use your hands with skill and precision? What tools or instruments can you use?

The first time a new connection is made in the nervous system many pathways are open. The connections seem to be made with some difficulty. The impulse must be guided by the brain to the proper motor nerves.

When you attempt some new movement, whether it is a forward pass or a new dance step, knitting or playing the piano, your motions are slow and awkward. They require undivided attention. If repeated many times, the movement becomes easy, graceful, and more automatic. It no longer requires all your attention.

Some scientists explain the learning of habits and skills by saying that nerve impulses establish pathways. Once an impulse crosses a synapse, the synapse is changed in some way. Other impulses can cross more easily. They will follow the old path in preference to a more difficult new path. Repeating an act many times establishes a fixed path something like a reflex. These scientists believe habits and skills are like chains of reflexes. One motion automatically sets off another one.

Many other scientists believe such an explanation is too mechanical. They point out that even a simple skill like catching a ball is not a fixed set of motions. Each catch is a slightly different series of motions precisely adjusted to a new set of conditions. Each catch requires observation and judgment and must be controlled by the brain.

Habits and skills are not set permanently. They can be controlled or changed by conscious direction and by practice. In some way a person's brain, mind, and purpose remain in control even of habits and skills.

Attempts to explain human behavior, actions, and learning are interesting. You may like to read more about them from the books described on page 215. If you do read, read critically. Remember that none of the theories is accepted by everyone. The same facts can be explained by different investigators in equally convincing ways. Facts can be fitted into many patterns, especially if many of the pieces are missing. You do not have to believe any theory just because the author of the book you are reading is convinced it is true.

Much of the evidence behind theories of human behavior is based on experiments with animals. The earliest research in any field is usually done with animals. Valuable information and clues are often obtained in this way. But theories based almost completely on animal experimentation are likely to lead to serious errors. Man is so much more complex than any other living thing, especially in the organization and influence of his mind and nervous system, that he is unique among living creatures.

Most scientists believe more and more that the nervous system as a whole somehow governs the activity of all parts of the system. Simple mechanical explanations cannot explain everything about a human being. Thinking and feelings are important influences on our nervous systems.

How can you control your nerves?

A person with good control of his nerves reacts quickly, but accurately and efficiently. He is the boss of his nervous system. Even under pressure he is cool and controlled.

What makes nerves fast? Good athletes have fast reactions. A good batter can follow the path of a ball along its route to the plate, judge its speed and path accurately, and react quickly to get a hit. How do abilities to play football or basketball, to box, or to drive a car depend upon fast and accurate reactions?

People differ in the speed with which they respond to stimuli. Some people respond more quickly than others. Their nervous system makes connections more rapidly. Can you think of some explanations for this fact? Do you think age, experience, training, or general health would have any effect?

The length of time required for a nerve impulse to get results is called the *reaction time*. It can be accurately measured. Using various devices found in the laboratory, scientists measure the time it takes a person to react to a stimulus. For example, they note the time it takes a person to press a buzzer after seeing the flash of a signal. Traffic experts have measured the time it takes a person to apply brakes after receiving the stimulus of a sound or a light.

Such tests show that some people respond more quickly than others. They also show that an individual's reaction time is affected by the condition of the blood supply to the nerves. A person's reactions are greatly slowed down by the presence of fatigue, narcotics, and alcohol. For example, an average driver takes one-fifth of a second to apply brakes after he receives a signal. After drinking a couple of teaspoons of alcohol in a glass of water, he takes twice as long. Fatigue has a similar effect. Persons whose nerve reactions have been slowed by fatigue are less accurate and efficient. They do less work. They are more likely to have accidents.

Nerves are quickly affected by lack of food or oxygen. Tests made by aviators show that at high altitudes lack of oxygen affects nerve co-ordination. A pilot's writing becomes illegible and he is unable to handle controls efficiently. Poor circulation or fatigue can also cause nerves to be poorly supplied with oxygen. Have you ever tried to thread a needle when you were very tired, or to throw a baseball when you were very cold?

Why are nerves jumpy? Even when you are asleep your nervous system is busy. It regulates the vital processes of digestion, breathing, heartbeat, and the flow of blood to various parts. When you are awake, the activity in your nervous system is greater than the activity in the busiest place you can think of. Your sense organs are bombarded by stimuli—sounds and noises, sights, odors, heat, cold, pressure, and pain. Your mental and emotional states—fear, joy, anger, worry, and resentment— also stimulate nerves.

Harold M. Lambert

Self-control is one of the marks of a good athlete. Feelings and thoughts affect your nerves, your co-ordination and control. How can you develop self-control?

Some people respond to many of the stimuli around them. They are distracted by every sight and sound, upset by every emotion. They seem unable to control their responses. They jump and wiggle, respond quickly and impulsively.

Other people are less jumpy. They are able to concentrate, to ignore small distracting sights and sounds and ideas. They can control their responses.

Increasing self-control is a mark of growing up. Self-control is necessary to improve skills, habits, and muscular co-ordination. The first steps in learning new skills are always accompanied by many unnecessary motions and tensions. To become skillful you must be able to check the unnecessary motions and relax the muscles not needed. Forming new habits often involves the breaking of old ones.

Inhibition, or the power to restrain movements, seems to come from the mind. Special nerves probably carry inhibiting impulses that prevent the spinal cord from sending out motor impulses even when strong stimuli are received. A person whose brain is not exerting good control will jump suddenly if a door slams.

Restraining impulses are important because they make possible almost complete self-control. Even some automatic responses, like a sneeze or cough, or withdrawing your hand from a painful stimulus, can be restrained by brain control.

Inhibition, or self-control, makes you the boss of your nervous system. You can control your own actions or change poor habits. Without self-control you become the slave of your habits. You block your own development. You respond automatically, thoughtlessly, and impulsively without applying your best knowledge and judgment.

It is as important to develop self-control as it is to develop skills and habits. You can develop self-control by thought and practice. You can develop habits of being alert, looking ahead, controlling your temper, and making your body respond to your judgment and will, just as you develop skills and habits of making home runs or brushing your teeth.

How do tea and coffee affect your nerves? Your nerves carry messages that cause the parts of your body to work slowly or rapidly. Anything that speeds up body activity is said to stimulate it. There are many natural stimulants that act to speed up the activities of the nervous system: food; sunshine; cool, fresh air; exercise; cleanliness; and happy feelings. They make you feel alert, sensitive to stimuli, and ready to respond.

H. Armstrong Roberts

Fresh, cool air, pleasant surroundings, and new experiences are natural stimulants. They give you a feeling of well being. Do you take part in some activities that are pleasantly stimulating?

Some drugs contain substances which stimulate the body. Some drugs are so powerful that even small amounts are too stimulating. They speed up bodily activity enough to cause fatigue. They overwork the nervous system. They cause nerves to become sensitive so they are difficult to control. Sense organs may thus be impressed by stimuli that ordinarily could be ignored.

You probably have noticed overstimulated people. Their muscles are tense. They are unable to rest or relax. Their nerves are so sensitive and so little subject to their control that they jump at unexpected sounds. Their movements are likely to be jerky and unco-ordinated. They are

likely to be touchy and irritable. An overstimulated person presents a striking contrast to the poised, relaxed, controlled person most of us would like to be.

Coffee and tea contain a stimulative drug called *caffeine*. Some soft drinks contain caffeine. Small amounts of caffeine, as much as contained in a cup or two of coffee, increase nervous activity. Larger amounts may interfere with nervous control and the ability to concentrate. In some people it causes headache, dizziness, and inability to sleep.

Regular drinking of tea and coffee by growing boys and girls is condemned by all medical opinion. Boys

207

and girls need food to supply energy and material for growth. They are learning self-control and need less, not more, stimulation. Any nervous or excitable person may suffer ill effects from even moderate amounts of tea and coffee. Moderate use of tea and coffee by stable grown people may cause little harm. Excessive amounts are probably bad for everyone. People who feel the need of stimulation would do better to get fresh air, rest, exercise, and some enjoyable relaxation.

How do other drugs affect you? Some drugs, called *narcotics*, act to slow down bodily activity. They particularly interfere with the working of nerve cells. They can cause nerve cells to stop working altogether. Some of them may be used to prevent sensory nerves from carrying pain messages. Others deaden parts of the central nervous system, beginning with the highest centers, judgment and meaning, and working down through the centers that control coordination and consciousness. Increased amounts may even affect the centers that control breathing and cause death.

Many narcotics are extremely valuable when administered carefully by skilled doctors. They may be used as anesthetics to relieve pain or to produce sleep. Most narcotics are extremely dangerous to use without medical supervision because they are habit forming.

Drugs such as morphine, cocaine, opium, and marihuana affect the central nervous system. When taken in sufficient quantities they may lead to complete lack of self-control. Normal people usually find drugs unpleasant.

Some weak and unstable personalities use drugs to dull their reason and sense of values. They want to escape from reality and from problems they do not want to face or are too weak to solve.

Everyone feels sure that he would never be so foolish as to become a drug addict. Actually you cannot be sure. People differ in their susceptibility to drugs just as they differ in other ways. The first use of a drug weakens self-control and makes it easier to acquire the drug habit.

Often drugs recommended by advertisements or by friends are taken to relieve weariness, pain, or mental suffering. They sometimes are taken to induce sleep. To an already upset nervous system they are particularly dangerous. The nervous system may very quickly come to depend upon drugs and be unable to get along without them.

Education and law enforcement are the most effective ways to protect people from dangerous and habit-forming drugs. The government rigidly controls the sale and the use of narcotics valuable as medicines. The sale or possession of marihuana is prohibited. Medicines containing habit-forming drugs must be plainly labeled. The United States Public Health Service provides special hospital treatment for addicts.

People need to protect themselves, too, by being aware of the dangers. They can avoid the first step toward addiction by carefully reading labels and by refusing to experiment. Unscrupulous people often try to make addicts of young people by giving them marihuana cigarettes. Boys and girls can protect themselves and others by being alert and informed about such dangers.

How does alcohol affect you? Contrary to common belief, alcohol is not a stimulant. Alcohol taken into the body in a drink passes directly from the stomach and small intestine into the blood stream and is carried to all parts of the body. It especially affects nerve cells, interfering with their ability to receive and pass on nerve impulses. Therefore, it is a *depressant* drug or a narcotic.

Nerves in the brain are affected first. Experiments show that even small amounts of alcohol interfere with a person's ability to judge, to tell how much time elapses between two events or which of two lights is brighter, or to criticize his own actions. The ability to do work requiring skill, speed, or accuracy is decreased. Other mental abilities such as reason, memory, and self-control are weakened. Increasing amounts affect more and more nerve centers. Senses are dulled, co-ordination impaired. Increased amounts of alcohol in the blood cause a person to stagger, to slur his words, and to lose his reasoning powers. With larger doses he may become unconscious or even die.

By depressing the higher nerve centers alcohol gives a false sense of stimulation. A man who becomes intoxicated loses judgment and self-control first. He thinks he is being witty and clever, moving more easily and rapidly. Actually experiments show that he makes more mistakes, is more awkward, tires more easily, and says and does things he would not do or approve with his normal reason and judgment.

Opinions differ very widely about drinking. All are agreed that alcohol can impair judgment, skill, speed, co-ordination, endurance, and self-control. People need to avoid alcohol when they are working. Some people handle machines and instruments so powerful and sensitive that the slightest move in the wrong direction or at the wrong time may cause serious damage. Automobile drivers, pilots, engineers, and skilled craftsmen of all kinds need all their mental and nervous ability. Doctors, judges, managers, public officials, and all others whose judgment and reasoning are important should not drink, since their work might be affected.

Alcohol is especially damaging to growing boys and girls. Their whole system is delicately balanced and undergoing many important changes. Their habits of co-ordination, judgment, and self-control are not well established. Even small amounts of alcohol may interfere with the establishment of sound physical, mental, and emotional balance.

How can you help your nerves work efficiently? Anyone who wants his body to respond quickly and accurately needs to know some of the factors that affect his nervous systems.

Like all other cells in the body, nerves need a constant supply of clean, nourishing blood. They need to obtain food and oxygen and have wastes removed.

Chapter 8 explains some ways you can help to keep all parts of your body supplied with blood. Useful health habits for this are tall, uncramped posture; loose clothing; balanced diet; vigorous exercise; and plenty of rest and sleep.

What foods are good for your nerves? Experiments indicate that a poor supply of vitamin B lowers the efficiency of the nervous system. Severe deficiencies cause such dangerous nerve disorders as polyneuritis and beri beri. You can help to keep your nerves working efficiently by eating foods containing good supplies of vitamin B. Vitamin B is found in many foods, but especially good supplies are present in milk, green leafy vegetables, and whole grains. Some breads and cereals are enriched with extra supplies of vitamin B. Read the labels on packages to make sure you are buying healthful foods.

In their natural form cereal grains are good sources of vitamin B. Whole grains like wheat and rice lose most of their vitamin B when they are refined. One of the reasons for the low supply of vitamin B in modern diet is the increased use of refined flours and cereals, sweets, and fats. All of these foods are low in vitamin B.

Vitamin B is not stored in the body. It must be provided daily. High, dry temperatures reduce the strength of vitamin B. Vitamin B dissolves in the water in which foods are cooked. Can you figure out ways to prepare foods to save vitamin B?

No foods are "nerve foods." To have good nerves you need all the kinds of food that make up a balanced diet. Your nerves depend upon other parts of your body. They cannot be healthy if other parts are not working well.

How can you protect your nerves from overwork? Modern living keeps nerves working overtime. The world is noisy and brightly lighted. It is full of dangers, excitement, difficult social relationships, and conflicting ideals and values. It constantly bombards our senses with stimuli, urges us to act, urges us to be charming and popular, and wants us to keep up with our neighbors. It attacks our ideals and standards, making us waver and worry.

We like life to be stimulating. We like to think and have feelings and to respond and act. Natural moderate stimulants, like fresh cool air, pleasant thoughts and sights and sounds, and new experiences, make us feel refreshed and invigorated.

Many stimuli, though, are harmful and unnecessary. Stimulation that is extreme, intense, or long continued tires the nervous system. Experiments have shown that fatigue lessens the efficiency of the nervous system. Tired people work more slowly and make more mistakes. Fatigue and overstimulation of the nervous system may even cause some diseases.

Strong or continuous stimulation weakens self-control. It may make a person irritable and impulsive. It may make him insensitive to simple, natural, less-intense stimulation. Often overstimulated people are not able to enjoy the quiet pleasures of friendly talks and games. They miss the opportunities to find beauty and pleasure in ordinary, everyday contacts with people and with nature. They are restless and unhappy.

One of the cruelest tortures is to give a person constant intense stimulation, with no opportunity to recover by sleeping. If you read accounts of the "third degree," used to break down a prisoner's morale, you will notice the same pattern: bright lights, sound, constant questioning, no sleep. Such torture will completely break down self-control and personality.

There are many ways of eliminating useless and harmful stimuli. Experiments by business and industry have produced evidence that people work better and are easier to get along with when places of work are quiet and well lighted. Many cities have ordinances prohibiting irritating stimuli, such as unnecessary noises.

You can do much to eliminate harmful overstimulation. Do you try to study in a place free from distractions? Do you have a good light? Are your materials handy? Is the radio or television set turned off? Is your mind on what you are doing? Do you avoid stimulating drugs like tea, coffee, and tobacco?

You can eliminate unnecessary work for your nervous system by taking care of your sense organs and protecting them from intense and unnatural stimuli. Pain or discomfort in any part of the body irritates the whole nervous system. You will find some suggestions for taking care of sense organs in Chapter 14. The same chapter discusses some of the values and behavior of pain impulses.

Regular medical and dental checkups, immunizations, and prompt medical attention for illness and injury do much to prevent unnecessary illness and pain. Chapter 17 has some suggestions about securing medical attention, preventing disease and infection, and taking care of small injuries and illnesses.

Keeping your body comfortable prevents irritation. One annoyance is clothing that is too tight, too warm or too cool, dirty, or unsuitable. Ill-fitting shoes can upset the whole body. Suggestions for choosing and caring for attractive comfortable clothing are found in Chapter 16.

Being with other people is stimulating. Everyone needs a chance to be quiet and by himself for a part of each day. Especially if your life is hectic, exciting, and crammed with activity, try to plan for some quiet recreation occasionally. Take up reading, fishing, quiet conversation, or just plain loafing. Slow down and enjoy your life.

You can give other people's nerves a break too. You do not have to be noisy all the time. After a day's work your parents could probably use a little peace and quiet. To tired people your cute behavior may be merely irritating. Teasing and begging and quarreling will not improve anyone's disposition.

If you can help members of your family relax and rest, you will do much to improve all your family relationships. Are there some little jobs you could do to relieve Mother or Dad? Do you have any idea how many things they have on their minds (and nerves) at the same time?

You can be sensible, too, about asking for favors. Try to present your case fairly at a time when they (and you) are rested and able to consider a new problem with understanding and judgment.

Take over some family responsibility for a time. See if it does not pay big dividends in improving your relationships with your family and increasing your own feeling of being grown up, independent, self-confident, and responsible.

How can you protect your nerves from fatigue? Tired nerves make you awkward, slow, and irritable. Athletes know they do not perform as well when they are tired or stale. Protecting your nerves from overstimulation helps to keep them from getting tired. You can protect them in other ways too.

Experiments show that haste produces unnecessary and tiring tensions in nerves and muscles. When you try to work faster than your skill permits, you tense muscles that are not needed. Have you ever observed the quickened breathing, the tension, the awkward movements of someone trying to work hastily? Employers have found that people do better work—and more work—if they proceed at a slower pace. Do you work at a pace that suits you, that feels comfortable? Schedule your time so you do not have to hurry. You will not tire so quickly if you are relaxed and comfortable, using only the nerves and muscles you need.

Rhythmic movements are less tiring than jerky ones. Try tapping with a pencil slowly and rhythmically. You

Our modern world keeps nerves working overtime. They become tired and hard to control. Do you enjoy some quiet forms of recreation and relaxation?

will find you can keep it up for a long time. Then try tapping rapidly with no rhythm and notice how quickly you get tired. Have you ever noticed the rhythmic motions of a good athlete?

All cells need to alternate between periods of activity and rest. Often a change of activity provides a rest by calling into action different groups of nerves and muscles. After studying, a vigorous game that makes you use many large muscles may be more restful and relaxing than a nap or rest period. In monotonous work, where the same actions are repeated over and over, frequent short periods of rest or relaxation are especially valuable. Why?

Sleep is the best method of resting all the nerves of the central nervous system. Sufficient regular sleep improves mental ability, self-control, and co-ordination. It makes a person less irritable, more cheerful, more friendly, and easier to get along with.

People differ in the amount of sleep they need. Growing boys and girls usually need 9 or 10 hours every night. More is needed by people who are active and vigorous and whose lives are full of stimulation and excitement. You can judge for yourself how much sleep you need to feel rested and refreshed. If you tire easily, or do not feel refreshed and ready to go when you get up in the morning, experiment to see what more sleep will do for you. Give it a long fair trial.

What habits help your nerves? Taking time to perfect the skills and habits needed for daily activities saves much nervous energy. You can make almost automatic acts out of washing, dressing, brushing your teeth, hanging up clothes, getting up early enough in the morning, studying, playing, and helping at home. You can probably name many other activities that can be practiced enough to relieve the higher brain centers of much work.

Nerves are stimulated by thoughts and feelings as well as by sights and sounds. Efficient habits of thinking and of solving problems help the nervous system. Controlling emotions or expressing them in appropriate ways prevents much nervous tension and fatigue.

People who are unable to make up their minds or to make decisions and carry them out are almost constantly under nervous strain. Much nervous strain comes from fearful anticipation of an activity or from useless regret after it is done. Actually doing a thing produces less nerve strain than worrying about it. Developing standards and ideals, a goal, and a philosophy of life will help you make difficult decisions. Practicing such virtues as honesty and fairness will help you to act in ways that harmonize with your ideals. You can increase your self-control by practice, by living up to your ideals, and by avoiding impulsive, self-indulgent actions. Chapters 18 and 19 have many suggestions that may help you to face and solve problems.

Save your nerves by forming habits of solving personal problems as they come up and getting difficult things done and off your mind. Learning to concentrate helps to eliminate unnecessary stimuli. Athletes must learn to

213

Denver Public Schools

ignore crowds and keep their minds on the game. You can train yourself to respond only to stimuli that are important. How could you drive a car through traffic if you paid heed to every stimulus along the street?

Learning common courtesies and manners saves you emotional and nervous strain. There will be less friction and nervous tension in your life if you can develop attitudes of tolerance and consideration for others. You will be more relaxed if you can develop an attitude that helps you accept some of the unpleasant things of life. Such incidents are bound to happen and must be taken along with the joys and happiness.

In many of our favorite activities the split-second counts! Mind and muscle work together with speed and precision. How can you develop such co-ordination?

Reviewing the chapter

Test yourself

I

You should answer "yes" to the following questions.

1. Do you try to form good and useful habits?

2. Do you learn muscular control by practicing slowly at first?

3. Do you try to co-ordinate your muscles rhythmically and accurately?

4. Do you have a regular bedtime?

5. Do you have a regular schedule for routine activities?

II

Complete the following sentences by supplying the missing words. Do NOT WRITE IN THIS BOOK.

1. The .... nervous system controls voluntary actions.
2. The .... nervous system operates without conscious direction.
3. The spinal cord is a .... of ....
4. The largest part of the brain is the ....
5. A nerve cell is called a ....
6. Nerves carrying messages from sense organs to the brain are .... nerves.
7. .... nerves carry messages to the muscles.
8. The simplest nerve reaction is a ....
9. Nerves are affected by lack of .... or ....
10. The power to control or check reactions is called ....

III

What would you think, say, or do if:

1. You wished to form a desirable habit?
2. You wanted to learn a new dance step?
3. You felt jumpy and irritable much of the time?
4. A stranger offered you a cigarette?

Reading to help you grow up

How Your Body Works, by Herman and Nina Schneider, has interesting experiments with senses and nerves.
Health for Young America by Burkhard and others.
Working Together for Health by Burkhard and others.
Life and Health by Almack and others.
A Clear Case against Narcotics, by Almack and others, tells how various narcotics affect the body.

Films to help you understand

Functions of the Nervous System. Knowledge Builders.
Nervous System. Encyclopedia Britannica Films.
The Spinal Cord. Brandon.
Ways to Good Habits. Coronet.
It's the Brain That Counts. Association. A doctor shows two young people how alcohol affects the nervous system.

Picture Preview:

Chapter 12

Ewing Galloway

Certain glands in the body set off the changes that cause boys to become men. Along with physical growth go changes in feelings and interests. What are some signs of growth in the interests and behavior of high school boys?

The endocrine gland timetable usually causes girls to mature at an earlier age than boys. When do boys catch up?

H. Armstrong Roberts

The "giant" is eight feet, seven inches tall. His small companion is only 23 inches high. How can you account for the difference in size?

Ewing Galloway

Supreme effort put forth by an athlete is made possible by secretions of the adrenal glands.

Denver Public Schools

Chapter 12

HOW DO GLANDS HELP TO REGULATE YOUR BODY?

Teamwork among the parts of your body is not entirely controlled by nerves. The special organs called *endocrine glands* play an important part in regulating the way your body grows and operates.

Endocrine glands manufacture fluids called hormones. In some way, not clearly understood, hormones influence growth and the development of normal physical and mental powers. Some of them regulate the body's use of calcium, iron, and other substances. Some govern the rate at which the cells burn food to produce energy.

Knowledge concerning hormones is new. Much of it is still in the experimental stage. However, enough is known to show that normal health and development are dependent upon proper functioning of the endocrine glands.

Normally the glands manufacture just the right amount of hormones to enable your body to function properly, to grow and develop. They maintain their delicate balance and set off their complex chains of reaction according to some inner order. The natural laws governing them are for the most part still a mystery.

Once in a while, glands for some reason manufacture too little or too much of certain hormones. Abnormal amounts of certain hormones may cause an individual to be too big or too small, too fat or too thin, slow and dull, or irritable and nervous.

Once in a great while glands may manufacture too much or too little secretion. Then they may cause the unusual growth patterns that produce midgets or giants or bearded women. They may cause diseases like diabetes or goiter.

Although little is known about glands, some knowledge of them helps us understand ourselves better. Often we are afraid of things we do not understand. Everyone needs reliable information about how his body is constructed and how it works. He needs to satisfy his curiosity and prevent worry and fear. Correct information will help to do both.

Looking ahead

Questions and suggestions

1. Glands help your body to develop harmoniously, to make constant delicate adjustments and to maintain its balance in a changing world. Ordinarily when glands are working well, we pay no attention to them. Probably you know more about signs of gland disorders than about the marvelous jobs performed by healthy glands. What do you already know about glands? What glands are important in digestion? Do you know about any others?

2. The endocrine glands that help to regulate your body processes do not have ducts. What are ducts? Do you know or have you heard of any body processes that are affected by the hormones from the endocrine glands?

3. Have you ever had stage fright? What are the symptoms? What is "second wind"? The hormone called adrenalin plays an important part in causing these body changes.

4. What do you know about goiter, diabetes, giants, and midgets? Do you know other signs of glandular disturbance?

Committee planning

Some of the most exciting important research being carried on today concerns the effect of glands and hormones on body processes. Probably everyone can bring clippings from magazines and papers telling about some interesting experiments. What is a sensible attitude to take toward these articles?

Reading

Do you know what these words mean? You will come across them as you read this chapter:

Function, govern, complex, abnormal, chains of reaction, stimulate, exhibit, sensitive, research, metabolism.

What do glands do?

Endocrine glands are small organs located in various parts of the body. Some have been recognized for a long time. Others are so little known that no one knows for sure what they do. There may be others that have not yet been discovered.

What are endocrine glands? Glands are special organs which produce chemicals or secretions that help keep the body running smoothly. Some glands send their secretions through tubes or ducts directly to the places they are to be used. For example, sweat glands secrete perspiration into ducts leading to pores (openings in the skin). Salivary glands secrete saliva through ducts leading into the mouth.

But endocrine glands have no ducts. They pour their hormones directly into the blood stream for transfer to all parts of the body. Their effects are widespread and difficult to trace. A hormone from one gland may act directly on cells to produce activity. It may stimulate into activity other glands or a part of the nervous system. Another hormone from the gland thus stimulated may stop the activity of the first gland; or it may set off a whole chain of glandular actions. The workings of your body are as complicated as an atomic-bomb

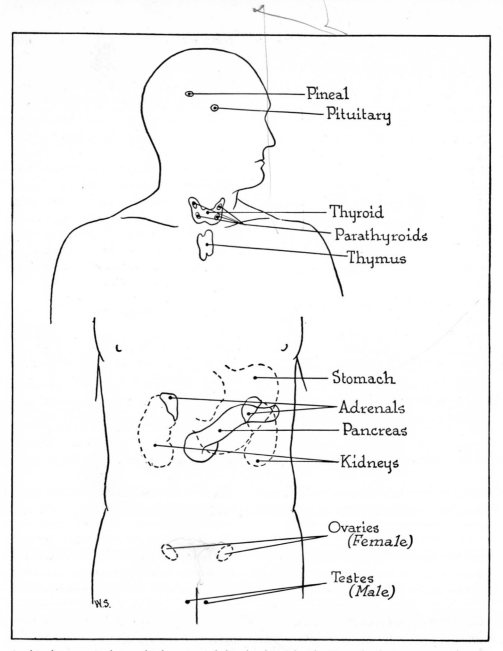

Pineal

Pituitary

Thyroid

Parathyroids

Thymus

Stomach

Adrenals

Pancreas

Kidneys

Ovaries
(Female)

Testes
(Male)

W.S.

In this diagram is shown the location of the ductless glands. How do their secretions reach the cells?

chain reaction! The specialized study of endocrine glands is called endocrinology.

The four best known endocrine glands are the *thyroid,* the *pituitary,* the *adrenals,* and the *pancreas.* The thyroid is located in the lower neck just in front of trachea. The adrenals are like small caps on the kidneys. The pituitary is almost in the center of the head, attached to the base of the brain. The pancreas nestles close to the stomach.

Other endocrine glands are the sex glands, the parathyroids, the thymus, and the pineal body.

Some of the glands manufacture several hormones. The pituitary manufactures at least 15 different ones. Some of the endocrine glands are parts of organs that have other duties. The pancreas secretes juices that help in digestion, in addition to producing the hormone *insulin.*

How do hormones act? Scientists have discovered the exact composition of some hormones. They have been able to manufacture some. They have been able to extract others from the glands of animals. Others they know almost nothing about.

Each hormone acts in a special way. Insulin, secreted by the pancreas, makes it possible for the body to burn sugar as fuel. *Thyroxin,* manufactured by the thyroid, governs the amount of sugar burned. One of the hormones of the pituitary governs growth. Another hormone of the pituitary has three effects: it causes blood vessels to contract, causes more sugar to enter the blood, and acts on the kidneys to inhibit loss of too much water. The actions of some hormones are not clearly understood.

Hormones act directly on body tissues, and indirectly through their effects on other glands. A deficiency of thyroxin affects the pituitary and thus affects growth indirectly. Hormones from the pituitary affect the development of the thyroid and sex glands. The pituitary may be a master-control gland that affects all the others. In such circular action, in which glands act on each other, it is hard to tell where the action starts or how or why.

Hormones are remarkably powerful. An amount as small as one part in a million in the blood stream can produce noticeable effects in the body.

How do glands affect you?

Individual differences in height, weight, mental ability, and nervous and emotional control are greatly affected by the balance and proportions among the various hormones in the blood. The balance is so delicate, the reactions are so mysterious, and the hormones are so powerful that any attempts at self-treatment using hormones are extremely dangerous.

What does the thyroid do? The largest and best known of the endocrine glands is the thyroid, located in the neck. For a long time people have recognized the thyroid enlargement known as *goiter.* They have realized there was some connection between the gland and a kind of mental and physical dwarfism called cretinism.

The thyroid is a butterfly-shaped organ, weighing about an ounce. Its two lobes lie one on each side of the neck. The thyroid secretes a powerful hormone called thyroxin. Thyroxin acts on cells to regulate the rate at which they burn food for energy. Nerve cells are particularly sensitive to it. When you want a car to run faster you speed up the rate at which it burns gasoline. Thyroxin, by governing the amount of sugar the body burns, regulates the speed of body activities.

The activity of the thyroid gland may be determined by a *basal metabolism test*. In this test a person resting quietly, and using the least possible energy, breathes into a special container on a machine. The machine, by measuring the amount of oxygen used, indirectly measures how fast food is being burned in the body.

If the thyroid gland is overactive, sugar burns more rapidly and the heart beats faster. There is an increase in nervous activity. The person is likely to be irritable and jumpy. Often he is underweight. An overactive thyroid may be treated by medicines or surgery.

A deficiency of thyroxin causes food to burn more slowly in the cells. The heart action is slow, the body gains weight, and the mind becomes dull and slow. A deficiency of thyroxin in infancy leads to a very

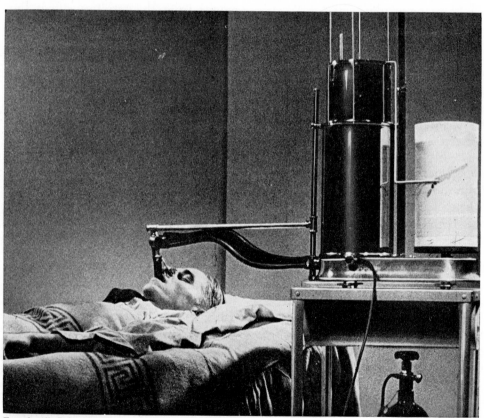

Encyclopedia Britannica Films

In the basal metabolism test a rotating cylinder measures the amount of oxygen consumed by the body. This test detects any disturbance in the normal functioning of the thyroid gland.

stunted physical and mental development called cretinism. In adults, if the thyroid is destroyed by disease or accident, a similar condition develops called myxedema. A thyroid deficiency may be treated by a physician by prescribing proper amounts of pure thyroxin.

In drug form, thyroxin (the extract of thyroid gland), is powerful and dangerous. It should never be used except under the supervision of a physician. Some advertised methods of weight reduction are dangerous because they contain thyroxin. Physical, mental, and emotional health depends upon a delicate balance of hormones. Upsetting the balance can have far-reaching consequences.

Four small glands in back of the thyroid, called the parathyroid, control the body's use of calcium. Little is known about them, although much research is being carried on.

What is goiter? Most goiters are enlargements of the thyroid gland caused by a lack of *iodine* in the diet. In order to manufacture thyroxin, the thyroid gland requires a small amount of iodine. If the body fails to receive enough iodine in food and drink, the thyroid gland works harder to overcome the deficiency. It may increase in size and show a swelling in the neck. Usually there are no other effects, and the disease is called simple goiter.

In most places iodine is found in the soil and water and is present in foods grown there. Sea foods, such as fish, oysters, clams, and lobsters are usually good sources of iodine. In some regions there are inadequate supplies of iodine. One such region,

called the goiter belt, extends across the central part of the United States. Residents of such iodine-free regions often have goiter, unless they obtain iodine from other sources. The addition of iodine to the diet is effective in controlling simple goiter. Little is needed and it may be supplied in various ways. The most practical way is the use of iodized salt. Many scientists believe that general use of iodized salt would almost completely eliminate simple goiter.

Another type of goiter, the exophthalmic, is different from simple goiter. In exophthalmic goiter, the thyroid gland is overactive, and the

Why does your body need iodine? How can you make sure you are getting enough iodine? What are some of the signs of an underactive thyroid gland or an overactive thyroid gland?

patient has the symptoms of thyroid overactivity. He is nervous and trembling. His pulse and breathing are rapid. His eyes are staring and may bulge. His metabolism rate is high and he loses weight. This kind of goiter may be treated by removing part of the gland or by drugs. Nobody knows what causes the gland to become overactive. There is some evidence that emotional shock may play a part.

How do anger and fear affect glands? One of the quickest-acting and most powerful of the hormones is *adrenalin,* produced by the adrenal glands.

When adrenalin is secreted into the blood, the body gathers all its re-

Philip Gendreau

Fear, anger, and other emotions cause the adrenal glands and the sympathetic nervous system to become active. How can you get rid of the energy released by emotions?

sources. Adrenalin, acting with the sympathetic nervous system, brings about many body changes. *Glycogen* stored in the liver is changed to sugar and released into the blood, ready for use by the muscles. Under adrenalin stimulation the arteries to big muscles enlarge, the arteries to digestive organs contract, the heart beats faster and harder, and the blood is able to clot more quickly.

The adrenals respond actively to feelings of fear and anger. You have probably noticed some of the effects of strong feelings. Your muscles tense, your heart pounds, your hands perspire, and your face flushes or pales. When you notice these signs of adrenal activity, you will know that other internal changes are taking place. The sympathetic nervous system and the adrenals have prepared your body to take action in response to your stirred-up feelings. The adrenals and the sympathetic nervous system work as a team to help the body respond to emergencies, to prepare for action.

Extraordinary feats of strength and daring have been made possible by the effects of strong emotions on the body. Emotional stimulus is important in athletic contests, in catastrophes, in war, and in great creative enterprises.

Causes or activities in which you are emotionally concerned call forth your greatest energy, your best performance.

What is diabetes? The *pancreas,* called the sweetbread in animals, is an organ lying below and in back of the stomach. It gives a digestive juice into the intestine through a duct and also has cells which produce a hormone called *insulin.*

Insulin enables the body to burn sugar. When insulin is lacking, the individual develops diabetes. He is unable to use or to store sugar. Sugar collects in the blood and is given off in the urine. A person with diabetes eats heartily but does not gain weight. He urinates frequently to get rid of excess sugar, and he has an unnatural thirst to replace the lost water.

One of the most important achievements of modern medicine was the discovery of insulin. In 1922 a group of Canadians led by Dr. Frederick Banting obtained insulin from the pancreas of animals. One million diabetics in this country can continue normal life because of this medical triumph. For his discovery Dr. Banting received the Nobel prize for medicine in 1923. (You may like to look up the achievements of other winners of the prize.)

Insulin does not cure diabetes. It does not restore the body's own ability to produce proper amounts of insulin. The patient is normal only so long as he takes insulin regularly. The amount is difficult to determine and needs careful medical supervision. What are some factors that would influence the amount? An overdose is dangerous or may even be fatal.

In spite of our ability to detect and to control diabetes, it is now one of the leading causes of death in the United States. The U. S. Public Health Service estimates that there are over two million persons in this country who suffer from diabetes. Only slightly more than half of them know that they have the disease. When diabetes is allowed to go unrecognized, serious complications are likely to occur.

Much suffering can be avoided if all persons have periodic medical examinations which include a test for sugar in the urine. Doctors and druggists have made up kits that can be used by individuals to test urine for sugar. The kits are inexpensive and simple. If widely used, they would help people to discover unrecognized diabetes and enable them to obtain early treatment.

How do glands make midgets and giants? The pituitary gland is an organ about the size of a small marble. It is located at the base of the brain, almost in the center of the head.

Recent investigations indicate that the pituitary may be a "master gland," influential in controlling, to some extent, the activities of the thyroid, adrenals, and sex glands. For example, the increased activity of the thyroid that causes exophthalmic goiter probably is caused by a hormone secreted by the pituitary.

The pituitary secretes many hormones and influences directly many activities in the body, including growth, body weight, mental ability and alertness, and blood pressure.

If the pituitary is too active during childhood the long bones grow too rapidly, producing a giant. If there is insufficient secretion from the pituitary, a person may attain a height of only two to four feet. Pituitary dwarfs are well proportioned and ordinarily intelligent. Other types of dwarfs, resulting from other causes, usually have heads too large or legs too short. Of course, the pituitary gland is not the only thing that affects a person's size. The way he lives—eats, plays, works, and sleeps—is very important.

How do glands help you grow?

As you grow up your body undergoes an orderly sequence of change. It changes in size and shape and the way different organs work. A number of glands are believed to work together to produce these changes. Individuals vary a great deal in the age at which changes take place. Each has his own unique glandular balance but all go through the same sequence sooner or later.

Which glands help you grow up? The pituitary regulates normal growth in body size and weight. Another small gland, the thymus, is located just behind the breastbone or sternum. It is believed to hold in check the development of sex characteristics until physical growth is appropriate. The thymus is often called

Harold M. Lambert

As you grow up, you usually take a new interest in schoolwork and assume more responsibility for doing a good job. Do you have any responsibilities?

the gland of childhood. It grows from birth, attains its greatest size before the age of fourteen, then decreases rapidly in size. Only a tiny remnant is left after the age of 30.

Another tiny gland, the pineal body, is located between the two hemispheres of the brain. Little is known about the pineal body although much research is being done. It is believed to have some ability to regulate growth in childhood.

At some time when a person is between the age of about 10 and 14, a hormone from the pituitary causes a rapid increase in growth.

What is adolescence? Hormones secreted by the sex glands produce the physical sex characteristics of the mature man and woman. The time of life when these changes are taking place, when boys and girls are becoming men and women, is known as adolescence.

Just before adolescence begins, there is usually a period of slow growth, followed by increases, first in height, then in weight. Physical changes are accompanied by other kinds of changes. Boys and girls change in feelings and interests. They begin to play a new role in life, to prepare for independence, marriage, and parenthood.

Boys and girls need to become adult in thoughts and feelings as well as in looks. They need to broaden their education, choose a job, and develop a philosophy that helps them feel secure, hopeful, and tolerant.

Growing up mentally and emotionally is not so automatic as growing up physically. It requires thought and

Philip Gendreau

Do you have satisfying and appropriate ways of expressing your feelings or working off unhappy feelings? Do you consider other people's feelings?

attention. Growing up and acting your age are discussed in Chapters 18, 19, and 20.

What are the problems of adolescence? Adolescence is an important time, exciting and challenging. You change almost completely in appearance and in the way you feel. Different things now begin to interest you. It is a wonderful time to take stock of yourself, to learn more about yourself, and to direct your growth into the channels you choose.

Adolescence brings many problems. You may grow so rapidly that your body has a big job co-ordinating new cells, different proportions, and new functions. You may feel that you are all hands and feet. Changes in hormone secretions may upset the chemistry of your body for a while. You may experience sudden changes of feeling; you may be easily moved to tears or laughter and have "moods." The increased activity of oil and sweat glands may cause problems of pimples, acne, and body odor.

Adolescence brings problems of feelings and attitude. Individuals vary greatly in the time they enter adolescence. You may find yourself developing at a different rate from

Look Magazine

Some of the signs of growing up are a widening of friendships to include both boys and girls, increased interest in personal appearance, and interest in social activities and sports which include both boys and girls.

your friends. Then your interests will be different for a while.

If you grow rapidly, people often expect too much of you. You may assume too soon that you are ready for adult independence. Mental and emotional development are more important than physical development. Most unhappiness in the world is caused by people who never grew up in thoughts and feeling.

Mental and emotional development is orderly, like other growth. You need to expand your horizons slowly, accumulating experiences that help you to think and feel, and behave as an adult. Leaping from

the complete self-interest, irresponsibility, and dependence of a child to complete independence naturally will result in many poor adjustments. Growing up is a *gradual* job.

Your developing social interests and your interest in members of the opposite sex call for new skills. You need to know how to get along with people and how to make yourself liked and accepted.

Most important is your attitude toward yourself, other people, and life in general. Physical development takes place automatically, that is, without conscious direction from you beyond eating and sleeping and exercising. It requires much more attention and practice to grow up mentally and emotionally. Some boys and girls are frightened or embarrassed about their physical development. Boys and girls who regard sexual development as shameful or funny are not growing in understanding. They need to know what is normal in growing up, to accept and take pride in their new roles, and to help themselves become mature, happy men and women.

How can you help your glands work?

The same factors that affect other parts of your body affect your glands. You can help them most by leading a reasonably balanced life, by

developing a cheerful, idealistic philosophy. You can help them by developing efficient ways of solving problems, by preventing excess nervous and emotional stimuli, and by developing ways of discharging emotional energy.

Do you need medical help? The role of hormones in the body is one of the most complex of medical problems. Experimental work on animals is difficult enough. It is much more difficult to apply even established facts to the treatment of humans.

A human being is a complicated organization of thoughts, feelings, and structures. He reacts as a whole, and it is hard to single out specific causes and effects of his reactions. In spite of the difficulties, great practical progress is being made in use of surgery and medicine for treating persons whose glands do not function properly. Almost miraculous results have been obtained using hormone extracts of the thyroid, the pancreas, and the pituitary.

Generally a person has no trouble with glands if he follows reasonable rules of good health—balanced diet, sufficient sleep and rest, and moderate exercise. The body maintains a natural balance.

Occasionally a gland may fail to work properly. The reasons for the failure often are not known. Poor functioning may be due to a deficiency of a certain mineral, for example, iodine. It may be due to emotional shock, nervous strain, or other factors hard to trace. Even without knowing the cause, doctors are often able to compensate by surgery or medicine for glands that are not working.

Periodic medical examinations help to discover hormone deficiencies. If glandular difficulties are discovered early doctors are usually able to treat them effectively or to control

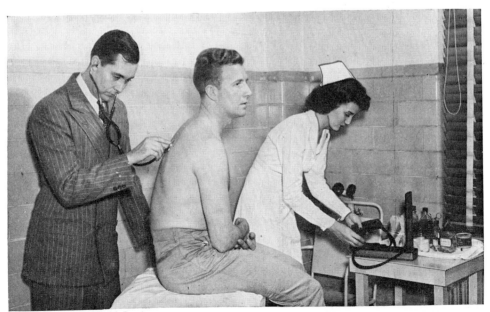

United States Public Health Service

How do medical tests help to discover glands that are not functioning properly?

229

them by administering gland extracts. How do basal metabolism and urine tests help to discover gland deficiencies?

A doctor should be consulted by anyone who has any unusual symptoms—for example, abnormal thirst, unexplained loss or gain of weight, undue fatigue, extreme nervousness, or chronic pains. If you feel any concern about your health or growth, a medical check-up is very reassuring. Prompt treatment can prevent or control almost any disease. If nothing is wrong, the reassurance will prevent unnecessary worry and fear.

You may like to read some of the many theories about the effect of hormones on the body. Some of the theories are based on careful research and much evidence. Others are based on little or almost no evidence. Be careful to distinguish between reliable research facts and imaginative but convincing theories.

One interesting theory traces to the hormone deficiencies the development of many diseases, including arthritis, arterial and heart diseases, and even mental diseases like schizophrenia. Some scientists believe that emotional shock or continued emotional strain affecting the adrenals may be the trigger that starts glandular overwork which may result in eventual breakdown. They have collected some evidence and are still carrying on research. Such interesting theories open new fields for research. They offer new hope for millions of people suffering from glandular diseases.

Can you help yourself? Glands help other parts of your body to work and to grow and to develop. They help your body to meet changing conditions and emergencies. There is evidence that glandular balance may be upset by extremes of various kinds; overeating or eating inadequate meals; overexertion or lack of exercise; fatigue; continual unnecessary nervous stimulation; and lack of either emotional control or emotional expression. You help yourself by maintaining general good health. You help by being temperate and moderate and by trying to maintain a balance in your life.

Emotions release energy and need to be followed up with action of some sort. Actions use up the extra energy. They seem to restore the normal body balance. If you do not use the energy, your nerves remain tense and your feelings remain upset. You may feel restless and irritable. Soldiers, athletes, and actors feel upset and irritable before the big game or show or battle. When they go into action their tensions disappear. You probably have had the same experience. Have you ever had "butterflies" before it was your turn to perform in a game, or in class, or at a party? How did you feel when you were actually doing something? Physical activity brings feelings of satisfaction and relaxation.

We cannot control the internal responses to emotion. Instruments that measure blood pressure, heart action, breathing rate, or perspiration can detect even brief emotional responses. You might like to report on how a lie detector works. A shrewd observer can often detect even small emotional changes. Are you sensitive and observant enough to notice and respect other people's feelings?

As we grow up we learn to express

The "lie detector" makes a graph showing changes in the body set off by emotions and the nerves and endocrine systems. What changes do you feel in yourself when you are excited or afraid?

our emotions in mature ways. We learn that direct, impulsive action may bring more trouble. If we run from our fears, they are more frightening next time. So we learn to control ourselves. We learn to understand and overcome our fears. We try to obtain more lasting satisfaction than mere relief of emotional tension. Chapter 19 has some suggestions that may help you to control your emotions and to express them in ways that are useful and happy.

Everyone needs to know how to get rid of uncomfortable feelings of tension and excitement. You can work off the extra energy by a brisk walk or getting into some active game. Have you ever known anyone who worked off a "mad" feeling energetically cleaning or sweeping or maybe punching a bag?

Many doctors believe that constant emotional strain, fear, anger, worry, jealousy, and the like may cause nervous and glandular disorders. Nervous and glandular upsets may, in turn, cause many kinds of diseases such as ulcers, headaches, indigestion, high blood pressure, and mental illnesses. People who are "mad" at something all the time put a real but unnecessary strain on themselves.

You can protect yourself by avoiding unnecessary or extreme emotional stimulation. Do you think some movies can be over-stimulating? Do you spend some time each day in quiet relaxation?

Everyone needs to have satisfying and appropriate ways of expressing feelings of friendship, affection, sympathy, and joy. Do you practice expressing these feelings? You can practice at home little acts of thoughtfulness. Try to develop habits of generously expressing praise and gratitude and affection so that you feel at ease with emotions. Life without emotions would be colorless and dull. You can learn and practice ways of working off emotional energy. You can develop more grown-up attitudes toward people or situations that upset you often.

Chapter 19 has some suggestions that may help you to deal with such problems.

What can you do about problems of growing up?

Everyone has problems, things that worry him, decisions he must make. No one can tell you how to solve your problems, but some information about people in general may help you. For more specific help you may do additional reading on your own particular problem. You may consult a doctor for help with your physical problems. To help with your emotional problems you can go to your parents, your spiritual advisor, a teacher, or some trusted older friend.

Adolescence is a period of rapid physical change. Most boys and girls take the changes of adolescence in their stride. Their body maintains its balance through all the changes. They mature in their thoughts and feelings. Growing up is a happy process.

Some boys and girls go through stages of awkwardness, skin troubles, and being a different size from their friends. Some tire easily or develop whims of appetite. Physical problems are complicated by emotional reactions. Some boys and girls are worried or afraid. They feel different and conspicuous.

You can help yourself most to prevent and improve physical troubles by establishing regular good habits of eating, getting sufficient sleep, and exercising. Extra attention to personal cleanliness will do much to prevent skin blemishes. Working slowly and practicing skills will help overcome awkwardness. Other chapters have more detailed suggestions about subjects such as skin care, skills, fatigue, and diet. If you have particular problems, look up the topics related to them in the index. Use other references too. Perhaps you can have a doctor or nurse or some other expert discuss common problems with your class.

The biggest problems of growing boys and girls are emotional. Most physical troubles are of short duration. Your body naturally balances itself. You achieve a well-proportioned adult body as the glands become adjusted. If you can take things easy, reassure yourself by having a medical check-up, and develop a sense of humor, you can do much to overcome temporary embarrassments or difficult times.

Other chapters in this book have suggestions that may help you to acquire poise and self-confidence, to make the most of your abilities and opportunities, and to grow up mentally and emotionally.

Reviewing the chapter

Test yourself

I

You should answer "yes" to the following questions.

1. Do you get plenty of rest?
2. Do you have regular physical check-ups?
3. Do you have a balance of quiet and exciting activities?
4. Do you eat a variety of nourishing foods with plenty of fresh fruits and vegetables?
5. Do you have an older person to whom you can take problems when you need help?
6. Do you exercise vigorously outdoors every day?

II

Complete the following sentences by supplying the missing words. Do NOT WRITE IN THIS BOOK.

1. The .... and .... system regulate and govern body processes.
2. Endocrine glands secrete ....
3. Endocrine glands have no ....
4. ...., secreted by cells in the pancreas, enables the body to burn sugar.
5. The .... governs growth.
6. The .... may be a master control gland.
7. Goiter is an enlargement of the .... gland.
8. The activity of the thyroid may be determined by a .... test.
9. Strong emotions cause .... to be secreted.

III

What would you think, say, or do in the following situations?

1. If something made you very angry?
2. If you wished to make sure you were getting enough iodine?
3. If you were worried about your own development?

Reading to help you grow up

Men against Death by Paul De Kruif. The story of the discovery of insulin.

Hepatica Hawks, by Rachel Field, tells the story of a girl six feet tall and how she made satisfactory adjustments.

Life and Health, by Almack and others, has an interesting chapter on nerves and glands and their role in personality.

Your Health and Safety, by Clemenson and LaPorte, has an interesting discussion of glands.

The Wonder of Life, by Levine and Selegmann, describes the changes that transform boys and girls to men and women.

Films to help you understand

Human Growth. University of Oregon. A group of junior high students discuss a film on how a baby is born.

They Live Again. Teaching Films Custodian. Discovery of insulin.

Endocrine Glands. Encyclopedia Britannica Films.

How Can You Make the Most of Yourself?

Most of us would like to improve ourselves in many ways. Often we wish we were stronger, more graceful, better in our schoolwork, healthier, and happier. We wish but fail to try to make our wishes come true. We are more likely to feel sorry for ourselves and to blame our shortcomings on others.

Actually everyone has many opportunities to improve himself. Human beings are capable of achievements not dreamed of by those who lack spirit. Think of some of the human achievements of body, mind, and spirit. Some people have accomplished almost unbelievable physical feats of endurance, speed, and skill. The human mind is responsible for the scientific discoveries and inventions that have made modern civilization possible. The human spirit is capable of rising to great heights of generosity, sacrifice, and heroism. Many of these great achievements have been made in spite of handicaps. Do you know some of the stories of human achievements in the face of great difficulties?

Do you know of athletes who have overcome handicaps of frail bodies, crippling accidents, and disease? Do you know of scientists, artists, and statesmen who overcame obstacles of poverty, injustice, prejudice, and lack of understanding? Do you know of ordinary boys and girls, men and women who have achieved happiness only after overcoming obstacles that would have discouraged the faint hearted?

You, too, can make the most of your abilities. You can take advantage of scientific discoveries and of the experiences of others to improve yourself. You can develop your mental abilities and your abilities to read, to memorize, to concentrate, to remember, to think, and to judge. You can learn to use your senses—your abilities to see and to hear and to feel—with more skill and satisfaction. You can be better looking and stronger, healthier, and happier.

H. Armstrong Roberts

How do your nervous system and brain help you to get a hit?

Picture Preview:

Chapter 13

Books are shortcuts. They enable you to share the experiences of others. Do you know how to read for pleasure or for information?

Denver Public Schools

As you grow up you enjoy challenging games that require mental skills like alertness, concentration, ability to learn rules. Do you like to match wits as well as physical ability? What games do you like to play?

H. Armstrong Roberts

What is the simplest way to memorize a set of tables or formulas? Does it make learning easier to arrange the parts in order so you can see a relationship between them? Can you memorize more quickly if you put the letters in groups like EIS, TMO, and AN?

Chapter 13

HOW CAN YOU MAKE THE BEST USE OF MENTAL ABILITY?

What do you mean when you say a person uses his head? Do you think you are growing in ability to use yours? Are you developing efficient methods of studying? Do you think you are increasing your ability to solve your own problems and to control your emotions?

In any class or group there are many people of fairly equal ability. They may differ greatly in the way they use their mental ability. Some do well in their studies. They seem to learn easily, to be able to remember and to use what they learn. Others make little or no progress. They are not able to study efficiently. They have no confidence in their ability to learn and use childish, emotional methods of solving their problems.

It is just as important to develop good mental habits as good physical habits. You can develop skills in thinking, organizing, remembering, observing, and other mental abilities. Probably you have worked out some methods of your own to help you learn. Consciously or unconsciously, you have formed habits of studying, remembering, and solving your problems. What are your study habits? Are they efficient or could they be improved? Have other people worked out any fundamentals of learning that might help you?

Scientists have worked for a long time trying to find out how the brain works and how people use their mental ability. No one has been able to find out exactly how the brain acts in thinking, remembering, and performing other mental functions. From their observations and experiments, scientists have accumulated a great deal of evidence about the work done by various parts of the brain.

Some of the observations of psychologists and other scientists may help you develop your own mental ability. You can try some of their suggestions and change some of your own unsatisfactory habits.

Looking ahead

Questions and suggestions

1. What is mental ability? What are some mental skills?

2. When do you use mental ability? For which of your daily activities do you use it?

3. In what ways would you like to improve your mental ability?

4. Recall your own study habits. How do you go about learning a new lesson in school? A new skill or technique in a game or sport?

5. Take a look at your memorizing techniques. Choose a piece of about 100 words of poetry or prose to be memorized by everyone in class. Let each keep a record of his time and method. Do you learn easily? Forget quickly? Test from time to time to see how quickly people forget. How can you improve your ability to remember? After you have finished studying the unit, memorize a similar selection to see if you are improving.

6. Examine your own learning habits. Are you satisfied with them? Do you learn about as well as other people? Have you worked out some habits you think are good? What inefficient habits do you have?

7. Any new learning is based upon skills you have already acquired. What are some fundamental mental skills that you need now? Do some of your skills need improvement?

8. Do you think it would be helpful to take some tests to discover fundamentals in which you are weak, so that you can work to improve them? Do you read as well as you should?

9. Do you know how to use all kinds of books, the library, and other aids? Can you organize your thoughts? Can you say what you mean orally and in writing? Can you use and understand numbers, maps, charts, and graphs?

Committee planning

1. The field-trip committee can arrange a visit to the library. Do you know how to find the kinds of books you want? Can you use the magazines and guides and catalogs?

2. A committee may organize a treasure hunt for facts to help you learn how to use the library and all the various reference books and guides.

3. A committee may organize some games or stunts that are tests of memory or concentration or other mental abilities. For example, the committee can arrange on a tray or table 15 or 20 objects, such as a pin, a penny, a thimble, a pen, and an eraser. Allow everyone to look at the objects for a minute or two; then remove them. See who can remember and write down the largest accurate list of objects. The committee can find many other good games that require mental ability.

How does your brain work?

The human brain is so complicated that no one knows exactly how it works. Somehow, the workings of its billions of cells make possible memory, consciousness, feelings, sensations, will power, learning ability, thoughts, dreams, and ideas.

What is your brain like? The average human adult brain weighs about three pounds. It consists of several different parts or sections. Each section performs certain specific duties. At the base of the skull is the medulla, an enlarged continuation of the spinal cord. The medulla controls involuntary activities like breathing and circulation. Above the medulla is the cerebellum. It serves in co-ordinating actions of the muscles and can take over the control of established skills and habits.

The largest part of the brain is the cerebrum. This is the part most people refer to as the brain proper. The cerebrum fills all the top part of your skull. It is divided into two halves, or hemispheres, and resembles the shape of a half-walnut meat.

The cerebrum is a peculiar-looking soft mass of nerve tissues folded in deep wrinkles. A layer of gray nerve cell bodies about one-seventh of an inch thick covers the entire outer surface. This is the cerebral cortex where all the mental functions such as thinking and remembering are carried on. The inner part of the cerebrum is made up of a complicated network of white nerve fibers running to and from cells in the gray matter.

The brain is protected by three membranes: a tough lining next to the skull; a thin, delicate covering which carries blood vessels next to the brain; and a very thin membrane between these two. Between the two inner membranes is a space filled with clear fluid, a continuation of that in the spinal cord, which serves as a cushion against shock and injuries.

How does the brain work? In the cerebrum messages are received from nerves which are connected to sense organs and muscles in all parts of the body. Here the messages are relayed and organized. They are given meaning somehow by being combined with impressions already stored in the mind. Somehow the brain produces thoughts and the will to act.

Observation and experiments show that special areas of the brain seem to control certain kinds of activity. The middle part of the cortex controls the voluntary muscles. Nerves from the two hemispheres cross so that the right side of the brain controls muscles on the left side of the body, and vice versa. Directly behind the *motor* (voluntary muscle control) *area* is a *sensory area* that receives impressions of touch and taste and smell. Below the sensory area is the special area for receiving sound impressions. The back part of the cortex receives impressions of sight from nerves connected to the eyes.

Outside the special motor and sensory areas, all the other parts of the brain are called *association areas*. They relate the work of one part of the brain to another and let it work like a huge switchboard. The brain is much more than a switchboard. It not only communicates, records, and organizes but in some way it compares, judges, and creates. Reason and thought and will power seem to come from the working of the whole brain.

The most marvelous work of the brain, and the least understood, is the way it puts impressions together, relates them to previous experience, gives them meaning, and orders appropriate action. The sensory areas do not see or feel or hear. They receive impressions from nerves and send them to the association areas to be interpreted. If 30 people are looking at an object, each "sees" something

Many activities in our modern world require alert use of mental ability. Handling machinery calls for good co-ordination, concentration, and ability to judge speed and distance. Can you think of other mental abilities needed by the operator?

different as he adds to the actual object his previous experiences, his expectations, and his feelings.

Does your brain need special care? The delicate, important tissues of your brain are well protected by the bones in the skull. If injuries are received that might affect the brain, they should have immediate medical attention.

The brain is helped by healthful habits of eating, exercising, and resting that keep the whole body in good condition. There is no special food good for the brain. The brain is nourished by the blood and naturally is affected by all the things that affect the blood and circulatory system. The brain has a large blood supply and is quickly affected by lack of oxygen or by the presence of drugs in the blood.

Areas of the brain are affected in regular order. Persons suffering from lack of oxygen, or going under an anesthetic, or being affected by alcohol may go through the same changes. First affected are the higher functions —judgment, memory, and will power.

and heart action. The danger point occurs when the eye reflex disappears. (The eye reflex is the closing of the pupil when more light is admitted.) Soon after, the heart and breathing are affected. This is the comatose stage of either too deep an anesthetic or extreme drunkenness.

Your brain needs exercise and rest. Brainwork does not seem to use much energy. Mental fatigue is probably boredom or physical fatigue caused by eyestrain, poor circulation, or overstimulation of the nervous system, or other conditions. Each individual must learn for himself how to avoid being either bored or tense. Alternating short periods of work and rest help many people. Some other good mental and emotional habits are discussed on pages 370–375.

Philip Gendreau

How does your brain help you to be an expert diver? What parts of your brain take over as you become more experienced in any activity?

A person is likely to talk excitedly; to laugh or cry without control; and to be unable to judge distance, time, color, or his own behavior.

Later the senses are dulled; muscular control becomes poorer; and speech and writing are uncertain. Then, co-ordination, walking, and balancing suffer. This stage could occur when a person is drunk, when he "blacks out" in an airplane, or when he is partially under an anesthetic. Finally paralysis sets in, slowing the automatic actions, reflexes, breathing,

Ewing Galloway

Change provides rest and relaxation for your brain. A camping or fishing trip makes a good vacation for city people.

People differ in their ability to think and to learn just as they differ in their ability to do other activities such as running or sewing or playing basketball. The ability to do mental work improves as you grow up.

By observation and experiment psychologists have worked out some principles and techniques that make learning easier.

How do feelings affect learning? You have probably noticed that people learn more easily if they are interested. Some boys learn the names and batting averages of entire baseball teams but cannot spell ordinary words. You can learn really difficult things if they are interesting or important to you.

Pleasant feelings make learning easier. Feelings of resentment or anger increase tension and reduce skill and learning ability. Have you ever failed on a job that was really easy because you did it in a mood of anger or defiance?

Interest, pleasant feelings, and learning usually go hand in hand.

Denver Public Schools

Learning is easier when it is built directly on knowledge and interest already present. Learning about an airplane motor is easier for some of these boys. Why?

Some things are naturally interesting because they help us to get the things we want—a place on the basketball team, approval of the gang or a friend. Other things are interesting because they result in pleasant feelings of success and accomplishment. We usually are interested in and like to do the things we do well.

Lack of interest, unpleasant feelings, and failure often form a circle. It is difficult to tell which comes first. Indifference or resentment may cause failure. Repeated failures often cause unpleasant feelings that make learning difficult. You can break the circle at any of the links. Trying to realize the importance of what you are learning, and applying it to your own life, usually makes any subject interesting. If you are growing up mentally, you

All skills, mental and physical, are perfected by practice. What skills are required to build a column of blocks?

should be constantly expanding your interests, realizing the importance of ideas and people and events in the world around you.

Boys and girls often must learn things that do not seem to them either interesting or important. Yielding too easily to early feelings of displeasure or failure builds habits of laziness and inefficiency and makes success more difficult. You can control your feelings and expand your interests. Deliberate, cheerful persistence at a task which seems disagreeable may cause it to become interesting from sheer sense of accomplishment. Do you think it could happen with piano lessons?

How does repetition help you learn? Even with interest and good will some people learn with difficulty. They lack the skills to make efficient

Do you think the boy is learning much? Why? What should he do?

use of their mental ability. The development of useful mental skills and habits is as important as the development of physical skills and habits.

Learning requires *repetition* and *understanding*. Few people learn much the first time they study a lesson. Whether you are learning to swing a baseball bat, to drive a car, or to work a new kind of problem, your first attempt is likely to be unsatisfactory.

Failure is a natural part of learning. You can learn a great deal from mistakes and failure. Thomas Edison tried over a hundred times to make an invention work, failing every time, before he learned the right combination.

Do you think he tried exactly the same thing a hundred times?

Repetition for learning is more than a dull pattern of doing a thing over and over. Learning requires constant alertness, criticism, and correction. This is where an instructor or coach is useful. He can help you to find and correct mistakes before they become practiced. Directors and instructors help you to avoid mistakes; they help you to skip many trials and errors. They are like guides who have been through the same country before you.

Psychologists have discovered that you learn more efficiently if you read every lesson at least three times. Read once, rapidly, for a bird's-eye view.

Why is drill helpful in learning? What makes drill interesting and enjoyable?

Try to figure out the main idea and purpose of the lesson without worrying about details. The second time, read slowly and carefully. Look for details and proofs of main points. Look up the words you do not understand. The third reading is another rapid one. See how the main ideas and details fit into a complete picture. In the long run those systematic readings will save you time.

How does understanding help you to learn? Which is easier to learn—15 words in a sentence or 15 unrelated words? Has a picture or puzzle or problem ever become suddenly clear to you? You learn best when you understand how one thing is related to another. Understanding is the ability to see a pattern or relationship between separate parts.

Learning is easier when you can associate new ideas with ideas you already have. Few studies are difficult if you can see a relationship between what you know and what is new. Difficulties arise when you try to grasp ideas before you are properly prepared.

Using a variety of methods helps you to learn. How would you go about learning to play a new game like golf? Would you read about it, or talk it over with some friends who wanted to

H. Armstrong Roberts

You can improve your ability to recite in class or to talk to a group of people by attention and practice. Do you take advantage of opportunities to improve yourself?

play, or watch someone, or take lessons, or just go out with a ball and club and try it? Probably you would do all these things and maybe think of some more. Some people who fail to learn by one method may learn easily by another.

A variety of methods helps you to learn lessons in school. You can learn from reading, writing, listening, talking, experimenting, looking at pictures and charts, and many other activities. Think while you learn. Try to fit in things you read and learn in school with your other experiences. Apply your knowledge as soon as you acquire it. Test it. See what it means to you and how it fits into your life. Try to make it interesting and important.

How can you study efficiently? One of the most important modern ways of learning is studying from books. Books are short cuts to learning. Good books are organized to lead you along step by step from things you know to new knowledge. They give you, in a short time, experiences that other people have acquired with great time and effort. To learn efficiently from books you need to develop such study skills as reading, concentrating, and fitting in book learning with other things you know. Investigations and experiments have revealed some principles and rules that can help anyone develop study skills.

Any learning takes a certain amount of time. Allowing sufficient time for study and using this time efficiently are the marks of a good student. The habit of letting work pile up is found most often among poor students. Insufficient time may be due to too many social or recreational ac-

Studying is a skill. Practicing good study techniques will make learning easier and more enjoyable.

Denver Public Schools

Can you carry on an interesting conversation or discussion? Do you think such a skill is valuable? How can you improve?

tivities. Usually it is caused by lack of planning.

Planning a regular time and place for study is extremely helpful. Doing

247

What are some mental skills that help you to use the library? How can you learn to find the material you want? To concentrate? To make efficient notes?

anything regularly helps form habits that save you time and energy. Studying under good physical conditions helps to prevent fatigue and wandering attention. A good place to study is well lighted, well ventilated, and free from such distractions and annoyances as radios, conversation, and noise or activity. Good posture, changes of position, and short periods of relaxation help prevent fatigue and make studying pleasant and effective.

Although good physical conditions make studying easier, everyone should learn to concentrate and to overlook little disturbances. If you work with a purpose, toward a goal you have set yourself, little discomforts will distract you less and less. As you grow up you should be able to concentrate your attention for longer and longer periods.

A definite goal is a great help to concentration. Make up your mind to accomplish a certain reasonable amount of work in a certain time. Break large goals, like understanding the backgrounds of American history, into a series of subgoals, like reading from page 620 to 632 in your book before taking a stretch. Make yourself stick with it. The satisfaction you feel from achieving a goal helps you to form habits of concentration and persistence.

How can you improve your memory? Many investigations have been made to see what study techniques help you to remember what you learn. Memory is part of the whole process of learning and is improved by methods and habits of learning.

You remember best the things that you understand, the things that add on to a pattern of things you already know. Try to put yourself into the place of others. As you study history, imagine yourself an American colonist in the Revolutionary War, or a congressman voting on a bill. What would you know, what would you think?

You remember best the things that you use. Try to apply immediately and often your new knowledge or ideas. Relate new learning to your own activities, to other things you are studying or expect to study. Talk about it; explain it to others; try it out.

All your learning experiences can reinforce and support each other. Some boys and girls try to shut each little thing they learn into a separate box instead of allowing all of them to make a pattern. Which is easier to remember—a paragraph of 50 words or a list of 50 unrelated words? Relate your history lesson to the novel you study in literature.

Spaced study periods help you remember. "Cramming" is an inefficient method of learning. Three 20-minute study periods are better than one 60-minute period. Periods of review and periods of rest after study help you to collect and organize new learning and to recall other experiences that are related.

Experiments show that forgetting is most rapid at first. Review new learning frequently at first. Then review at longer intervals. Since some

Denver Public Schools

Expressing yourself on paper is another skill that improves with attention and practice. Boys and girls your age should be able to write interesting, friendly letters and clear accurate descriptions. Do you need practice?

249

forgetting always happens, go beyond the point of barely successful learning. When you finally succeed in doing correctly that new dance step or football play, do it right several times while it is still fresh and you still have the swing of it.

Do the same for that poem you memorized for English or that new arithmetic process. It will save you some relearning later.

At the end of a study period, review and try to recall what you have learned. At the beginning of the next study period call to mind what you have learned previously. When you finish a large section of learning, review all you know about it.

Reviewing the chapter

Test yourself

Would you like to learn something about your study habits? You can find your own learning difficulties. Look over this check list of suggestions for study and see what habits you need to improve.

1. **Do you study under good physical conditions?** Are you physically fit and free from fatigue, illness? If you have defects of sight or hearing, have they been corrected? Is your study place well lighted, well ventilated, and reasonably free from distraction? Do you relax or take a stretch at intervals?

2. **Do you plan your time?** Do you allow enough time for study so that you can do a good job and feel a sense of satisfaction? Do you use several short study periods rather than one long one?

3. **Do you profit from mistakes and failures?** Do you observe your own limits and stop when work is no longer profitable? Do you try to find the reasons for failure? Do you realize that no one is perfect and refuse to be discouraged by failure? Do you set reasonable goals to be accomplished in a definite time so you can experience the satisfaction of achievement?

4. **Do you try to make serious reading interesting to yourself?** Do you try to realize the importance and meaning of what you are studying? Do you ask your-self, "How can I use this information now and in the future?" If previous knowledge or skill is required, do you get it? Do you try to acquire interest in a dull subject by finding out more about it? Everyone has had the experience of becoming interested in a subject as he finds out more about it. Do you alternate hard and easy work?

5. **Do you concentrate?** Do you know exactly what you are trying to do? Do you set a goal for yourself? Do you stay with each page until you understand as far as you have gone? Do you keep your mind on what you are doing? Do you avoid distractions by radio, daydreaming, or other means?

6. **Do you use good reading techniques?** Do you read a lesson three times: once rapidly, once carefully, once again rapidly? On the second reading do you look up unfamiliar words and use charts and other study aids? Do you try to recall what you have learned by stating it in your own words either by writing or telling?

7. **Do you try to understand what you learn?** Do you pick out the main ideas? Do you try to relate the main ideas to each other? Do you try to recall other things you know that are related?

8. **Do you apply what you learn?** Do you try to use new learning immediately? Do you apply book learning to practical situations in your own life?

Reading to help you grow up

How Man Discovered His Body, by Riedman, has an interesting chapter entitled "Your Thinking Cap."

To Live in Health, by Burnett, discusses mental health.

Do Your Own Thinking by C. H. Scheaf. You will be interested in these chapters: "How We Learn," "Study Helps Thinking," "Humor and Intelligence."

Films to help you understand

The Brain. Brandon.

Nervous System. Encyclopedia Britannica Films.

Encyclopedia Britannica Films

Imagine that you are standing beside this lake. What information and sensations will your senses bring you? Which of your senses seems the most important?

Your senses protect you from many dangers. Can you recognize traffic signs by their shapes? How do other senses warn you of dangers?

National Safety Council

SPEED LIMIT 40   STOP   RAILROAD CROSSING   R R

They protect us only when we observe them; they are useless when we don't.

252

Sense can be highly trained. Are you developing a sensitivity and precision in the use of your senses? What are some jobs that require highly trained senses?

All of your senses work together. Sometimes one must substitute for another. Which senses can help to make up for the loss of sight? Of hearing?

Many people who do not hear well can learn to understand speech very well by lip reading. Can you read lips?

Chapter 14

HOW CAN YOU MAKE BETTER USE OF YOUR SENSES?

*I*magine yourself unable to see, hear, touch, taste, or smell. If you were then taken to a strange place what impression of the place would you have? Could you find out anything about it?

Information about the world we are living in comes to us through our senses. Special kinds of nerve endings are affected by light, sound, odors, tastes, and touch.

Although we commonly speak of five senses there are really many more. Sight includes the ability to see light, color, and form. Hearing includes the ability to detect differences in pitch and intensity. Nerves of smell can detect thousands of different odors. Sensations of taste include sweet, sour, bitter, and salt. Touch includes sensations of pressure, strain, and changes of shape. Special nerves are sensitive to heat and cold. A mechanism in the inner ear gives sensations of upright position. Some sensations probably blend to give us a sense of motion and position and space. We receive impressions of pain from nerves. We have a sense of time, perhaps from the rhythm of body activity.

Only a human being has such varied and rich impressions of the world. Many animals live in a world lacking color, or sound, or some other sensory impression.

Our senses are sources of satisfaction and pleasure as well as information. We can receive pleasure from the rich color of a jewel or the texture of a silky fur. We receive comfort from warmth, a touch, and a friendly voice.

We can improve our ability to use our senses. A trained musician hears variations of sound unnoticed by many people. A farmer or an artist looking at a field of grain would see things that others would not.

Knowledge of how sense organs work can help you care for them and use them more efficiently. Experience and practice in using all your senses will add greatly to your knowledge and enjoyment of the world.

In this chapter will be discussed the function and care of the eyes and ears.

254

Looking ahead

Questions and suggestions

1. Your senses bring you all kinds of messages from the world around you. We often speak of the five special senses. What are they?

2. Each of the five senses has many subdivisions. Knowing and using them makes life more pleasant and interesting.

Sight includes the ability to recognize light, colors, and shapes.

Hearing includes ability to recognize pitch and intensity. What is pitch?

Touch includes the ability to recognize changes of shape, pressure, strain, and vibrations.

The nose can distinguish over 6000 odors. There are only four taste sensations—sweet, sour, bitter, and salt.

Special nerves bring messages of heat and cold, pain, muscle position, and balance. You may like to try some experiments to test your own senses.

3. You can improve your ability to use your senses. Let them register. Use them. Take a real look at the world around you. Part of using your senses consists of paying attention and noticing things. Could you go to another room and describe all the sights and sounds and other sense impressions that are coming to you now?

Some authors and poets have the ability to re-create a scene so the reader feels he is there. How many interesting things—people, buildings, flowers, insects, and sounds—did you notice on the way to school this morning?

Do you ever stop to enjoy the beauty in the sky, in flowers, or in a snowflake?

4. Senses can be made keener by training. Many adults are not good observers. Without looking again, can you describe accurately the boy or girl sitting beside you? Can you tell about people who have trained various senses?

5. Ability to use your senses is enriched by experiences. Children acquire ability to use their senses because they are curious. They handle and touch and taste everything.

Indifference causes many adults to limit their abilities to use and enjoy their senses. Do you explore your world? Do you visit places outside your own neighborhood? Do you experiment with new foods, listen to all kinds of music, or learn to handle many things—from machinery to clay? Can you recognize flowers, birds, kinds of wood, musicians, and painters?

Your ability to use your senses can grow throughout your life. Senses can be ways of learning and sources of pleasure. They are well worth your care and protection.

Committee planning

Committees can collect materials for experiments with various senses. Some experiments are suggested at the end of the chapter. The committees can find others in the books suggested there and in other reading material.

1. A committee may be able to arrange to have vision and hearing tests for the class.

2. You may be able to visit an art gallery or to listen to recordings of many kinds of music. Are you more interested in a symphony or opera when you understand it?

3. A committee might like to make a collection and exhibit of optical illusions, that is, of pictures that deceive you.

4. A science committee can experiment with lenses.

How can you see better?

Of all your senses, probably sight contributes most to the ease and joy of living. Yet most of us abuse our eyes. We fail to use them as effectively as we might. Understanding how your eyes work can help you to form efficient habits of using and caring for them.

What is the eye like? In many ways the eye resembles a camera. A camera is a box whose interior is completely dark. Light may enter only by passing through a lens (a curved piece of glass) set in the front of the box. A screen or shutter in front of the lens regulates the amount of light that enters. The lens bends the light rays so that they focus on a film and form an image. Examine a camera. Notice the arrangement of the shutter, lens, and film. Experiment with a lens to see how it bends light rays to focus them at a point.

The eyes are somewhat like ball-shaped cameras about an inch in diameter. At the back they are connected to the brain by a thick cable of nerves, called the *optic nerve*. A small almond-shaped *lens* is suspended in the front center of the eyeball.

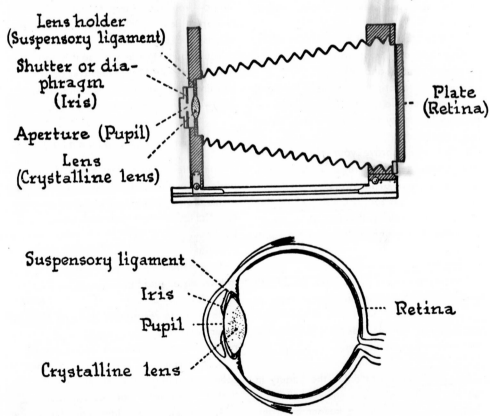

Lens holder
(Suspensory ligament)

Shutter or dia-
phragm
(Iris)

Aperture (Pupil)

Lens
(Crystalline lens)

Plate
(Retina)

Suspensory ligament

Iris

Pupil

Crystalline lens

Retina

Using these diagrams, compare the parts of the eye with a camera. How does the eye differ from a camera?

The inside of the eyeball is a transparent jelly. Covering the jelly-like interior are three coats. The outer one is a tough protective covering. The middle coat contains the tiny blood vessels that nourish the cells of the eye and a dark pigment to shut out all light. The inner coat is a sensitive film, called the *retina*.

The tough outer layer, or *sclera*, covers the entire eyeball. In front, it is visible as the "white" of the eye. Where it passes in front of the lens, it is transparent and bulges slightly. You can see the transparent bulging part, or *cornea*, by looking at a friend's eye from the side as he looks straight ahead.

The dark middle coat, or *choroid*, covers all the eyeball except for a small hole in front of the lens. Where the choroid is visible through the transparent cornea, it forms the *iris*, or colored part of the eye. The color of the eye varies from light blue to dark brown according to the amount of pigment present. Most new-born babies have blue eyes. Later the pigment may change to brown, grey, or black.

The iris contains circular muscles which can contract and relax to

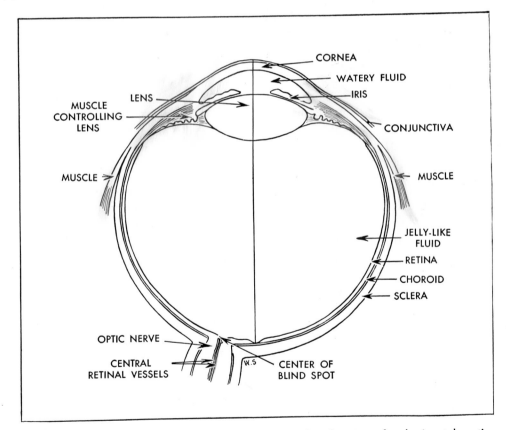

Note the various parts of the eyeball, as shown in this diagram of a horizontal section of the eyeball. Is the eyeball hollow?

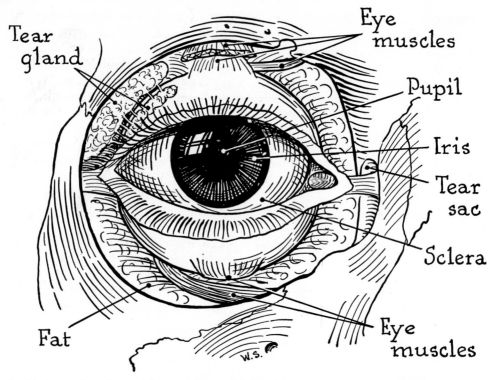

In this front view of the right eye, the eyelid has been partly removed to show the tear gland. Where is the cornea? The lens?

change the size of the opening in the center. The hole in the center of the iris is called the *pupil*. It appears black because it looks into the dark interior of the eyeball. The pupil changes in size to regulate the amount of light entering the eye. You can watch the pupil in a friend's eye grow larger in dim light and smaller in bright light. Directly in back of the pupil is the lens.

The space between the lens and cornea is filled with a watery liquid, called the aqueous humor.

What is the optic nerve? The optic nerve is a cable of thousands of nerve fibers leading from the back part of the brain to the eyeball. It enters the eyeball at the back by penetrating the two outer coats. Inside the eyeball, it

branches into millions of nerve endings. The nerve endings form a sensitive film, called the retina. The retina lines all the back part of the eyeball.

All sight impressions pass instantly from the retina through the optic nerve to the brain. Unlike a film, the retina does not retain the image. It is immediately erased, and the retina can receive new images in rapid succession. Damage to any of the paths along which sight messages travel results in more or less loss of vision.

The optic nerve itself is not sensitive to light stimuli. Where the optic nerve enters the eyeball there is a spot where light rays make no impression. This is the "blind spot."

How is your eye protected? Your eyeball is protected from injury by its position in a bony socket and by eyelids and eyelashes. The upper lid closes over the eye like a curtain. The lashes are rows of curved hairs along the edges of the lids. They help to screen the eyes from dust and insects.

The inner surfaces of the eyelids are lined with a thin membrane, called the conjunctiva. This membrane also covers the front of the eyeball and gives the eye its moist, glistening appearance.

The front of the eye is kept moist and washed free of small particles by tears. Tears are secreted by the tear glands which lie near the upper outer edge of the eye socket. Tears spread across the eyeball in a thin film and flow down into the nose through two tubes at the inner corner of the eye.

How does the eye work? Light entering the eye passes in order (1) through the transparent cornea, (2) through the aqueous humor, (3) through the pupil (or hole in the iris), (4) to the lens, and (5) on to the retina. The lens bends the light rays so that they focus on the retina.

In a camera the focusing of an image is performed by sliding the lens backward and forward. Look through a pair of field glasses or a microscope. What do you do to get a clear image? The human eye focuses in a different way. It changes the shape of the lens, making it flatter or more rounded. The lens is held in place in the eyeball by a frame of ligament. The ligament is controlled

Harold M. Lambert

How do you focus a pair of field glasses? How does your eye change its focus?

by a tiny muscle. A pull on the muscle causes the ligament to relax, and allows the lens to thicken. Relaxation of the muscle tightens the ligament and causes the lens to become thinner. The thickening of the lens is called *accommodation.*

In the normal eye a slight tension of the accommodation muscle holds the lens so that images about 20 feet away are in sharp focus. For work at close range, the muscle must work to thicken the lens. Continuous work at close range may cause strain on the eye muscles.

How can experts help you take care of your eyes?

Your eyes have many natural protections. They can make adjustments to compensate for some defects. However, our modern life often makes our eyes work under difficult conditions for long periods of time. We can often use help from experts to help our eyes work better and to prevent them from being overworked or damaged.

Why do some people need glasses? Many eyeballs are imperfectly shaped. They may be too deep from front to back, or they may be too shallow. If the eyeball is too long, parallel light rays from distant objects come to a focus in front of the retina. Near objects may be seen clearly without accommodation. Distant objects appear blurred. Such a condition is called *nearsightedness.*

In *farsightedness,* the eyeball is too short. A person is likely to see distinctly both near and far objects, but he sees with extra effort. Such an eye uses accommodation for near objects just as a normal eye does. It also must use accommodation for distant objects, which the normal eye does not. Farsighted persons use the accommodation muscle all the time. They are likely to suffer eyestrain without realizing there is anything wrong.

All persons are born farsighted. Eyeballs tend to grow deeper. They may grow too deep, causing nearsightedness. They may not grow deep enough, causing farsightedness. From early childhood the lenses gradually become more rigid and less capable of accommodation. A young child with normal eyes can see objects plainly as near as four inches or less. A person of forty years with normal eyes may be able to see them plainly at six or seven inches. By forty-five years, the minimum distance for sharp vision will probably increase to ten inches. Older people often need glasses to bring small close objects into sharp focus.

Defects in the shape of the eyeball usually cannot be cured. They can be corrected by wearing a properly fitted lens in front of the eye. A concave lens will spread light rays before they reach the lens of the eye and cause them to focus further back. A convex lens causes rays to come closer together before they reach the eye and thus to focus farther forward.

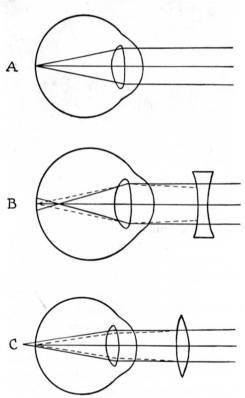

In a normal eye (A), parallel light rays from distant objects focus on the retina to produce a clear image. In a nearsighted eye (B), the eyeball is too long; rays meet in front of the retina, producing a blurred image. The dotted lines show how a concave lens corrects the focus by spreading the light rays. In the farsighted eye (C), the eyeball is too short; rays fail to reach a focus. The dotted lines show the path of the light rays after correction by convex lenses.

Astigmatism is another eye defect that causes blurred vision. It is often due to slight irregularities or differences of curvature in the cornea, or lens, or both. Rays of light are bent irregularly and a sharp focus is not possible from any distance.

Nearsighted people need concave lenses to help them to see at a distance. Those slightly farsighted do not need glasses to see clearly, but they do need glasses to save the accommodation muscles from the strain of constant use. People with astigmatism need glasses with a combination of curves to counteract curves in the eye surfaces.

Eyeglasses are precision instruments which require careful handling. The frame holds the lens precisely centered in front of the eye. If the frame is bent, this accurate centering is disturbed and the glasses are less effective. Film or particles on the lens may blur vision enough to cause fatigue. The lens should not be touched by the fingers and should be polished with a soft cloth or tissue.

Who needs an eye examination? The fact that more eyeglasses are used all the time may not signify that eyes are growing weaker. Under modern conditions eyes are used more strenuously. Also, techniques for corrections are constantly being improved.

Boys and girls who neglect wearing needed glasses often damage their eyes, harm their nervous system, and reduce their general efficiency. Much poor schoolwork and many accidents and injuries are due to eye defects that can be corrected. The eyes of every schoolchild should be examined each year or two. If the test made by

Denver Public Schools

Poor schoolwork, nervousness, irritability, accidents, and headaches are caused in part by eye defects. Most eye defects can be corrected with properly fitted glasses.

the school nurse or teacher shows defective vision or suggests the presence of strain, examination by an eye specialist is recommended.

Vision is usually tested by using a chart with numbers, letters, or other symbols. The person tested usually sits 20 feet away and attempts to read from the chart. Each eye is tested separately. Why? The vision is usually expressed as a fraction. Above the line is put the distance at which the person being tested reads the symbols. Below the line is the reading distance for a normal eye. Normal vision is usually considered as 20/20. Can you demonstrate this on a few classmates with a reading chart?

An *oculist* or *ophthalmologist* is a physician who specializes in the treatment of all eye disorders, defects, or diseases. An *optometrist* is one tech-

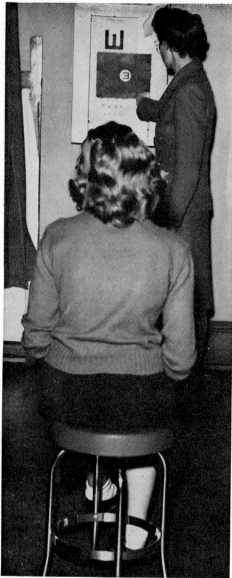

Vision is often tested by using a chart with letters or symbols of graded sizes. What does 20/20 vision mean? Why might such a test fail to detect farsightedness?

lenses for eyeglasses according to a formula or prescription.

How do the eyes work together? The eyeball is moved in various directions by three pairs of muscles fastened to it and controlled by nerves. Proper control of the muscles causes the eyes to work together.

Ordinarily the two eyes receive separate, slightly different pictures. In the brain, experience and intelligence blend the two pictures into one which gives a sense of depth or perspective. By experience, a person learns to compare the two pictures to estimate size, shape, distance, and rate of motion. A person with one eye, or one who has not developed this sense of perspective, cannot judge accurately whether he is seeing a large object far away or a small object nearby. He would have trouble judging things like how far away a car is and how fast it is approaching. Why are perspective tests important for pilots?

If the two eyes do not focus on an object together, double vision may occur, or the stronger eye may do most of the work while the weaker eye gradually loses its sense of sight. If one muscle of an eye is weak, the eyeball tends to turn in the direction of the strongest pull. A pull to one side or the other causes squint or cross-eyes. Some kinds of cross-eye are caused by birth defects or by paralysis of the eye muscles. Most cases in young people are related to farsightedness, and, if cared for early, can be relieved by wearing proper lenses. Some squint and cross-eye can be corrected by muscle training or by surgery. Eye defects should be treated as early as possible by an oculist.

nically trained to measure vision and to correct defects of vision with glasses. An *optician* is one who grinds

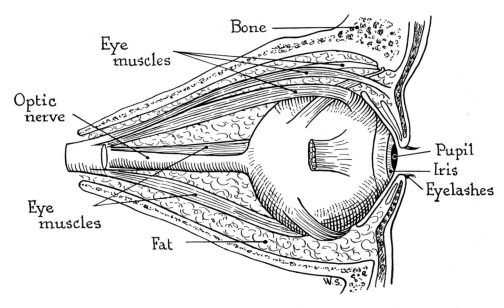

Six slender muscles control the movements of the eye. What happens if some muscles are weak?

What is color blindness? Color blindness is an inherited defect found most often among men. In the commonest form, a color-blind person cannot distinguish red from green. In the most extreme form all colors are seen as varying shades of gray. There is no correction for these defects. Color blindness may be dangerous in activities that depend upon colored signal lights. Trainmen, sailors, pilots, and sometimes even automobile drivers may be disqualified for color blindness.

In dim light no one can see clearly and sharply. A person with normal eyes has a short interval of *night blindness* when he changes from a brightly lighted place to a dark one. In the dark, even a faint light may be temporarily blinding. Usually after a few minutes in the dark, nerve end-

ings become sensitive to dim light. Some people, however, do not regain their vision and remain almost blind while in dimly lighted places. Lack of vitamin A in the diet contributes to night blindness.

Experiments have shown that a person can see more clearly in dim light by looking sideways at an object. Nerve endings which are sensitive to dim light are located mainly away from the center of the retina. How is this fact of value to night fighting pilots?

Another important disorder of the eye, called a cataract, occurs rather frequently in older people. The lens, normally transparent, becomes cloudy, sometimes to the point of causing blindness. The only remedy is to remove the lens and put a strong convex glass in front of the eye.

Have you ever seen a poor picture taken by a fine, expensive camera? Improper use of your eyes can also result in poor vision.

What causes eyestrain? There are many symptoms of eyestrain. The eyes themselves may look strained. They may be red rimmed, be bloodshot, or have crusty lids or sties. Sometimes the symptoms appear in other parts of the body. Eyestrain may cause repeated headaches, dizziness, nausea, vomiting, twitching eyelids, or even a general tired feeling. If properly balanced rest and exercise and a good diet fail to relieve such symptoms, an eye physician should be consulted.

Defects of vision are one cause of eyestrain. Strain due to eye defects can be overcome by wearing properly fitted glasses. Some people refuse to wear glasses. They think glasses spoil their looks or prevent their participating in activities. A little observation will convince you that such fears are unnecessary. Many attractive people wear glasses. Anyone can find a becoming style. By taking away that strained, tired look glasses actually may make a person better

The pupil reacts to light and to accommodation. It is contracted (left) when exposed to light or looking at a near object. It is dilated (right) when light is withdrawn or in looking at a distant object.

looking. Modern glasses need not interfere with activity. Even big-league baseball stars wear them. George Mikan, the famous basketball player, wears glasses with special unbreakable lenses to overcome nearsightedness. Do you know other athletes who wear glasses?

Improper use of normal eyes may also cause strain. Anything that causes the eyes to make continuous adjustments may be tiring. Dim light, dazzling light, or glare may tire the eyes. Light that shines directly into the eyes or that is reflected by a shiny surface may fatigue the muscles and retina. It may cause a painful contraction of the pupil or even damage the retina. Eyes may be seriously injured by looking directly at the sun. At the beach or on snow, eyes often need the protection of tinted glasses.

Eyes become tired when they must constantly change focus. Reading on a moving train or streetcar may be tiring. Unsteady motion pictures or sitting too close to the screen may cause eyestrain.

Hold your head erect and look at objects straight ahead, then above, below, and at the side of your direct line of vision. Notice how the visibility of a printed page is reduced as you move it from a position directly in front of the eyes to a position flat on the desk. Eyestrain may be caused by reading material that is held at an angle away from a direct line of vision.

Proper lighting and correct use of the eyes in close work will help to protect your eyesight. Good light should come from a steady source, be bright enough to light without glare, and produce no shadows on the reading or working surface. For general use, light reflected from a wall or ceiling produces less glare and casts less noticeable shadows. For close work an additional direct light, shaded so as not to shine into the eyes, may be preferable.

Material being read should be held still, perpendicular to the line of vision, and 13 inches or more away from the eyes. If you are writing, light coming from over your left shoulder will prevent interference from the shadow of your hand.

When reading or doing close work, look away from your work at frequent intervals. Blinking the eyes helps to clear and to rest them.

How can you protect your eyes? Eyes that are healthy and functioning properly do not need special protection in ordinary circumstances. Some habits are helpful in protecting and making the best use of your eyes.

The membrane lining the eyelids and covering the front of the eyeball is usually washed free from dust by tears. It may become irritated or inflamed when exposed to too much dust. Goggles can be used to protect

General Electric Company

A combination of gloom and glare is hard on eyes. How do these people show the effects of strain? What other symptoms may be caused by eyestrain?

265

Can you find six common errors of study desks in the top photo? How have they been corrected in the bottom photo?

the eyes from glare and dust in some occupations.

Small particles that are caught in the eye are usually washed out by tears. Splashing clear water in the eye may help to wash out a foreign particle. An experienced person may remove a particle by grasping the lashes on the upper lid to hold the eye open and touching the particle gently with a corner of a clean handkerchief. Never press or rub the eye as a particle may scratch the delicate membrane or may become imbedded. If a foreign object does not come out easily, see a physician.

The membrane lining the eye may become infected. The most common infection is known as pinkeye. It is a communicable disease. Those in-fected should keep away from others. Infections are commonly carried to the eyes by dirty fingers or by towels or washcloths that have been used by others. The safest rule is to keep everything away from your eyes. For any severe inflammation an eye physician should be consulted as soon as possible.

Eyes of newborn infants are treated with a weak solution of silver nitrate to prevent infection. Persons recovering from measles need to take special care not to strain their eyes.

A black eye, like a bruise anywhere, is due to the breaking of blood vessels in the soft tissues. The most helpful treatment is to apply ice or cold wet compresses as soon as possible.

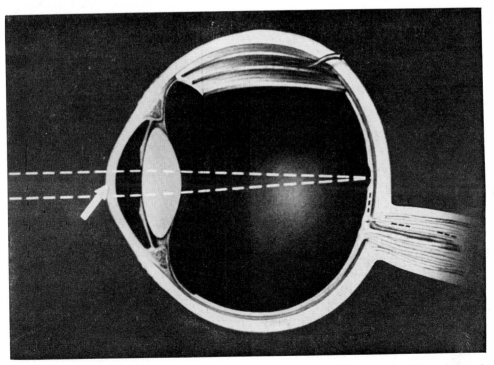

This diagram shows the important parts of the eye. Can you tell the names of the parts and what each parts does?

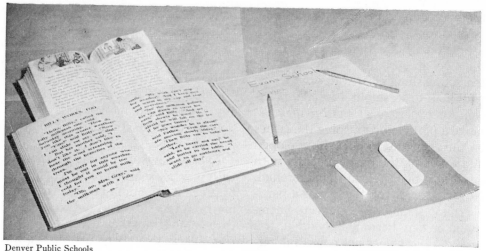

This picture compares ordinary school materials with those used in sight-saving classes. How does your community or school help people with defects in vision or hearing? How can you help them?

Examinations every year or two will enable you to find defects while they are easy to correct. Prompt medical attention for symptoms of strain like burning, itching, blurring, and headache may prevent damage to your eyes.

Some blindness is due to faulty structure of the eyeball. Most blindness is acquired, and much is preventable. Accidents and burns from fires and chemicals account for many cases of blindness. Foresight and consideration for others will do much to prevent injuries in games and from air rifles, firecrackers, rubber bands, snowballs, and other missiles.

Progressive nearsightedness causes some blindness. Many schools now have sight-saving classes to help people with vision defects to protect and use their eyes.

How can you hear better?

Next to sight, hearing is probably the most important of our senses. Our ears are delicate receiving instruments that are sensitive to sounds. Through our ears we become aware of sounds that vary greatly in quality and intensity.

How do you hear? Sound waves are created when objects vibrate. Pluck a tightly stretched wire or strike a tightly stretched membrane so that it vibrates. Listen to the sound that comes from it.

The ears are constructed to pick up sound waves and conduct them to nerve endings. The ear is commonly said to consist of three parts: the outer or external ear, the middle ear, and the inner ear. Most important is the delicate inner ear where the sound waves are picked up by the auditory (hearing) nerve.

The external ear consists of a visible sound collector like a funnel, and a canal. The sound collector on the outside of your head collects sound waves from all about you. Have you ever helped it to collect sound by cupping your hand behind it? Sound waves travel along the canal to a drum membrane at its inner end.

The canal is constructed so that objects are not likely to get in to injure delicate inner parts. It is a curved tunnel. Wax is secreted by the skin along the canal. Normally the wax is pushed out soon after it is secreted. Wax helps to keep the canal clear. It lubricates the canal and eardrum, keeping them flexible. In some people wax accumulates and hardens in the ear canal. It may cause temporary deafness or an annoying buzzing sound. If this occurs, a physician should be consulted. Attempts to clean out wax yourself may injure the drum membrane. Cleaning your own ears should be done carefully with a cloth over your fingertip. Nothing smaller than a fingertip should ever be inserted in the ear except by a physician or nurse.

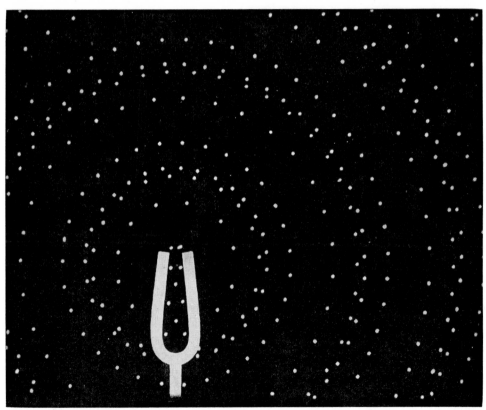

Sound waves are created when objects vibrate. The diagram shows how successive waves of sound move out in all directions from a vibrating fork.

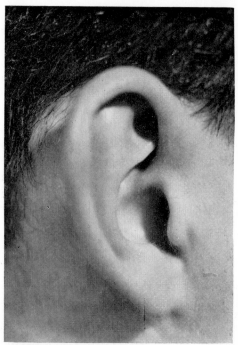

The external ear is a funnel-like sound collector. Cup your hand behind your ear. Do you collect more sound?

Three small bones in the middle ear connect the membrane or drum at the end of the canal with the inner ear. Because of their shape the three bones are called the hammer, anvil, and stirrup. One theory is that the bones soften certain vibrations before they reach the inner ear. Another theory is that they intensify vibrations.

A tube, called the Eustachian tube, leads from the middle ear to the throat. The purpose of the tube is to equalize pressure inside and outside the eardrum. The throat end of the tube opens when you swallow.

The inner ear is in two parts. One, called the cochlea, is like a tiny snail shell. It is filled with fluid and contains the sensitive endings of the auditory nerve. When set in motion, the fluid causes the nerves to carry impulses to the hearing area of the brain.

How does the ear help maintain balance? Another part of the inner ear is called the semicircular canal. The semicircular canal contains fluid which moves as you change position. The movement of the fluid causes pressure on delicate nerves in the canal. Signals from the nerve to the brain stimulate orders to the body to right itself and maintain balance. Dizziness may be caused by sudden changes of direction or position, like sitting up too suddenly from a lying position, or sudden ascent or descent in an elevator. Repeated change of direction, like that in an airplane or a swing or a ship, may set up many contrary impulses and cause a feeling of nausea. The degree of sickness is usually greater where unfamiliar motions—up and down or sidewise—are involved. Many persons get used to the new motions and become less subject to motion sickness. You can prevent some sickness by gradually becoming used to various kinds of motions. If you begin to feel dizzy, lie down to lessen vertical motion, which seems to be the worst.

Other sense impressions also help maintain balance. For example, it is easier to balance with your eyes open. Other nerves in muscles, tendons, joints, and skin seem to be stimulated by motion and pressure to give a sense of position and balance. A person with his eyes closed can tell the position of his body and its parts and the

270

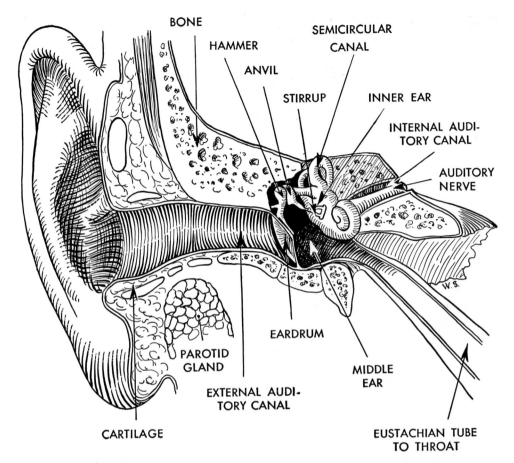

BONE
HAMMER
ANVIL
SEMICIRCULAR
CANAL
STIRRUP
INNER EAR
INTERNAL AUDI-
TORY CANAL
AUDITORY
NERVE
EARDRUM
PAROTID
GLAND
MIDDLE
EAR
EXTERNAL AUDI-
TORY CANAL
CARTILAGE
EUSTACHIAN TUBE
TO THROAT

The diagram shows the external, the middle, and the internal ear. Why is it dangerous to allow any object to enter the auditory canal?

direction of motion. These senses become keener from experience. Some adults have a highly developed sense of balance.

What are hearing defects? Many people do not know they are hard of hearing. We are likely to get used to what we hear, and we think it is normal. You can experiment to test the hearing of your classmates and yourself. Use some instrument that makes a small clear noise. Blindfold the person being tested. Let him sit in a chair in the middle of the room. Have him point to the location of the noise. Try various distances with each ear separately and with both ears.

Moderate deafness may account for apparent backwardness and lack of spirit. A person who does not hear well is often fearful and timid. A very deaf person tends to develop an attitude of irritability. He often becomes suspicious and may withdraw from others. Most elderly persons lose some sense of hearing. Such deafness may

271

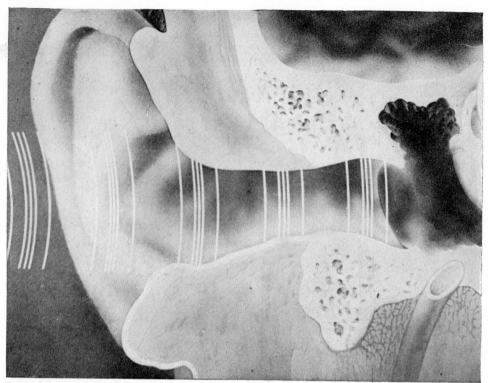

Encyclopedia Britannica Films

Sound waves travel down the short canal leading to the eardrum and middle ear. What is the tube opening on the inner side of the eardrum?

be due to increased rigidity of parts of the middle ear. Or it may be due to changes in the nerve paths.

The so-called deaf and dumb are rarely dumb in any sense of the word. Usually their failure to speak is due to their inability to hear. Normal people learn to speak by imitating others. Individuals deaf from birth or early childhood have never had the opportunity to imitate speech. They can be trained to read lips and then to speak. The art of lip reading has become well developed in recent years and is bringing comfort to many people.

Many cases of deafness can be helped by electrical hearing aids or other kinds of appliances which intensify sound vibrations. We can do our part to help those who are hard of hearing by being especially patient with them. They should be encouraged to use hearing aids. In these ways we can make them feel that they can participate in everyday activities.

How can you protect your hearing? Good hearing requires that the ear canal be open, that the eardrum and bones in the middle ear be free to vibrate, that the inner ear and nerves be in good condition, and that

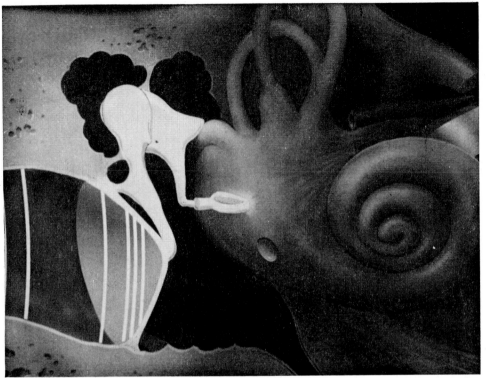

The eardrum is shown curved inward. Three small bones connect it with the inner ear. Can you find the cochlea? The semicircular canals? What does each do?

the hearing center in the brain be ready to interpret the sound.

Nose and throat infections may cause ear trouble by traveling along the Eustachian tube to the middle ear. At such times inflammation and swelling may cause temporary deafness, and occasional permanent damage. Blowing the nose too forcibly may carry nasal secretions into the middle ear.

Diseased tonsils or enlarged adenoids may cause partial deafness by blocking the Eustachian tube or by causing infection in the tube. Various infections like scarlet fever, measles, and influenza often cause inflammation. Pus may form and cause pain and pressure.

Middle-ear infections may cause the eardrum to break or rupture. Sometimes to prevent a rupture, a physician may help the pus drain by making a small hole in the eardrum. Such a small opening usually heals readily.

Earache may be relieved by applications of heat in the form of hot, dry cloths or a hot water bottle placed against the side of the head. Severe earache or a running ear should have immediate medical attention. An in-

Can you find two hearing devices in the picture? How do they work?

fection may cause deafness. The infection may extend into the mastoid bone behind the ear, or even into the brain, causing serious illness or death. Ear infection and mastoiditis are some of the most dangerous possible complications of a cold.

The eardrum needs to be protected from injury or infection from the outside as well as from the inside. Water should be kept out of the ear. When swimming, and especially when diving, you can protect your eardrums by wearing a cap or using earplugs. Wax, foreign objects, or insects should be removed by a physician.

All persons should have their hearing tested from time to time. Those whose hearing is defective can learn ways of compensating by lip reading and by observation. More serious hearing defects can often be overcome by use of hearing aids. In the schools of some cities, all pupils are tested for acuteness of hearing with an apparatus called the audiometer. This apparatus consists of a phonograph with earpieces for each member of the class. In a quick, accurate way, slight hearing defects can be easily discovered. Does your school have any hearing tests?

What special protection do your ears need in sports and other activities? Why is an earache always serious? How should it be cared for?

Denver Public Schools

Reviewing the chapter

Test yourself

I

You should answer "yes" to the following questions.

1. Do you rest your eyes occasionally?
2. Do you never read in a moving vehicle?
3. Do you always have proper light for eye work?
4. Do you use your own clean washcloth, towel, and handkerchief?
5. Do you keep your hands away from your eyes?
6. Do you blow your nose properly?
7. Do you treat every earache as serious?
8. Do you have regular eye and ear check-ups?

II

Which of the following statements are true and which are false? Reword each false statement to make it true.

1. Gradual loss of hearing is always noticed by the person affected.
2. The middle ear is connected with the throat by the semicircular canal.

Denver Public Schools

This is a hearing-conservation class. The electrical appliances magnify sounds so the pupils can learn to associate sights and sounds. How can you sharpen and train your own senses?

3. Many hard-of-hearing persons are helped by mechanical hearing aids.

4. Light enters the eye through an opening called the ears.

5. Eyestrain caused by a defect in the structure of the eyeball may often be cured by exercise.

6. The only part of the eye which is sensitive to light is the cornea.

7. Sewing and books should be held about 6 inches from the eyes.

III

What would you think, say, or do in the following situations?

1. If you were not able to see words on the blackboard clearly?

2. If your eyes often felt strained or irritated?

3. If you noticed you often had to ask people to repeat what they said?

4. If your friends were going to scare someone by exploding a firecracker or popping a paper bag close to his ear?

5. If you wanted to make life easier for a person who was hard of hearing?

6. If distant objects appeared blurred?

7. If you had frequent headaches, especially after reading or attending motion pictures?

8. If you wished to protect your eyes from glare?

276

Reading to help you grow up

How Your Body Works, by Herman and Nina Schneider, describes many interesting experiments with taste, smell, sight, and hearing.

Man in the Air, by Herbert Zim, discusses the importance of eyes and ears in flying.

How to protect and use your eyes and ears is discussed in these books:

Your Health and Happiness by Burkhard and others.

Builders for Good Health by Burkhard and others.

The Human Body by Brownell and Williams.

A Sound Body by Charters and others.

Sound, by Bertha Morris Parker, has some interesting experiments for you to perform.

Story of Sound by James Geralton, explains sound phenomena like echoes, musical instruments, telephones, and noise.

Films to help you understand

Ears and Hearing. Encyclopedia Britannica Films.

Eyes and Their Care. Encyclopedia Britannica Films.

Eyes for Tomorrow. National Society for Prevention of Blindness.

Light Is What You Make It. Pennsylvania College for Women. Disney color cartoon.

Your Eyes. Young America. A magician and an artist provide entertainment and instruction in function and care of eyes.

Williston Academy, Easthampton, Massachusetts

Good form in an athlete does not just happen. It results from correct habits of living, attention, and practice.

Good looks are the result of health and happiness. What are some habits that help you keep your skin, hair, and teeth clean, healthy, and attractive?

Ewing Galloway

H. Armstrong Roberts

Routine jobs are done more easily and efficiently if you form regular habits. Do you have a schedule that allows you a definite time for study, sleep, recreation, and home duties?

Active exercise outdoors speeds up the circulation, helps to keep muscles firm, and skin clear and healthy. What exercise do you have daily?

Denver Public Schools

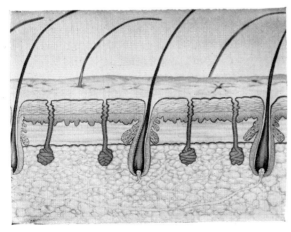

This section of skin, greatly magnified, shows hairs, oil glands, sweat glands, pores, and small arteries. Can you identify each without referring to the explanation in the chapter?

Encyclopedia Britannica Films

Chapter 15

HOW CAN YOU BE BETTER LOOKING?

A desire to be good looking is natural. We know that, fairly or not, we often judge other people by their appearance. We realize that others form their first ideas about us from the way we look. Everyone likes to have his appearance tell people that he is a person who would be an interesting and pleasant companion.

Our looks reflect the way we think and feel about ourselves and others. They also affect the way we feel and act. An attractive appearance can make us feel more cheerful and self-confident. Good looks help us to satisfy two desires that are strong in everyone—a desire for self-respect and a desire to be liked and accepted by others.

Probably you know many people of all ages and descriptions that you consider good looking. What makes them attractive?

Good looks are not dependent upon the features you inherit. The perfect features, proportions, and coloring that we call beauty are not an essential part of good looks. A beautiful face may be spoiled by a disagreeable expression. Physical flaws may go unnoticed because of attractive grooming and expression. A person who faces defects and handicaps cheerfully may earn great admiration and liking.

The basis of good looks is good health—mental and physical. A healthy, happy person is always attractive. We are attracted by the appearance of a clean, alert, pleasant person, because we think he looks intelligent, considerate, and self-respecting.

To be as good looking as possible you need to know how to be healthy and happy. You need to make the most of your appearance. You can learn how to keep your skin, hair, and teeth healthy and clean. You can form habits of taking care of yourself that help you to feel better and to look as if you would be nice to know.

Looking ahead

Questions and suggestions

1. What makes a person attractive looking?

2. What do you dislike in a person's appearance?

3. What is the first thing you notice about a person?

4. Are you more aware of appearances now than when you were younger?

5. In what way do you think your standards change as you grow up?

6. How do fads and styles affect your ideas of what is good looking?

7. Why do you think people like to be good looking?

8. If you were listing the qualities you like in a friend, how would you rate appearance?

9. Do you think good looks are important for appearance or for revealing character, personality, disposition, and habits?

10. How does your appearance indicate that you are growing up socially, mentally, and emotionally? Does it show you are developing self-discipline and regard for others?

11. How do mannerisms and little habits affect your appearance?

12. Do you have any little habits that detract from your appearance, such as nail biting, lip chewing, standing on one foot, gum chewing, or combing your hair · in public?

Committee Planning

1. A committee interested in dramatics might like to demonstrate how posture and facial expression are used to express feelings and ideas. They could demonstrate how to play charades. Then the class might arrange a charade party or program.

2. The movie committee might like to take moving pictures of the class so you can see yourself as others see you.

3. The speaker's committee could invite someone, perhaps from a modeling or photographic studio or class, to give tips on standing and moving gracefully.

4. If you can locate a large mirror, everyone can watch himself standing and walking and performing other movements.

5. A committee might arrange a fashion show. They could exhibit clothing suitable for different occasions and activities, characteristics of various materials.

6. Committees interested in science can prepare experiments to show cleaning ability of water of various temperatures, with and without soap. Or they can evaporate a salt solution to show how perspiration leaves waste products behind. Or they can examine skin with a magnifying glass.

Reading

By now you should have established the habit of reading the chapter at least twice —once rapidly, and again more slowly.

How can you have a good complexion?

Normal healthy skin is clean and smooth and soft. Pimples, coarseness, roughness, dryness, acne, and other skin troubles may have a variety of causes. If you know how the skin functions, you may be able to figure out some remedies for your own skin troubles.

What is your skin like? Your skin is made up of two distinct layers. The outer layer is called the *epidermis* and the inner layer is called the *dermis*.

The outside cells of the epidermis are like scales, flat and hard. They are constantly falling off as tiny flakes of dead skin. The scaling is very noticeable when the skin has been unusually dry. The scales are washed off when you bathe and rubbed off on your clothing. Accumulation of dead scales makes your skin rough and dirty-looking. The inside cells of the epidermis are round and soft. They contain no blood vessels but are nourished from capillaries in the dermis directly beneath. They are constantly multiplying and pushing up the layer of old, practically dead, cells above.

Hairs and sweat and oil glands are located in the dermis. The sweat glands open to the outside through tiny openings called pores. Oil glands open into the pits (follicles) from which the hairs grow.

Sweat glands take water and some wastes from the blood and carry them to the surface. The water evaporates, but salt and other solids remain on the skin.

Oil glands secrete an oil which keeps the skin soft and flexible. On the scalp, oil from oil glands softens the hair, gives it luster, and keeps it from becoming brittle.

What causes freckles? The dermis also contains tiny grains of brown or reddish-yellow matter called *pigment*. The amount of pigment determines the color of your skin and hair. Blond people have very little pigment, Negroes a great deal, albinos none. The amount of pigment in your skin is inherited.

Your coloring also is affected by sunlight, which increases the amount of pigment either in spots called freckles or in an even tan. Rosiness of cheeks and skin and lips depends upon the thinness of the outer layer of skin, the number of blood vessels in the inner layer of skin, and the quality of the blood. A pale complexion may be due to ill health but is often merely a family trait.

What causes moles and warts? *Moles* are flat or raised spots on the skin varying in color from light yellow to black. Sometimes they have coarse hairs growing out of them. Their cause is not known. Ordinarily moles cause no trouble. If they seem to be a source of worry because they are painful or growing, they may be removed by a physician. Irritating a mole may produce cancer.

Warts may be harmless outgrowths from the skin, or they may be due to a virus infection. In children, warts sometimes come out in numbers and then suddenly disappear. This sudden disappearance of warts has given rise to superstitions regarding their removal. If troublesome warts persist, increase in number, or occur on the soles of the feet (plantar warts), a physician should be consulted.

What causes pimples? Openings of oil glands may become clogged with dirt and oil from the skin. The collection of dirt and grease in a pore makes a *blackhead*. Blackheads occur at any age but are most common during adolescence. People whose oil glands are overactive or who are careless about cleaning their skin are most likely to have blackheads. Sometimes they can be removed by pressing gently with clean fingers on either side of the blackhead. Great care must be taken so that the pressure is not

How does the sun affect your skin? How much sunshine should you have? Why?

great enough to break the skin or to cause bleeding. Usually blackheads cause no trouble unless they become infected.

If the oil glands become clogged and infected, they become hard, reddened bumps or pimples filled with pus. Infections around hair roots may become sties, boils, or carbuncles. These should not be self-treated. Infection may spread and cause serious trouble. Infections are dangerous, especially on the face where blood and lymph vessels go directly to the brain and eyes.

Chronic pimples or *acne* occur most frequently in the early teens. At this time the activity of many glands is greatly increased. Acne is not fully understood. It seems to be related to

the hormones at adolescence. Ordinarily a balanced diet, plenty of rest and exercise, and careful cleanliness will prevent or eliminate acne. Sometimes bad cases develop in spite of care. Then medical attention may be necessary to prevent scarring. Picking or squeezing skin infections is likely to spread them. Surrounding cells are injured, the skin is broken, and other infections may gain a foothold. If your body cannot take care of an infection, consult a physician.

What are some other skin disorders? There are many kinds of skin disorders. Some are caused by pressure, some by cuts or wounds, some by infection, and some by burns. Some rashes are symptoms of disease.

Continued pressure or rubbing of

skin causes the outer layer to thicken into a hard protective pad or *callus*. A fallen arch often allows a large callus to form on the ball of the foot. Properly fitting, low-heeled shoes that allow the body's weight to be balanced on the arches of the feet help prevent calluses.

Pressure of poorly fitted shoes may cause the skin to thicken over an irritated area on the toes with gradual formation of a *corn*. This will usually disappear if shoes are properly fitted.

A *blister* may be formed by rapid and persistent rubbing of the skin, especially in the palms of the hands or on the feet. This rubbing separates the outer and inner layers of skin. The space between fills with clear watery lymph, forming a blister. As long as the skin is not broken, there is no danger of infection and the fluid will gradually disappear. If the outer skin is broken, an antiseptic bandage should be applied over the blister.

If the blister is large, it may be broken. Often it is necessary to drain blisters to relieve pain or to avoid accidental breaking and infection. Use a sharp needle; sterilize it by holding it in a flame or dipping it in alcohol. Hold the needle flat against the skin at the edge of the blister and make a small puncture. Gently force the fluid out of the blister by pressing it with a sterile pad. Keep it covered—this is important—until a new layer of skin is grown.

Athlete's foot is a skin disorder caused by a tiny plant called a fungus. The fungus lives usually in warm, moist places such as shower rooms and runways of swimming pools. It sticks easily to feet that are moist from perspiration or water. The first symptom of athlete's foot is scaling and itching between the toes. These symptoms are followed by blisters, which sometimes open, giving a raw surface that itches and spreads on the foot. An early case of athlete's foot can be cured by using a mild antiseptic and by washing the feet every day and wearing clean hose every day. A physician should be consulted if the infection persists or spreads.

To help prevent spread of athlete's foot, most locker and shower rooms are washed regularly with strong chemical solutions. Persons known to have athlete's foot are excluded from showers until cured. You can protect yourself by carefully washing and drying between your toes, by wearing clean hose, and by keeping your bare feet off surfaces likely to be infected.

Cold sores or *fever blisters* come from virus infections or irritations that cause blisters to form around the mouth and lips. They usually appear when resistance has been lowered by a cold or by excessive exposure to sunlight. They may be very annoying but usually go away in a few days if they are left alone. Picking may cause them to become infected. Spirits of camphor or alcohol may be beneficial if applied when the sores first appear.

Hives is a skin irritation that may result from certain foods, from various drugs, or from contact with irritation. Repeated or persistent attacks of hives should have the attention of a physician.

Chicken pox, measles, and other diseases may cause skin eruptions. Impetigo, exzema, and rashes are still other skin diseases. You may like to look up some in which you are particularly interested. Any sudden skin eruption may be dangerous. It may be a warning of a disease—call a physician.

Practically all skin troubles are best treated by allowing the body's natural defenses to work. Keeping the skin unbroken, clean, and dry will prevent most infections. Patent salves should be avoided and the family physician should be consulted if the skin irritation persists. If the skin should be broken, antiseptic or sterile dressings should be applied. Widespread infections or breaks in the skin should be treated by a physician.

How does the sun affect your skin? Sunlight in moderate quantities has a good effect on normal skin. It causes vitamin D to be formed in the skin. In most people it increases pigment to form an attractive tan.

Pigment forms a protective layer for delicate cells underneath. Some people with little pigment sunburn easily. Anyone can be sunburned. The ultraviolet rays of sunlight are deceptive. They are present in light reflected from water, snow, ice, and clouds. People often are burned on cloudy days or when they are exposed to sunlight reflected from water or snow. You can tan or even burn without your skin feeling hot or looking red.

To acquire a suntan, begin gradually. Expose your skin for only five or ten minutes the first day. Begin your suntan during the time shortly before or after the sun's rays are most intense. Remember that the rays are most intense around the middle of the day. Increase the time of exposure by adding five minutes each day.

What causes body odor? Some sweat or perspiration is being given off from the body at all times. An ordinary person loses two to six pints of liquid daily, depending on his activity, the amount of water he has taken in, his clothing, and the weather. The water evaporates, but the body wastes which were dissolved in the water remain on the skin. Other substances which accumulate in the skin include oil, bacteria, dirt, and flakes of dead skin. If allowed to remain on the skin, they decompose and cause an unpleasant odor.

Bathing with warm, soapy water is necessary to remove substances from the skin and to prevent odors. Certain areas of the skin, such as the feet and armpits, have many sweat glands and should receive special attention. Underclothing absorbs much of the moisture given off by the body. Frequent change of underclothing is as important as bathing in eliminating body odor.

Some people perspire a great deal. Exercise increases perspiration. Nervous reactions to fear or embarrassment increase the amount of perspiration. Hot weather does too. When you perspire a great deal, you need to bathe more often.

What about baths? The obvious reason for a bath is to clean the skin. In reality a bath serves many other purposes. It may stimulate or soothe nerves. It may tone up or relax muscles. It may speed up the circulation of the blood. Bathing of the right sort at the right time improves health. It makes you look and feel good. No one needs to be afraid of work or play that makes him dirty. Your skin is a dirt-proof covering that can be easily cleaned. Only accumulated dirt is objectionable.

285

Perspiration is being given off from the body at all times. Exercise greatly increases the amount. What is a good routine to follow after strenuous exercise?

A warm bath with soap is most effective for cleaning the body. The water should be just a little above body temperature. Bathing in warm water expands the blood vessels in the skin and draws blood away from the brain. It often makes one feel comfortably sleepy. Such a bath is best taken at bedtime.

Soap is necessary to help remove dirt and especially oil. Any mild soap that lathers well and does not irritate the skin can be used. Colored and scented soaps are no better than plain, mild soaps. Often they are not as good. For average skin no medicine in a soap gives it any advantage over plain, ordinary mild soap.

The skin should be thoroughly rinsed before it is dried. Soap remaining on the skin may cause irritation. All parts of the body should be thoroughly dried, especially where skin surfaces are in contact, as between the toes.

The body should be thoroughly bathed with soap or warm water as often as necessary to keep it clean. If you cannot take a daily all-over bath, every day you should thoroughly wash your face, ears, neck, hollows under the arms, and feet. At least twice a week most people should take an all-over sponge bath, tub bath, or shower with warm water and soap.

Shower baths should follow strenuous exercise. Bathe before going to a party or social event. It shows consideration of your companions and increases your feeling of well-being and self-confidence.

Face and hands should be washed morning and evening and during the day as often as they are dirty. For health's sake, the hands should be washed thoroughly before eating and after going to the toilet.

A hot bath is the proper type for one who is chilled. The warmer the bath, the more necessary is protection against chilling after the bath. After a very hot bath, you should at once get into a warm bed in a warm room. A hot bath temporarily increases the size of blood vessels in the skin. It helps the blood to carry away waste products and often relieves muscle soreness or stiffness.

A cold bath will contract blood vessels in the skin. The cold bath should be followed by a brisk rubbing to help the blood vessels enlarge again so that the skin becomes warm and glowing. If no such reaction follows, the bath may have been too cold or too long, or the body may not be strong enough to respond well to the temperature change. If cold baths are not followed by a warm glow, they should be discontinued. For a healthy person who responds well, cold baths may be pleasant and stimulating, good for the skin and blood vessels.

No bath of any kind should be taken within an hour after eating. At that time blood is needed for digestion, and circulation should not be

Encyclopedia Britannica Films

The chief purpose of a bath is to cleanse the skin of accumulated dirt and perspiration. What are other benefits of a bath?

disturbed. How would a cold bath alter the blood supply to the digestive organs?

What about cosmetics? The well-cared-for skin of a healthy person generally does not need cold cream to soften it, powder to remove the shine from it, or artificial coloring to brighten it. Before resorting to beauty aids it is well to find out what can be done by diet, exercise, and cleanliness.

There is no substitute for healthy hair and teeth. There is no substitute for the clear complexion that comes from proper diet, rest, exercise and regular elimination. Nor can anyone improve on bright eyes that are not shadowed or hollowed from lack of sleep or some kind of overindulgence. A good complexion cannot be bought in a box or bottle, no matter how appealing its advertising may be.

Skin roughness or dryness may be due to accumulated dead skin, harsh soap, soap left on the skin, or washing with water that is too hot or cold. Overheated houses, dry climates, and

287

Clapps Baby Food Division

Healthy young people have no need for cosmetics. Older people use them to counterfeit the clear complexion, bright eyes, and rosy cheeks that result from good habits of diet, rest, and exercise.

exposure to sun or wind may cause the skin to become dry and scaly. In such cases, cold cream may be used to keep the skin soft. Cream containing lanolin, the oil from sheep wool, most nearly takes the place of natural human skin oils.

Being pale may be natural to the individual or it may indicate poor health —a condition that should be given proper treatment and not merely disguised with rouge. Healthy blood and exercise that keeps the blood flowing near the surface of the cheeks bring color to the face and give the skin a healthy appearance.

Some cosmetics involve special risks. Hair removers, dyes, and eyewashes may be irritating or poisonous. Using other people's lipstick or powder puffs may be an easy way to pick up skin and mouth infections. Products that make unusual or extravagant claims often are dangerous.

Use of cosmetics is general. Cosmetics are artificial aids to charm. If selected with care and used wisely, ordinary cold creams, face powders, and rouge should cause no harm. But they cannot take the place of health and thorough cleaning with soap and water.

Use of rouge, lipstick, and powder requires a careful study of what is suitable to your own individual features and coloring. Provided the materials are not injurious, use of cosmetics is a matter of taste. It requires knowledge and judgment. No artificial aids can surpass a clean, healthy young complexion. Girls are often misguided by advertisements and ruin a good, clear, natural skin. At best, the use of cosmetics is in large part an attempt to imitate a natural, healthy complexion.

How can you have attractive, good-looking hair?

Smooth, glossy hair adds a great deal to a person's appearance. Do you know why your hair is like it is—curly or straight, soft or stiff, oily or dry? Do you know how you can improve its appearance?

Your hair is one of the first things about you anyone notices. Dirty, un-

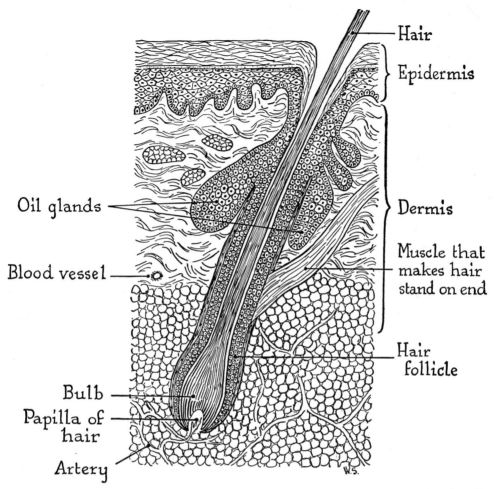

Hair

Epidermis

Oil glands

Dermis

Blood vessel

Muscle that
makes hair
stand on end

Hair
follicle

Bulb

Papilla of
hair

Artery

W.S.

Hairs grow out of pits, or follicles. They get their blood supply and nourishment only through the bulb or root. How can you help your hair receive plenty of necessary food materials to keep it healthy and attractive?

combed hair spoils your appearance.

What is hair and how does it grow? Hairs grow out of small pits in the outer layer of skin. These little pits, called follicles, push down into the dermis, even into the layer of fat beneath.

Hair usually grows at the rate of about one-half inch a month. Cutting or oiling hair at the ends may prevent splitting and breaking. It does not make hair grow faster, for the visible part of the hair shaft is dead tissue. The only part of the hair that is alive is the root, under the skin.

Near the hair root opening into the follicle are one or two oil glands. Oil secreted by these glands keeps the skin flexible and the hair soft and glossy. Hair is nourished through the root from the blood supply beneath the scalp.

Whether hair is straight or curly depends upon the shape of the individual hairs. Round hairs are straight. Oval hairs are wavy or curly.

Curling straight hair requires something to flatten the hair and press it into the shape of a curl. Permanent-wave solutions soften the outer layers of cells so they can be forced to assume the shape of curly hairs. Why are they not "permanent"?

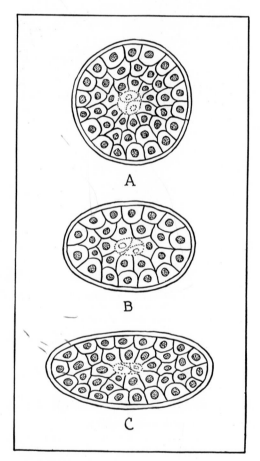

A

B

C

Cross-section views of three kinds of hairs show the difference in shape of straight (A), wavy (B), and curly (C) hair.

The color of the hair depends on the pigment in the dermis around the living hair cells. The color of hair, like that of skin, is inherited.

How do nails resemble hair? Fingernails and toenails grow out of special cells in the skin, much as hair does. At the base of each nail, the skin folds down into a pit. From the bottom of the pit, living, growing cells push outward the thin, horny layer of cells that are the inert and dead tissues of the nail. The white half-moon at the base of the nails marks the place where the living cells end.

How can you make your hair shiny and manageable? Lustrous, manageable hair is largely a matter of good health and cleanliness. The glow of clean, healthy hair is more beautiful than the stickiness and shine due to oil.

To be lustrous and manageable, hair must be clean, with its natural oil spread smoothly over its entire surface. Too much oil causes the hair to accumulate a coating of dust and scaling skin. Too little oil leaves hair dry, brittle, and dull.

Your hair naturally picks up dust, perspiration, oils, and scales of old skin. It needs to be washed with soap and warm water every week or two. In between shampoos it can be kept clean by daily brushing.

Vigorous brushing is good for your hair. It removes dry skin scales and loose hairs. It improves circulation. Improving circulation in the scalp helps to nourish the living roots of your hair. There is a constant flow of oil from all the oil glands of the skin, including those of the scalp. Brushing makes hair glossy and flexible by spreading oil smoothly over the whole surface.

When you brush your hair, brush small separate strands from the scalp to the ends. Keep the brush clean by wiping it on a towel several times. If you lean over as you brush, circulation to the scalp is improved.

Massage also improves circulation. You can massage your scalp by pressing the balls of your fingers hard against your head, and rotating them enough to move the scalp.

How can you keep your hair clean? Hair needs to be washed often enough to keep it clean. For most people a washing every week or two is enough. Many boys wash their hair every day. Unfortunately some people believe that frequent washing destroys the natural oil in hair, increases dandruff, or causes splitting of the ends.

Washing removes oil from the hair itself but does not distrub the oil glands. There is a constant flow of oil from glands in the scalp. If hair is dry, frequent shampooing may cause ends of the hair to split because they are brittle.

Dry hair should be protected from the sun and from excessive heat, such as may come from hair dryers. Oil production may be stimulated by scalp massage. Brushing helps spread oil over the entire surface of the hair. A small amount of liquid vaseline or olive oil applied to the ends of the hair may help. Boys who wash their hair every day often use a little liquid oil on the hair to make it lustrous and managable. Too much oil makes hair sticky and greasy.

In washing the hair and scalp, soap-

Ewing Galloway

Clean, healthy hair is shiny and soft. How could this girl make her hair more attractive?

suds should be rubbed with the fingers into the scalp itself, not merely into the hair. Any good soap may be used. Cake soap rubbed directly on the hair is difficult to rinse off. More satisfactory is a soap solution or a liquid or cream shampoo. Washing is more thorough if two successive soapings are used instead of one. Oil and dirt usually make difficult the first lathering. A thorough rinsing gets rid of most of the dirt and enables you to work up good penetrating foam on the next soaping.

The most neglected part of a shampoo is usually the rinsing. Soap film that remains on the hair makes it sticky and dull. Many of the shampoos on the market are not real soaps.

Philip Gendreau

Washing removes oil and dirt from hair. Why are brushing and rinsing such important parts of a shampoo?

They require no special rinsing and leave no film on the hair. The hair should be rinsed two or more times. When the hair is free from soap, it will give a little squeak as the hands are rubbed over it. The rinse is not complete until this stage is reached. If water is hard, a little vinegar or lemon juice in the rinse water helps to remove the last traces of soap and alkali.

What can you do about scalp trouble? Like the rest of the skin, the scalp sheds dry, flaky scales. This scaling is a normal, healthy process. The scales are removed by daily brushing and by regular shampoos.

Dandruff consists of an accumulation of these scales with extra oil secreted by the oil glands. The cause of dandruff is not known. Sometimes it clears up itself if general health is im-

proved and the scalp is kept clean. Some persistent cases may be caused by a germ and require medical attention.

Occasionally oil treatments lubricate the scalp, help keep scalp and hair clean, and prevent the accumulation of dry flakes.

All the time some hairs are falling out and being renewed. There is no cause for alarm unless hair falls out more rapidly than it is renewed. The cause of baldness is not known. It seems to run in some families. It may also be associated with the functioning of the endocrine glands. It is far more common in men than in women. In some illnesses the lowering of general vitality is accompanied by loss of hair.

The growth and strength of each individual hair depends upon its

Brushing distributes natural oil evenly over the hair making it lustrous and manageable. How can you choose an attractive hair style?

Ewing Galloway

blood supply. Circulation can be stimulated by massage and brushing. Good general health and cleanliness promote the health of the hair.

Certain insects called lice attach themselves to the hair and scalp if they get a chance. They are easily spread from one person to another. No one needs to feel disgraced if he finds head lice on himself. It can happen to anyone. No one, however, needs to provide a permanent home for lice. There are several good medicines that get rid of them quickly.

You can probably avoid lice if you use only your own clean comb and brush and wear only your own hat.

How can you have a good figure?

Probably the first thing you notice about a person is his general size and shape. This general size and shape depends partly upon inherited body build. It also depends upon acquired characteristics, like posture, weight, muscular development, and co-ordination.

Why should you control your weight? Most people are concerned about their weight because it affects their appearance, their self-confidence, and their relationships with other people. There are other reasons for watching your weight, too. Life-

insurance statistics show that you have a better chance to be free from disease and live a long life if you do not become too heavy.

It is often said that the most healthful weight when you are young is slightly heavier than average, and when you are over thirty is slightly lighter than average. Extremely thin young people have little reserve for extra activity or for fighting disease. They tire easily and may not get enough exercise to develop strong, well-co-ordinated muscles. Rapidly growing boys and girls who are too

293

thin may become anemic or develop tuberculosis.

Extreme overweight crowds the internal organs and puts an extra burden on the feet. Extreme overweight may make you feel "different" and invite teasing from your classmates, decreasing your self-confidence. Overweight makes it difficult for you to take part in athletics and social activities. In general, overweight decreases good looks, self-confidence, and good times.

The ideal weight and figure produces a body that is smoothly rounded but not bulgy. A good figure looks streamlined and strong and is capable of moving gracefully. It performs skillfully the actions required for work, play, athletics, and social activities.

How can you control your weight? Some things about your body shape you cannot control. You inherit a certain type of body build. Some people are naturally short and stocky; others are tall and slender. Some are tall and large; others are short and slender.

There is no normal size and weight to be reached by all persons of a certain age. When you read weight tables remember that variations of 10 per cent or more are perfectly natural for some people. If you really think that you are much underweight for your age and body type, talk with your doctor or a nurse or your gym teacher before you start trying to gain or to reduce.

Your body grows and puts on weight only by using food. All your body systems co-operate to use the food you eat. If you are eating the proper amounts of a balanced diet and your body is working as it should, your weight will be normal. Any extremely underweight or overweight person should be examined by a doctor. Abnormal weight is usually related to food intake. But it may be influenced by poor functioning of glands or the digestive system. It is also altered by infection or disease. All these conditions need to be treated by experts. Advertised short-cut methods to reduce weight are either useless or dangerous.

Extra fat is usually simply the result of eating more food than the body requires. When you eat more food than your body needs for growth and repair and energy, the extra carbohydrates and fats are stored. Some carbohydrates are stored in the liver for emergency fuel. Most is stored as fat in layers around some organs and just under the skin. Fat serves as padding and as an insulation. Some fat is useful; too much is a burden.

By a little self-control you can avoid extra weight caused from overeating. You will have to change your eating habits. A fat person is not necessarily well nourished. Too much carbohydrate and fat in the diet often means too little protein and minerals. Fat people often have little energy. Often they have poor teeth, bones, and muscles.

An overweight person needs a better balance between food taken in and food used. He often has a tendency to withdraw from sports and social activities. Lack of exercise, stimulation, and activity makes the condition worse.

To lose weight you should reduce the amount of sweets and fat you eat. For best growth boys and girls usually need to increase the amount of fruits, vegetables, milk, meats, and eggs in their diet. These foods give the essential minerals, vitamins, and proteins you need.

An overweight person can help balance the amount of food taken in and the amount used by his body by being more active, as well as by eating less food. Vigorous outdoor exercise and more participation in school and social activities will improve his figure, his complexion, and his disposition.

Growing boys and girls are more likely to be underweight than overweight. They may need more or better food. Sometimes a glass of milk at each meal will help. Often needed is an extra meal of bread, butter, fruit, and milk. Extra supplies of sweets, especially between meals, may make the condition worse. Candy and some other carbohydrates furnish no vitamins or minerals. They spoil the appetite and may actually reduce the use of foods necessary for healthy growth.

Boys and girls who are too active may need to choose their activities more carefully. They should get some rest before and after meals and more sleep at night. Underweight people should avoid unnecessary stimulation, worry, excitement, and stimulants like tea or coffee, so they will get more food and rest to gain weight.

How can you have a graceful figure? A graceful figure is well shaped and rounded. It is strong and well coordinated and moves smoothly and easily. A graceful, attractive figure depends more upon muscles and posture than upon size and weight.

Unnatural-looking bulges, particularly of the hips, abdomen, and back of the neck, are usually caused by poor posture, weak muscles, and overweight. A strong, erect, well-proportioned body need not have any special size or measurements to be attractive.

Even a well-proportioned body can be spoiled by round shoulders, sagging and flabby muscles, and bulges. Good athletes, dancers, actresses, and actors know the importance of good posture.

The kind of muscles you develop affects the appearance of your body. Muscles that are not exercised lose tone and become flabby. They allow the body to sag and droop. Strong muscles are necessary to hold the body erect and easily balanced. You can learn some exercises for developing various muscles from your health or physical-education teacher. Some activities like swimming are particularly good because they exercise many muscles of the arms, legs, and trunk.

It is a good idea to learn some activities that furnish exercise. Learn some that you can participate in when you are older if you want to keep your youthful figure. Many sports considered "minor" in school are really of major importance because you can continue them into adult life. Well worth learning are golf, tennis, bowling, skating, skiing, archery, hiking, and swimming. These sports can be continued beyond school days.

What is good posture? Posture is simply the way you hold your body balanced as you stand and sit and move. Good posture is comfortable, healthful, and good looking. When

295

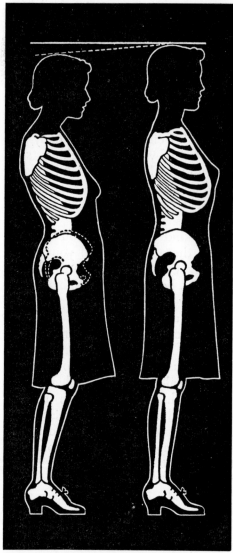

Samuel Higby Camp Institute for Better Posture

In these drawings you can see the change from poor posture (left) to good posture (right). In good posture the head is high, shoulder blades flat, chest up, abdomen up and in, and lower back flattened. Developing the muscles that hold you in this position makes good posture easy. Why is good posture important? How does it affect the way your clothes fit?

your body is balanced and held correctly it obeys natural laws of mechanics. Bones are in the position for which they were constructed, joints are not strained, and internal organs have room to work without sagging or pressure. Weight is distributed on structures designed to support weight. Your body is balanced and can move with little effort.

Good posture is largely habit. You can train muscles to assume their responsibilities. You can learn the principles of good posture and practice them. When your body is growing rapidly you need to be particularly careful not to fall into bad habits.

To stand easily erect, try the following suggestions:

1. Stand with feet parallel, a few inches apart. Have your weight over the arch of your foot so you can raise either heels or toes without much change of position.

2. Your knees should be slightly flexed. Limber knees are especially important in sports. Can you tell why?

3. The lower back should be almost flat.

4. The abdomen should be up and flat. Abdominal muscles that lose their tone permit organs to sag.

5. The chest should be high but relaxed.

6. The shoulders should be relaxed. The arms should hang easily. The head should be poised above the shoulders; it should not be stretched forward.

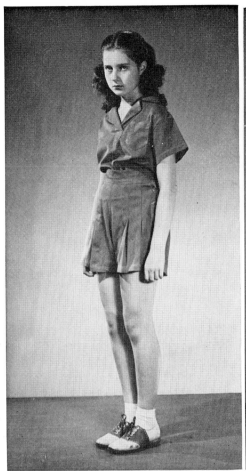

Your posture affects your looks, the impression you give people, and your comfort. How do feelings affect your posture?

It may help you stand correctly if you stand with your feet parallel a few inches apart and if hips and abdomen are held in as if squeezing through a narrow space. Imagine yourself being lifted by hands pressed over your ears. Relax your arms and shoulders and press up with the top of your head.

When you have acquired the habit of standing easily and have developed the muscles that hold you erect, you will look and feel your best.

Good sitting posture is similar to good standing posture—tall and relaxed. Hips should be against the back of the chair. If you need to bend forward, bend from the hips without curving your spine.

How can you move gracefully? To look your best you must be able to move gracefully. Graceful movement

Graceful movements require balance, muscular development, co-ordination, and self-confidence. Are you learning to play and enjoy a wide variety of activities?

demands balance, muscular development, co-ordination, and self-confidence. Previous chapters have had suggestions for developing self-confidence. You can get other suggestions from other sources. Find some that help you, and practice until graceful movements become easy.

The foundation for strong, skillful movements is healthy nerves, muscles, and bones. The ability to move with speed and flexibility is gained by practice. You need practice in fundamental body motions as well as in special techniques of various sports. The fundamental body motions are standing, walking, sitting, running, jumping, climbing, vaulting, hanging, throwing, striking, lifting, and carrying. You can improve all these techniques by instruction and practice.

Good walking posture is erect and relaxed. Your feet should point nearly straight ahead. Place your feet ahead of each other as though walking along a narrow board. Keep your weight balanced over the arch of your foot. Lead with your knee, not your nose.

How can you be well-groomed?

A well-groomed person is more than healthy, clean, and neat. He is fresh and well-cared-for to the smallest detail. His skin, hair, nails, and clothing show that he is self-respecting and considerate of others. He knows how to keep himself in good condition and takes time to do it. Good grooming adds the extra little touches that make a person especially attractive. Being well groomed gives you a feeling of self-confidence.

What about B. O.? Frequent bathing will not always prevent body odor. In addition to washing under the arms daily, most adolescents and adults use antiperspirants or deodorants that check perspiration. Excess perspiration causes unsightly stains on clothing and has a disagreeable odor. For some people a little talcum powder, such as baby talcum, is enough to absorb the excess moisture. Others find help temporarily by using deodorants after bathing.

There are many commercial deodorants that are perfectly safe if used according to directions. Keep them away from your eyes and wash your hands thoroughly after applying them. If a deodorant is irritating, stop using it.

Excess hair on the face, under the arms, or on the legs may be removed easily and safely by a safety razor. Shaving does not make hair thick or coarse. When shaving, be careful not to nick the skin. Cuts are unsightly and may become infected.

How can you take care of nails? Fingernails require extra care to be attractive. They should be trimmed weekly. Fingernails should be filed round to follow the shape of the finger. Toenails should be cut straight across to help prevent ingrown nails. After bathing you can easily push back the cuticle around your fingernails with a wash cloth or an orangewood stick. This will expose the moon at the base and help prevent painful hangnails.

If your hands and nails get very dirty you may need to use a hand

Harold M. Lambert

Would you like to know this boy and girl? Why? Could they make themselves more attractive?

brush. Many boys use one daily. If your hands become rough, a little hand lotion or lanolin cream will soften them and help prevent cracking and infection.

How can you improve your smile? A friendly, attractive smile can make the plainest person good looking. But a smile can be spoiled by dingy teeth or unpleasant breath. Fresh breath and attractive teeth are the result of good health and care. Teeth that are not cleaned daily accumulate tartar (a dull yellow or brownish material). Tartar is formed from saliva and food. It usually remains soft for 12 hours or so and can be removed by brushing. Many people gradually accumulate tartar in spite of brushing and must have it removed by a dentist. Teeth must of course be sound and healthy as well as clean. How can you have healthy teeth?

How can clothes make you attractive? To be attractive, clothing must be clean and well cared for. It is easier to be attractively dressed if you choose clothing that is simple, appropriate, and easy to care for. Clothing for school, play, and work should be comfortable and sturdy. Clothing that cannot be washed and pressed easily is likely to be worn soiled and wrinkled because it is too expensive or difficult to keep fresh. Run-over heels and dirty shoes make any outfit look sloppy.

Styles change rapidly and boys and girls like to keep up with the times. The use of principles of design can help you make the most of any style.

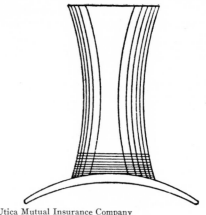

Utica Mutual Insurance Company

The brim of this hat is as wide as the crown is high. Vertical lines make you look taller and thinner. How can you take advantage of this optical illusion in selecting clothing?

Lines and colors do certain things for your figure and complexion. Vertical lines, for example, make you look taller and thinner. Horizontal lines make you look shorter and wider. There are many lines on clothing where you can take advantage of these optical facts. Edges of lapels, belts, closing lines, necklines, and trimmings all form lines. Accent those that help your figure. Make them stand out by contrasting colors, or with buttons or on trim. Why would anklets make your legs appear shorter?

Colors affect both the eye and the feelings. Dark colors make the skin seem to have less color. Pinks and reds reflect in the skin and add color. Certain colors seem warm, cool, gay, or sad because they are associated with fire or the sea or sky or some personal experience.

Reviewing the chapter

I

You should answer "yes" to the following questions.

1. Do you eat every day some fruit, green or yellow vegetables, milk, and an egg?
2. Do you sleep 9 or 10 hours a night?
3. Do you bathe frequently with soap and warm water?
4. Do you change your underclothing and stockings often, and always after a bath?
5. Do you keep your hands, face, and fingernails clean?
6. Do you keep your clothing clean and neat?
7. Do you shampoo your hair when it becomes oily or dirty and brush it every day?
8. Do you use only your own towel, wash cloth, brush, and comb?
9. Do you exercise in the sunshine every day?

II

Complete the following sentences by supplying the missing words. DO NOT WRITE IN THIS BOOK.

1. The top layer of the skin is the
....
2. Nerves and blood vessels in the skin are located in the ....
3. Openings of the sweat glands are called ....
4. .... is the secretion of the sweat glands.
5. A beautiful complexion depends largely upon ....

III

What would you think, say, or do in the following situations?

1. If you wanted to improve your posture?
2. If you were troubled with blackheads?
3. If your hair and skin were very oily?
4. If someone wanted to borrow your lipstick or comb?
5. If you were buying your own school clothes?

Reading to help you grow up

Builders for Good Health and *Your Health and Happiness,* by Burkhard and others, have helpful posture exercises, meal plans, and habits to improve your looks.

Life and Health, by Almack and others, has a detailed chapter on care of the skin, hair, and nails.

Walk Your Way to Better Dancing, by Hostetler, has a helpful chapter on body balance and control.

These booklets by the National Dairy Council offer helpful pictures, information, and a check list for checking your own appearance and personality:
"Straight from the Shoulder."
"Who—Me?"
"Get on the Beam."

Films to help you understand

Body Care and Grooming. McGraw-Hill Book Company. Helpful daily habits.
Cleanliness and Health. Coronet.
How To Be Well Groomed. Coronet.
Posture Habits. Coronet.
Scrub Game. Modern. Care of skin.

Denver Public Schools

Everybody has eating habits. Why not practice good ones until you naturally like and select foods that help you to be healthy? What does a good lunch include?

Do you enjoy a variety of recreations? Is this a good recreation? Always?

Philip Gendreau

Encyclopedia Britannica Films

Football players spend much time practicing fundamentals—ball handling, passing, tackling, and other skills. How are good health habits like the basic skills of a game?

Good health habits make you healthy, vigorous and attractive. Can you name ten fundamental health habits?

American Institute of Bakery

Chapter 16

WHAT ARE SOME SIMPLE WAYS TO KEEP HEALTHY?

Everyone likes to be healthy and attractive and active. Most people also like to be comfortable, to do things the easiest way, and to avoid discomfort, pain, and injury.

Somehow, for many people, "good" health, "good" posture, "good" diet, and other things that are "good" for them sound disagreeable. They sound stiff and uncomfortable and uninteresting. Actually, correct ways of caring for and of using your body are called "good" because they are comfortable and efficient. They get the most done with least effort, allow your body to work at its best, and enable you to have the most fun and fewest pains and regrets.

Good health practices seem difficult only if wrong habits have been practiced so often they have become easy. Nobody wants to think about health all the time. And it is not necessary. Athletes do not have to think about balance and what their feet are doing. Good health, good form, and balance are fundamentals. They are the basis of enjoyable activities, not an end in themselves.

If your body is operating efficiently, you look good and feel good. You rise in the morning rested and refreshed, ready to go. You have energy and enthusiasm for work and play. Other people like you because you are cheerful, optimistic, and considerate. Your senses and mind are alert, and you grow in knowledge and understanding as well as in size.

You spend your life eating, sleeping, playing, working, and resting. Learning the best ways of doing these things bring pleasure and ease, as well as good health. When you eat, eat properly; when you work and play, use your body correctly. Learn to rest and relax. Why not practice habits that will build your health, keep you comfortable, and help you have fun, all at the same time?

Looking ahead

Questions and suggestions

1. In order to stay alive every cell requires certain things. What are they?

2. The cells in your body require food, exercise, and rest. For what purposes do they use food?

3. What are calories, minerals, vitamins?

4. How would an explorer plan for food to be taken along on an expedition?

5. Can you plan the food to be taken on a two-week camping trip?

6. What foods should you have every day?

7. People eat meals at different times. Is there any advantage to eating at regular times? Why should breakfast be a large meal? What about lunch and dinner?

8. Some persons require extra food between meals. Why?

9. What kinds of foods supply quick energy for that lift between meals?

10. Cells require a sensible balance between rest and exercise. Why?

11. Why do adolescents need extra rest?

12. How can you keep rested as you go?

13. Recreation should provide a change. What kind of recreation would be good for an office worker? For a factory worker? For a construction worker? For you?

14. Do you know the hobbies or ways of relaxing of some famous people?

15. What hobbies or recreations do you enjoy?

16. What is good form in a sport? Do you know the principles of good form in several sports?

17. Do you know and practice good form in your daily activities like standing, walking, sitting, lifting, or climbing stairs?

18. How does your body maintain an even temperature? Why is it a good idea to (a) keep moving when exposed to cold? (b) Wrap up if obliged to remain quiet? (c) Change damp clothing as soon as possible, or cover it with something dry? (d) Use insulating material when sitting on cold ground (layers of newspapers will do)? (e) Cool off gradually when hot and perspiring?

Can you give examples of times when these rules are useful?

Committee Planning

1. Make a survey in the lunchroom to see how many have good lunches. What are common mistakes? Can anything be done to improve lunches?

3. Make a survey of recreational activities of members of the class. Report on recreation facilities in your community.

4. Plan a party. Arrange to learn some new games, such as folk dancing. Plan good refreshments.

5. Make displays of good meals.

How can you eat properly?

Most people like to eat. We enjoy snacks after school, light lunches after ball games, and party refreshments. At the same time, they are habits that build health, good looks, and strength. How can you learn good form in eating and increase both your pleasure and profit?

Why does diet seem so complicated? As you recall all the kinds of foods needed by your body, it may seem very complicated to choose a good diet. Your body needs fats and carbohydrates for heat and energy. It needs proteins for cell growth and repair. It needs minerals and vitamins for certain kinds of growth and activity.

Scientists know of at least 14 *minerals* essential for a healthy body. Calcium and phosphorus are known to be necessary for building of bones and teeth, for clotting of blood, and for proper working of nerves. They are found in muscles and other soft tissue and may have other important jobs. Iron seems to be a necessary part of every cell in the body. In blood an iron compound carries oxygen to the cells and stimulates cell activity. Iron seems unable to work alone; it must be helped by copper. Iodine is important in the production of thyroxin. What gland makes thyroxin? Can you find some other minerals needed by the body?

Before 1900 it was known that certain amounts of protein, fat, carbohydrates, and minerals were necessary in a healthful diet. It was also known that a person must have a variety of foods and some fresh fruits and vegetables to keep all body tissues healthy. No one knew why variety was necessary. Since 1900 scientists have discovered substances called vitamins that make a varied food diet necessary. The vitamins are usually named by letters of the alphabet; they have descriptive names too.

Scientists are constantly finding out more about vitamins. They keep discovering new vitamins and breaking old ones down into new parts. For example, the substance first called vitamin B was found to be a whole family. We now know six kinds of B vitamins.

The *kinds* of food are important, but you must also consider *amounts*. *Fats* and *carbohydrates* are stored in your body. Extra amounts build unnecessary weight. Proteins, minerals, and vitamins are not stored; therefore, they must be supplied daily in sufficient amounts.

Proteins are made up of simpler substances known as amino acids. At least 22 of these acids are known and others may be discovered. Some of these are manufactured by the body, but at least 10 must be supplied by food. Proteins which contain all the amino acids necessary for life and growth are called *complete proteins*. Among foods supplying complete proteins are milk, meat, eggs, cheese, fish, poultry, and soybeans. The most abundant complete proteins are of animal origin.

Is there a simple way to choose a good diet? Fortunately, there are simple ways of choosing a good diet. Nature usually puts many essential foods together. Healthful diets were enjoyed by primitive people who ate everything available, including internal organs of animals and many parts of plants that we discard.

Modern people need to eat fewer refined starches and sugars. They should eat more whole, natural foods like fruits, vegetables, whole grains, meat, and milk. No one food is perfect in meeting all the requirements of good nutrition. We need to learn to like and to eat a wide variety of foods. Two foods which come nearest to containing all the essentials are milk and whole-grain cereals.

What kinds of food supply quick energy? What would you take along on a hike to furnish you with renewed strength?

Only four minerals need to be especially planned for in a diet. If these four—calcium, phosphorus, iron, and iodine—are present, we may be fairly sure of getting the others along with them. Milk and cheese are the best sources of calcium and phosphorus. Egg yolks are another good common source. Especially good sources of iron are dark-colored foods, such as liver, lean meat, and whole grains; fruits, such as apricots, prunes, and raisins; and green vegetables. Iodine is found in sea foods, in veg-etables grown in soils containing io-dine, and in iodized salt.

Most of the vitamins are found to-gether. Large quantities of most vita-mins are supplied by milk, green leafy vegetables, liver, lean meat, and whole grains. Additional supplies of vita-mins D and C may be necessary. Fish and liver oils and irradiated foods are the best food sources of vitamin D. What is another source? Because it is destroyed by heat, vitamin C must be obtained from fresh raw fruit and veg-etables like oranges, grapefruit, cabbage, green peppers, and sprouted seeds.

Nutrition experts have picked out seven groups of foods that contain all the essential carbohydrates, fats, proteins, minerals, and vitamins. These groups are often called the *basic seven food groups*. If you eat a wide variety of food from all these groups every day your diet will be balanced. The essential groups are (1) milk; (2) fresh fruits and raw leafy vegetables; (3) other fruits dried or cooked; (4) other vegetables cooked or raw; (5) whole-grain cereals; (6) meat or fish; and (7) butter or other oily spread like margarine or peanut butter. See the chart on this page.

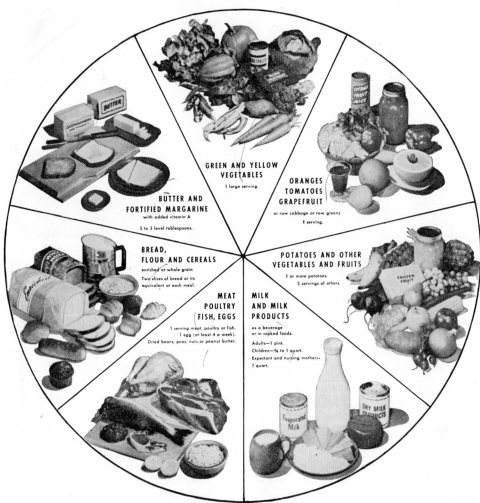

GREEN AND YELLOW
VEGETABLES
1 large serving.

ORANGES
TOMATOES
GRAPEFRUIT
or raw cabbage or raw greens
1 serving.

BUTTER AND
FORTIFIED MARGARINE
with added vitamin A
2 to 3 level tablespoons.

BREAD,
FLOUR AND CEREALS
enriched or whole grain
Two slices of bread or its
equivalent at each meal.

POTATOES AND OTHER
VEGETABLES AND FRUITS
1 or more potatoes.
2 servings of others.

MEAT
POULTRY
FISH, EGGS
1 serving meat, poultry or fish.
1 egg (at least 4 a week).
Dried beans, peas, nuts or peanut butter.

MILK
AND MILK
PRODUCTS
as a beverage
or in cooked foods.
Adults—1 pint.
Children—¾ to 1 quart.
Expectant and nursing mothers—
1 quart.

American Institute of Bakery

If you eat some foods from each of these groups daily, your body will be receiving all the kinds of foods it needs. Why do growing boys and girls need extra vitamin D? How can they get it?

Eggs should be included at least every other day. Once you have foods from all these groups every day, you may add any other foods you like to supply the additional food needed for energy.

If you find that eating from all these groups gives you too much food, you can cut down the size of your servings, but maintain the good mixture. Eat some food from all the groups daily. Few people have allergies that will not allow them to get essentials in natural foods. These few can have concentrated minerals and vitamins prescribed by a physician. There is no reason for promiscuously taking extra vitamins or minerals. If a vitamin deficiency is suspected, a physician should be consulted before money is spent on pills and capsules. Scientists are not sure of the effect of too much concentrated minerals and vitamins. They may be harmful.

How much water should you drink? Although water is not a food, it is an essential part of your diet. About two-thirds of the body weight is water. Practically all body processes are dependent upon water. It controls body temperature; it dissolves food substances; it acts as the base of all body fluids; and it carries food material to the cells and waste products out of the body.

The body must replace water lost in urine, perspiration, respiration, tears, and saliva. This amount varies in different individuals according to the amount of exercise, temperature, and body activity. A man of average size loses two or three pints a day unnoticed. About one or two pints a day are perspiration that evaporates unnoticed, and about a pint is from the lungs. In addition, from two to five pints are lost by the kidneys and bowels. This loss of water will be partly replaced by the three or four pints taken in with an ordinary mixed diet, leaving about two pints, or four glasses, to be drunk as water. Even moderate activity causes more perspiration; so six to eight glasses of water are often considered a good daily average amount of water to be drunk.

Excessive sweating rapidly removes water and salt from the body. Ten pints of sweat may be lost in an hour during hard exercise. Taking extra salt to make up for the loss is advised for persons who work hard physically or who exercise or work in heat.

How can you get the most value from food? Both the value and the enjoyment of food are affected by several factors. The most valuable parts of food are often discarded. Vitamins are found in the outer shell and in the germ of some cereals. Consequently dark-colored, whole-grain cereals and breads are more valuable than the white, refined ones.

Some manufacturers enrich their flours and cereals by putting some of the vitamins and minerals back into the refined product. Enriched products are better than the refined. They are not as good as the whole grain. Read the labels to see what food values you are buying. Whole grains usually have a richer, more satisfying flavor, too. Get your money's worth.

We often lose valuable parts of foods by discarding peelings, tops of some vegetables, and water in which minerals and vitamins have been dissolved. Try to eat raw and unpeeled some vegetables and fruits like apples and carrots. Some vegetables are better when cooked. They are more digestible and appetizing. Meats should be thoroughly cooked. Why?

Because several of the vitamins, as well as many of the minerals, are soluble in water, methods of preparing fruits and vegetables are of great importance. Vegetables and fruits should be pared and cut just before using. Exposure to the air destroys some vitamins. Vegetables should be cooked in a small amount of boiling water until slightly tender. Overcooking destroys flavor and food values. The water in which vegetables are cooked may some times be used in soups, gravies, and sauces in order to save the minerals and vitamins which are dissolved in it.

Balanced meals need not be expensive. If you learn to like many kinds of food you can use less expensive sources of essential foods. You can buy foods when they are in season. Fresh and raw foods are usually cheaper than prepared ones. Cooked cereals are less expensive. Learn to read labels to get the most for your money, in weight and in food value.

National Cranberry Association

Are these good party refreshments? Why?

Does everyone need the same diet?
Everyone needs adequate supplies of the essential food materials and water. Everyone needs foods from all the basic groups. People differ in the amounts they need according to their size, age, and activity. The science of using food for special purposes is called *dietetics*. People of different ages have different needs. Growing boys and girls need more protein, calcium, and vitamin D than adults do. Adolescents also need extra-energy food and good supplies of fresh fruits and vegetables for minerals. The amount of energy supplied by foods is measured in calories.

Individuals of the same age and size may have different needs. Different people can grow fat or thin on the same diet. Some body cells use food more rapidly than others. Some people may need extra supplies of minerals to make up deficiencies. Very active young people need extra supplies of carbohydrates for energy.

During and after illness the body needs easily digested foods to supply energy and rebuilding material. Fruit juices, milk dishes, and meat broths are especially good.

Ordinarily your appetite, weight, and feeling of well-being indicate whether your diet is adequate. If you desire more detailed information to guide you, you can consult calorie charts and tables of food values. Consult a physician if you are underweight or overweight. He can give you tests to determine where your diet is deficient.

How can you plan family meals?
All the members of a family can satisfy their own requirements by eating

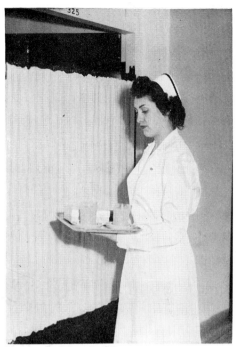

Encyclopedia Britannica Films

What kinds of foods are needed during and after illness?

different amounts of the same foods. Which members of the family require the most food?

Good basic plans for the day's meals insure your getting all the essential foods. The basic plans are simple, are easy to remember, and leave room for interesting variations. You can use great freedom in planning your meals, especially if you have learned to like many kinds of food. Get all the foods you need sometime during the day in about the correct proportions. Most people like to balance each meal to make it more interesting and appetizing.

Breakfast especially should be a good meal, containing about one third of the day's food. Breakfast

Ewing Galloway

Dinner

Milk

Whole-grain bread

Meat or substitute

Potato

Vegetable

You can add whatever you like to the basic plans to obtain sufficient amounts of food. For breakfast popular additions are eggs, meat, and jam. For lunch you can add sandwich filling, hard-boiled eggs, cookies, and additional fruits or vegetables. For dinner try salads, fruits, sauces, and desserts.

Notice the most nearly perfect foods—milk and whole-grain cereals —are included with every meal. Growing boys and girls should have every day at least one quart of milk and five or six slices of bread, at least part of it whole grain.

You need not worry about food fads and fancies. Any wholesome foods may be eaten in any combination. Modern refrigeration and transportation enable you to enjoy favorite foods from all over the world. Only a dull or unimaginative person needs to eat the same things all the time.

Boys who are active and growing rapidly may need more food. They can take larger helpings or have some bread or fruit and milk between meals. The sample meals listed below contain the basic pattern and also contain enough food to supply 2500 calories.

comes after a long period without food. It must furnish most of the energy to be used during the day. Try eating a good breakfast if you feel tired after a little exercise, if you are unable to keep your mind on your work, or if you get touchy and cranky before the day is over. You may be surprised at how much better you get along when you have lots of good fuel.

Here are some good meals following a "basic plan."

Breakfast

Milk

Whole-grain cereal or bread

Fruit or juice

Lunch or supper

Milk

Whole-grain bread and spread

Fruit or vegetable

The day's food supply should be divided fairly evenly among the three meals. What are disadvantages of making any meal extra large or small?

Breakfast

An orange
Cooked whole-wheat cereal
with milk and sugar
Soft-boiled egg
Two slices of buttered toast
with jam
Glass of milk

Lunch or supper

Hot soup
Peanut-butter sandwich
or whole-wheat bread
Banana
Glass of milk

Dinner

Meat
Baked potato
Cooked spinach
Carrot strips
Two slices of bread and butter
Gingerbread
Glass of milk

A well-balanced meal usually has a variety of colors. It is attractive and well flavored as well as healthful.

What habits help you enjoy meals? Manners and consideration for others help you to get more pleasure and profit from your meals. Your digestive system makes the best use of food when it has a good blood supply. Prepare for your meals by slowing down your physical and emotional activity. Help other members of your family

Ewing Galloway

calm down too, by assuming some responsibilities about meal preparation. An attractive table, a spirit of friendly co-operation, neat and considerate table manners, and pleasant conversation make mealtimes enjoyable events. Cleaning up before meals makes us more pleasant companions and protects us from germs.

Ordinary good manners serve the same purposes. One should use the serving fork or spoon, not his own silver, to take food from a serving dish. When food is passed, you should take the first piece you touch. Drink only from your own glass.

After eating, avoid violent exercise or cold baths or anything that would take the blood supply away from digestive organs. If your responsibilities include cleaning up after meals, develop a routine so you can take care of it quickly and cheerfully.

How can you enjoy between-meal snacks and help yourself to health at the same time?

Many boys and girls eat between meals. Eating between meals can be both pleasant and healthful. You can take advantage of between-meal snacks to provide some foods you need. Especially good are milk in any form, bread and butter, and fresh or dried fruits. Fruits are a good source of quick energy. Fruit sugar does not require much digestion, and it goes quickly into the blood. Fruit juice is a wonderful source of energy.

With a little imagination you can work out milk and ice cream combinations, spread for crackers or bread, and fresh dried fruit confections that make the best kind of refreshments. It is a dull teenager who has to rely on soft drinks and sweets for snacks and refreshments.

How can you keep relaxed and rested?

Everyone gets tired. Fatigue is the natural result of activity. A certain amount of fatigue is desirable. Strength is not built up unless activity is continued long enough to cause some fatigue. Only when activity is too prolonged and fatigue becomes too great is any harm done. Waste

314

products accumulate in the muscles and blood stream, and general bodily health is lowered.

Those who are continually over-fatigued lose their healthy good looks, enthusiasm, energy, and mental alert-ness. They are less able to get along with others. Fatigue lowers resistance to disease and interferes with recovery from infection.

How can you avoid unnecessary fatigue? If a person feels well, sleeps well, eats well, and is happy, there is not much danger of overdoing activities, even though he may feel tired at the end of a day. The amount of work and play you can do depends upon your own individual strength and health. You can learn how to save your strength for the things you want to do. You can build your strength and energy.

Your supply of energy may be compared to a water supply, continually refilled by nature. To thoughtless people the supply of energy often seems inexhaustible. Actually there must be a balance between replenishment and outgo. Energy must be spent wisely. The body must have a chance to build up new supplies, or the reservoir goes dry.

Many people allow their energy to be lost, like water dripping from an open or leaking faucet. They waste so much energy on small things that little energy is left for necessary activities.

Mental and emotional excitement keep the nerves and internal organs working overtime and keep the muscles tense. Any kind of tension uses energy and increases fatigue. Violent emotional shock or strain may have much the same effect on the body as

Denver Public Schools

Some fatigue is desirable. Why? When is it harmful? How does good posture help you to avoid fatigue?

violent exercise. Under such a strain the body becomes tired out.

Emotions are extremely valuable, but they must be controlled. Strong emotional stimulus can cause a person to draw on the body's reserves of energy and exert unusual strength. Persons who put forth such unusual effort are likely to collapse when the strain is over.

One of the surest ways to develop fatigue is to have a feeling of disgust or resentment toward the work you

315

are doing. A feeling of irritation toward your companions can use up energy that might be better spent.

You can work more efficiently if you can overcome unhappy feelings about your job. Everyone has some disagreeable tasks to do. Learn to do jobs you dislike as well and as quickly as you can. Do them promptly and cheerfully. In that way you save part of your energy for things you like to do. Some people let one unpleasant job or disagreeable person use up their supply of energy for a whole day.

We do not know as much about mental fatigue as we do about muscular fatigue. Nerve impulses seem to require little energy. Nerves can carry impulses for a long time without much fatigue. Mental fatigue may be caused by congestion of blood vessels at the base of the brain. A remedy for this type of fatigue is exercise that forces blood to circulate rapidly.

You probably become tired *of* mental work, not tired *by* it. So-called mental fatigue from study probably results from eyestrain or poor posture, plus lack of interest and will. The poor health of the bookworm is due not to mental strain but to bad habits of living, such as lack of exercise, late hours, and poor nutrition.

How can you rest? You rest by allowing muscles to relax. They then receive enough blood to replenish food and oxygen and carry off wastes. Erect, easy posture and loose comfortable clothing help you keep rested. Muscles and nerves are a team. To relax one you must also relax the other.

Frequent change of activity may be a desirable way of resting. New sets of nerve and muscle cells are used, giving the cells a chance to recover their normal state. Variety often gives pleasure and reduces the effort required to pay attention. However, one of the signs of growing up is an increasing ability to stick to a job until it is done and to control your attention for longer periods of time. Yielding too easily to feelings of fatigue and boredom tends to develop habits of laziness and inefficiency. If you have a job to finish you can rest by taking a few minutes of every hour to relax.

Several intervals of complete rest during the day are a necessity to relieve tension and to maintain health. With a little planning, several opportunities for rest can be provided daily at home, at work, or at school. At school put your head down and close your eyes a few minutes, if possible. Think of something pleasant and let your muscles go limp. Some active people have trained themselves to relax so completely that they can even go to sleep in a few minutes.

Trained hikers prevent fatigue by stopping to rest at regular intervals of 15 or 20 minutes standing relaxed and at ease. Industrial experiments have shown that 15-minute rest periods in the morning and afternoon reduce fatigue and result in increased efficiency. Many physicians say that boys and girls should observe periods of rest as regularly as they do periods of sleep.

If you have been maintaining the same position for a long time, a few minutes exercise may provide the best rest. Poor circulation increases fatigue.

How can you keep rested as you go? By alternating periods of activity and rest you can prevent the accumu-

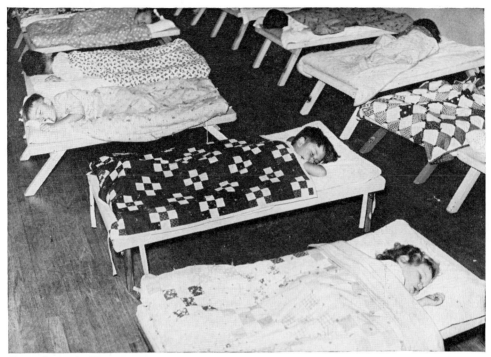

Intervals of complete relaxation during the day relieve tension and prevent fatigue from accumulating. How can you plan for rest periods in school? In games? On hikes?

lation of fatigue. Rhythm keeps muscles clean, fed, and rested by allowing frequent intervals of rest. Standing is more fatiguing than walking, because in walking each muscle is relaxed half the time. All the body processes have a natural rhythm of their own. The heart works and rests at every pulse beat. The lungs work rhythmically. Nerve impulses stimulate muscles in smooth rhythm. In some occupations a definite rhythm of movement tends to lessen fatigue. There is rhythm in the movements of a skilled athlete.

You can establish a rhythm of movements for the organs of digestion and elimination by having regular habits of eating and elimination. You can also establish regular habits for going to sleep, waking and getting up, exercising, and resting. Establish habits for doing routine tasks, for dressing, for washing, for caring for hair, nails, teeth, and clothing, for home responsibilities, and for studying. These habits save mental and emotional tension and enable your body to work more efficiently.

A balance of activities in the day's program helps you keep rested. Work, play, social life, vigorous activity, and quiet activity should all have a part in your daily program.

Modern life requires much use of small muscles and fine co-ordination.

317

Many activities require the use of small muscles and fine co-ordination. What are some other activities that use small muscles?

Large muscles may lose tone and strength unless exercised in recreation or hobbies.

Self-control is an important part of keeping rested. When you control your motions and emotions, your energy is concentrated on important activities. Good athletes usually have developed such self-control that they can alternately relax or call all their reserves of energy into strong co-ordinated movement. You improve your self-control by developing muscular skill and by practicing emotional control.

Athletes who lose control of their tempers waste energy. They are likely to suffer loss of attention, accuracy, and endurance. Keeping your attention on what you are doing and keeping your eye on the ball help you use energy efficiently.

You keep rested as you go if you use your energy efficiently. You can avoid wasting your energy on unimportant things by developing self-control. You can concentrate your energy by doing wholeheartedly one thing at a time. You can save energy by relaxing and taking rest periods at regular intervals, long and short.

Everyone should do activities suited to his own strength. He can learn to work at a rhythm and pace suited to his body's ability to recover. Experiments have shown that working at high speed increases fatigue. A steady rhythmic pace accomplishes more and is less tiring than bursts of speed. Every athlete must learn to pace himself. If you desire to improve your strength and endurance, you must do so slowly. The reason for this is that overfatigue does not build muscles, and it may destroy them.

How can you get enough sleep? Of all the methods of getting rest, sleep is the most efficient. Cells of many organs, such as the brain and nerves, work hard all the time we are awake. During sleep all parts of the body, even the heart, slow down. Body repair and growth take place during sleep, when the demand is low for energy for other purposes.

The amount of sleep needed varies with individuals. It depends partly upon the rate at which body cells work. Some people naturally use energy faster than others. It depends partly upon the rate of growth, partly on daily activity. A very young baby sleeps 22 out of the 24 hours. A growing boy or girl sleeps, or should sleep, 9 or 10 hours. An adult should sleep 8 or 9 hours. Extra sleep is required to gain weight, to fight disease, to gain strength after illness, or to recover from strenuous activity.

You are getting enough sleep if you wake up naturally, rested and refreshed. Too little sleep results in loss of weight, good looks, and energy and often leads to illness.

Sleep should come easily to a healthy body. Going to bed at a regular hour is a great help, because you develop the habit of becoming sleepy as the time approaches. Besides irregularity in the time of going to bed, other factors that interfere with sleep are light, physical discomfort, unusual noises, overeating, worry, and too much excitement during the evening.

Sleep and relaxation should go together. Tenseness may cause sleep to come slowly. If you can relax you need not worry about sleeping. You will at least be resting, and you will drop off to sleep sooner or later. Drugs for sleep should never be used unless prescribed by a physician.

There are various ways for preparing for sleep. Some of these suggestions may help you: Take a short walk in fresh air. Spend the half hour before retiring in some quiet activity —reading, listening to music, or the like. Exercise a few minutes. Take a warm bath. Have a glass of warm milk or some very light food. Relax every muscle in bed. Put worries out of your mind. Count or recite in bed.

Ewing Galloway

Fishing is enjoyed by all ages and kinds of people. Why is it a good recreation?

What is good exercise?

Good exercise increases your bodily efficiency, helps you relax, and gives you pleasure. No one exercise can do all of these things for everyone. Each person must decide for himself how long and how vigorously he should exercise. He must select exercise that he enjoys and that helps him to have a balanced life.

How much exercise do you need? Exercise is necessary for developing and giving tone to the muscles. Muscular exercise stimulates all body functions. During exercise heart action and circulation through the body are increased. This results in a general speeding up in the supply of blood to all the organs. Exercise within reasonable limits improves digestion and helps to overcome constipation and poor complexion. It clears the mind, steadies the nerves, and leads to better co-ordination of all bodily activities.

319

A young person in good health, who wishes to remain well, must have some strenuous exercise each day. Growing boys and girls need at least two hours of vigorous exercise, outdoors if possible, every day. The exercise should be brisk enough to stimulate faster breathing and increased heartbeat. Boys and girls need to discover and heed their own limitations. You can prevent exhaustion by avoiding exercise strenuous or prolonged enough to cause pounding heart, extreme breathlessness, and excessive perspiration. No one should be ashamed to rest. Take frequent short rests and longer ones at greater intervals.

It is a serious mistake to attempt to keep up in games when the effort involves strain. Competitive track, basketball, and football are often temptations to too much exercise. Those who participate in very strenuous or competitive sports should have a physical examination. An activity should be selected that will cause you to associate with others of about the same strength and endurance. In an easy game, further strength and skill are not readily developed. On the other hand, competing beyond your strength is discouraging and dangerous. It is natural to be tired after exercising, but after some rest and food, you should feel refreshed. Usually you should be able to recover in an hour or two. Feelings of fatigue should never carry over from one day to the next.

If you desire to build your strength and endurance, do it systematically. Increase your exercise gradually, without exhaustion. At the same time, be sure you are getting proper food and rest.

What kinds of exercises are good? Good exercise is enjoyable and healthful. Exercise should be taken out-of-doors if possible. It should be suited to the individual. It should require the use of many muscles. It should bring a feeling of well-being.

Outdoor exercise has several advantages. It provides interesting variety and change for people working and studying indoors. If the skin is exposed to direct rays of sunshine, vitamin D is formed in the body. The air outdoors is cleaner and more invigorating. Sounds and odors are not so distracting. Fresh air, blue sky, and other beauties of nature are natural stimulants.

All muscles need exercise to develop and to maintain tone. Exercise

Denver Public Schools

Can you play several games fairly well? Do they give you a good variety of activity the year around?

320

Special exercises help in physical development. What are some sports that use many muscles?

that uses many large muscles is especially beneficial to circulation and general health. Games are usually better than set exercise. They are usually more vigorous and use a wider range of movements. Systematic exercises are helpful in developing certain muscles, or when other exercise is not possible. Often exercise can be combined with routine duties. You can make a game of housework, learning more efficient and enjoyable ways of working. Many games provide for a wide variety of body movements, such as running, throwing, and jumping. Some games are especially good for certain groups of muscles. Swimming is probably the best-balanced all-around exercise. Playing different kinds of games that use many muscles is usually the most helpful and enjoyable form of exercise.

Games and the spirit of play take your mind off yourself. Good games supply a mental and emotional stimulus that makes muscular exertion easy and enjoyable. You should develop an interest in outdoor sports that will continue in later life. It pays to become proficient in several sports. Games and sports that you can play with both boys and girls help you to have many friends of both sexes. Skill in activities like tennis, golf, swimming, bowling, volleyball, ping pong, skating, and skiing help you to have fun and to be popular. How many games can you play?

Do not overlook the values of simple activities, like walking and hiking. An adult can keep in good muscular condition by taking a daily walk of a couple of hours. The greatest amount of benefit comes from walks taken regularly and for recreation. An interest in the out-of-doors, country or city, gives zest and interest to the daily walk. To be a member of a hiking or bicycling club is an excellent way to maintain healthful activity.

How can you keep comfortable?

You naturally are comfortable if your body is healthy and working efficiently. Anything that interferes with the functioning of your body is likely to cause a feeling of discomfort, strain, fatigue, or even pain. Besides good health, your body needs a favorable environment. It needs to be able to maintain a normal temperature.

What makes air uncomfortable? People used to believe that air in a room was bad because it contained much carbon dioxide and little oxygen. They thought lack of oxygen made a person uncomfortable. Scientific experiments have shown, however, that even in a badly ventilated room, crowded with people, it would be almost impossible for the oxygen supply to become so low, and the carbon dioxide content so high, as to endanger life. Experiments prove that temperature, moisture, and air movement in a room are what usually make the room comfortable or uncomfortable, the air "good" or "bad." Within ordinary limits the amount of oxygen or carbon dioxide makes no difference. What are some extraordinary conditions where lack of oxygen is a real threat to health and even life?

We are most comfortable in a room with a temperature about 68° Fahrenheit, with some moisture in the air, and with the air in motion. Under those conditions the body loses heat just about as rapidly as it is produced. If we exercise vigorously and produce more heat, a comfortable room may become uncomfortable.

Heat will be lost more rapidly, due to evaporation, if the air is drier or moving more rapidly. You can notice the cooling effect of evaporation if you allow a little water or alcohol to evaporate from your arm or hand. Wave your wet hand and notice how more rapid evaporation cools it. A temperature of 95° Fahrenheit with a breeze may feel more comfortable than still air at 80°.

How can you make a room comfortable? To make indoor air comfortable, it is best to let in outside air by proper *ventilation* (changing of air), warming or cooling it if necessary. Air seeps in and out around doors and windows, and through walls, so that there is considerable natural ventilation at all times, even if doors and windows are closed.

At night rooms need to be only a little cooler than in daytime. Windows may be opened if necessary to provide a comfortable temperature. Extremely cold air, or drafts, may cause dangerous chilling of a person whose body activities are slowed down in sleep. In the treatment of common colds and other respiratory disorders, cold air is a detriment. Clean, balmy air with moderate moisture (humidity), moving rapidly enough to keep the body comfortable, seems most desirable. Healthful air is also free from disagreeable odors, irritating dust, and other impurities.

The air inside most buildings, especially in winter, is far from ideal. It is often too dry and too still. Window ventilation is used in most homes to provide fresh, moving, moist air from outdoors. The circulation is important, not the cold.

Air can circulate if windows are opened from both the top and bottom, or on opposite sides of a room. You will have to adjust the windows so that air is moving enough just to circulate, but not enough to cause a draft or rapid cooling.

When many people are in a room, the amount of moisture, germs, and odors may accumulate. Air needs to be changed more often.

How does clothing help keep you comfortable? Clothing helps to regulate the amount of heat that escapes from the body. Clothing does not add heat, but it may check the loss of body heat.

The amount of heat that clothing retains depends upon the weave of cloth, kind of material, and fit.

Clothing that fits snugly allows less heat to escape. Snug bands at neck, wrist, and ankles add greatly to the warmth of winter clothes. Close-fitting belts and collars are uncomfortable in warm weather. Loose clothing permits air to circulate around the skin and helps perspiration to evaporate, cooling the body.

The amount of body surface covered by clothing is important. Chilling in one spot can cause a general drop in body temperature. In cold weather you should cover your head, hands, and legs, as well as the other parts of your body.

Tightly woven materials are warm. Materials that have been coated to make them waterproof and windproof allow little body heat to escape. Many waterproof garments do not allow perspiration to evaporate and should be worn over a layer of clothing that can absorb perspiration. After removing waterproof garments, you should be careful to avoid drafts that might cause rapid evaporation and cooling.

Materials that hold water so that it evaporates slowly, or materials that contain small pockets of air, are warm. Materials that allow heat to travel rapidly away from the body are cool.

Smooth vegetable fibers, like cotton and linen, are cool. They have few air pockets and allow perspiration to evaporate rapidly. Rayons and silk are cool too. Several layers of cotton, or cottons woven so that they have a fuzzy pile, contain air spaces and are much warmer.

Animal materials like wool and fur are warm. Their fuzzy surface has many air pockets. They also hold water so that it evaporates slowly. The leather part of fur materials also keeps out wind and water.

The warmest outer garment is an electrically heated one. Pilots flying at altitudes above 30,000 feet, where the temperature is 50° below zero, use electrically heated suits. The next warmest garment is sheepskin, worn with the thick fluffy wool inside, the leather outside.

For ordinary use, experiments have shown that several thin layers of clothing are warmer than one thick layer. The air spaces between layers serves as insulation. The most successful combination for active wear is a layer of absorbent cotton material next to the skin, as many wool layers as necessary, and an outer windproof garment. Why is this combination the most comfortable?

Clothing to keep you cool should be thin and porous—cotton, linen, rayon, or silk. It should cover as little of the body as the occasion permits, fit loosely, and be light in color.

In winter, indoor clothing should be suitable to a temperature of about 65° Fahrenheit. Extra layers of clothing should be worn outdoors. Wearing sweaters, coats, and overshoes indoors is uncomfortable, unhealthful, and shows lack of consideration for others. Why?

How can you take care of your clothing? Clothing contributes to your mental comfort. You feel more relaxed and confident if your clothing is clean and suitable for the occasion. Most boys and girls like to wear different clothing for school and for play. Sports and play clothing should be sturdy and washable and allow plenty of muscular freedom.

You can establish habits that help keep you dressed comfortably for any occasion. Changing from school to play clothes immediately and regularly gives you a chance to hang your school clothes so they shed wrinkles and are aired. Stockings and underclothes should be fresh each day. If you form the habit of washing them each night you will be surprised at how little time and attention it takes to be always fresh and clean. Boys as well as girls can easily learn how to keep their clothes pressed. You can usually save some pressing if you can allow clothing to hang for a day between wearings. Clothes should be hung neatly on hangers.

How does your posture make you comfortable?

The way you stand and move is important for several reasons. Posture affects your body efficiency and also affects the impression you make on others. Actors and actresses can express feelings, mood, and character by the way they hold their bodies erect or slumped.

How can you form good posture habits? The way you hold and control your body is chiefly habit. Your skeleton is held upright by muscles. These muscles are strengthened and trained by use and posture.

At birth your spinal column forms a straight line but as you begin to walk it takes on four slight curves, like a straightened-out "S". These curves should remain slight. If one curve is increased the others usually become exaggerated, to keep the body balanced. If the head is constantly bent forward, the shoulders are likely to become round; the back of the waist develops a hollow; the hips project back; the chest becomes flat; and the abdomen looks prominent.

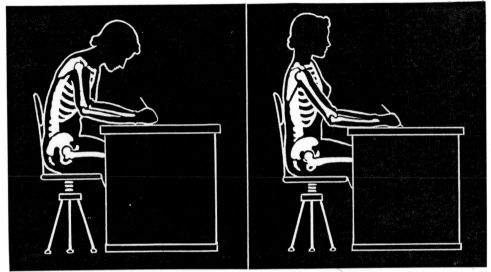

Why is the posture shown in the picture on the left more tiring?

Such posture is poor because it is inefficient. Extra effort is required to hold the body balanced. Endurance and skill are decreased. It puts undue strain on the joints of the spine, hips, knees, and ankles. It cramps internal organs and interferes with circulation. It is uncomfortable and unattractive.

Poor posture can be due to weakness, fatigue, old age, or simply poor habits.

Poor posture may be caused by high-heeled shoes that throw the body out of balance. It may be caused by carrying loads on the same side or by always humping over a desk, slumping in a chair, or standing with your weight on one foot.

You can improve poor posture by exercising weakened muscles and by a constant effort to remember to stand tall. Once you have overcome poor habits, good posture is natural, easy, and relaxed.

You can increase your body's efficiency if you learn and practice good form in lifting, bending, walking, and climbing. Keep your spine straight when you bend or lift. When you bend forward, bend from the hips. When you lift, squat down with knees bent and spine straight. Lift as you stand up.

The chief rule for good posture is to sit and stand tall. When you have established good habits and strengthened muscles weakened from disuse, you will find that good posture is relaxed and comfortable. It requires little effort and is not tiring. It makes you look and feel balanced and alert. Practice until you have the feel of good posture and it becomes almost automatic.

How can you use your feet efficiently? Your feet are the foundation which support your body. No part of your body is more closely related to your comfort. You appreciate this if

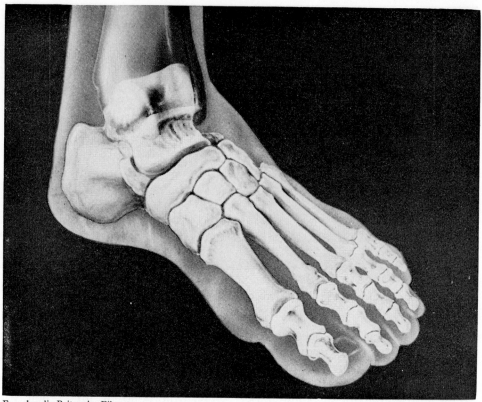

The entire weight of your body must be supported by these small bones and the ligaments and muscles that hold them together.

you have ever worn a pair of ill-fitting shoes. You realize that if your feet hurt, you hurt all over. Although most foot troubles can be prevented, few persons reach adulthood without some type of foot trouble.

The framework of the foot consists of small bones held together by ligaments. The bones are arranged in two *arches*. The long arch extends from the heel to the ball of the foot. The short arch runs across the ball at right angles to the long arch. The body's weight rests on the bones of each ankle, which in turn is supported by the bones in the foot. The foot is really a tripod. The weight rests on

three points; the heel and the ends of the short arch. The slight curvature of the arches gives spring and elasticity to the action of the feet. You can see the shape of your arches by examining a print of the sole of the foot. Make a footprint by placing your wet foot on a piece of brown wrapping paper.

The bones of the foot and ankle are supported by muscles. Some muscles are in the foot. Most of them are in the leg. If you want, you can feel the muscles in your leg contract and relax as you move your toes. The muscles are attached to the bones by tendons.

326

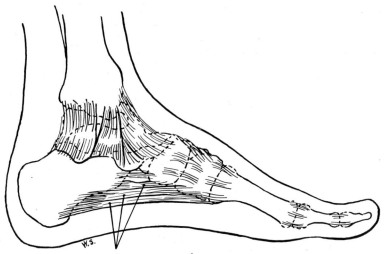

Ligaments of arch

A

The bones of your foot are arranged in two arches. The long arch runs from the heel to the ball of the foot. Arches give strength and spring to your feet.

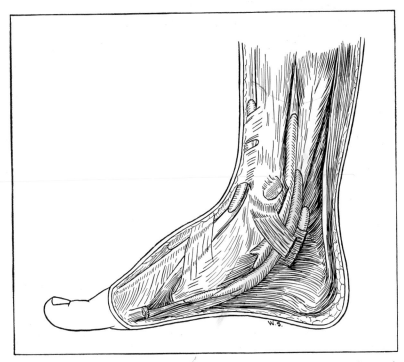

Tendons and muscles support the arch of your foot. Can you feel the muscles in the calf of your leg that move the bones in your foot?

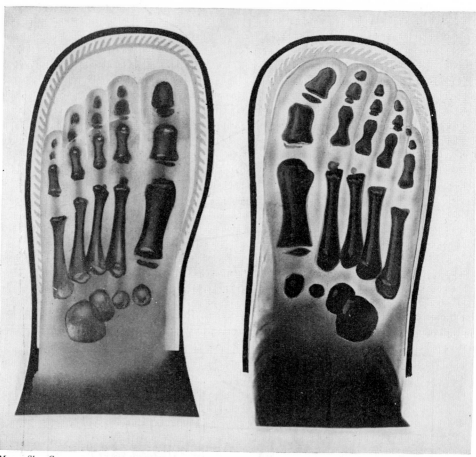

The well-fitted shoe on the left gives the bones in the foot room to lie naturally without bending or crowding. Why will the shoe on the right be uncomfortable? What will it do to a child's foot?

In a weak foot, the body's weight does not fall where it should, on the bones of the feet. Instead the ankle rolls inward and bulges. The inner edge of the foot approaches the floor. Weak feet are often flat. They often cause a person to run his shoes over on the inside edge. Examine your shoes to see if they wear evenly.

For all standing and walking, feet should be parallel, toes gripping, and ankles upright. You can experiment with placing your weight properly on your feet. Stand, without shoes, in front of a mirror if possible, with the feet parallel, about four inches apart. Stand firmly, gripping the floor with your toes. Try to throw the weight of your body toward the outer side of the foot. You can feel leg muscles tighten and notice the ankle straighten. The inner edge of your

Friends Magazine

Denver Community Chest

Why is horseback riding a good form of recreation? What kinds of recreation do you enjoy? Would you like to learn some others?

329

sole from ball to heel will be raised slightly from the floor.

A healthy foot is strong and flexible. If yours is not, ask your physical-education teacher for some strengthening exercise and practice them. A good exercise for strengthening weak ankles and feet is to stroke the shin of one leg with the sole of the other foot. You can feel the sole of your foot arch as the tendon is tightened by the contraction of its muscle below the knee. Picking up marbles or pencils with your toes is good exercise.

Choosing shoes is highly important to help use your feet correctly.

Shoes should be sufficiently long and wide so that toes can be flat and be used in gripping and so that the arches have room for spring action. For all active pursuits, heels should be low and as broad as the heel of the foot. The heel should fit snugly. The shank of the skin should fit up against the side of the foot.

Shoes that slip or cause pressure or that gape and twist when the ankle is held upright are ugly and uncomfortable. They tend to wear unevenly and may cause lasting damage to your feet. Examine your own shoes. Are they wearing evenly?

Reviewing the chapter

Test yourself

I

Your answers to the following questions about your routine habits will help you in your daily life.

1. Are your routine habits efficient? Are you getting your time and money's worth each day?
2. Do you have a good balance of activities and relaxation? A good balance of foods?
3. Can you make and experiment with a more pleasant and efficient daily schedule?
4. Which habits need to be improved? How can you change them?

II

Follow one day's routine in these questions. See how many you can answer correctly now that you have read the chapter.

1. Did you wake up naturally? When? How did you feel? Why?

2. Did you have time to wash, dress neatly, and take care of your room and other household responsibilities?
3. What responsibilities do you have in the morning? Do you perform them cheerfully, without prodding?
4. How was your disposition? Why?
5. What did you have for breakfast?
6. Did you wash your hands with soap and water after going to the toilet?
7. Did you start for school in plenty of time to enjoy the walk?
8. How did you spend your time before school?
9. Were you on time and prepared for class?
10. Did you wear suitable indoor clothing?
11. Were you able to get to work promptly?
12. Did you relax and rest at intervals?
13. Did you become tired and restless during the morning?
14. Did you sit and stand in a comfortable, healthful position?
15. Did you observe rules of safety

and courtesy in the rooms, halls, and playgrounds?

16. Did you wash your hands before eating?
17. What did you have for lunch?
18. How did you feel in the afternoon?
19. How much water did you drink?
20. What did you do after school?
21. Did you have outdoor exercise?
22. What did you eat?
23. Were you clean and relaxed for dinner?
24. What did you have for dinner?
25. How did you spend the evening?
26. How did you prepare for bed?
27. What time did you go to bed?

Reading to help you grow up

Good Health Is Fun, Your Health and Happiness, and *Builders for Good Health,* by Burkhard and others, have simple interesting suggestions for building good health habits.

Outwitting the Hazards, by Francis L. Bacon, will help you to think clearly and perform skillfully to avoid accidents. It has many suggestions for activities and check lists of do's and don'ts with which to check your own practices.

Films to help you understand

Fit To Win. Teaching Films Custodian. Many famous athletic champions demonstrate health habits and conditioning exercises.

Care of the Feet. Encyclopedia Britannica Films.

Beauty from Within. Princeton Film Center. The blood stream and its relation to nutrition.

Something You Didn't Eat. USAD (loan). Castle (purchase). Cartoons by Disney combine entertainment with basic instruction in the seven major food groups necessary to good health.

If It's Health You're Seeking. National Motion Picture. Deals with all the habits that make for good health.

In Every Day. Brandon. An American boy shows how an ordinary day is related to good health habits.

Modern Guide to Health. Young America. A cartoon showing common sense rules of personal hygiene.

Picture Preview: Chapter 17

All children should be protected by immunizations from smallpox, polio, diphtheria, whooping cough, and tetanus. What immunizations have you had?

United States Public Health Service

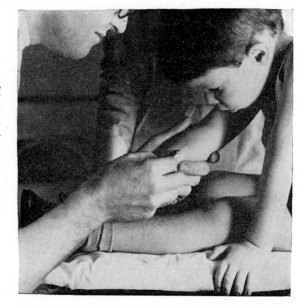

How does this store protect food from contamination and spoiling? How should you protect food at home?

Ewing Galloway

Most of the drownings that occur every year could be prevented. How well can you swim?

All wounds and injuries should receive immediate attention. Germs may enter through scratches that seem unimportant. Do you know how to treat minor injuries?

Chapter 17

HOW CAN YOU PROTECT YOURSELF FROM DISEASE AND INJURY?

*A*ny plans to make the most of yourself must include some ways of avoiding and fighting disease. Disease has always been one of man's most serious problems, interfering with his plans and hopes, bringing suffering and untimely death.

One of the most important parts of the scientific attitude is a belief in an orderly world, where everything has a cause. Scientists believe that diseases do not just appear. If your body develops tuberculosis, rickets, or cancer, something must cause the disease. Until the cause is known, progress in preventing any disease is slow.

In general, there are two causes of disease. Some diseases are caused by germs, and are therefore catching. Others are caused by changes in the body cells.

The changes in cells are little understood and apparently very complicated. The changes may be in the form of growths, unusual abnormal actions of glands and other organs,

mental and emotional disturbances, or other kinds of changes from normal functioning. Usually it is possible to find out *what* has gone wrong. It is more difficult to find out *why*. Medical scientists are working hard to find out why people get cancer, diabetes, heart trouble, arthritis, and many other diseases.

Remarkable progress has been made in the last hundred years in the prevention of many of the diseases caused by germs. Some diseases have been practically eliminated. Many others could be, if scientific knowledge could be applied everywhere.

You can help to prevent disease if you understand something of the nature of your own body and of the nature of disease. Naturally, you do not need to know nearly as much as a doctor does. You do need to know enough to avoid foolish and unnecessary risks, to help your body fight disease, and to seek medical aid when necessary.

334

Looking ahead

Questions and suggestions

1. What diseases have you had? What injuries, large and small, have you had? Which ones might have been prevented? How?

2. What have you learned from experience about avoiding disease and injury? How can you detect and take care of beginning illness? How can you care for small injuries—cuts, sprains, blisters, insect bites, and minor burns? How much first aid should an ordinary person attempt? Why?

3. Most people today must depend on their communities for healthful environment. How does your community obtain water? How does it keep its water supply pure? How does your community dispose of wastes—garbage and sewage?

4. How does your community control epidemic diseases?

5. How does your community provide for traffic safety? For industrial safety? For building inspection? For fire and police protection?

6. Which diseases do you think are the chief causes of sickness and death today? Are they different at different ages? Why? Are they different in various parts of the country? Of the world?

7. What do you think are the chief causes of accidental injury and death? Does age make a difference?

8. What are some skills that contribute to the safety of a modern boy or girl?

9. Does your community supervise housing conditions? Do you have any housing units or areas unfit for human living?

10. Does your community provide adequate recreation?

11. Is your community clean? Is the air free from smoke and dust? Are street and sidewalks clean? Are public buildings and vehicles clean and safe?

12. Are food handlers in your community inspected and supervised?

If you do not know the answers to these questions, they will make interesting topics for surveys, field trips, and reports.

Committee planning

1. The field-trip committee can arrange trips to community water supplies, sewage- and garbage-disposal plants, and public-health facilities like clinics and general hospitals.

2. Many committees can work on surveys to get better acquainted with your community. What facilities are available for recreation? Are there free and low-cost health services? How many hospitals are there? Is emergency help available for accidents? What are quarantine regulations?

3. Boy Scouts or other camping experts can report on ways of keeping a camp comfortable and safe.

4. You may be able to secure a trained first-aid team from a Red Cross class to demonstrate various techniques of first aid.

5. A committee can arrange other trips to see how people are protected from disease and injury while at work. Try to visit or have talks about a variety of kinds of work—farming, mining, big industry, and small individual jobs. How do workers pay for the care of disease and injury?

Reading

This is a long chapter. After you have read it rapidly once, study each section in more detail.

Many diseases are caused by living organisms called germs. Germs invade the body and poison the cells. They multiply and spread from person to person. At one time germ diseases were the leading cause of death. At times they swept over entire countries, killing thousands of people in great plagues.

Today we know enough about germs to fight them, both inside and outside the body. Against some of them we can be completely protected. Many others we can avoid or destroy before they do much harm. There are still many things we do not understand. Research goes on constantly.

What are germs? Since Leeuwenhoek, peering through his crude microscope, first saw what he called the "wee beasties," men have known about the existence of microscopic living things. Some microscopic living things are plants, some are animals, and some are so tiny that no one knows what they are. The tiny plants are called *bacteria;* the animals are called *protozoa;* and the small unknowns are called *viruses.* They exist almost everywhere and multiply rapidly under favorable conditions of warmth, moisture, food, and darkness. You can examine almost any moist substance—a drop of pond water, a fingerprint on a slice of potato, or saliva—under a microscope and find tiny living things. Fortunately only a small proportion are harmful.

About a hundred years ago Louis Pasteur proved that certain microscopic living things were the cause of fermenting, souring, and certain disease. Those that cause disease are called germs. Diseases caused by germs are called infections or infectious diseases. Each kind of infection is caused by a certain kind of germ.

Most germs are bacteria. The special study of bacteria is called the science of bacteriology. Bacteria are classified according to their shape. A round one is a coccus; a straight one is a bacillus; and a twisted one is a spirochete. Infections are often named for the germs that cause them. Tuberculosis, for example, is caused by the tubercle bacillus.

Scientists have identified many of the germs that cause diseases. Even with the best instruments and techniques they have been unable to find all of them. They now believe that many infectious diseases are caused by germs so tiny they cannot be seen even with a microscope. These tiny germs are called viruses. By means of special microscopes and techniques a few viruses have been seen as tiny living particles. Many are still unidentified. The common cold, influenza, smallpox, chicken pox, polio, and measles are believed to be caused by viruses.

How do germs affect the body? Each kind of germ has a special chemical make-up. It may be poisonous itself, or it may make materials poisonous to the cells. The poisons made by germs are called toxins.

Each kind of germ causes a special reaction in the body. Many kinds cause inflammation. They cause tissues to swell, to become red, and to feel hot and painful. Such infections are often named by adding *itis* to the part of the body affected; for exam-

Anyone who is ill should be put to bed away from others and kept quiet and warm. What are some signs of illness?

Encyclopedia Britannica Films

ple, tonsill*itis* and appendic*itis*. Pimples, boils, and infected wounds are other examples of such infections. Some germs cause specific diseases. For example, only the typhoid bacillus causes typhoid fever. Only the malaria parasite causes malaria.

The seriousness of a disease depends partly upon the kind of germ. Some, like those causing tetanus, are highly destructive. Others are less harmful. The number of germs and the kind of tissues attacked also make a disease more or less serious. Some kinds of tissues are more easily harmed than others. Internal organs, as a rule, are most easily and severely damaged. It is wise to care for all infections in their early stages, before they can spread and attack vital organs. Often such infections as scarlet fever, measles, or rheumatic fever may not seem particularly serious at the time; but toxins in the blood stream later may damage internal organs like the heart, kidneys, or ears.

Like many other living things, germs divide to multiply. Some are capable of dividing every 20 minutes. At that rate, if none died, the offspring of a single germ could amount in weight to over a ton in 24 hours. Fortunately, most germs do not multiply that fast. Inside the body they are checked and destroyed by the body's defenses. Outside the body they can usually exist only a short time. Since germs multiply, infections spread. A cold in the nose may spread

to the throat, sinuses, ears, or lungs. Infections may spread to nearby cells or get into the blood stream and be scattered over the body.

Often, when germs get into the body, nothing happens. The body is able to destroy them easily. In other cases nothing may seem to happen for a few days. This is the incubation period, when germs are getting established and multiplying. When enough germs are present they begin to cause certain symptoms. Depending on the germ you may have an inflammation, a sore throat, chills, fever, or other disease *symptoms* (signs of a war between germs and your body).

Usually your body overcomes the germs and the symptoms subside. Infections which last only a short time are called *acute*. Sometimes the body is able to control the invaders, but does not destroy all of them. Germs which remain in the body, not able to cause much trouble, but ready to take advantage of any lowering of body resistance cause the *chronic* stages of an infection.

How do germs travel? The specific illnesses caused by germs are called *communicable*, because they may travel from one person to another, as well as from one body cell to another. Most germs can live only in the body, and for a short while in materials discharged from the body. They are present in secretions from the nose and throat, in the excretions of the kidneys and intestines, in the matter from infections, or on articles soiled with such discharges.

Germs enter the body through body openings such as the nose and mouth, with food or water, or in breathing. They enter through breaks in the skin or mucous membrane, such as cuts or insect bites.

Germs may travel directly from one person to another by means of coughs, sneezes, shared food, kisses, or even forceful talking close to another person's face. Any material may carry germs for a while. The personal belongings of an infected person, or any article he touches, such as eating utensils, pencils, or doorknobs, are likely to have some of his germs deposited on them. Usually the germs die when they become dry, but they may be picked up by another person before that happens.

Germs are often transferred by a person's hands. You may pick up germs or leave them on the things you touch. When you think of all the ways you use your hands and how many objects you touch, you can see how likely they are to be carrying germs.

Malaria, one of the most widespread of all diseases, is carried from one person to another by the Anopholes mosquito.

Germs from infected people may contaminate food, milk, and water and be transferred to other people. Some germs can even contaminate the soil and gain entrance to new victims through wounds.

Some of the most dangerous disease germs are carried by insects or animals. Certain mosquitoes, ticks, fleas, and lice carry special disease germs like malaria, yellow fever, and tick fever. Fleas and other insects, like ants and cockroaches, can carry disease germs from filthy materials upon which they alight.

When you know how germs travel, can you figure out some logical way of stopping them? Compare your methods with those discussed on page 344.

How does your body protect itself from germs?

Your body has many natural defenses against germs. It has barriers to keep them out and ways of destroying them if they do enter. When your body is stricken by disease or injury, doctors do all they can to restore the normal functioning of the body. At the same time they try to locate and remove the cause of the illness.

Body defenses may be weakened by unhealthful living habits. They may be strengthened by good living habits and by proper use of scientific discoveries.

How does your body keep germs out? Germs are with us all the time. They are on food, in water, on objects we handle, and even in the soil and air. They can do us no harm unless they, or their toxins, can get into a tissue or into the blood.

Your skin is a protective covering over the entire outer surface of your body. Oil glands keep the skin lubricated and free from cracks. Fluid from the sweat glands helps to wash germs out of the pores in the skin. Both fluids help to make the skin surface slightly antiseptic.

Tiny glands in the mucous membrane lining of openings into the body produce a slimy secretion, called mucus, that helps to check the growth of germs and helps to remove them from the passages. The tonsils and glands catch some germs entering by way of the mouth.

How may germs penetrate the body's barriers? Germs are always present on the skin and membranes. They may enter through the tiniest cuts and breaks. Blackheads, or clogged oil pores, may imprison many germs. Squeezing or scratching that breaks the skin, or injures nearby tissue, allows the germs to enter the body. Insect or animal bites that break the skin may introduce germs into the body.

Some diseases caused by viruses may possibly pass directly through the skin or membranes. Germs of common colds, smallpox, polio, and tularemia may enter the body this way.

Germs may travel to parts of the intestinal tract if they are in food, in water, or on other objects put into the mouth. They may travel in droplets from the nose and throat of infected persons to tissues in the respiratory organs.

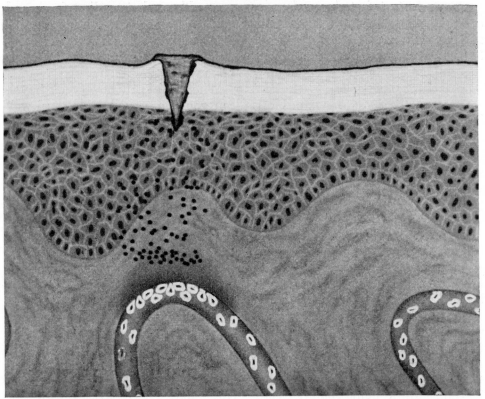

Germs (the black dots) enter the body through a break in the skin (top). White corpuscles have gathered at the scene of invasion (bottom). Many of them have already gone through the capillary walls and are destroying the germs. See the drawing on the opposite page.

How does your body fight germs? Once germs have penetrated the body's outer defenses, the skin and membranes, they are met by other kinds of resistance. General resistance to germs of all kinds is offered chiefly by *white corpuscles* and by the *lymphatic system*. White corpuscles devour and destroy many germs, both in the blood and in the *lymph* surrounding the cells. The presence of germs seems to stimulate the production of white corpuscles. A high "white count" may thus indicate the presence of an infection.

Dead bacteria, toxins, and damaged white corpuscles are absorbed by the lymph and carried in its circulatory system. At intervals, along the lymphatic drainage system, are special structures called *lymph nodes*, or *lymph glands*. They act as filters to strain harmful materials out of the lymph, before it re-enters the blood stream. If lymph nodes collect much harmful materials they may themselves become enlarged and tender. For example, an infection in the hand may cause lymph nodes in the armpit to become noticeable.

Your body attempts to keep invading germs "localized," or walled off in

340

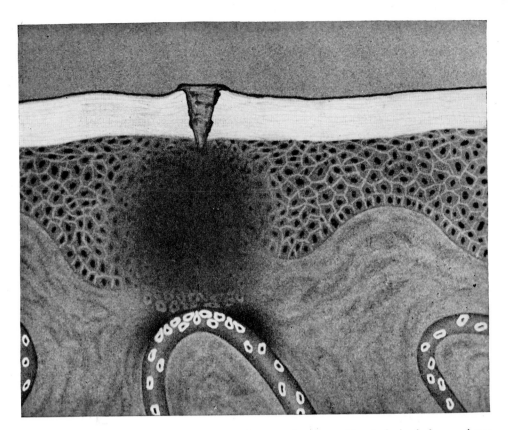

Here we see the victory of the white corpuscles over the germs. The dark shaded area shows where the germs were. (See the drawing on the opposite page.) After the bacteria are thoroughly destroyed, the skin will return to normal.

as small an area as possible. Materials pass out of the blood into the lymph, near the invading germs, and build a kind of wall. In the walled-off area, white blood cells destroy the bacteria. It is believed that body temperatures higher than normal also destroy bacteria.

Infections that have been localized in a small area often accumulate a white or yellow, thick, liquid material, known as *pus*. Pus consists chiefly of living and dead germs, white corpuscles, lymph, and destroyed tissue. Pus is the material discharged from the nose in late stages of a cold; it is visible at the top of a pimple.

Pus may be absorbed in the lymph or it may form a passageway to the outside and drain. If not drained, the increasing pressure may make the infection tender and painful. Any collection of pus is dangerous and a likely way to spread infection. Deaths occur every year from blood poisoning caused by opening pimples with unsterile instruments.

What is immunity? In addition to general resistance, your body has special kinds of defenses against certain disease germs. Each kind of germ acts

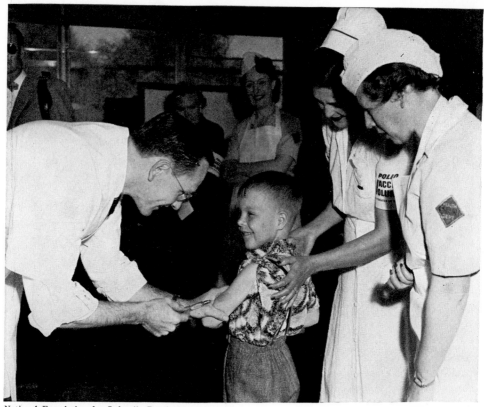

Vaccines can give protection against certain diseases. How? Can you tell how vaccines are prepared?

as a stimulus to cause the body to produce a special chemical. These special chemicals are called *antibodies,* because they are against (*anti*) the bacteria. They destroy the bacteria or neutralize its toxins. Those that neutralize toxins are called *antitoxins.*

Usually antibodies begin to form as soon as the germ enters the body. If they are formed rapidly enough, they destroy the bacteria and its toxins. The protection furnished by antibodies is called immunity. Some diseases produce only temporary immunity.

Against some infections extra antibodies are formed. These may remain in the body for varying lengths of time, even for life.

A person who has stored in his body antibodies for a certain disease is immune to that disease. Some diseases produce no extra immunity; they also seem to leave the body with less ability to make antibodies against that disease. Colds, influenza, pneumonia, and rheumatic fever seem to leave a person even more susceptible to a secondary infection right after the first one. After attacks of these diseases it is important to take extra precautions, such as plenty of rest, very light exercise, and careful avoiding of chilling and drafts, and exposure to crowds.

Most adults are immune to many common diseases, either because they have recovered from an attack, or because they have had repeated slight, unnoticed infections that caused antibodies to be produced. For a few months a new-born baby has the same immunities as his mother. People who have never been exposed to even a slight infection of a disease have no antibodies and often have very little resistance to that particular disease. For example, when smallpox was introduced into Mexico by the armies of Cortez, the Indians were easy victims of the disease. It is estimated that about half of the 12 million Indians in this hemisphere died of smallpox.

Americans going into tropical countries are likely to be easy victims of diseases rare in this country. Fortunately, now we are able to gain immunity from many diseases by vaccinations or innoculations.

How do vaccinations and serums protect you? *Vaccines* are harmless material introduced into the body to stimulate it to produce antibodies. Some vaccines are called *toxoids*. The advantage of vaccines is that they enable the body to prepare antibodies before it is ever exposed to the disease. If an immune person is exposed to a disease, he is ready to destroy those particular germs when they enter the body, before they have a chance to do any damage.

Modern vaccines are prepared in laboratories in various ways, most usually from dead bacteria. They are produced with extreme care and cannot possibly cause the disease. They are a simple, safe method of protecting yourself from diseases to which you are likely to be exposed.

Vaccines and toxoids have been produced to prevent several of the most serious epidemic diseases. If they were used widely enough, these diseases could be eliminated. In spite of proof that immunization will protect against certain diseases, only a comparatively few children are vaccinated against even such common diseases as whooping cough and diphtheria.

Serums are the clean portions of animal fluids—usually blood—in which antibodies are concentrated. They may be derived from the blood of persons who have recovered from the disease, or from the blood of animals that have been purposely vaccinated until their blood contains many antibodies.

Serums can be given when the body is already infected and in immediate need of antibodies. In any infection there is always the danger that the body may not be able to manufacture enough antibodies to overcome the disease. Serums are available for many diseases. The antitoxin for diphtheria was the first to be produced and has a dramatic record of cures. Serums are also available for treating several types of pneumonia, measles, tetanus, meningitis, scarlet fever, and other diseases. What diseases have members of your class been vaccinated against?

How can you help your body protect itself from germs?

You cannot avoid all contact with germs. They are everywhere. However, you can avoid unnecessary contacts. You can help your body resist germs by keeping its barriers strong and by improving its general resistance. General methods of protecting yourself against infection can be used to help prevent such widespread diseases as colds, infantile paralysis, and tuberculosis, for which specific methods have not yet been developed.

How can you destroy germs? One of the best ways to fight disease is to

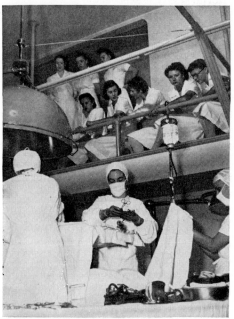

University of Colorado Medical Center

In the modern operating room everything is done to make the operation safe, painless, and successful. Physicians and nurses have their mouths and nostrils covered with gauze masks, their hands with rubber gloves. Instruments are sterilized.

destroy germs before they have a chance to cause disease. In general, most germs are destroyed by extremes of heat or cold; by dryness; by direct sunlight or ultraviolet rays; and by certain chemicals, called germicides or disinfectants. Many germicides are harmful to body tissues as well as to germs. They can be used only to destroy germs before they have a chance to enter the body. Materials free from germs are called sterile.

The most certain way to destroy germs is by *burning*. One effective way to help prevent the spread of respiratory diseases is to use paper handkerchiefs that can be burned. In emergencies, the point of a needle, used to remove a splinter or to insert between the layers of skin to drain a blister, may be sterilized by holding it in a flame a few minutes.

Boiling destroys nearly all germs in a few minutes. It is an easy way to make doubtful water safe to drink. You should boil articles, such as dishes, soiled underclothing, or soiled bedclothes, used by persons with respiratory or intestinal infections. Surgical instruments may be sterilized by boiling.

Exposure to temperatures above 140° for a long time kills most germs. Germs ordinarily carried in milk are killed by *pasteurizing*, a process of holding the milk at a definite temperature for a certain length of time. Pasteurizing has no noticeable effects on the food value or the taste of milk. Persons who drink unpasteurized milk are taking a foolish and unnecessary risk.

Hot water, soapsuds, and *sunlight* ordinarily will keep homes safe from germs. Dishes are usually sterile if washed in hot soapy water, rinsed by pouring boiling water over them, and allowed to stand until dry. Household linens and clothing washed, sunned, and ironed in the ordinary way will usually be free from germs. Clothing that is not washed, such as coats, and linings of shoes, may be aired and exposed to sunlight frequently.

Hot soapsuds and airings in the sun will help to keep garbage pails and other household articles clean.

Methods of cleaning that reduce dust, that expose as many parts as possible of the house and furnishings to sunlight, and that prevent accumulations of dirt and debris are safeguards of health.

How can you help your skin keep germs out? The important rule in taking care of your skin is "keep it whole and clean." Keeping your skin free from cuts and scratches helps to keep out germs. Even tiny breaks in the skin should be treated with an antiseptic. A 2 per cent solution of iodine is a useful home remedy for small wounds.

Larger breaks should be covered with a sterile dressing to prevent new contamination. A pad of sterile gauze held in place with strips of adhesive tape is usually a practical, easy dressing. Iodine may be irritating to the more delicate body tissues under the skin. Deep or extensive wounds should be treated by a physician. He has many specialized antiseptics that check the growth of germs without injuring tissue.

Encyclopedia Britannica Films

How does wearing clean clothing protect you from infection? Why is clean clothing especially important in athletics and other strenuous activity? How often do you wash your gym suit?

Your skin and clothing should be kept clean. Cleanliness helps prevent infection. Dirt means dangerous germs! Some kinds of dirt are especially likely to have germs. For example, tetanus germs are often found in soils that contain animal wastes. People who come in contact with dangerous germs can protect themselves by wearing gloves, smocks, and other protective clothing. In many places, going barefoot can be a foolish, dangerous practice. Soiled clothing should be removed before it has a chance to contaminate other objects.

For most people warm, soapy water applied vigorously and often is enough antiseptic for the skin. There is no special value in soaps that are supposed to contain antiseptics. Hand lotion or cold cream may be used to keep skin from becoming rough and cracked. A brush is often helpful to remove dirt around fingernails. Keeping your fingernails trimmed helps to prevent dirt accumulating under them.

Boys, as well as girls, can form habits of wearing fresh underclothing every day. It takes only a few minutes at night to wash stockings and underclothing in warm, soapy water, roll them in a towel to absorb excess moisture, and hang them to dry overnight.

How can you avoid respiratory and intestinal infections? Many respiratory and intestinal diseases can be avoided by applying our knowledge of germs and how they can travel. You can protect yourself from respiratory diseases by keeping away from infected persons. Cover your mouth and nose when you cough or sneeze. Keep away from people who are spraying germs into the air. Stay away from crowds when infectious diseases are prevalent. Many dangerous diseases, such as scarlet fever and diphtheria, begin as respiratory infections. Many chronic and dangerous diseases of the respiratory tract follow cold infections.

A well-balanced diet with plenty of fresh fruits and green vegetables helps general resistance, builds up allaround health, and keeps mucous membranes healthy.

You can help to keep germs out of your intestinal tract by putting nothing in your mouth that does not belong there. Almost everything can carry germs.

Modern methods of sanitation protect food and water from contamination. In towns and cities, we usually depend upon government agencies to see that food and water are free from dangerous germs. We can help to protect ourselves by buying food that has been inspected and labeled or stamped. We can buy from dealers who protect their food from being contaminated by handling or by insects and vermin. We can eat only in restaurants which we know are sanitary. On trips, it is much better to buy packaged food and make your own meals than to eat in doubtful restaurants.

After you buy food, you can protect it from contamination. Keep it clean and cold. Cover it to protect it from germs and from insects. Keeping your home free from insects and rodents helps to protect your food from contamination. Food that is eaten raw or unpeeled should be carefully scrubbed.

Food handlers and food utensils are common sources of infection. Your hands should be washed thoroughly with soap and water before you handle food. Most communities require that cooks and waitresses in restaurants be examined regularly to make sure they are free from communicable diseases. They also should be careful in the way they handle food and dishes.

How can you improve your general resistance? Not all germs can be destroyed. Some slip past the body's outer defenses. Persons with good general resistance can destroy ordi-

Restaurants, food stores, bakeries, and other places where food is handled should be inspected and supervised to insure sanitary conditions. Have you inspected kitchens in places where you eat? What are some danger signs?

nary invading germs and show few or no effects. People with low general resistance seem to catch more infections and diseases.

General resistance to infection is not completely understood. It is probably favored by all the habits of living that promote general health and strength—an adequate diet, a balance between exercise and rest, plenty of sleep, cleanliness, and a forward-looking, optimistic attitude toward life.

The white blood corpuscles and lymphatic system play an important part in general resistance. Activities that improve circulation probably help build general resistance. You might like to review these activities in Chapter 8. They include (1) exercises that use many large muscles and stimulate increased heartbeat and breathing; (2) erect, relaxed posture; and (3) frequent changes of position.

Medical check-ups help to reveal chronic infections or other conditions that may be taxing the body's reserve strength.

General resistance seems to be es-

Encyclopedia Britannica Films

Many germs are carried by insects and animals. How can you protect food from contamination?

pecially reduced by fatigue or by chilling. Many people notice that they catch cold more easily when they have been getting too little rest or have become chilled. You may like to review Chapter 16 to recall ways of avoiding fatigue and chilling. Remember that fatigue may result from play, as well as from work. Remember that you can become chilled on warm days as well as cold days. How is this possible?

How does medicine help?

Out of long years of experience and scientific experimenting has developed the science and art of medicine. Doctors can help us to keep healthy. They can discover disease in its early stages. They help us to recover promptly without complications. They can help us fight infections that the body alone cannot overcome.

How does vaccination help? Vaccines and toxoids have been developed that give certain protection against many serious diseases. Several diseases have been practically eliminated from enlightened communities by means of widespread vaccination.

All people could be kept from getting smallpox, tetanus, typhoid fever, and paratyphoid fever by simple, safe vaccination. Vaccination is a method of making a person immune to a disease.

All children should be protected against polio, smallpox, diphtheria, whooping cough, and tetanus. Persons likely to be highly exposed can be protected from many other diseases, such as tuberculosis and yellow fever.

How do the new drugs help? In treating infections some drugs are helpful because they help the body in a general way. They may relieve pain, promote needed rest or sleep, or stimulate some organ, such as the heart. Other drugs are valuable because they attack certain germs.

Until recently only a few drugs, serums, and medicines were available for specific action against infectious diseases. Drugs that destroyed germs were usually also harmful to the body. Now successful serums have been developed for many diseases, including diphtheria, cholera, measles, scarlet fever, tetanus, several types of pneumonia, and meningitis.

Since 1938 many new drugs have been discovered that act specifically against certain germs. Among the new germ fighters are the sulfa drugs, penicillin, streptomycin, and related medicines. Each of the sulfa drugs acts specifically against one or more kinds of germs and is harmless to others. Penicillin has been used successfully against a wide variety of infections since its discovery in 1940. Your doctor has powerful new weapons to fight infections. Constant research is discovering and testing new germ killers. Many are extremely effective and are harmless to the body when used properly. None should be self-prescribed.

How can you treat infections?

Even a person who has done his best to keep well may become ill. Then he must do his best to become well as soon as possible. Many illnesses are cared for by the person himself or by members of his family. Others require medical or hospital care.

Not many boys and girls have to assume responsibility for the care of a sick person. Everyone, however, needs to know how to take care of minor injuries, to do simple first aid, to help care for a sick person, and to know when to get expert help.

How can you care for illness at home? In taking care of a sick person at home, you need to apply what you have already learned about promoting health and destroying germs. You need to consider the protection of members of the family as well as the comfort and welfare of the patient.

Encyclopedia Britannica Films

A comfortable, suitably equipped room helps a sick person to recover. How would you prepare a suitable sickroom at home?

If possible, the patient should have a room to himself. A comfortable, suitably equipped sickroom helps the sick person recover and protects other persons from infection. The room should be comfortably heated and ventilated. It should be free from drafts and disturbing noises and should be close to a bathroom.

A patient with an infectious disease should have his own dishes and personal articles, such as comb, brush, clothing, and towels. They should be kept separate. They can be sterilized by boiling. Paper handkerchiefs should be used to collect discharges from the nose and mouth. They can be collected in a paper sack and burned.

At least one person in every home should know how to follow the doctor's orders. He will give instructions for giving medicine, for feeding and bathing a sick person, and for preparing and serving the right foods. He will also explain the necessity of keeping the patient quiet and removed from other people.

The Red Cross offers courses on home care to people of high school age or over. Such training can be of great value to everyone. Even young members of a family can learn to do some helpful things when someone is ill. They can help to keep the household running smoothly and give extra thought to the patient's welfare.

A person who is sick is more sensitive than a well person to discomfort and annoyances. Too much noise or light, lack of ventilation, disorder, and disagreeable odors may be irritating or depressing. Boys and girls can often do much to keep a sick person more comfortable and happy. They can avoid unnecessary noise and confusion, slamming doors, running, yelling, and loud talking. Flowers, a radio, little gifts, and thoughtful acts often do much to cheer a sick person and help him recover.

What medical attention should you have? Everyone should have periodic medical examinations. Young people and old people need more frequent examinations than healthy, mature people do. Health examinations often disclose conditions that could be improved. Many people have habits and practices that are likely to do them harm. Routine check-ups often reveal these conditions before they have done damage and while they can be readily cured.

A health examination often helps a person to choose the right kind of work and play. A handicapped person may learn to overcome his handicap or to choose activities where it makes no difference. Even if the health examination reveals no disease, it gives a person a feeling of confidence and well-being.

When a person is ill he wants to become well as soon as possible. Ideally, this would mean having medical attention for any symptom. A person cannot know which symptoms are serious and which are not. Since any infection may prove to be serious, all illnesses are cured more easily and surely at their start.

No rule can be given for selecting a physician. Helpful information may be obtained from a local hospital, the medical society, or discriminating friends. Keep certain considerations in mind in making a choice. Persons using the title "doctor" vary greatly in knowledge and skills. A physician qualified to practice medicine will have a degree from a recognized school of medicine and a license from the state. Most good physicians belong to a recognized medical society and have connections with a good hospital. It is against the best medical ethics for a doctor to advertise in newspapers or pamphlets.

Some industries, schools, and businesses provide medical attention for any symptom. Most people, however, must decide whether or not to see a doctor. They consider several factors and balance them against their chances of having a serious or long illness. If a person decides he can get along without medical help, he should at least go to bed and rest. He should not attempt to doctor himself. Self-treatment may cause the disease to grow worse or hide important warnings that it is growing worse.

Generally a doctor should be called for any unusual symptoms, like rash, swelling, or earache. He should be called if ordinary symptoms are severe or prolonged. Medical attention

Why is it a good idea to have a family doctor even if you have had no illness in your family? How can you select a doctor?

351

should be given for severe sore throat, colds that hang on, abdominal pain that lasts over three hours, vomiting more than once, and sores that do not heal readily. Immediate medical aid should be given to severe bleeding, loss of consciousness, severe or prolonged pain, and accidental injuries.

How can you pay for medical care? There is a general impression that the cost of medical care is high. Yet each year more than twice as much money is spent by the American people for tobacco as is spent for the services of physicians and dentists.

However, some people are unable to pay for necessary medical care and others are unable to meet the large expenses for sudden illness. The nation as a whole suffers from much illness that would be prevented with adequate use of medical services.

Many plans for obtaining good medical service, at moderate cost, are being suggested and tried out in various parts of the country. Some colleges and organizations and industries have their own medical facilities and furnish complete medical service to their groups at low cost. Cities have hospitals and clinics that provide free medical examination and service for those unable to pay.

There is a definite but much-disputed trend toward medical care at government expense. This trend is apparent in the growth in number and size of city and county clinics and hospitals, which are serving more and more people. Bills have been considered by Congress that would provide for national health insurance for everyone. Another solution of the problem is being offered by plans for group health and hospitalization insurance. In such arrangements, the members of the group pay a fixed premium to provide for the cost of medical and hospital care when the need arises. Some plans pay any physician chosen by the member. In other plans a selected group of doctors and hospitals care for all the members of the plan.

Being able to secure adequate medical care is important to everyone. The problem requires intelligent thought and decision.

What are our health problems?

Since 1900 the infectious diseases of infancy and childhood and many of the great plagues have been greatly reduced and in some cases almost eliminated. So the average age of our population has been increasing, and many more persons live to be old. But those who have escaped the diseases of childhood face other dangers.

Cancer, diseases of the heart and circulatory system, diabetes, and mental illness are diseases becoming more and more important. Much research is being done on all of them. Associations of volunteers and professional workers conduct campaigns to raise funds both for research and for the care of victims. With enthusiastic public support they will probably be as successful in their battles as was the National Foundation for Infantile Paralysis in its fight against polio.

You may like to write to some of these disease-fighting associations to find out about the work they are doing. (See page 358 for the names of some of the organizations.) What are some ways you can be a disease fighter?

Is heart disease important to you? A few years ago heart disease reached first place as a cause of death and, in spite of better diagnosis and treatment, is still on the increase. Heart disease may be either valvular or degenerative.

Valvular heart disease usually develops in young people. Infections from diseases like diphtheria, scarlet fever, influenza, or rheumatic fever may damage the heart valves. Many of these diseases can be prevented. When they do occur, expert care and prolonged rest during convalescence can safeguard against heart injury.

Other types of heart disease are due to *degenerative processes*, more or less normal to old age, but often occurring too early in life. They may be due to severe general infections. You may like to refer to Chapter 8 for some suggestions on taking care of your heart.

Diseases of the heart, arteries, and kidneys are usually extremely complex and hard to understand. They often develop slowly as tissues gradually break down. They are still baffling medical science, although research is constantly piling up new facts.

The tendency to such degenerative diseases is probably aggravated by excesses in eating, by alcohol, by tobacco, by insufficient exercise, by overwork, by nervous and mental strain, by chronic infections, and by the rapid pace of modern living.

How dangerous is cancer? Cancer is probably the most dreaded disease of middle age and old age. It is the second leading cause of death. The cause of cancer is not yet understood. Some cells, for no known reason, begin to grow wildly and without control. They spread in every direction and destroy other cells that are in their way. They develop into a mass, some growing rapidly, some slowly. A cancer may be on the outside of the body or hidden inside.

As far as present knowledge goes, cancer is not a germ disease, is not communicable, and is not inherited. Research is being carried on constantly, and everything points to the conclusion that the cause of cancer will some day be discovered. It is already a less hopeless disease than it was a few years ago. At the present time, cancer in many instances can be cured if the right kind of treatment is given early.

There are only three reliable methods of treatment for cancer; by surgery, by X ray, and by radium. The best method, or combination of methods, can be determined only by an experienced physician. The sooner proper treatment is given, the better is the chance of recovery.

Everyone should know the common signs of cancer and consult a physician promptly if they appear. The common signs are (1) the presence of a lump; (2) persistent bleeding; (3) a sore that does not heal readily; (4) internal pain; and (5) unexplained loss of weight. No one should postpone an examination because of fear. If cancer is revealed early, chances of recovery are much better. Usually the examination will reveal that no cancer is present, and the patient is saved a great deal of mental torture.

Remember—no medicine, no diet, no serum exists that will cure cancer. Fake cures can do no good and may result in death by causing postponement of proper treatment.

What is the status of tuberculosis? Tuberculosis is completely unnecessary. We know how to find, prevent, and cure it. Yet it is the eighth leading cause of death in the United States. Over 1,200,000 people are suffering from the disease. More than 86,000 new cases are reported every year. This unnecessary suffering will decrease as more people learn the ways to prevent tuberculosis, to recognize early signs, and to seek early diagnosis and prompt treatment. You can help.

Tuberculosis is caused by a germ that may attack any part of the body. The most frequent location of the infection is the lungs. Little nodules or tubercles develop, poisons are produced, and lung tissue is destroyed.

Tuberculosis begins after germs are inhaled or taken into the mouth with food, water, or milk. It can be contracted from soiled hands or by direct contact with an infected person. The germs can live for several hours outside the body in moist sputum. Discharges from the mouth and nose of infected persons should be burned. Most people are able to fight off a few of the germs, and the disease may never develop. Most adults show in X rays and tuberculin tests that they have at one time been infected and have successfully resisted the disease.

If body resistance is lowered, the germs may gain the upper hand and an active case of tuberculosis may re-

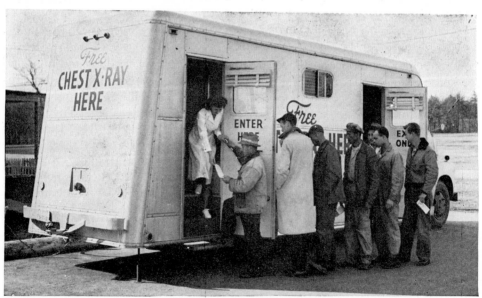

United States Public Health Service

The X-ray examination is the best and easiest way to detect tuberculosis infection. Mass examinations have been conducted in many communities, using mobile units as shown here.

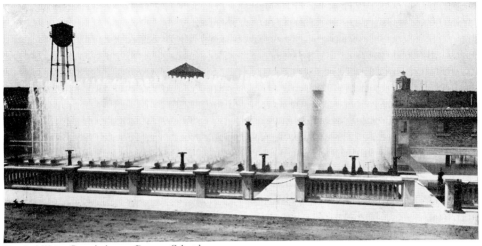

Board of Water Commissioners, Denver, Colorado

How does a city provide a safe water supply?

sult. Because tuberculosis often develops slowly, it may not be recognized until it has reached an advanced stage. It is in the high school and young adult years that the number of cases of tuberculosis increases. Young people often are careless about their diet and rest, and this may be part of the cause.

To avoid tuberculosis, body resistance should be maintained by observing the general rules of health—wholesome food, fresh air, rest, and exercise. Exposure should be avoided as much as possible. Cleanliness is important. Early recognition of the disease is a help to rapid recovery.

The tuberculin skin test is a way to discover whether a person is, or ever has been, infected with the germ. It does not prove he has tuberculosis. The X-ray examination is the best and easiest way to find active or inactive tuberculosis infection. If the infection is not active, an individual may live a normal life, if he lives sensibly, and does not become run down.

If the infection is active, careful treatment under medical supervision is essential. Treatment is not alone by medicines, but by complete rest in bed, wholesome food, and fresh air. Surgical treatment is sometimes necessary to provide a chance for damaged lungs to rest and recover.

Recent medical discoveries are helping to prevent and to cure tuberculosis. BCG vaccine has proved to be safe and to build some resistance. Because it is still being studied and tested, it is distributed only where it is most needed and its results can be studied. Generally, it is recommended only for people most likely to be heavily exposed, to those highly susceptible, and those who are living under extremely unhealthful, crowded conditions. The World Health Organization is helping conduct programs for mass vaccination of children in some foreign countries. The vaccination is being carried on in connection with other general control methods.

All young persons should have tests for tuberculosis every year or so. If the skin test reveals the presence of infection, past or present, a chest X ray should be obtained.

How can cities promote health? In order that the best standards of healthful living may prevail, careful planning for the whole city is necessary. The plans should include (1) a safe and adequate water supply, (2) sanitary disposal of waste and sewage, (3) food inspection and protection, (4) enforcement of isolation and quarantine laws, (5) protection against industrial hazards, (6) safety programs, (7) protection against epidemics, and (8) control of smoke and noise. Can you find out how your community takes care of these problems?

Although disease attacks all kinds of persons, it is usually most common among the poor. The resistance of many people is lowered by inadequate food, bad housing, overcrowded living conditions, overwork, and worry. Therefore the control of disease is partly an economic problem. A community that is a happy, healthful place in which to live gives people opportunity for useful, well-paid work and protection from poverty and exploitation.

Communities should offer opportunities for relaxation and play, for mental stimulation, for self-improvement. People like recognition, secu-

A city protects the health of its citizens by disposing of trash, garbage, and sewage. How does your community take care of these services?

356

Swimming pools promote both health and fun. How can they be kept safe?

rity, and a feeling of belonging. How can a community do this? What does your community do? Could you help it do more?

Learning to accept responsibility for community welfare must be learned. You learn and enjoy the learning by *doing* something.

Active participation in community enterprises brings a satisfaction, a sense of belonging and of responsibility, that cannot be valued in dollars and cents. You learn to think of others and understand their viewpoint. It is fun. Your world expands and you grow up with it.

What organizations help keep you healthy? A community which has a low standard of health is a menace to its neighbors, to its country, and to the world at large. At every government level—city, county, state, and nation—are departments of health and welfare that deal with health problems for large areas.

Various international agreements have been made in recent years, so that nations may assist each other in protecting public health. Leading nations that enjoy greater advantages and opportunities in health work realize the wisdom of making these ad-

357

Encyclopedia Britannica Films

vantages available to nations that are backward, or that lack the financial ability to carry on progressive measures. Sixty-one governments formed the World Health Organization in 1946 to extend health knowledge and practices throughout the world.

More and more governments are turning to WHO for help in controlling communicable diseases, strengthening public health services, educating medical personnel, and obtaining medicines and equipment.

There are many other organizations that deal with health problems, such as the National Committee for the Prevention of Blindness, the American Society for the Control of Cancer, the National Committee for Mental Hygiene, life-insurance companies, the Rockefeller Foundation, and the National Dairy Council.

The American Red Cross provides home nursing. It provides many services connected with the military in time of war. In time of peace it does much public-health work in connection with epidemic diseases, floods, fires, and other disasters. It provides nursing and nutrition services for public schools. It performs welfare work of many kinds. The American Junior

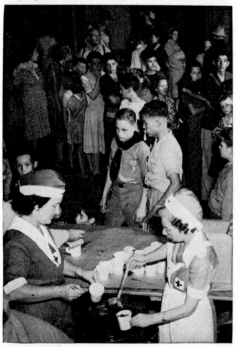

American Red Cross

The American Red Cross provides many health services—in connection with the armed forces, in disasters, and in safety and welfare programs. What are some other groups that work to promote health?

Red Cross operates in the public schools. It offers boys and girls opportunities to be of service to children who are sick, disabled, or troubled by war or other disasters. Financial support for the American Red Cross comes from contributions from its members.

The National Tuberculosis Association combats tuberculosis. It educates the public in matters of hygiene through newspapers, pamphlets, and moving pictures. It conducts clinics and X-ray examinations and encourages the establishment of special hospitals for the tuberculosis patients.

What can you do about accidents?

Do you sometimes feel that adults are too concerned about safety? If you look at the statistics, which tell the sad story of accidental death and injury, you will realize they have good reasons for being concerned. Although boys and girls have the physical equipment to react quickly and accurately, they have the worst accident records. Each year accidents cause nearly 100,000 deaths and over 300,000 disabling injuries. They cause almost ten million minor injuries. About a third of the deaths are caused by automobile accidents; about a fourth are caused by falls. Burns, drowning, and firearms are other major causes of accidents.

Safety practices are for everyone. Some childish persons feel it is a sign of weakness to follow safety rules. Talk to or read about the men who lead adventurous and thrilling lives. You may be surprised at the many safety precautions they take.

Athletes, adventurers, and intelligent leaders take all possible steps to protect themselves and others.

Well-conducted fire drills, practiced at regular intervals, can save lives. Are drills in your school efficient and realistic? How could they be improved?

How can you play safely? Each boy or girl needs to choose activities suited to his own particular ability and physical condition. Attempting to play games that are too strenuous or to play with others who set too fast a pace is not only dangerous but discouraging. Everyone can find some games which he can learn to play well and to enjoy.

If you do take part in competitive sports, have a thorough physical examination and follow the doctor's advice. Intensive competition requires a mind and body working at their best. Work up gradually to strenuous activity. Careful training helps to put you in good condition. Get nine or ten hours sleep every night. Eat plenty of vegetables, fruit, milk, meat, eggs, and fish. Have regular meals at least three times a day. Today training rules are usually not as rigid as they once were. It is up to the individual athlete to know and practice good habits.

In any game, avoid unnecessary contact or collision with other players. This calls for balance, alertness, and skill. Learn to fall properly. In falling, the weight should never be thrown forcibly on a knee, waist, shoulder, elbow, or hand. Be on the alert for unsafe places on the playing area—slippery spots, pieces of equipment, or broken apparatus.

It is always important to warm up thoroughly before strenuous exercise. Wear a sweater or coat when resting. Why? All equipment coming into contact with your body should be clean and sanitary. Use your own clean towel. Report to the coach all injuries, bruises, blisters, and scratches. Stop any activity when you do not recover quickly from breathlessness or fatigue after a short rest. Anything that injures your general health and vitality makes you more likely to have an accident. Why is attempting to reduce by excessive sweating a dangerous practice?

Training yourself to be constantly on the alert helps you to avoid accidents and makes you a better player.

All sports have certain hazards of their own. Skill in fundamentals, careful use of dangerous equipment, proper clothing and equipment, and safe playing areas help to prevent accidents and to make you a better player.

How can you be safe at home? Most home accidents are preventable. Records show that about one half the deaths in the home are caused by falls. The remainder are caused chiefly by burns, firearms, poisoning, suffocation, gas, and electric shocks. Stairways, yards, and kitchens seem to be the most dangerous spots. Can you think why?

Young children have many accidents. They experiment with anything they can reach—sharp pointed objects, gas jets, wall sockets, matches, pills, bottles, kettle handles, and hot-water faucets. They climb on chairs and ladders and boxes, fall down stairs and out of windows, and slip on loose rugs or slippery spots. What are some ways you can protect children? Are different methods appropriate at different ages?

Strangely enough, experienced older persons are injured by the same things that bring grief to babies. Adults trip over loose objects, fall down stairs, are burned in explosions, and are poisoned and shocked. Many serious accidents could be prevented by adequate lighting, uncluttered floors, protected stairways, and other simple precautions. Can you describe a safe home?

How can you care for sickness and injuries? In spite of all precautions, accidents and illness occur in most homes. Everyone should know what to do in cases of injury or illness.

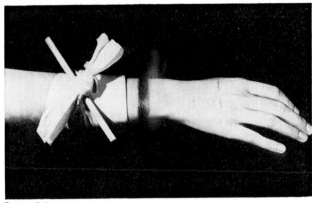

Ewing Galloway

A tourniquet is used only for severe, life-threatening hemorrhage. It should be applied close to the wound and above it. Once applied, it should not be released except by a physician.

It is advisable to know when and how to call a doctor and how to obtain emergency help such as the police or fire department. Police and fire departments usually have rescue squads to remove people from dangerous situations and to revive cases of asphyxiation from drowning, strangling, electric shock, or poisoning. Do you have an emergency card near your telephone with name, address, and telephone number of (1) the family doctor, (2) another nearby doctor, (3) the police department, and (4) the fire department?

For most beginning illnesses the patient should be put to bed in a warm room by himself and kept quiet and warm. Foreign bodies in the eye, ear, windpipe, or face should be removed by a physician. Emergency treatment may be given by qualified persons. Persistent bleeding or convulsions should have immediate medical attention.

What first aid should you know? Most of us are faced sooner or later with the question—how much first aid and when? It is better not to use first-aid procedures unless you are well informed as to what is safe. However, the right technique applied at the right time may save a life or prevent more serious injuries. All adults and boys and girls may be prepared by taking a Red Cross first-aid course. In severe injuries always call a physician.

Some accident victims require immediate care to prevent excessive bleeding that may cause death. If blood is bright red and flowing in spurts you will know an artery has been cut. Why? In such cases pressure should be applied either directly on the wound, on the artery near the wound, or on the side where the artery comes from the heart. A folded sterile compress or clean handkerchief can be used to put pressure on the wound. If the flow of blood is too strong to be stopped by finger pressure a tight bandage can be applied directly over the compress. A tourniquet may be applied if bleeding cannot be stopped by other methods.

Puncture wounds caused by rusty

nails, splinters, and other penetrating objects are particularly dangerous. Often they do not bleed well, are difficult to cleanse, and may contain tetanus germs. They should be treated promptly by a physician even if they seem unimportant.

A physician should treat any wound that develops much pus, that shows red streaks extending from it, or that is accompanied by any fever. Serious infections may develop into blood poisoning. Even small wounds, tiny scratches, cuts, and blisters should be treated with antiseptic and covered with a sterile dressing.

Reviewing the chapter

Test yourself

I

You should answer "yes" to the following questions.

1. Do you use a handkerchief when you cough or sneeze?
2. Do you wash your hands with soap and water before handling food and after using the toilet?
3. Do you help keep your home running smoothly when someone is ill?
4. Do you help to keep convalescent children in your family entertained quietly while they rest in bed?
5. Do you take steps to be immunized from such diseases as smallpox and diphtheria?
6. Do you have regular medical check-ups?

II

Complete the following sentences by supplying the missing words. Do NOT WRITE IN THIS BOOK.

1. Germs affect the body differently because they have different .... make-up.
2. The seriousness of a disease depends upon the ...., ..., and ....
3. Infections which last a long time are called ....

4. Germs may travel directly from one person to another by ...., ..., and ....
5. Body defenses against germs are ...., ..., ..., ..., and ....
6. The leading cause of death for persons between fifteen and thirty-five years of age is ....

III

What would you think, say, or do in the following situations?
1. If someone complained of feeling faint?
2. If you scratched your finger?
3. If someone was wounded by stepping on a nail?
4. If someone near you sneezed without covering his nose and mouth?
5. If someone in your family were ill and your mother were acting as nurse?

Reading to help you grow up

What Is Tuberculosis? The National Tuberculosis Association. See also other publications by this association.

First Aid and Diphtheria. The Metropolitan Life Insurance Company. See also other publications by this company.

Community health services and communicable diseases are discussed in the following list of readings:

The Human Body by Brownell and others.

Health in a Power Age by Charters and others.

Working Together for Health by Burkhard and others.

Life and Health by Almack and others.

Interesting discussions of safety and first aid are found in these readings:

The Road to Safety Series by Buckley and others.

Your Health and Safety by Clemenson and La Porte.

To Live in Health by Burnett.

Films to help you understand

Your Doctor and You. Filmstrip. Zunick.

Your Friend the Public Health Nurse. Filmstrip. Metropolitan Life Insurance Company.

Defending the City's Health. Encyclopedia Britannica Films. How a Public Health Department operates.

Red Cross News. American Red Cross.

Bacteria. Encyclopedia Britannica Films.

Body Defenses against Disease. Encyclopedia Britannica Films.

Defense against Invasion. Princeton Film Center Association. Combination of regular photography and Walt Disney animation showing the importance of vaccination.

Insects as Carriers of Disease. Inst. Inter. American Affairs. A Walt Disney production showing the fly, mosquito, and louse as disease carriers.

Triumph without Drums. TFC. The story of the Federal Food, Drug, and Cosmetic Act.

Water—Friend or Enemy. Princeton Film Center. A Disney production showing the dangers in water contamination.

Goodbye, Mr. Germ. National Tuberculosis Association. Uses animated drawings to tell the story of tuberculosis and prevention measures to combat it.

Winged Scourge. Princeton Film Center. A Disney production illustrating the dangers of mosquitoes in spreading malaria.

First Steps in First Aid. Modern. Basic information in the standard first aid course for beginners.

Help Wanted. Association. For beginners in first aid.

How Can You Act Your Age?

Have you ever been told to "act your age"? Have you ever been unhappy because you felt that you were being treated like a baby? Everyone recognizes that different feelings and behavior are appropriate to different ages.

As you grow up you play many different roles. First you are an infant —helpless, dependent, and selfish. Soon you are a child, active and curious, gaining some independence, becoming aware of other people. Next you are a schoolchild, testing yourself, beginning to want to "belong" to gangs and teams. Now you are a teen-ager, eager for independence, trying to acquire self-confidence and a place of your own in your world, seeking approval and acceptance among others your own age, and looking for solutions to your own problems.

In a little while you will be in a new role, an adult, independent and responsible. To be a happy adult you will need all the skills you have ac-
cumulated in your other roles. You will need to be an independent, responsible individual with a philosophy that helps you to see and understand the meaning of your life. You will need a philosophy that gives you standards for making your own decisions and that gives you hope and courage for facing inevitable griefs and disappointments. As an adult you will need to shoulder responsibilities and to be concerned for the welfare of others.

Acting your age requires that you develop the necessary skills. Some of the skills are physical. They require a healthy, well-co-ordinated body. Some skills are mental. They require increasing ability to use your mind, to behave reasonably and with self-control. Some are emotional. They require increased understanding of why people, including yourself, do the things they do and how everyone is affected by natural human desires and feelings.

As you grow up you change in many ways. Perhaps most important are the changes in your feelings and actions.

Harold M. Lambert

Children sometimes think clothes and manners make them seem more grown up. What are some ways you have seen older boys and girls use to appear more grown up?

Harold M. Lambert

366

The ability to see things that need to be done and to go ahead and do them is a real sign of maturity. What home responsibilities do you have?

H. Armstrong Roberts

A sign of maturity is the ability to concentrate and to stick with difficult jobs.

Ewing Galloway

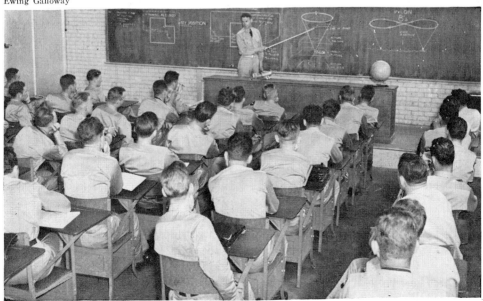

Chapter 18

WHAT FEELINGS AND ACTIONS SHOW YOU ARE GROWING UP?

Boys and girls are usually eager to grow up. They try to do things that will make them seem grown up. Unfortunately, they do not always realize that growing up does not depend upon clothes or artificial manners and habits. They are likely to think that imitating certain adult behavior, such as using cosmetics, smoking, or defying authority, shows that they are grown up. Actually a person never seems more childish than when he is imitating a role he does not understand. Do little children seem grown up to you when they dress up and imitate their parents?

Experiences at every age are valuable. Living one role successfully prepares you for the next. The child learns to walk. Later, he learns to run, to skate, to play basketball, and to dance. The five-year-old gains confidence in his own abilities. The ten-year-old learns to get along with playmates his own age. Later, in his gang and teams, he learns more of the skills necessary for getting along with others, to lead and to follow, to give and to take. He learns to play on a team, to do his share, to accept defeat and success. These skills, and the self-respect and self-confidence he acquires, help him to get along with other boys and girls, to consider the desires and welfare of other people.

The experiences at every age are enjoyable, too. However, it is important that you do not remain too long in any role. Everyone loves a baby, awkward and self-centered as he is. A teenager acting like a small child is an annoyance to himself and all who come in contact with him. An adult who is selfish and lacks self-control can cause great unhappiness to himself and to others.

Looking ahead

Questions and suggestions

1. What do you mean by chronological age? Physical age? Mental age? Emotional age? Social age?

2. What are some physical changes that take place as you grow up?

3. What are some mental changes that take place as you grow up?

4. How do your feelings about people change as you grow up?

5. Have you ever seen people behaving childishly?

6. What childish habits do you have?

7. Can you recall the last time you felt left out or treated unfairly by others? What did you do? Do you think you might have found a happier solution?

8. Do you expect other people to be friendly? The socially mature person likes other people and expects them to like him.

9. How does your sense of humor change as you grow up?

10. Has your taste in reading changed in the last year?

11. How have your other interests changed?

12. What do you think are some signs of childishness?

13. Do you really care about what happens to other people? What have you done today that showed consideration for others?

Committee planning

1. It might be interesting to poll the class to find out favorite comedians, jokes, comic strips, and books. Compare with favorites among other age groups.

2. You might be able to give commercial tests of social and mental maturity to members of the class.

Reading

Read quickly the entire chapter. Give the main ideas in the chapter in your own words. Read the chapter more slowly for details. Answer the questions that introduce the new topics.

What are signs of growing up?

A baby is dependent, is selfish, and lacks self-control. He is aware of only a small world and is interested only in himself and his immediate comfort. As he grows up, he moves from the center of a small world into a larger one. He gains control of himself, becomes independent and self-confident. His interests and affections expand. He gains insight into happenings and behavior; he becomes reasonable and considerate of others.

It is perfectly natural for a child to be awkward, unreasonable, and un-

social. We expect him to stumble and fumble, to yell and strike out in anger, and to be concerned only with his own immediate comfort and pleasure. As he grows up, we expect him to learn more reasonable, controlled, unselfish ways of behaving. No one ever reaches perfection, but we can move toward it. You can check your own progress if you know which are childish and which are mature ways of behaving.

What are signs of mental maturity? As you grow up you increase in men-

Small children cannot take turns or give in gracefully. They express their emotions directly.

tal abilities. You are better able to use your senses. You learn by seeing and hearing, and you receive pleasure from sense impressions. Are you learning to enjoy and use your senses? Do you know and appreciate more music and art than you did a few years ago? Can you observe and describe more accurately the things you see and hear and feel? As you grow up you gain in ability to control muscle responses. Are you stronger, more skillful and graceful than you were last year? Are you learning to play games that call for more skill and timing? Are you doing some manual arts like woodworking or clay modeling that help you to gain hand skills?

The mentally mature use reason to control their actions. They know and use the method of scientific problem solving. They are able to concentrate, to focus their attention for longer periods, and to disregard minor irritations. They can see things that need to be done, and they do them without outside urging. They have formed efficient habits to take care of routine activities but can control their habits when they want to. Do you follow an efficient routine for such things as homework, taking care of your clothes, going to bed, and getting ready for the day's activities? Do you ever do more work than has been assigned?

The mentally mature look for reasons and causes back of events and behavior. They carefully examine ready-made opinions and claims. They are able to think logically and have confidence in their own reasoning. Their increased understanding of how things work and why people act as they do helps them to solve many

As you grow up you can use your hands more skillfully. You can follow directions and enjoy doing a good job.

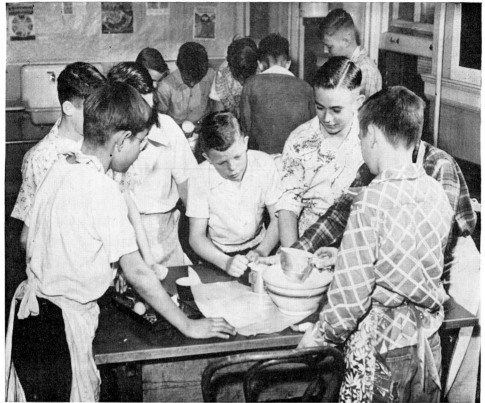

A wide variety of interests and skills are signs of growing up. Older boys enjoy learning many home skills, such as gardening and taking care of children.

problems without fear or anger. Do you believe all the ads and promises, everything you read or hear? Do you know where and how to get reliable information and guidance about your problems?

What are signs of emotional maturity? A person who is growing up emotionally lives in an expanding world. Gradually he notices more things and more people. He learns how the outside world brings him pleasure or discomfort. He learns how to use objects and get along with people. He wants to be liked and accepted. Slowly he becomes aware that other people are like himself, that they want much the same things, and that they have the same worries. He learns to consider the other person's point of view and to be concerned about the welfare and happiness of others. Do you always demand your own way, or do you sometimes do things for others' happiness? Do you see things to be done around home and do them without being told?

Some children expand their world rapidly. Successful experiences at each stage bring self-confidence and eagerness for the next step. Some

Older girls are strong, skillful, and careful. They can develop a wide variety of skills.

quite small children have learned to take turns and to consider other people's feelings. They can play on teams and co-operate with a group. Some adults never learn.

An important part of emotional development is increasing self-control. Is it adult behavior when grownups indulge in temper tantrums, fighting, or getting even? Interest in others helps mature people to overcome self-consciousness and timidity, bluffing and boasting. They can control their reactions to anger and fear. They can use up the energy generated by emo-

tions in socially acceptable ways, such as strenuous exercise or work. They can examine reasonably the causes of their fear and anger and try to overcome them. Do you have unreasonable fears, for example, of the dark, of being alone, or of animals? Do you become angry easily or express your anger in tantrums?

A mature person can put up with things that cannot be helped. He can sacrifice temporary pleasures to achieve a distant goal. He can save and plan for the future. Can you keep yourself at necessary work when you

372

Hobbies that require knowledge and skill are signs of growing up. What are your hobbies?

would like to play? A mature person can control his own actions. He can follow directions and obey laws, even if they cause him personal discomfort. Do you play without cheating, even in small ways? Do you obey your parents and other lawful authority promptly and cheerfully? Do you really understand why some rules must always be followed?

Children are easily satisfied to receive the attention and help of other people. Childish personalities may continue to be satisfied with friendships, which have all the benefits going one way. A mature person cannot enjoy the companionship of others unless they also enjoy his. He cannot enjoy friendships based upon flattery, threats, or envy. He learns that serving others can be more satisfying than being served. He learns that his ideals must include feelings of friendship and consideration for others, if he wishes to have worth-while friendships.

A mature person has a belief or philosophy that makes his life follow a consistent pattern. His behavior is not a series of disconnected actions. Probably most mental and emotional disturbances of adults are caused by the lack of a mature philosophy, which can give their life meaning. Finding such a philosophy should be one of the goals of all boys and girls as they grow up.

As you grow up, you can look critically at yourself, and accept responsibility for your own growth. It may help you grow up to recognize some common dangers and signs of failure to develop.

What are childish ways of behaving? See if you can recognize some childish habits and traits in small children you know. Many of these traits persist into adult behavior. You may know older people who behave in a childish manner.

Probably the most noticeable characteristic of a small child is his interest in himself. Other people exist simply to serve him. He can ignore others or demand their immediate and complete attention. Children like attention and will go to almost any lengths to obtain it. They like to tease but lack a sense of humor.

Children cannot put up with unpleasant things. They want to quit when they are not getting their own way. They are impatient and will not stick to difficult or uncomfortable jobs. They cannot pay attention to anything for very long.

Children are emotional. They become excited, angry, or frightened by many things. They cannot control their emotions, and they are easily moved to laughter, tears, hitting, or running away.

Children must learn to play and work with others. Have you ever noticed how independently small children play? Each one goes his own way and plays with his toys alone, even though he is playing in the same room with others. They dislike sharing toys.

Gradually their games become more co-operative and finally highly organized, with complex rules and team play. Do you enjoy working and playing with others?

What are some dangers? The greatest danger at any stage of development is that a person may get stuck. The baby who depends upon his mother for affection and companionship and comfort is happy and normal. The wise mother will help him to include his father and, later, other children in his world of interest and trust. He must build self-confidence and independence and the ability to get along with many people.

Teenagers are usually outgrowing self-centered childish habits. They often show flashes of childish behavior, alternating with more mature feelings and actions. Like physical development, mental and emotional growth is uneven and different for different people. Everyone can recognize some harmful habits in himself. Do you recognize any of these habits?

Some boys and girls still crave immediate, complete attention. They may laugh too often and too loud, wisecrack, show off, or do almost anything to gain attention. Some are practical jokers or teasers. They lack a sense of humor and do not like to play games or do work where they cannot appear to good advantage. They cannot bear to lose or to fail at anything.

Some boys and girls are still completely self-centered. They want to appear unnaturally perfect. They belittle the achievements of others to

374

make themselves seem better. Some people deliberately choose the company of younger boys and girls in order to seem big and important. They demand more than their share of time and attention from their friends, parents, teachers, or coaches. They demand more than their share of family money and consideration. They cannot give and take, take turns, and let other people have their way part of the time.

Many people never learn to accept all kinds of things. They cannot stick with a disagreeable job or follow a planned routine. They are easily discouraged by failure.

Many people never learn to control their emotions. If they are enjoying themselves, they never know when to quit. If they are angry or depressed, they let everyone know it. They do not stop to think but are easily moved to anger and respond quickly by threatening or fighting.

A child gets along fairly well, even if he is selfish and self-centered. He usually does not care what others are thinking. He simply likes attention and his own way. Other people accept his behavior, because it is only natural at his stage of development. As you grow up, you become more aware

Philip Gendreau

Teenagers should be able to write interesting, friendly letters. Do you keep in touch with absent friends? Do you write notes of appreciation and congratulation and sympathy?

of other people and are eager to "belong." Being self-centered may make you self-conscious or sensitive. You think everyone is as interested in you as you are. You may feel that everyone is looking at you or talking about you.

How can you help yourself grow up?

An experience that helps boys and girls to develop emotionally is to belong to a club or a team or a gang. Playing and working with a group of people of about your own age and of your sex gives you a chance to learn valuable skills. In gangs you have opportunities to learn about other people much like yourself and to observe people with the same problems as you. You learn to give and take, to co-operate, to lead and to follow, and to win or lose. You gain confidence in yourself when you are accepted by others. Close friendships give you a chance to find out what other people

375

Philip Gendreau

As you grow up you enjoy activities with mixed crowds of boys and girls. Do you have friends among both boys and girls?

your age think. They help you to realize that others have dreams and fears and face problems and disappointments much the same as yours.

Understanding many people and being accepted as a worth-while person gives boys and girls skill and confidence to move on to larger groups. In high school most boys and girls are ready for crowds made up of both boys and girls, rather than gangs of one sex. As you move into mixed groups, you may have to endure teasing. If you are growing up, you will not be too disturbed. Children cannot endure teasing, but more mature boys and girls develop a sense of humor.

Many friendships with persons of both sexes help you to develop emotionally. You learn more about all kinds of people. You obtain a better understanding of yourself from the way other people react to you, and from the way you react to them.

Growing up emotionally enables you to see people more clearly. People who were just a background for yourself become distinct individuals. You can understand how others are feeling and why they act the way they

376

do. As you become increasingly grown up, independent of your family, you should see its members more clearly as individuals. You see your mother, father, brothers, and sisters as persons with feelings and lives of their own. You may be surprised to find out what interesting people they are.

Some people find themselves naturally having the experiences they need to grow up. They belong to a gang, are on a team, and get acquainted with their family easily. Others need to make a deliberate effort. Sometimes it is difficult to overcome habits of shyness or selfishness, but it can be done. It may help you to learn some of the reasons you and other people feel and act the way you do.

Reviewing the chapter

Test yourself

Would you like to find out if you are growing up, or if you are childish? The questions that follow will help you to decide. If you can answer "yes" to most of the questions in the dark type, you can say that you are really growing up in the right way.

Do I try to think for myself?
or seek help on every little problem?
Do I admit facts?
or make up excuses?
Do I keep cool in a tight spot?
or give way to temper?
Do I accept ideas better than mine?
or hang on stubbornly?
Do I profit from experience?
or repeat the same mistakes?
Do I keep a good balance between work, play, and rest? Keep my body healthy?
or try to defy health rules?
Do I have friends among both sexes?
or are most of my friends boys (or girls)?
Do I see other's points of view?
or believe they have it in for me?
Do I have confidence in myself?
or enjoy other's failures?
Do I have a sense of humor?
or am I touchy?

Do I look to the future? Get along with parents and friends? Accept a moral code? Overlook slights?
or plan to get even?
Do I try to understand other's failings?
or expect perfection?
Do I find congenial friends?
or keep to myself?
Do I try to develop a pleasing personality?
or bluff to keep up?

Reading to help you grow up

Many stories of teenagers illustrate how it feels to grow up. These are very interesting:
The Yearling by Marjorie Kennan Rawlings.
Bright Island by Mabel Robinson.
My Friend Flicka by Mary O'Hara.
Blueberry Mountain by Stephen Meader.

Films to help you understand

Helping the Child to Accept the Do's and *Helping the Child to face the Don'ts.* Encyclopedia Britannica Films. Portrays a child learning to live in a world of people.

Ewing Galloway

*A crowd at a baseball game displays many emotions. How can
you use up some of the energy that accompanies strong feelings?*

*Sharing interests or hobbies helps
you to have friends. Do you have
friends among both boys and girls?*

Ewing Galloway

*Compliments from the coach on a
job well done make a person feel
happy and worth while. Do you try
to make others feel successful by
being a good sport?*

H. Armstrong Roberts

*Important to everyone's well-being are
ideals and a religious belief that help
him to solve his daily problems, to believe in something true and lasting.
How can you develop such ideals?*

Ewing Galloway

Chapter 19

WHY DO YOU ACT THE WAY YOU DO?

Unless you are a very unusual person you probably have many things about yourself that you would like to improve. Do you have some habits that are inefficient or irritating to others? Do you have feelings that make you fearful or self-conscious? Do you give up easily or become angry often? Do you sometimes feel discouraged, different, or out of things?

You are not the only one who has doubts and unhappy feelings. You have only to read the lives of famous people to see how common are feelings of shyness, insecurity, and doubt among even the most successful. For example, Mrs. Eleanor Roosevelt, a most gracious and able woman, tells of her painful shyness as a child. Do you know of other people who have overcome problems and emotional handicaps?

What makes people feel and act the way they do? Are some kinds of feelings and behavior natural for all people? Can you do anything to control the way you feel and act?

Human beings are such a complex blend of body and spirit that it is difficult to figure out why they act as they do. Physical needs for food, rest, and activity influence some behavior. Spiritual needs for self-respect, companionship, and a belief in something lasting help to determine how people act. Health, physical abilities, and mental abilities all play a part. Habits of behavior are built by the kinds of experiences people have, their surroundings, the way they learn to solve problems, and their reactions to fear and failure.

This chapter will discuss a few of the reasons why people act the way they do. If you are interested you will find additional references on page 393. No single explanation has been accepted by everyone. As you read, see which of the explanations seem true and useful to you, in the light of your own reason and experience.

380

Looking ahead

Questions and suggestions

1. Do you have some unhappy feelings or bad habits you would like to change?

2. What do you think is meant by security? Do you think everyone desires security?

3. What are some of the ways we try to gain security?

4. How are gangs, families, nations, laws, armies, insurance, religion, education, and savings all ways of trying to gain security?

5. What is Social Security?

6. What is meant by recognition?

7. Do all people like to be noticed and approved?

8. Can you bring advertisements that are based on the desire of people to be secure? To be recognized? To be loved? To have new experiences? To believe in something lasting?

9. If you had three wishes, what would they be? Are your wishes based on fundamental desires of every human being?

10. Try to list all the groups you belong to and briefly describe the size and character of each group—family, gang, class in school, and others. Why do you belong to each?

11. What is the scientific method of problem solving?

12. Have you ever felt self-conscious? What did you do?

Committee Planning

1. The speakers committee may invite someone to talk to you about developing your personality or self-confidence.

2. A committee may plan a program where everyone participates in some way.

3. Everyone can prepare and give a short talk about what he has done, what he hopes to do, and his favorite foods, books, games, radio comedians, and television plays.

4. A committee can make a survey to see how many boys and girls belong to gangs and what the gangs are like.

Reading

As you read the chapter rapidly, keep its purpose in mind. Read it a second time more carefully. Answer all the questions you meet in your reading.

What makes you act?

We all act in order to get the things we want. Everyone wants something. We may want food, a new dress, to be on the basketball team, or a thousand other things. Although we seem to want such a variety of things, psychologists and philosophers believe that there are certain basic kinds of satisfactions desired by all people.

Boys and girls who work to be on teams, those who try to be superior in school, those who act indifferent or belligerent, and those who are shy and avoid others may all be acting to get the same thing. They want to be liked and approved by others. A need for approval and recognition is natural for everyone. What do you think are some other basic needs or desires of all people?

What are some needs that affect you? Some students of human nature

381

Philip Gendreau

Everyone has unhappy feelings sometimes. What effect does a feeling of being inferior, of not being accepted by others, have upon you? What are some satisfactory ways of getting rid of unhappy feelings?

These desires are not separate and easily recognized. Often we act without knowing why we do. We are not always conscious of the forces that make us act. They are deep within us, built slowly through the years by the things we feel and believe and do.

We only know that sometimes we feel happy and satisfied. Other times we feel unhappy, restless, and discouraged. Our desires and feelings cause us to act.

How does a need for self-respect affect you? Everyone as he grows up develops some pictures of himself. He has ideas of the kind of person he would like to be. As you grow older, you see your real self more clearly. You learn to know your own abilities and your shortcomings. The way other people treat you adds to your picture of yourself.

Everyone needs a satisfying self-picture. He needs to be pleased with himself. He wants to feel that he is normal and sensible, possessed of virtues like honesty, loyalty, and courage. He likes to feel that he is of some importance as an individual, that his rights and feelings are being respected.

We all like to feel that we are living up to our own ideals. Our beliefs and ideals are involved not only in the great decisions of our lives, but in our simple everyday choices. Self-respect helps us to decide little things like whether to help with the dishes or go to the movies.

A need for self-respect makes us do the things we ought to do. Unconsciously we say to ourselves "I cannot do that, because I am not that kind of person," or "I must do this if I keep my self-respect." Self-respect

believe that people act as they do because they desire power, or pleasure and comfort, or security. Many agree that all human beings want security, recognition, love, new experiences, and a belief in something lasting.

Two important needs that affect our behavior are a need to like and respect ourselves and a need to be loved and accepted by others. Everyone needs self-respect. He needs to feel that he is normal and likable. He needs to feel that his ideals and plan of life are worth while and that he is living up to them. At the same time, everyone needs to feel that he is not too different from other people. He wants to be loved, recognized, and accepted as a member of a group, his family, gang, and community.

gives us strength to do difficult and dangerous jobs, to stand on our own feet, to be honest and truthful even though others will never know.

Forming a satisfactory self-picture is often difficult. Some people have impossibly glorified pictures of themselves. They feel they must always appear successful and important. They cannot bear to fail or to have people laugh at them. A person who feels he must always be superior has an unrealistic self-picture. No one can be good at everything.

Some people have too low an opinion of themselves. Their self-picture does not challenge them to make the best of themselves. Their experiences have made them believe they are inferior to other people. What kinds of training and experience help a person to build a satisfying self-picture? Is it possible to have different ideas about yourself in different situations? Have you known anyone who behaved like an entirely different person in different classes, or at home and at school?

A satisfying self-picture should be realistic, honest, and hopeful. In it you recognize your strengths and weaknesses. You glimpse the person you are capable of becoming.

How does a need to be liked affect you? Everyone wants to be loved, to feel that he is important to someone. He needs to feel that some one thinks of his well-being and happiness and will stand by him in any crisis. Everyone desires to be approved and accepted. We like to feel that we are not too different from other people.

Everyone likes to feel that he belongs. We do many things to make ourselves acceptable members of var-

Ewing Galloway

Families are the most important source of feelings of security and self-confidence. Can you help to develop happy feelings in your own family?

ious groups. As we grow up we add to the groups to which we want to belong. To the family group we add playmates, school friends, church groups, the gang, the whole school, and the community. The willingness to conform to group desires is valuable to society. It is the basis of custom and law. Could you explain fads and clubs and styles by people's desire for acceptance?

You cannot expect to be liked by everyone. Childish personalities are pleased by the liking and approval of anyone. They may mistake flattery or any kind of attention for liking and approval. They will not admit that they are popular with people of low ideals. They may do foolish things to gain attention and recognition.

Philip Gendreau

How do emotions affect personality? What do you mean by a colorless personality? Why must you learn to control your feelings and to express them in appropriate ways?

Older boys and girls want to be genuinely likable. They develop feelings and habits of friendliness and consideration for others. They try to live up to their own best possibilities. They know that if they live up to their own ideals, they will be liked and accepted by others with similar ideals.

However, a desire to be accepted may be carried too far. Blindly following a group may lead you into such harmful activities as needless extravagance, cheating, smoking, drinking, loafing, or defying authority. There are times when a person must be willing to be different, to stand on his own feet. It requires courage and

practice to do what you believe is right when the gang does something else. Many girls and boys, and adults too, lack the courage or have not practiced self-control enough to stand alone when necessary. One should be able to enjoy his own company at times, and to follow his own interests. Extremes either of loneliness or over-dependence on others are harmful.

What are emotions? Emotions are feelings like joy, fear, hate, anger, and love. Emotions underlie everything we do. Emotions vary in strength. Sometimes we are hardly aware of them and have only vague feelings of pleasure or tension. At times they are

384

so powerful they practically explode us into action.

Emotions are apparently inborn reactions that cause certain changes in the body. They affect the activity of various body systems like digestion, circulation, and glandular activity. Chapter 12 describes the internal activities that are set off by strong emotions. If emotions are pleasant, the body reactions give us a general sense of well-being and satisfaction. Unpleasant emotions cause us to feel tense and upset, ready to act.

Like other natural forces, emotions are good or bad according to how we learn to control them. Atomic energy may be useful or destructive. Energy released by emotions may enrich our lives or make them miserable. Unemotional people seem colorless and dull. Can you imagine a person who never laughed or got excited or sympathized with a friend in trouble? On the other hand, those who cannot control their emotions can cause much unhappiness for themselves and for others. A happy person must learn both to use and to control his emotions.

Emotions are related to our needs and desires. When our basic human wants are satisfied, we experience pleasant emotions. If you feel that you are doing a good job, are living up to your ideals, are a part of a group, and are liked and accepted by others, you feel happy and pleased with yourself. When you feel inferior or rejected by other people, you are likely to be angry or afraid. You will feel an urge to act to relieve your unhappy feelings. Often your feelings come out disguised. Bullying, boasting, jealousy, sarcasm, and withdrawing are only a few of the ways we disguise our feelings.

Why do people act in different ways?

Although people act to satisfy the same basic desires, they act in a variety of ways. They act in ways they have learned and practiced. A hungry man may do a number of things in order to eat. He may beg, borrow, get a job, hunt, or fish depending on where he is and what he has learned to do. A person may act in various ways to gain recognition or approval. He may work to gain real success. He may bluff or boast. He may try to make others seem inferior by criticizing or making fun of them. He may be shy and refuse to take a chance of failing.

How do we learn to act? People of all ages have problems to solve. They have feelings and needs. They do the things that they think will satisfy their needs and make them feel happy.

As we grow up we try out different ways of getting what we want. If a baby is fed only when he cries, he learns to cry for attention. By trial and error, by imitation, by training from adults, children learn to get the things they want. They learn what kinds of behavior bring them approval and happiness. They learn how to act to avoid disapproval and unhappiness.

Some children have many opportunities to succeed in doing little things for themselves. They learn satisfactory ways of getting along with people. Others have fewer opportunities to learn acceptable ways of behaving. They may find no ways of acting that bring them pleasure and approval. Children who fail in early attempts to do things for themselves and to be loved and approved learn to fear failure. They may try various kinds of behavior to gain attention or to avoid it entirely.

As we grow up our desires and interests change. Our feelings of self-confidence or fearfulness and our ways of acting to get what we want are likely to become well-practiced habits. The timid little girl will probably be a shy, withdrawing older girl. The friendly, self-reliant little girl will probably continue to develop more mature habits of independence and friendliness.

All of us grow up with some good habits and some poor ones. We may be successful and confident at home and in doing our work but fearful and timid with strangers or other boys and girls. None of us is perfect. Fortunately, we can improve or change our habits. We can learn to face our problems. We can examine our own behavior and recognize our second-rate habits. What kinds of habits do you have? Are you facing your problems and working out the best solutions you can? Or are you running away or trying to hide from problems? See if you are using any of these second-rate methods.

Are you running away from your problems? All of us have some difficult problems. Small children have many things to learn. They must learn to control their muscles, to form ideas of right and wrong, to talk, to read, and to get along with people. Teenagers have problems of their own. They must learn to stand on their own feet, to make friends with boys and girls their own age, and to make the most of their abilities. What are some of your own problems?

Solving problems in a mature way requires the use of reason and self-discipline. All of us solve some of our problems reasonably. Others we run away from. We may run away by such methods as daydreams, forgetting, and setting unworthy standards. Running away can become a habit.

Do you remember the story of the fox who was not able to reach some grapes he wanted, and went away saying, "Oh, well, they were sour anyway"? Many people run away from their problems by adopting a "sour-grapes" attitude. They try to make themselves and others believe they are not interested in anything that requires effort. They say they do not care to look well groomed, to be on the team, to earn good school reports, or to be a dependable member of a group.

Some people try to keep their self-respect by setting unworthy standards for themselves. They associate with people who know less than they do. They try only easy tasks, elect only the subjects in which they are already good, and play only the games in which they can star. They cling to their established position in their family or gang and hesitate to enlarge their circle of friends and interests. Sometimes they try to show their superiority by belonging to small select social groups.

Daydreaming can be a helpful way to plan your future. On the other hand, it can be a way of avoiding present problems by wishful thinking.

Daydreaming that causes you to withdraw from activities with other boys and girls can become a dangerous habit. You cannot live in a dream. You must learn to get along with real people in a real world. Now is the time to practice, while everyone else your age is practicing the same thing.

Some people run away from their problems by forgetting them. Have you ever noticed how easy it is to forget an appointment you did not want to keep? Or a lesson you did not want to prepare? You can forget almost any difficult task if you put it off and keep yourself busy with other activities.

Do you try to cover up your difficulties? Sometimes we cover up our problems instead of facing them. We try to make people think that our problems are solved or to distract attention from them. Often we can even fool ourselves.

Sometimes people try to cover up their problems by using methods that worked when they were children. Have you seen small children kick objects that were in their way? Emotional outbursts of rage or anger or tears may help you gain your own way with some people. Some people try to blame their failures on others. They try to distract attention from themselves by making others seem inferior. They play practical jokes, or make fun of others' achievements.

Often people rationalize or make up good reasons for their unwillingness to solve problems. They excuse themselves for not preparing their lessons by saying they have to help at home. Some people make up wonderful excuses. They avoid situations that

Denver Public Schools

Daydreams are often an escape from reality. They should be an inspiration for work.

will test their skills. They make up good reasons for not attending parties, or trying for good grades, or being friendly, or doing any other activity in which they fear they may fail. Are you good at alibis?

Some people try to gain feelings of being worth-while and important without really doing the things that make them grownup. They bluff and boast. They try to imply that they are smart by getting by without studying. They make fun of the "grinds." They imitate people who seem to be successful. They try to do things that seem symbolic of growing up. Symbols of growing up change. Once a boy put on long trousers and a girl put up her hair to show that they were growing up. Modern boys and girls sometimes try to appear grownup by driving a car, by smoking, or by defying authority.

Our natural desires and feelings push us into action. They do not tell us how to act. We must learn for ourselves the best ways to grow up and be happy. Many of our actions are habits. Examining our habits and improving the second-rate ones is an important part of growing up emotionally.

What is your emotional age? How do you expect to get the things you want? Do you expect to earn what you get out of life or do you want it handed to you? Everyone is tempted to try to get things the easy way. Sooner or later you will find that immature, unreasonable methods of getting what you want will fail you. Self-pity, deceit, irresponsibility, evasion, tantrums, or bluffing become a part of you. They make you an emotional midget.

Do you work for what you want? You want a strong, attractive body. Do you find out how it works and grows and how you can help it? You want to be recognized and considered a worth-while person. Do you try to improve your skills and natural abilities? You want love and affection. Do you deserve it? How much genuine affection and consideration do you give? You want to be treated like a grownup. Do you act it? Are you dependable and thoughtful? You want boy and girl friends. Do you take advantage of opportunities to know and like many people, or do you stay by yourself or with a small group? You want a good job. Are you developing skills and habits that will make you a valuable worker?

What habits help you to solve problems? You can apply the scientific method of problem solving to your own personal problems. The steps in the scientific method are these: (1) recognize the problem; (2) gather information about it; (3) think through some possible solutions; (4) try the most reasonable solution; (5) if it fails, use the experience you have gained to try again.

Many people refuse to face reality and recognize their problems. They have acquired habits of fooling themselves like those described in the last section. It takes experience, intelligence, and courage to face things as they are and to realize that some of the things you desire require much effort and that some are not possible at all.

All people at times have unpleasant feelings like anger, jealousy, fear, envy, and discouragement. When you are unhappy or uncertain, try to figure out why. It may help to talk your trouble over with some trusted older person. Reacting emotionally with outbreaks of tears or anger, catty remarks, lying, fighting, sulking, or withdrawing may bring temporary relief. In the long run, uncontrolled emotions make it difficult for you to live happily in an adult world.

When you recognize your problem, look for many solutions. Boys and girls often feel they have only two choices. Alice wants to go to a party. She thinks she cannot go without a new dress and knows her family cannot afford to buy her one. Alice is likely to state her problem by offering her family two choices. They buy her a new dress or she stays home. She may solve it purely from habit without thinking at all. She may have been unhappy at one party and learned to avoid them altogether. Can you think of other solutions? What is Alice's real problem?

Some mental and emotional habits help you to face and to solve problems. You can practice habits of accepting responsibility, tackling necessary jobs promptly and with good grace, methodically doing one job at a time, and sticking with a job until it is finished. Even a hopeless-looking problem becomes a simple one if you work on one part of it at a time.

You may need to develop a new attitude toward failure. Fear of failure can be almost paralyzing. Everyone must learn to fail without shame or discouragement. The only people who never fail are those who never try. Learn from your failures and losses. Laugh at yourself. Everyone feels embarrassed and ashamed at times. Can you recall your most embarrassing moment? How important was it then? How important does it seem now? Would you think less of a friend who was in that situation?

Beliefs and ideals help you to solve problems. Your ideals are involved not only in the great critical decisions in your life, but in small, simple, everyday choices.

How can you develop self-confidence? Growing up is naturally accompanied by some feelings of fear and uncertainty. People treat you sometimes like a child and sometimes like an adult. You are eager to be approved but are not sure what is expected of you.

H. Armstrong Roberts

Can you imagine the story behind this scene? What will happen next?

If you are interested in developing self-confidence, you have already taken the first step. You recognize your problem. You probably know quite a bit about self-confidence and its related problems like stage fright, timidity, and self-consciousness. You probably realize they are not your problems alone. Everyone suffers from them in some situations. Experienced public performers report that they feel the same stage fright as the greenest amateurs.

If you stop to think, you realize that this problem is being solved all the time. You can receive helpful suggestions from many sources.

Growth in self-confidence is built on many small successes. Your early successes were largely the result of training by others. You have reached

389

your teens with some poor habits and some good ones that need polishing. You may have learned to be overly sensitive to criticism. You may have learned to be thorough but not invariably to see a task through.

After childhood you must guide your own development. You must take the responsibility for having experiences that will help you develop a good personality and satisfactory mental and emotional growth. If you lack basic skills of any kind—reading or writing or speaking, dancing or skating, getting along with other people, or controlling your temper—you can start learning them. Plenty of people will be glad to help you if you give them a chance.

You grow in self-confidence when you do things. You probably have had the experience all public performers have of suffering chills, cold sweat, "butterflies," speechlessness, and fright before a big game or party. Then, when you are actually playing or talking, all your symptoms gradually disappear.

If you say something in class once in a while and participate in class parties and activities and teams, you will find your timidity and stage fright

Encyclopedia Britannica Films

Problems too difficult to solve alone often can be solved with the help of an understanding older person. Do you think trained, responsible persons like teachers, ministers, priests, and judges are better counselors than newspaper and radio columnists and people who sell advice?

vanishing. You can volunteer for little jobs and do them as well as you can.

Another helpful habit is to think about other people. Try to see opportunities to do something for others, to congratulate them, and to give them a chance to talk about things that interest them. This serves two purposes. It takes your mind off yourself and makes other people feel important and accepted.

The way you look and act affects the way you feel. Good health, cleanliness, and alert and thoughtful manners make you feel more cheerful and self-confident. If you act like a happy, friendly, considerate person, you cannot help having some pleasant feelings. You will meet with friendly responses from other people that help you gain confidence in yourself.

Being self-confident does not mean that you are sure of success, sure of being the center of things. It means that you are sure of yourself, confident that you will do your best and will live up to your own ideals for yourself. You can be sure of yourself if you practice daily doing your best, facing your problems with courage, and behaving with consideration for others. If you practice such habits you can relax and be yourself, confident that you are a worth-while, likable person. You need no special tricks or techniques to sell yourself.

Are gangs harmful? Boys and girls have a particularly strong natural desire to be liked by others of their own age. Gaining acceptance in your own gang is an important step in growing up. Most youthful gangs are idealistic and help their members develop skill in getting along with people. They encourage habits of loyalty, co-operation, and responsibility. They help boys and girls to widen their circle of friends and to become less dependent upon their families.

Philip Gendreau

What are some of the emotions people feel when they think they are being left out? How may they express their emotions? What is the best way to handle such feelings?

Gangs may hinder normal development. If you learn to depend completely on gang approval and fail to develop your own standards, you will be a misfit in a very short time. Some gangs set up standards of their own that conflict with personal ideals. Their members learn habits and behavior that make them less likely to be accepted by other people.

Such unprogressive gangs may last a long time. Their members have not learned to get along with many kinds of people. They cling to the group where they feel they have a place. Fearful of the outside world, they

391

often attempt to show that they are not afraid. They defy authority; they dress and act to attract attention.

Boys and girls who depend too much upon gangs have a real problem. They need to find ways of gaining recognition and approval in worth-while ways. Sometimes they can solve their own problems. They can make friends and join in activities outside their gang. Often they need help from others. Most of all, they need friendship and acceptance from other boys and girls who are their own age.

People who cannot find a place in a responsible adult world often become antisocial or even criminal. They remain emotionally immature and cannot be interested in the welfare of people outside their own small circle. They deprive others of their rights if they can.

It is important that all people have opportunities to satisfy their needs for self-respect and acceptance. If we deny these opportunities to others we are endangering ourselves. We are blocking our own emotional development. We are physically endangering ourselves because people who are denied opportunities may act in dangerous and antisocial ways. They may turn to crime and, on a larger scale, even to war in an effort to gain self-respect and acceptance.

Reviewing the chapter

Test yourself

I

You can find out how much self-confidence you have by answering the following questions. You should answer "Yes" to most of them.

1. Do you keep your clothes neat and clean?
2. Do you keep your body healthy and well groomed?
3. Do you express your ideas in good language?
4. Do you keep informed on news and sports?
5. Do you join in school activities?
6. Do you treat others fairly, omit gossip?
7. Do you have good manners?
8. Do you think for yourself as much as possible?
9. Do you discuss difficult problems with wise advisors?
10. Do you accept criticism in a friendly way?
11. Do you try to be clean minded and cheerful?
12. Do you try to think of other's happiness?
13. Do you follow a high moral code?

II

You can find out how self-reliant you are if the following statements reflect your own actions and thoughts.

1. I never become extremely excited.
2. I rarely feel nervous.
3. I usually solve my problems without help.
4. My feelings are not easily hurt.
5. Starting conversation is easy for me.
6. I make it a point to meet important persons.
7. I do not mind making a speech.
8. Having someone watch me work does not disturb me.
9. I think I am self-confident.
10. I enjoy spending some time by myself.

11. When ill, I prefer no company.

12. I prefer to study out difficult problems myself.

13. If I feel needed, I am inclined to help.

14. I do not need close supervision to keep me hard at work.

III

What would you say to someone who stated his problem in these words?

1. I dislike getting up stunts at a party.

2. Making up my mind is usually difficult.

3. Criticism makes me unhappy.

4. I feel discouraged when others disagree.

5. I think I am shy.

6. I often go out of my way to avoid meeting someone.

7. Others seem to take advantage of me.

8. I get stage fright easily.

9. Scoffing and teasing make me uncertain.

Reading to help you grow up

Psychology You Can Use, by William Roberts, has interesting discussions and experiments on how you think and feel —watching a habit grow, optical illusions, remembering and forgetting, and thinking.

Personal Problems, by John B. Geisel, describes the wants and feelings that make us act as we do, tells how we kid ourselves and how we can grow up emotionally.

Health and Human Welfare, by Burkhard and others, helps you understand how personality develops, how it is affected by emotions, heredity, environment, and intelligence.

Health and Fitness, by Meredith, has a section on mental and social health.

Finding Yourself, by Rosely, has an excellent personal analysis chart.

Films to help you understand

Attitudes and Health. Ideal (rental), Coronet (purchase). The story of two disappointed students—a boy who fails to make the team and a girl who does not get an expected promotion. Shows how right attitudes and self-confidence are vital to good health.

Shy Guy. Ideal (rental), Coronet (purchase). The story of a shy boy who learns to make friends.

Picture Preview:

Chapter 20

Getting along with your family is the real test of your personality. Do you treat them with as much consideration as you do your friends? Do they accept you as a responsible person?

Philip Gendreau

Do you have one or two close friends? What are qualities people like in their friends?

Belonging to teams and gangs helps boys and girls learn to understand and to get along with other people, to be good sports. How can such groups limit the development of your personality?

Ewing Galloway

Chapter 20

HOW CAN YOU GET ALONG WITH OTHERS?

*A*re you interested in such problems as getting along with your family, having friends, and feeling comfortable and at ease in groups of people? If you are, you are like most of the other people in the world. Books and articles about making and keeping friends and being popular are eagerly read by millions. Advertisers appeal to the universal desire of people to be liked and accepted by others.

Getting along with people is a social skill. You learn it gradually and improve upon it with practice. Small children learn from experience how to get along with their parents and the few people around them. If they are successful in their efforts to be approved and loved at home, they gain confidence in themselves. Then they can learn more easily to get along with other people. As children grow up, they need opportunities to associate with more people. They must learn social skills of sharing, obeying rules, and considering others.

Being grownup for your age—physically, mentally, and emotionally—helps you to get along with people. Do you think physical skills like playing games, skating, and dancing help you to have friends? Do you think people like you better if you can control your temper and are dependable and loyal? Are you attracted by people who have many interests, who like to try new activities, and who accept responsibilities?

Developing a sincere interest in other people helps you to get along with them. If you are interested in other people, you will be considerate of their feelings. You will try to make them feel comfortable and happy. This chapter has some suggestions that may help you to understand people and to start developing attitudes and habits and manners that will make you a more likable person.

Looking ahead

Questions and suggestions

1. Think about some of the people you like. What is it you especially like about them? The class might like to make up a list of things they like about people. What are some traits or habits you dislike?

2. Have you had any unhappy experiences with people? What do you think caused the trouble? Could you have handled the situation better?

3. Have you ever been embarrassed because you did not know the proper thing to do at a party or social event?

4. Do you think your family gives you enough freedom?

5. What home responsibilities do you have?

6. What generous, friendly, or thoughtful act have you done for another today?

Committee Planning

1. A committee might like to dramatize scenes showing good manners at home, at school, at a party, or in public.

Various groups can dramatize some of their own problems of getting along with people—family or friends. Any little scene— last night's argument over who should wash dishes, for example—gives you a chance to see yourself. In order to get the other fellow's viewpoint, try acting the part of the person with whom you could not get along.

2. You might like to plan a party for another class. Each member of your class can be responsible for seeing that guests are introduced and that everyone has a good time. A committee can plan good refreshments for the time of day. They can plan and try out some appropriate new games. Plan carefully and practice as much as necessary so that everything goes smoothly.

Reading

1. Can you pick out the main ideas of any chapter by a quick scanning?

2. When you read more carefully for details, do you look at the pictures, read the legends (the sentences under the picture), and look up new words?

3. When you finish reading do you try to discuss it with someone or write down the important ideas in your own words?

How can you understand others?

If you want to get along with other people, you must understand them. It is not easy to learn understanding. Knowing why people act as they do is not enough for understanding. Plenty of people know why people act. They use their knowledge for self- ish purposes. They flatter or frighten people to induce them to act. In adult life some salesmen and politicians use their knowledge of people to cause them to buy, to vote, or even to go to war. Understanding people means that you know and share their feelings, that you are concerned for their welfare. Growing up and understanding yourself helps you to understand others.

How does understanding yourself help you to get along with others? How do you react when people seem to like you and to value your opinions and your friendship? What do you do when others make you feel inferior or different or unwanted?

Showing consideration for other people's feelings helps you to get along with them. You know how to consider other people's feelings be-cause in many ways they are the same as yours. People behave differently, but like you they all desire some things like self-respect and approval.

Believing in yourself helps you to get along with people. If you believe and behave as if you were a likable and worth-while person other people are attracted to you. People who whine and who are sure no one likes them are not giving themselves a chance.

Like yourself, other people are happier and easier to get along with when they are pleased with themselves,

Ewing Galloway

Getting along with people takes practice. How do you take advantage of opportunities to know many kinds of people under different conditions? Are you friendly and willing to participate in many kinds of activities?

when their desire for self-respect and approval are satisfied. They like a person who makes them feel worth while.

If you stop to think about people and habits that irritate you, you will find that you know some habits to avoid. Do you like the person who must always be the center of attention, who constantly teases or makes fun of you? What other habits do you dislike? Do you have some of them yourself?

You already know many ways of making people feel pleased with themselves and with you. You compliment a teammate for a good play. You include others in your activities. You greet your friends as if you were glad to see them. You listen to the opinions and ideas of others, and often try their suggestions or do some of the things they like to do. From experience you have learned that people like you better when you are cheerful, friendly, and co-operative.

Understanding yourself can make you less sensitive and easy to get along with. You realize that actions are not always what they seem. You know that your own actions are often impulsive or awkward attempts to cover up unhappy feelings. Your actions may seem to others to be signs of unfriendliness or lack of interest. Other people's behavior may be just as misleading. You can make allowances for apparent unfriendliness or rudeness when you realize that actions are not always deliberate and thoughtful. You can give other people a chance to be cheerful and friendly. Have you ever known people so friendly and generous and cheerful that anyone could get along with them? They seem to bring out good qualities in others.

How does growing up help you to get along with people? Being interested in other people is one of the signs of growing up. At the same time, being interested in other people is the best way to get along with them. A sincere interest in people is based on understanding.

When you are really interested in others, you can share their feelings. You want them to feel happy and you enjoy helping them to get what they want. When you understand others you cannot stand by indifferently when your father is worried about finances or when your little sister is unhappy. You not only know how they feel, you can share their feelings. You want to do something to make them happy. Not only can you make allowances for people who are sick or tired or upset, but you feel a desire to help them.

As you become more mature you can sympathize with people outside your own circle of family and friends. You know how the neglected, shy boy at the party feels. Instead of teasing or ignoring him you receive pleasure from including him in your fun.

When you are more mature you feel you are a part of all humanity, sharing its hopes and fears. You can understand the feelings of the unknown boy who cannot find a job because of his race, the parents whose children are deprived of health and educational opportunities, the girl who is unfairly excluded from a social group—every individual unjustly denied the right to life or freedom of conscience.

You increase your understanding of people by your own experiences as you grow up. If you have never felt the pleasure that comes from sharing another's happiness, try it. See if you can find a way of helping some member of your family do something or get something he wants. Even a little effort like volunteering to wash the dishes so your mother can get away for a movie may bring unexpected pleasure. The Boy Scout's good turn a day can play an important part in helping him to grow up.

Reading can add to your understanding. Some reading gives little opportunity for you to use your imagination, to put yourself in the place of the characters in the story, and to feel as they do. A good story helps you to understand people. It pictures for you the feelings, desires, and behavior that are repeated over and over by people of all times and places. Try reading a story by a sensitive, skilled author and see how well you understand the characters.

How can you get along with your family?

Some boys and girls find it more difficult to get along smoothly with their family than with outsiders. They feel that their family has to put up with them. They make no effort to win their friendship or regard.

Getting along with your family is important. Your family is a part of you. Your experiences with the people in your home permanently influence your personality. Learning to live and work with your family is the best possible preparation for getting along with all kinds of people. Getting along with your family is the real test of how grownup you are. The way you behave around home reflects your emotional age. How do you measure up?

How can you get along with your parents? For a long time you have been dependent upon your family. They have furnished you with food, shelter, and other life necessities. They have satisfied most of your emotional needs for security, affection, and approval. Now you are growing up. Naturally you want to be independent, able to stand on your own feet. You want approval from a wider world, from people your own age.

Your parents want this for you, too. They want you to be an independent, happy person. They can be your biggest help in gaining independence, if you understand each other.

Many misunderstandings arise because parents and children do not see each other as individuals. Parents naturally remember their children as helpless and dependent. Sometimes they have difficulty in accepting them as self-reliant, independent persons. Boys and girls often fail to realize that their parents are people. They regard them as necessary but outgrown parts of themselves. Have you ever really talked with your mother and father? Do you know their thoughts and hopes, the kind of life they lead apart from you?

You get along better with your parents if you show them that you love them and desire their approval. Your father and mother love you and can understand your faults and selfish-

Ewing Galloway

Doing things with your family, whether it be hiking or reading, helps you to know and get along with each other. Does your family have any customs or special little ceremonies you all enjoy together?

ness, but they are human too. Like other people, they are pleased by signs of affection and approval.

Do you talk things over with them? Do you try to understand their viewpoint? Are you especially considerate and helpful when they are sick or tired or upset? Try to get acquainted with your parents. You can share many interests, both work and play. You may be surprised to find how much your parents know, how interesting and what good company they are. You may surprise them, too, if they have been in the habit of thinking of you as a baby.

How can you be more independent? You can help your parents to realize that you are becoming a responsible, independent person by behaving like one. Many boys and girls who act quite grownup away from home are childish and emotional around their parents. They show no evidence of being able to take care of themselves, to obey rules, or to consider the rights of others. Before you blame your parents for not under-

H. Armstrong Roberts

standing you, try to see yourself as you must appear to them.

Are you a selfish, thoughtless, irresponsible child? Do you make selfish demands on family money and possessions? Or are you growing up, trying to be dependable and thoughtful, ready for responsibility and freedom?

H. Armstrong Roberts

Everyone can learn to be responsible and independent. A small child acts as he does because of his training. Older boys and girls can do things if someone points out what needs to be done. More mature boys and girls can see things that need to be done and do them without being told. How are you progressing? Do you do the routine jobs assigned to you at home and school and work? Do you ever do extra jobs?

How can you get along with brothers and sisters? You are very lucky if you are growing up in a family with brothers and sisters. They help you to grow up; they give you opportunities to learn to share, to give and take, and to sympathize with other people's viewpoints. They give you a pleasant, safe sense of belonging to a group that cares about you.

Brothers and sisters usually have more affection for each other than for outsiders. Often they do not get along smoothly. Sometimes feelings of jealousy and rivalry develop. Habits of quarreling, teasing, being sarcastic, or being contrary may be established. Differences in ages and personalities

Do you enjoy playing with your younger brothers and sisters? How can you help them to grow up? How do they help you?

American Red Cross

make understanding difficult. Among people who live closely together, sharing many things may lead to lack of regard for personal belongings and feelings.

No family gets along perfectly all the time. Growing boys and girls need to learn to get along with people. They make mistakes and often behave unreasonably. As you grow up you should improve in your ability to control your own emotions. You can recognize that habits of using sarcasm and ridicule, of teasing, or of indifference are unsatisfactory methods of solving problems and getting along with people. You can overcome your own bad habits. You can help your brothers and sisters to learn better methods. Usually one person who uses reason and consideration for others can prevent quarrels and violent disagreements. If you can just resist that urge to have the last word, to make that snappy, cutting remark, you can avoid much trouble.

Brothers and sisters can help each other to feel comfortable and happy. Do you play with younger members of your family and help them to gain

skills and self-confidence? Do you show your brothers and sisters that you like them and are proud of them?

Ewing Galloway

Home responsibilities can be fun if done cheerfully and well. Your method of tackling tasks can help to convince your parents you are becoming responsible and independent. Do you require supervision?

403

How can you get along with boys and girls?

You grow up with your family and have many opportunities to learn to get along with them. How can you make new friends and be accepted in new groups? Are there any ideas that will help you to have friends and to be popular?

Why are some boys and girls more popular? You probably have some ideas of your own about what makes people popular. You know what things you like about people. You have ob-

Ewing Galloway

Informal outdoor activities help you to enjoy yourself and to make friends. Are you a cheerful, co-operative companion on hikes and picnics?

served other boys and girls who are well liked. Before you read the suggestions in this section, you might like to list your own ideas, or to take a poll to see what your class believes makes a person popular.

A popular person is usually grown up for his age. He has the skills other boys and girls his age admire. Small boys usually like active, boisterous leaders. They ignore clothing and grooming. Teenagers usually admire self-confidence and independence. They like people who have developed considerable skill in something, whether it be football, music, public speaking, or dancing. They like people who belong to important groups.

A popular person helps the people around him to feel comfortable and worth while. He has a cheerful, friendly way of noticing people and including them in activities and plans. Everyone likes to be a member of a group that is doing things. We like the people who help us achieve that desire. We avoid people who make us feel uncomfortable or unhappy.

A popular person has enthusiasm and vigor. He has a variety of interests and skills. No matter what activity is going on, he enters in. If he is not skilled, he tries to learn. We all like people who are willing to do the things we like to do at least part of the time. We like to show off our own skills.

Usually a popular person has an attractive personality. He has desirable ways of expressing his feelings. He appeals to many kinds of people of all ages because he has traits of self-respect and consideration for others.

Philip Gendreau

What are some traits boys and girls like in their friends?

Sometimes people may enjoy a brief popularity by using second-rate methods. For all the traits that others admire, they may develop substitutes. Instead of real interest and concern for other people, they may use flattery. Instead of developing skills, they may boast or cheat. Instead of becoming dependable and independent, they may defy authority. Some people may be fooled by these techniques for a while. In the long run, the people who are fooled will turn against the person who deceives them. His false popularity will cause him to be more alone than ever.

Some adults make use of second-rate ways of becoming popular. A person with a selfish desire for power often can win followers by pretending to be interested in the welfare of certain groups of people. He can use little tricks that take advantage of his knowledge of people. He can appeal to their desire for recognition and approval. He can take advantage of human tendencies to escape uncomfortable problems by blaming others.

How can you help yourself get along with people? Getting along with people depends mainly upon your being able to look at things from the other fellow's point of view, and to give him a break. You acquire this ability as you grow up. You can help yourself acquire the ability to share the feelings of others by taking advantage of opportunities to practice. Do you notice when other people are unhappy or upset? Do you try to help them? Do you try to avoid hurting other people's feelings?

People are not good companions if they are tired, unhappy, or irritated. Satisfactory habits of taking care of your health, getting plenty of good food and rest and exercise help to make you good company. Good mental habits of facing and solving your problems, forgetting injuries and grudges, being cheerful and optimistic, help you to be popular.

You get along better with others if you develop some social skills. You can overcome old habits of laziness, carelessness, and discourtesy. Habits of being too curious, fault finding, complaining, or too outspoken make others uncomfortable.

You get along better with others if you can do some of the things they like to do. Can you play several different kinds of games, both active and quiet, with large and small groups? As you go into high school you will need skills in activities in which both boys and girls take part. Are you learning to skate and dance, play tennis, hike, and carry on a conversation? If you can do a number of things well you will be included in more groups and activities. Even skills as a dishwasher or firebuilder are assets if they are used with good humor and enthusiasm.

Dating is an opportunity to widen your circle of friends and to broaden your interests. Before you start dating you will probably enjoy doing things with groups of boys and girls. Picnics and parties and games and gatherings in clubs and friendly groups are fun and help you to develop skills in getting along with people. Most high school boys and girls like to date many different people. You have more fun and a better opportunity to develop your own personality if you know many people with varied interests. Steady dating encloses you in a tiny circle just when you should be expanding.

Your ability to get along with people improves with practice. Some people are so eager to be popular they hinder themselves. They are discouraged at little setbacks and not willing to appear as less than perfect while they are learning social skills. Talking things over with friends often helps you. It may relieve your mind, may help you see your problems clearly, and may provide helpful suggestions.

Do you need to know any manners?

Manners are not something you can take or leave. They are simply the way you express yourself; so everyone has them, good or bad. Good manners are good because they help you to act in ways that maintain your self-respect and gain the approval of others. They help you to feel confident and at ease. They help you to feel at home anywhere.

How do you learn good manners? You need never worry about good manners if you realize that they are founded on consideration for others. Any acts that make others feel comfortable and pleased with themselves are good manners. Actions that make others uncomfortable are discourteous.

As you grow up and become genuinely interested in other people, their feelings and approval, you will naturally perform many acts of courtesy. You do not have to read a book about manners to know that friendly greetings, expressions of congratulation, sympathy, and thanks are considerate and courteous. Actions that make people feel different or rejected are both cruel and discourteous.

Good manners help you to keep your own self-respect. You want to be honest, loyal, and sportsmanlike. Strong, young people naturally like to assist older or weaker people in any way that they can. Waiting your turn, speaking well of others, and obeying rules and customs are the natural courteous acts of a good sport.

Like good form in any game, good manners require attention and practice. You can learn good manners the

Ewing Galloway

Good manners make any social occasion more pleasant. What are some basic rules for courteous behavior on any occasion?

same way you learn the techniques and rules of any game. You can observe and imitate others. You can learn from movies and books. Knowing what to do in any situation gives you poise and self-confidence. Practice makes your actions smooth and easy.

What are some everyday good manners? Practicing daily good manners at home and school and play makes life more pleasant. Your family and the friends you associate with all the time are surely deserving of consideration. The daily practice of good manners makes you feel more at ease on special occasions when you want to appear at your best.

With your family and friends you can form habits of speaking pleasantly and listening attentively. You can practice saying "please" and "thank you" until it is easy and natural.

Manners at home include picking up after yourself, taking care of family possessions, being presentable and pleasant company. Do you practice good home manners? You should observe the following suggestions:

Do your share cheerfully.

Use your own personal articles like towels and combs. Keep them clean and orderly.

Do not monopolize the bathroom. Leave it clean and orderly.

Respect the privacy of others—their mail, belongings, and room.

Never discuss family affairs with outsiders.

At school you can practice habits of being friendly and cheerful, obeying rules, and helping to keep the school clean. You can practice self-control and poise. Can you control yourself in class? Do you settle down

to work and control noisy boisterous behavior, clowning, and giggling that distracts or irritates others? Do you practice good school manners? You should observe the following suggestions:

Bring your own materials.

Obey school rules.

Help keep your school clean and attractive.

Speak to all in a friendly, cheerful manner.

Do you need to know any rules? Some manners are like rules of a game. They are a uniform way of doing things, accepted by a group. They eliminate much confusion and misunderstanding. If you know some of the rules of courtesy you feel more self-confident. You can be sure of doing the right thing at the right time.

Some of our modern manners are now only symbols. We use them to show others that we wish to consider their feelings. We use them as little ceremonies to make life more interesting and colorful. These kinds of manners are not simply natural expressions of consideration. We learn them because they make us feel at ease in groups of people who use them. They are something like the signs and ceremonies of a club. They differ from country to country or even between groups of different ages and backgrounds.

Some ceremonial manners at one time had real meaning. In other ages men lifted the visors of their helmets to show themselves as friends. They extended their hands to show that they were not armed. They protected the women in their group by walking next to dangerous roads. Today men still tip their hats, shake hands, and walk next to the curb in order to show friendliness and consideration. You may like to find out the origin of some of our other customs and manners.

Everyone needs to learn at least enough rules of courtesy to get along well and feel at ease with people he ordinarily sees. You may even learn some different ceremonial manners to use with different groups. If you enjoy ceremony or live with a group that does, you may learn many elaborate manners. If you learn a few customs that are acceptable by almost all people, you will feel more comfortable and self-confident in any situation.

What are some simple rules for introductions? Everyone has to meet and to introduce people. Learning and practicing a simple ceremony makes introductions easy. For informal introductions you can say "Mary, this is Bill Jones. This is Mary Davis." Or, "Dad, this is Mary Davis." For more formal occasions, you say, "Miss Smith, may I present Bill Jones?" All you need to remember is to say first the name of the woman, or an older or distinguished person, and present the other person to her. If you are introducing a friend to a whole group of people you can say, "I want you to meet Bill Jones. Bill this is Mary Wright, Sally Davis, and Jack Wilson."

The usual way to respond to an introduction is with a simple "How do you do" or "I am happy to meet you." In very informal introductions, you may say "Hello, Bill." Repeating the name of the person to whom you have been introduced helps you to remember it. You will make a better impression if you look interested and pleasant.

Boys always stand when they are introduced. Girls stand only to honor older or distinguished persons. Boys usually shake hands with other boys or men. Girls may shake hands if they like. Girls or older people usually offer their hand first, but either person may make such a friendly gesture.

If you have not been introduced in a group, you may introduce yourself. You can say "I don't believe we have met. I am Bill Jones." The person you are with should immediately introduce himself. It is considerate and polite to see that newcomers meet the others in a group.

What are some simple rules for eating? Everyone needs to know how to eat courteously. The common-sense rule is to make the meal pleasant for everyone—look clean and pleasant, eat quietly, and carry on pleasant conversations of general interest.

Eat slowly and inconspicuously. Do not criticize or make excuses for not eating. If you have an accident, like tipping over a glass of water, apologize briefly, then drop the subject.

If using the correct silverware is a problem, most people can do very well by watching the hostess. Generally silver is arranged in order to be used from the outside. Most food is eaten with a fork. Very soft foods are eaten with a spoon. When you put your silverware down, place it across your plate. Used silver should not be placed on the tablecloth or balanced against the side of a plate.

Avoid touching food with your fingers. Always use the serving spoons provided and take the pieces closest to you.

How can you act in public places? In public places strangers judge you by your manners. Some boys and girls give themselves and their families and schools a bad reputation by their careless and inconsiderate manners. The safest rule is not to make yourself conspicuous. Talking in a loud voice, chewing gum, eating—all make poor impressions in public.

Some polite phrases are helpful. "I am sorry" can save many an embarrassing situation. "Pardon me" often clears a path pleasantly. Except for these phrases and to give directions if asked, it is usually better not to talk to strangers in public places.

Speaking politely to clerks in stores and to other people who serve you in restaurants, buses, and taxis helps to make your dealings with other people more pleasant. You should observe the following suggestions:

Practice courtesies in your daily life.

Give others a chance to see and hear at movies and games.

Dress appropriately for the occasion —sturdy, informal sports clothes for play, simple clothes for school.

Express thanks for favors and courtesies.

Accept compliments graciously.

Reviewing the chapter

Test yourself

I

How do I rate as a friend?
1. How many friends do you have?
2. How many boys and how many girls?
3. What are their ages?
4. What do you like about them?
5. Are they good for you?

II

Do you choose friends wisely?
A variety of friends helps you to expand your personality. Lasting friendships usually are based on similar interests and ideals.
1. Am I inclined to be friendly to all?
2. Do I have several real friends?
3. Do I keep friends after they know me a long time?
4. Do they know me as I really am?
5. Do I trust them?
6. Do they seem to trust me?
7. Would they stand by me?
8. Do they help me live up to my ideals?
9. Do they make me feel worth while?
10. Do I think of them as equals?
11. Do we seldom quarrel?
12. Can I take their criticism?
13. Do I avoid hurting their feelings?
14. Do I avoid catty remarks about them?
15. Do I refuse to be jealous?
16. Is my circle of friends expanding?
17. Can I have a good time away from my closest friends?
18. Do I make friends easily with both boys and girls?
19. If you have many "no's" to questions 1 to 18, what can you do?

Are you good company?

Are you tolerant and considerate?

1. Do you avoid unpleasant topics and questions?
2. Do you make necessary disagreements tactfully?
3. Do you have friends among all kinds of people?

410

4. Do you congratulate people sincerely?

5. Do you notice and comment on people's good qualities and performances?

6. Do you let other's faults go without comment?

Are you dependable?

7. Do you stick with necessary jobs even when they are disagreeable?

8. Do you do your share of work?

9. Do you tell the truth?

10. Do you do your best without cheating or bluffing?

Are you good-natured?

11. Do you speak pleasantly to all?

12. Do you overlook minor irritations?

13. Can you laugh at yourself?

Are you a good sport?

14. Do you obey rules?

15. Do you enter into games and activities even if you are not good?

16. Do you know how to play several games fairly well?

17. Do you win without boasting?

18. Do you lose without excuses?

Are you self-controlled?

19. Do you hold your temper?

20. Do you face your problems honestly?

21. Do you avoid sarcasm and ridicule?

Are you loyal?

22. Do you avoid gossip and criticism of others?

How popular should you be?

I

1. Are you unselfish?

2. Do you always demand your own way?

3. Do you gossip or tell everything you know?

4. Do you pout or have temper tantrums?

II

You should answer "yes" to the following questions.

1. Do you have a friendly and cheerful disposition?

2. Do you have an interest in many activities?

3. Do you tolerate mistakes and things that cannot be helped?

4. Do you take time to congratulate and sympathize with friends?

5. Do you try to look attractive and to avoid being conspicuous?

6. Do you keep your conversation light and pleasant?

7. Do you enter actively into games and work and make a good partner?

8. Do you take the first step to be friendly, invite people to join in your activities?

Reading to help you grow up

New Frontiers, edited by Breggs and others, has many stories about getting along with people.

Have a Date by Caroline Ramey. From this book boys will enjoy finding out what girls expect of them.

I Was Shy, by Helen Ferris, will help those who can't have a good time because they are shy. How do you get over it? The story tells one way.

Questions Girls Ask, by Helen Welshimer, is a book girls will be interested in. A few topics discussed are: "That First Date" and "The Boy Friend Looks You Over."

Youth Thinks It Through, by Bacon and others, has short stories, poems, and essays about homes and families. Do you have any of the troubles of the boy in "Aren't Parents Queer?" You can probably find yourself in many of the stories.

Manners Made Easy, by Mary Beery, is an entertaining book describing manners for teenagers.

You and Your Life, by Randolph and others, has interesting chapters on school life, friendships, family, work, leisure and recreation, personality, ideals, and standards.

Films to help you understand

Your Family. Ideal (rental), Coronet (purchase). Happy family relationships at work and play.

Are You Popular? Ideal (rental), Coronet (purchase). Illustrates social problems of teenagers.

Sharing Work at Home. Coronet.

You and Your Friends. Association. Teenagers rate each other on friendship traits.

THE HEALTH LIBRARY

General References

Some reference books containing a wide variety of information relating to most of the topics in this book are listed below. Some are easy to read; others are more difficult.

Some well illustrated general reference books are:

Compton's Pictured Encyclopedia. Chicago: F. E. Compton and Company.

The Book of Knowledge. New York: The Grolier Society.

The World Book Encyclopedia. Chicago: Field Enterprises, Inc., Educational Division.

Adams, Alice B.; Buckley, H. M.; Silvervale, Leslie R. *Road To Safety Series*. New York.

American Book Company. *Around the Year. On Sand and Water. Who Travels There?* 1942.

American Red Cross First Aid Textbook. Philadelphia: The Blakiston Company, 1947.

Burkhard, William E.; Chambers, Raymond L.; and Maroney, Fred W. *Health, Happiness, and Success Series*. Chicago: Lyons and Carnahan, 1946. *Good Health Is Fun. Your Health and Happiness. Builders for Good Health. Health for Young America. Working Together for Health.*

Charters, W. W.; Smiley, Dean F.; and Strang, Ruth M. *Health and Growth Series*. New York: The Macmillan Company, 1941. *Healthful Ways. Let's Be Healthy. A Sound Body. Health in a Power Age.*

Schneider, Herman and Nina. *How Your Body Works*. New York: William R. Scott, Incorporated, 1949.

Stories

Some stories that may help you to understand other people and yourself are suggested below. You can find many others.

Baker, Louise. *Out On a Limb*. New York: McGraw-Hill Book Company, 1946.

Beim, Lorraine. *Triumph Clear*. New York: Harcourt, Brace and Company, Incorporated, 1946.

Brink, Carol. *Caddie Woodlawn*. New York: The Macmillan Company, 1935.

Ferris, Helen. *This Happened to Me*. New York: E. P. Dutton Company, 1929.

Field, Rachel. *Hepatica Hawks*. New York: The Macmillan Company, 1932.

New Frontiers. Edited by Briggs, Jackson, Bolenius, and Hergberg. Boston: Houghton Mifflin Company, 1936.

Wilder, Laura Ingalls. *Farmer Boy*. New York: Harper and Brothers, 1933.

Special References

Books suggested for special topics are listed below:

Accident Facts. Chicago: Lumbermen's Mutual Casualty Company, 1949.

Almack, John C. *A Clear Case Against Narcotics*. Mt. View, California: Pacific Press Publishing Association, 1939.

Almack, John C.; Bracken, John S.; and Wilson, Charles. *Life and Health*, Indianapolis: Bobbs-Merrill Company, 1945.

Andress, J. Mace; Goldberger, I. H.; Hallock, Grace T. *Helping the Body in Its Work*. Boston: Ginn and Company, 1945.

Bacon, F. L. *Outwitting the Hazards*. New York: Silver Burdett Company, 1941.

Bayles, Ernest E., and Burnett, R. Will. *Biology for Better Living*. New York: Silver Burdett Company, 1946.

Beery, Mary. *Manners Made Easy*. New York: McGraw-Hill Book Company, 1949.

Bretz, Rudolf. *How the Earth Is Changing*. Chicago: Follett Publishing Company, 1936.

Brownell, Clifford Lee, and Williams, Jesse Feering. *The Human Body*. New York: American Book Company, 1946.

Burkhard, William E.; Chambers, Raymond L.; and Maroney, Fred W. *Health and Human Welfare*. Chicago: Lyons and Carnahan, 1944.

Burnett, R. Will. *To Live in Health*. New York: Silver Burdett Company, 1946.

Clemensen, Jessie Williams, and LaPorte, William Ralph. *Your Health and Safety.* New York: Harcourt, Brace and Company, Incorporated, 1946.

DeKruif, Paul. *Men against Death,* 1932 and *Microbe Hunters,* 1939. New York: Harcourt, Brace and Company, Inc.

Floherty, John J. *Youth at the Wheel.* Chicago: J. B. Lippincott Company, 1937.

Garland, Joseph. *The Story of Medicine.* Boston: Houghton Mifflin Company, 1949.

Geralton, James. *Story of Sound.* New York: Harcourt, Brace and Company, 1948.

Geisel, John B. *Personal Problems.* Boston: Houghton Mifflin Company, 1949.

Goldberger, Irving H., and Hullock, Grace T. *Understanding Health.* Boston: Ginn and Company, 1950.

Hostetter, Lawrence. *Walk Your Way to Better Dancing.* New York: A. S. Barnes and Company, 1942.

John Hancock Life Insurance Company. Boston: Various publications.

Leving, Milton, and Selegmann, Jean. *The Wonder of Life.* New York: Simon and Schuster, Inc., 1948.

Metropolitan Life Insurance Company. *Health through the Ages, Health Heroes,* and other publications. New York.

National Dairy Council. *Straight from the Shoulder. Who—Me? Get on the Beam* Chicago.

Parker, Bertha Morris. *The Basic Science Education Series.* Evanston, Illinois: Row, Peterson and Company, 1948. *Our Ocean of Air. Sound. Stories Read from Rocks The Earth's Changing Surface.*

Reedman, Sarah R. *How Man Discovered His Body.* New York: International Publishers, 1947.

Roberts, William H. *Psychology You Can Use.* New York: Harcourt, Brace and Company, Inc., 1943.

Robinson, Victor. *Dr. Jad.* Evanston, Illinois: Row, Peterson and Company, 1941.

Shacter, Helen. *Getting Along With Others.* Chicago: Science Research Associates, 1949.

Scherf, C. H. *Do Your Own Thinking.* New York: McGraw-Hill Book Company, 1948.

Speer, Robert K.; Lussenhop, Roy; and Smither, Ethel. *Living In Ancient Times.* New York: Johnson Publishing Company, 1946.

White, Anne Terry. *Lost Worlds.* New York: Random House, Inc., 1941.

Youth Thinks It Through. Edited by Bacon, Wood, and MacConnell. New York: McGraw-Hill Book Company, 1941.

Zim, Herbert S. *Man In the Air.* New York: Harcourt, Brace and Company, 1943.

FILM SOURCES

You may secure films from these organizations, by loan, rental, or purchase. All the films suggested are 16 mm. sound, one reel (about 12 minutes), unless otherwise noted.

AAA: American Automobile Association, 17th Street at Pennsylvania Avenue, N.W., Washington, D. C.

Aetna: Aetna Life Affiliated Companies, Public Education Department, Hartford 15, Connecticut.

American Heart Association: American Heart Association, 1775 Broadway, New York 19, New York.

American Red Cross: American National Red Cross, 30 Rockefeller Plaza, New York 20, New York.

Association Films, 35 West 45th Street, New York 19, New York.

Bakery Engineers: American Society of Bakery Engineers, Department of Visual Education, 208 Third Avenue, Minneapolis 14, Minnesota.

Brandon: Brandon Films, Inc., 1700 Broadway, New York, New York.

Bray: Bray Studios, Inc., 729 Seventh Avenue, New York 19, New York.

Castle: Castle Films Division, United World Films, Inc., 1445 Park Avenue, New York 22, New York.

Central Washington College of Education, Ellensburg, Washington.

Columbia University, Public Information Office, New York, New York.

Coronet: Coronet Instructional Films, Coronet Building, Chicago 1, Illinois.

Encyclopaedia Britannica Films, 64 East Lake Street, Chicago 1, Illinois.

EFLA: Educational Film Library Association, 1600 Broadway, New York, New York.

Frith: Frith Films, P.O. Box 565, Hollywood 28, California.

General Electric Company, Distribution Section, Advertising and Sales Promotion Department, 1 River Road, Schenectady 5, New York. (Films also available from General Electric regional offices in principal cities.)

General Mills: General Mills Film Library, 400 Second Avenue, South, Minneapolis, Minnesota.

General Motors Corporation, Department of Public Relations, Film Section, Detroit 2, Michigan.

Ideal: Ideal Pictures Corporation, 28 East Eighth Street, Chicago 5, Illinois.

Institute of Inter-American Affairs, 499 Pennsylvania Avenue, Northwest, Washington 25, D. C.

Instructional Films, Incorporated, Division of Films, Incorporated, 330 West 42nd Street, New York 16, New York.

Jam Handy: Jam Handy Organization, 2821 East Grand Boulevard, Detroit 11, Michigan.

Knowledge Builders, 625 Madison Avenue, New York 19, New York.

March of Time, Forum Edition, 369 Lexington Avenue, New York 17, New York.

McGraw-Hill: McGraw-Hill Book Company, Text-Film Department, 330 West 42nd Street, New York 18, New York.

Metropolitan Life Insurance Company, 1 Madison Avenue, New York 10, New York.

National Dairy Council, 111 North Canal Street, Chicago 6, Illinois.

Modern: Modern Talking Picture Service, Incorporated, Rockefeller Plaza, New York 20, New York. (Branch offices in principal cities.)

National Safety Council, Film Department, 425 North Michigan Avenue, Chicago 11, Illinois.

National Motion Picture Company, West Main Street, Mooresville, Indiana.

National Society for the Blind: National Society for the Prevention of Blindness, Incorporated, 1790 Broadway, New York 19, New York.

National Tuberculosis Association, 50 West 50th Street, New York City, New York.

Pennsylvania College for Women, Film Service, Pittsburgh 6, Pennsylvania.

Popular Science: Popular Science Publishing Company, Incorporated, 353 Fourth Avenue, New York 10, New York.

Princeton Film Center, Princeton, New Jersey.

Public Affairs Films, 1600 Broadway, New York 19.

RKO-Radio: RKO-Radio Pictures, 16mm. Educational Division, 1270 Avenue of the Americas, New York 20, New York.

State College of Washington, Divison of General College Extension, Bureau of Visual Teaching, Pullman, Washington.

SVE: Society for Visual Education, 100 E. Ohio Street, Chicago 11, Illinois.

TFC: Teaching Film Custodians, 25 West 43rd Street, New York 18, New York.

U. S. Children's Bureau, Federal Security Agency, Social Security Administration, Washington 25, D. C.

USDA: U. S. Department of Agriculture, Office of Motion Picture Services, Washington 25, D. C.

U. S. Public Health Service, Federal Security Agency, Washington 25, D. C.

United Nations, Information Center, 535 Fifth Avenue, New York 17, New York.

United World: United World Films, Incorporated, 1445 Park Avenue, New York 22, New York.

University of Oregon, Medical School, Portland, Oregon.

Young America Films, Incorporated, 18 East 41st Street, New York 17, New York.

Yurich: Yurich Insurance Companies, Safety Zone Films, 135 South La Salle Street, Chicago 3, Illinois.

ā as in āble
ȧ as in chȧotic
â as in câre
ă as in ădd
ȧ as in ȧccount
ä as in ärm
à as in àsk
a as in sofa

ou as in out
oi as in oil

ē as in ēve
ê as in êvent
ĕ as in ĕnd
ĕ as in silĕnt
ē as in makēr

ī as in īce
ĭ as in ĭll
ɤ as in charɤty

ū as in cūbe
û as in ûnite
û as in ûrn
ŭ as in ŭp
ŭ as in circŭs
ü as in menü

ō as in ōld
ô as in ôbey
ô as in ôrb
ŏ as in ŏdd
ô as in sôft
ô as in cônnect

ōō as in fōōd
ŏŏ as in fŏŏt

ch as in chair
g as in go
ng as in sing
th as in then
th as in thin
tû as in natûre
dû as in verdûre
y as in yet
zh = z as in azure

The accented syllable is marked ′. The secondary accent is marked ′.

abdomen (ăb·dō′mĕn)₋ the part of the body between the diaphragm and the pelvis.

abdominal cavity, space below the diaphragm containing the intestines, liver, stomach, pancreas, kidneys, spleen, and reproductive organs.

abscess (ăb′sĕs), a collection of pus enclosed in any part of the body.

acne (ăk′nĕ), a disease of the skin that causes pimples.

adenoids (ăd′ĕ·noidz), masses of lymphoid tissue behind the nose.

adolescence (ăd′ŏ·lĕs′ĕns), period of development between childhood and maturity: in boys from 14 to 25; in girls from 12 to 21.

adrenal (ăd·rē′năl) **gland,** gland located at the top of each kidney.

alimentary (ăl′ĭ·mĕn′tȧ·rĭ) **canal,** the digestive canal extending from mouth to anus.

amputate (ăm′pû·tāt), to cut off, as a limb or projecting part.

anatomy (ȧ·năt′ŏ·mĭ), the structural make-up of an organism or its parts.

anemia (ȧ·nē′mĭ·ȧ), insufficiency of red corpuscles or hemoglobin.

anesthetic (ăn′ĕs·thĕt′ĭk), a substance which abolishes feeling or sensation.

antibodies (ăn′tĭ·bŏd′ĭz), defensive substances developed in the blood during an infection. When they remain in the blood after the disease is cured, they confer immunity to the disease.

antiseptic (ăn′tĭ·sĕp′tĭk), a substance that prevents growth of bacteria in or on the body. The word is also applied to methods tending to prevent bacterial growth.

antitoxin (ăn′tĭ·tŏk′sĭn), substance in the blood that neutralizes the toxin or poison produced by bacteria. The antitoxin that is injected in the treatment of diphtheria is blood serum from horses that have been made immune to diphtheria.

anus (ā′nŭs), opening from colon to outside of body.

aorta (ȧ·ôr′tȧ), the main artery carrying blood from the left ventricle of the heart to all parts of the body excepting the lungs.

appendix (ȧ·pĕn′dĭks), wormlike outgrowth at the junction of the small and large intestine, on the right side of the abdomen; vermiform appendix.

appetite (ăp′ĕ·tīt), desire for food.

artery (är′tĕr·ĭ), blood vessel that carries blood from the heart to various parts of the body.

417

astigmatism (á·stĭg′má·tĭz′m), a defect of vision in which light rays from any single point of an object cannot be focused at a single point on the retina.

athlete's (ăth′lēts) **foot**, ringworm of the foot, often acquired by athletes in gymnasiums.

audiometer (ô′dĭ·ŏm′ĕ·tẽr), an instrument for measuring the acuteness of hearing.

auditory (ô′dĭ·tō′rĭ) **canal**, air passage in the external ear leading to the eardrum.

auricle (ô′rĭ·k′l), the upper or anterior chamber of the heart that receives blood from the veins.

autonomic (ô′tŏ·nŏm′ĭk) **system**, system of nerve cells and fibers that control involuntary action.

bacilli (bá·sĭl′ī), plural form of **bacillus**.

bacillus (bá·sĭl′ŭs), a rod-shaped bacterium.

backbone. See **spinal column**.

bacteria (băk·tē′rĭ·á), extremely small one-celled plants that are ball-shaped, rod-shaped, or spiral in form.

bile (bīl), a bitter, yellow or greenish fluid secreted from the blood by the liver.

blister, a saclike cavity between the epidermis and the true skin which is filled with fluid.

blood pressure, pumping force of the heart against the elastic resistance of the blood vessels.

blood vessels, tubes in which blood circulates in the body, as an artery or vein.

boil, an inflamed swelling arising from a hair follicle caused by bacterial infection.

bronchi (brŏng′kī), branches of the trachea or windpipe.

caffeine (kăf′ĕ·ĭn), an alkaloid obtained from the dried leaves of tea or the dried seeds of coffee, and present in the beverages made from them.

calcium (kăl′sĭ·ŭm), a soft, silver-white metal, occurring only in combination. An important element in the chemical composition of bone.

callus (kăl′ŭs), hard, thickened skin.

calorie (kăl′ŏ·rĭ), a unit of heat. A large calorie is the amount of heat needed to raise the temperature of one kilogram of water one degree centigrade, or four pounds of water one degree Fahrenheit.

cancer (kăn′sẽr), a deadly disease in which a growth of tissue is caused by unlimited multiplication of certain body cells.

canker (kăng′kẽr) **sore**, a small sore discharging pus, affecting the mouth and lips.

capillary (kăp′ĭ·lĕr′ĭ), one of the fine, thin-walled blood vessels connecting arteries and veins.

carbohydrates (kär′bŏ·hī′drātes), food substances—including sugars, starches, celluloses—which contain carbon, hydrogen, and oxygen in certain proportions.

carbon dioxide (kär′bŏn dī·ŏk′sīd), a heavy, colorless gas given off in respiration, decomposition, and oxidation of carbon compounds.

carbuncle (kär′bŭng·k′l), a painful local inflammation of the skin, larger than a boil, which is sometimes fatal.

cardiac muscle (kär′dĭ·ăk mŭs′′l), the muscle of the heart.

carrier (kăr′ĭ·ẽr), a person who has the germs of some disease in his body but is not affected by them.

cartilage (kär′tĭ·lĭj), a tough, elastic animal tissue; gristle.

cell, one of the units of protoplasm of which all living things are composed; it consists of a nucleus in a mass of cytoplasm, which is usually enclosed within a cell wall.

cerebellum (sĕr′ĕ·bĕl′ŭm), the part of the brain lying below and behind the cerebrum which co-ordinates movement.

cerebrum (sĕr′ĕ·brŭm), the larger part of the brain, occupying the upper part of the skull, which controls voluntary movement and thinking.

chest cavity, the space above the diaphragm containing the heart and lungs.

chloroform (klō′rŏ·fôrm), a colorless, volatile liquid used as an anesthetic.

choroid (kō′roid), middle coat of eye, between between retina and sclera, made up of blood vessels and pigment.

circulation (sûr′kṵ·lā′shŭn), movement of the blood in the body.

circulatory (sûr′kṵ·lá·tō′rĭ) **system**, the system of organs by means of which the blood is carried through all parts of the body.

coccyx (kŏk′sĭks), the end of the vertebral column.

cochlea (kŏk′lĕ·á), the part resembling a snail shell, in the inner ear which contains the endings of the auditory nerve.

cold sore, an eruption of tiny blisters about the mouth or nostrils, usually appearing during a cold or fever.

colon (kō′lŏn), the part of the large intestine that extends from the cecum to the rectum.

conjunctiva (kŏn′jŭngk·tī′vá), the mucous membrane which lines the inner surface of the eyelid.

constipation (kŏn′stĭ·pā′shŭn), a state of the bowels caused by inactivity of the colon, in which food residues become overdry and packed, delaying elimination.

contagious (kŏn·tā′jŭs), spreading by contact from one person or animal to another.

convalescent (kŏn′vá·lĕs′ĕnt), recovering health after illness.

co-ordination (kō·ôr′dĭ·nā′shŭn), a working together or harmonious adjustment of parts.

cornea (kôr′nē·á), transparent region of the sclera, in the front of the eye.

corpuscle (kôr′pŭs′l), small body, such as a blood cell.

cortex (kôr′tĕks), outer layer of an organ.

cosmetic (kōz·mĕt′ĭk), substance for improving the appearance of the complexion.

cranial (krā′nĭ·ál), relating to the skull or cranium or to an organ within the skull, as the brain.

cretin (krē′tĭn), a deformed idiot, whose condition is brought about by a deficiency in the secretion of the thyroid gland.

cross-eyes, condition in which one eye turns toward or away from the other instead of being directed with the other eye toward the object looked at.

dandruff (dăn′drŭf), small dry scales that form on the scalp.

degenerative (dē·jĕn′ĕr·ā′tĭv) **disease,** disease which causes deterioration of vital organs; more or less normal to old age but often occurring prematurely.

dermis (dûr′mĭs), inner layer of skin.

diabetes (dī′á·bē′tēz), disease in which the sugar of the body is not completely oxidized or burned, caused by lack of hormone from pancreas.

diagnose (dī′ăg·nōs′), to recognize disease from its symptoms.

diaphragm (dī′á·frăm), the dome-shaped sheet of muscle separating the chest cavity from the abdominal cavity; used in breathing.

digestion (dĭ·jĕs′chŭn), process by which foods are changed to certain liquids which can be absorbed and used by the cells.

disease, any condition in which there is a departure from health and which presents marked symptoms.

disinfect (dĭs′ĭn·fĕkt′), to destroy disease germs or other harmful microorganisms.

dislocation (dĭs′lŏ·kā′shŭn), displacement of a bone from its normal position in a joint.

electrocardiograph (ē·lĕk′trŏ·kär′dĭ·ŏ·gráf), a device for recording variations in action of heart muscles.

embryo (ĕm′brĭ·ō), plant or animal in its earliest stages of development, before it is fully formed.

endocrine (ĕn′dŏ·krĭn) **glands.** See the diagram on page 220.

epidermis (ĕp′ĭ·dûr′mĭs), outer layer of skin.

epiglottis (ĕp′ĭ·glŏt′ĭs), the tissue which closes the windpipe when anything is swallowed.

esophagus (ē·sŏf′á·gŭs), the portion of the alimentary canal leading from the throat to the stomach; the gullet.

Eustachian (û·stā′kĭ·án) **tube,** the tube which leads from the middle ear to the throat.

excreta (ĕks·krē′tá), waste matter given off from the body; excretions.

excretory (ĕks′krĕ·tō′rĭ) **duct,** a duct discharging waste products, as sweat.

eyestrain, weariness or strained condition of the eye from overuse or uncorrected defects of vision.

fainting, loss of consciousness caused by sudden reduction of the brain's blood supply.

farsightedness, a condition of the eye in which vision for distant objects (though not as good as in the normal eye) is better than for near objects; hyperopia.

feces (fē′sēz), the intestinal wastes of animals.

fluoroscope (floo′ŏ·rŏ·skōp), device consisting of a fluorescent screen and an X-ray tube by which shadows of objects between the two are made visible.

focusing muscle, a muscle that controls the shape of the lens of the eye so as to bring light rays from a given point to a focus on the retina.

follicle (fŏl′ĭ·k′l), a tiny cavity, sac, or tube.

fontanel (fŏn′tá·nĕl′), one of the intervals, closed by membranous structure, between neighboring bones of an infant's skull.

fracture (frăk′tŭr), a break or crack in a bone.

gastric (găs′trĭk) **juice,** a digestive fluid secreted by the glands of the stomach.

genes (jēns), small particles of a chromosome that have the power to produce definite traits in the offspring.

419

germicide (jûr′mĭ·sīd), any substance that destroys disease germs.

germs (jûrms), microorganisms, either bacteria or protozoans, that cause disease.

gland, a secreting organ which separates and elaborates fluid from the blood.

glycogen (glī′kŏ·jĕn), a form of carbohydrate, known as animal starch stored in the liver.

goiter (goi′tẽr), an enlargement of the thyroid gland, causing a swelling in the front of the neck.

heart, a hollow, muscular organ which, by contracting rhythmically, keeps up the circulation of the blood.

heartburn, a burning sensation about the heart, caused by a flowing back of acid from the stomach into the esophagus.

hemoglobin (hē′mŏ·glō′bĭn), the iron compound in the red blood corpuscles, which unites with oxygen.

heredity (hĕ·rĕd′ĭ·tĭ), the passing on of qualities or traits of the parents to their offspring.

hives (hīvz), an inflammatory disease of the skin accompanied by intense itching.

hormone (hôr′mōn), a chemical substance produced by a ductless gland that passes directly into the blood and controls the activity of some organ of the body.

immunity (ĭ·mū′nĭ·tĭ), condition in which an individual does not develop disease even when the causative agent is present.

impulse (ĭm′pŭls), the change which travels like a wave along a nerve fiber when it is stimulated and is responsible for sensation or motion.

infection (ĭn·fĕk′shŭn), a condition due to microorganisms within the body multiplying and producing toxins.

inhibition (ĭn′hĭ·bĭsh′ŭn), restraint of the action of an organ.

insulin (ĭn′sŭ·lĭn), hormone made in the pancreas; regulates use of sugar in the body.

intestine (ĭn·tĕs′tĭn), tubular portion of the alimentary canal following the stomach; the bowels.

involuntary (ĭn·vŏl′ŭn·tẽr′ĭ), not under the influence or control of the will.

iris (ī′rĭs), colored part of the eye surrounding the pupil.

kidneys (kĭd′nĭz), two bean-shaped organs in abdominal cavity which excrete urine.

larynx (lăr′ĭngks), part of the windpipe where the voice is produced; voice box.

laxative (lăk′sȧ·tĭv), anything that causes looseness of the bowels.

ligament (lĭg′ȧ·mĕnt), a band or sheet of fibrous tissue connecting two or more bones or cartilages.

liver, a large gland located on the right side of the body between the diaphragm and the stomach. It secretes a liquid called bile.

lymph (lĭmf), a nearly colorless fluid, contained in the lymphatics, consisting of blood plasma and colorless corpuscles.

lymph nodes, bodies scattered along the lymphatic vessels in which the lymph is purified.

lymphatic (lĭm·făt′ĭk), tube carrying lymph back into the blood stream.

marijuana (mär′ĭ·wä′nȧ), Mexican term for the dried leaves and flowers of hemp which are smoked in cigarettes and which contain a habit-forming drug.

marrow (măr′ō), soft tissue which fills the cavities of most bones.

medulla (mĕ·dŭl′ȧ), the extreme upper part of the spinal cord, forming the connection between the cord and the brain; spinal bulb.

membrane (mĕm′brān), a thin, sheetlike layer composed of epithelial cells, serving to line a cavity or tube.

metabolism (mĕ·tăb′ŏ·lĭz′m), all chemical change in living plants or animals, including building-up processes and breaking-down processes.

microorganism (mī′krŏ·ôr′găn·ĭz′m), any organism of microscopic size; applied especially to bacteria and protozoa.

molar (mō′lẽr), back tooth with broad surface, adapted for grinding. Man has twelve molar teeth.

mold, any fungus producing a wooly growth on damp or decaying organic matter.

motor nerve, nerve that carries impulses that result in movement of a muscle or activity of an organ.

mucus (mū′kŭs), a watery secretion from the mucous glands.

muscle tone, slightly contracted condition of a muscle.

narcotic (när·kŏt′ĭk), a sleep-producing drug.

nausea (nô′shē·à), a feeling of a need to vomit.

nearsightedness, seeing distinctly at short distances only; myopia.

nerve, cordlike bands of nervous tissue that connect parts of the nervous system and conduct nervous impulses to and away from these parts.

nutrition (nū·trĭsh′ŭn), processes by which an animal or plant takes in, absorbs, and utilizes food substances.

occlusion (ŏ·klōō′zhŭn), shutting or closing a passage; bringing the opposing surfaces of the teeth of the two jaws into contact.

oculist (ŏk′ū·lĭst), a specialist in diseases of the eye.

ophthalmologist (ŏf′thăl·mŏl′ŏ·jĭst) a physician specializing in the study and treatment of defects and diseases of the eye; an oculist.

optic (ŏp′tĭk) **nerve,** nerve of sight, carrying impulses from the retina of the eye to the brain.

organ (ôr′găn), a part of the body that has a special work or function to perform.

palate (păl′ĭt), roof of the mouth.

pancreas (păn′krē·ăs), digestive gland lying below the stomach.

parathyroids (păr′à·thī′roidz), four small bodies that control calcium balance in the body.

pasteurize (păs′tēr·īz), to heat milk from 140° to 150° F. for at least 20 minutes in order to destroy harmful bacteria.

pelvis (pĕl′vĭs), the basin-shaped, bony hip girdle supporting the spinal column, resting on the lower extremities.

peristalsis (pĕr′ĭ·stăl′sĭs), the wavelike motion that forces the food through the intestines, stomach, and esophagus due to the contraction of the muscles of these organs.

perspiration (pûr′spĭ·rā′shŭn), secretion of the sweat glands; sweat.

pharynx (făr′ĭngks), the region or cavity at the back part of the mouth through which air passes to the windpipe, and food and drink to the esophagus.

pimple (pĭm′p′l), a tiny, pointed swelling on the skin.

pituitary (pĭ·tū′ĭ·tĕr′ĭ) **gland,** a ductless gland projecting from the lower side of the brain.

plasma (plăz′mà), liquid part of the blood.

platelets (plāt′lĕts), colorless disks in the blood, smaller than either the red or white corpuscles, important in the clotting of the blood.

protein (prō′tē·ĭn), a complex chemical compound containing nitrogen and other elements in addition to carbon, hydrogen, and oxygen; the basis of protoplasm.

protozoan (prō′tŏ·zō′ăn), a one-celled microscopic animal

pulse, regular beating or throbbing in the arteries caused by the contraction of the ventricles of the heart.

pupil, the opening in the iris of the eye through which rays of light pass to the retina.

pus, a yellowish-white matter containing bacteria and the remains of white corpuscles.

radium (rā′dĭ·ŭm), a rare metallic element which gives off invisible and extraordinarily energetic particles.

rectum (rĕk′tŭm), lower end of the large intestine.

reflex (rē′flĕks) **action,** bodily action controlled by spinal nerve centers without conscious direction from the brain.

relax, to loosen or lessen tension.

renal (rē′năl) **circulation,** circulation of blood to the kidneys.

reproduction (rē′prŏ·dŭk′shŭn), the process by which plants and animals produce offspring.

respiration (rĕs′pĭ·rā′shŭn), process by which oxygen is taken into, and carbon dioxide is given off from, the cells.

retina (rĕt′ĭ·nà), the innermost layer of the eyeball, formed by the branched endings of the optic nerve.

sacrum (sā′krŭm), the parts of the vertebral column forming a part of the pelvis. It consists of five united vertebrae.

saliva (sà·lī′và), digestive juice secreted by salivary glands, active chiefly in the mouth.

sanitation (săn′ĭ·tā′shŭn), use of measures for improving conditions that influence health.

sclera (sklē′rà), white outside coat of the eyeball.

secretion (sē·krē'shŭn), substance given off by a cell or group of cells differing in properties from the material from which it is produced.

semicircular (sĕm'ĭ·sûr'kû·lēr) **canals,** loop-shaped tubes in the inner ear.

sensation (sĕn·sā'shŭn), being conscious of an external stimulus, as sensation of color caused by action of light on retina of eye which results in impulses affecting brain cells.

sensitive (sĕn'sĭ·tĭv), having sense or feeling; capable of receiving impressions from external objects.

septic sore throat, a sore throat with severe systemic infection due to streptococci in the general circulation.

septum (sĕp'tŭm), a dividing wall separating cavities.

serum (sē'rŭm), plasma of the blood without fibrinogen, the liquid left after the blood has clotted; also may mean the material used for immunizing purposes.

sinus (sī'nŭs), a hollow space in a bone or other tissue; one of the cavities connecting with the nose.

skeleton (skĕl'ĕ·tŭn), bony framework of the body.

skull, skeleton or framework of the head.

spinal column, a series of similar bones, joined by cartilage, giving a strong, flexible support for the body; backbone.

spinal cord, cord of nerve tissue lying in a canal in the spinal column.

sprain, injury to a joint with tearing or separation of ligaments.

sterilization (stĕr'ĭ·lĭ·zā'shŭn), process by which all living bacteria are destroyed by heat or by chemicals.

stethoscope (stĕth'ŏ·skōp), an instrument for examining the heart, lungs, and other organs of the body by listening to the sounds produced by them.

stimulant (stĭm'û·lănt), a substance, force, or condition that excites action in the body by acting on the nerves in the skin or by entering the circulation.

stimulus (stĭm'û·lŭs), anything that starts the activity of a nerve (impulse) or produces an impression on a sensory organ.

stomach (stŭm'ăk), an enlargement of the alimentary canal that serves to hold food while it is being acted upon by digestive juices.

strain, undue stretching of a muscle or ligament.

sweat glands, glands that give off moisture through the pores of the skin.

symptom (sĭmp'tŭm), a sign or indication that serves to point out the existence of some condition or disease.

synapse (sĭ·năps'), a place of meeting of the dendrites of one neuron with the ends of the dendrites of another neuron.

synovial (sĭ·nō'vĭ·ăl) **fluid,** fluid in a joint.

tear gland, gland that secretes watery liquid to moisten the eye.

temperature (tĕm'pēr·a·tūr), the degree of heat of the human body; sometimes refers to the excess over the normal temperature.

tendon, cord of connective tissue terminating the fleshy part of a muscle and binding it to a bone; sinew.

tension (tĕn'shŭn), state of being strained or under pressure.

theory (thē'ŏ·rĭ), a more or less reasonable or scientifically acceptable explanation of an observed fact.

thymus (thī'mŭs), ductless gland in neck and upper chest.

thyroid (thī'roid) **gland,** ductless gland in the neck, lying on each side of the windpipe, which secretes a hormone that regulates the rate of metabolism.

thyroxine (thī·rŏk'sēn), substance in thyroid secretion that stimulates rate of oxidation.

tissue (tĭsh'û), a group of cells of one kind, forming a continuous mass or layer.

tonsil, mass of lymphoid tissue on each side of the throat near the base of the tongue.

tonsillitis (tŏn'sĭ·lī'tĭs), inflammation of the tonsils.

tourniquet (toŏr'nĭ·kĕt), a device or bandage which, when properly placed and twisted tight, controls the flow of blood and stops bleeding.

toxic (tŏk'sĭk), poisonous.

toxin (tŏk'sĭn), poison produced by bacteria and capable of causing disease.

toxin-antitoxin, material injected in a person to develop immunity to diphtheria.

toxoid (tŏk'soid), a modified toxin used for producing immunity to diphtheria.

trachea (trā'kĕ·a), air tube between larynx and bronchi; windpipe.

transfusion (trăns·fū'zhŭn), transferring blood from the blood vessels of one person to those of another.

tuberculin (tû·bûr'kû·lĭn) **test,** a test for determining the existence of tuberculosis.

tuberculosis (tū·bûr′kū·lō′sĭs), a disease caused by *Bacillus tuberculosis*, forming tubercles in any part of the body.

tympanic (tĭm·păn′ĭk) **membrane,** membrane like the head of a drum between outer and middle ear; eardrum.

urination (ū′rĭ·nā′shŭn), passing urine.

urine (ū′rĭn), fluid secreted by the kidneys, stored in the bladder, cast off as waste from the body.

uvula (ū′vū·lȧ), small, fleshy projection hanging from the soft palate above the back part of the tongue.

vaccination (văk′sĭ·nā′shŭn), the process of developing in man immunity to a disease by introducing the dead germs or the germs of a less severe related disease.

vaccine (văk′sēn), inoculating material originally taken from the cow, now including any inoculating material for the prevention of disease.

valve (vălv), a fold in the wall of a blood vessel, canal, or other organ which allows the contents to flow in one direction only.

ventricle (vĕn′trĭ·k'l), either of the two lower chambers of the heart having muscular walls.

vertebra (vûr′tĕ·brȧ), any one of the single bones of the spinal column.

vertebrae (vûr′tĕ·brē), plural form of **vertebra.**

villi (vĭl′ī), plural form of **villus.**

villus (vĭl′ŭs), small fingerlike projection on the mucous membrane of the small intestine, increasing the absorbing surface.

virus (vī′rŭs) **disease,** any disease caused by a filterable virus.

vital organs, organs that are necessary to life.

vitamin (vī′tȧ·mĭn), any of a group of substances occurring in many foods, essential to the proper functioning of the body.

vocal cords, folds of mucous membrane which project into the cavity of the voice box.

voluntary (vŏl′ŭn·tĕr′ĭ) **muscle,** muscle regulated or controlled by the will.

white corpuscle, colorless body in the blood, irregular in shape, possessing the power of movement and ability to destroy disease germs.

X ray, a ray of very short wave length, capable of penetrating many substances ordinarily opaque; used in medical diagnosis and treatment of certain diseases.

INDEX

Sharon Lee Waddell

This is a fly sheet
I'm writing on.